INUYASHA 犬夜叉

ANI-MANGA™

VOL. 13

**CREATED BY
RUMIKO TAKAHASHI**

Inuyasha Ani-Manga™
Vol. #13

Created by
Rumiko Takahashi

Translation based on the VIZ anime TV series
Translation Assistance/Katy Bridges
Lettering/John Clark
Cover Design & Graphics/Hidemi Sahara
Editor/Frances E. Wall

Managing Editor/Annette Roman
Director of Production/Noboru Watanabe
Vice President of Publishing/Alvin Lu
Sr. Director of Acquisitions/Rika Inouye
Vice President of Sales & Marketing/Liza Coppola
Publisher/Hyoe Narita

© 2001 Rumiko TAKAHASHI/Shogakukan Inc.
© Rumiko TAKAHASHI/Shogakukan, Yomiuri TV, Sunrise 2000.
First published by Shogakukan Inc. in Japan as "TV Anime-ban Inuyasha."
Ani-Manga is a trademark of VIZ Media, LLC. New and adapted artwork and text © 2006 VIZ Media, LLC.

Printed in the U.S.A.

Published by VIZ Media, LLC
P.O. Box 77010
San Francisco, CA 94107

10 9 8 7 6 5 4 3 2 1
First printing, February 2006

www.viz.com
store.viz.com

Story thus far

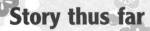

Kagome's mundane teenage existence was turned upside down when she was transported into a mythical version of Japan's medieval past! Kagome is the reincarnation of Lady Kikyo, a great warrior and the defender of the Shikon Jewel, or the Jewel of Four Souls. Kikyo was in love with Inuyasha, a dog-like half-demon who wishes to possess the jewel in order to transform himself into a full-fledged demon. But 50 years earlier, the evil shape-shifting Naraku tricked Kikyo and Inuyasha into betraying one another. The betrayal led to Kikyo's death and Inuyasha's imprisonment under a binding spell...and Inuyasha remained trapped by the spell until Kagome appeared in feudal Japan and unwittingly released him!

In a skirmish for possession of the Shikon Jewel, it accidentally shatters and is strewn across the land. Only Kagome has the power to find the jewel shards, and only Inuyasha has the strength to defeat the demons who now hold them, so the two unlikely partners are bound together in the quest to reclaim all the pieces of the sacred jewel. To prevent Inuyasha from stealing the jewel, Kikyo's sister, Lady Kaede, puts a magical necklace around Inuyasha's neck that allows Kagome to make him "sit" on command.

Inuyasha and Kagome gradually begin to feel affection for one another, but the situation becomes complicated when Kikyo is raised from the grave through witchcraft. The resurrected Kikyo still burns with hatred and jealousy over Inuyasha's supposed betrayal and his relationship with Kagome, but Inuyasha can't suppress his abiding love for Kikyo. Now Koga, the leader of a wolf-demon tribe, has kidnapped Kagome so he can use her ability to detect jewel shards in his clan's war against the vicious Birds of Paradise. Inuyasha and the others chase after Kagome in hopes of rescuing her, but they run into the Birds of Paradise and come under attack!

INUYASHA™

ANI-MANGA™ Vol. 13

Contents

37
The Man Who Fell in Love With Kagome!

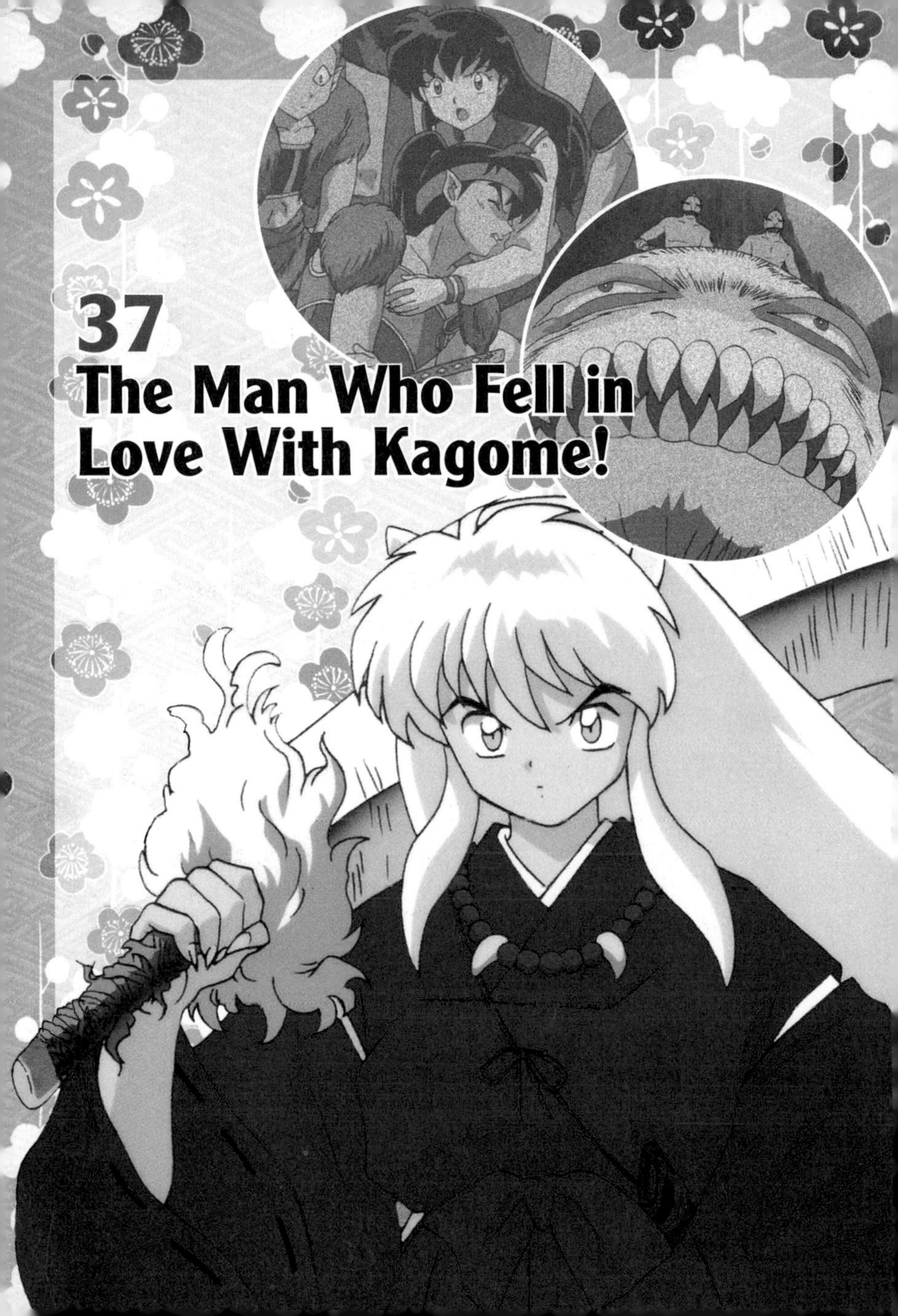

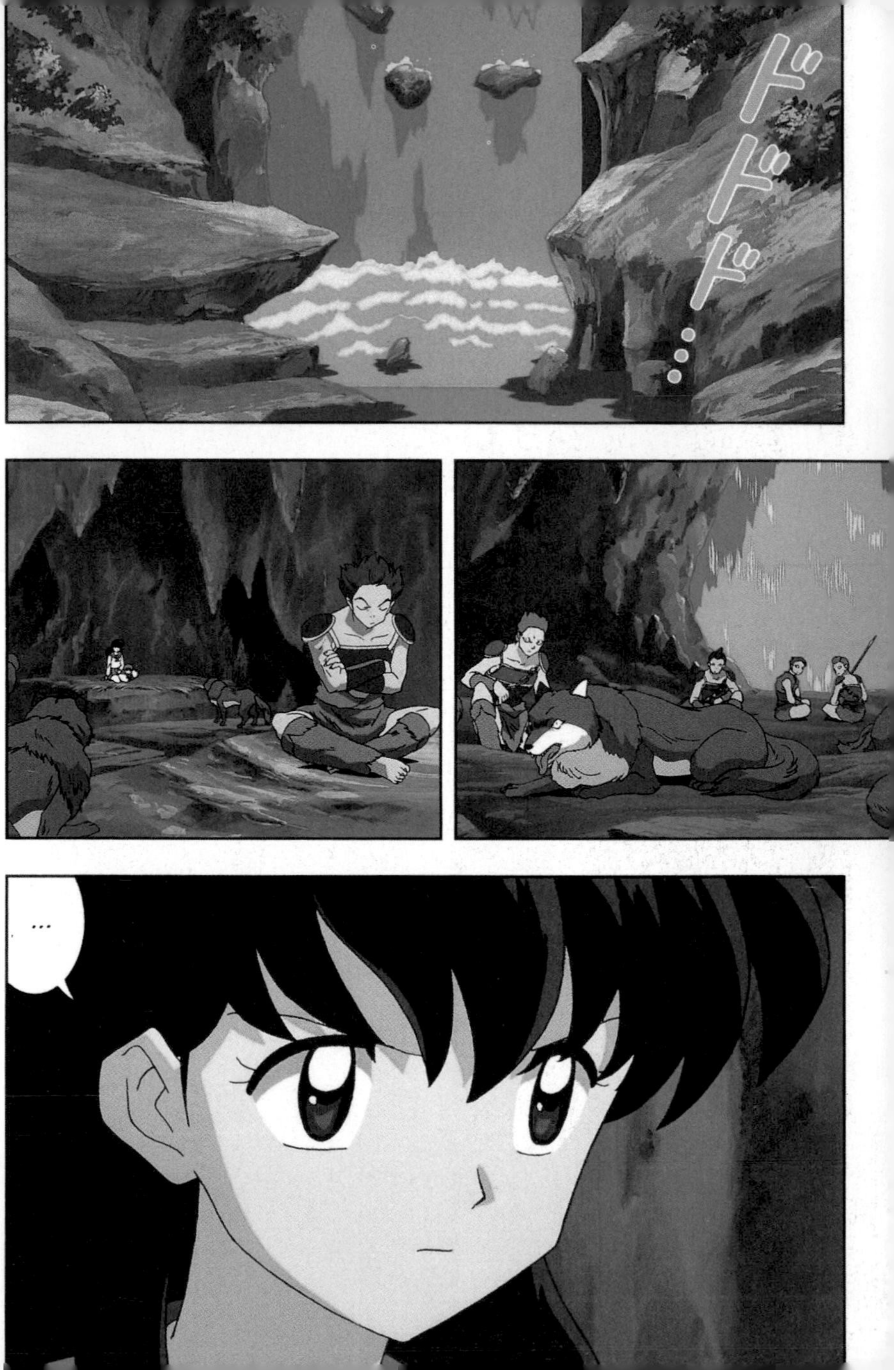
ドドド…
...

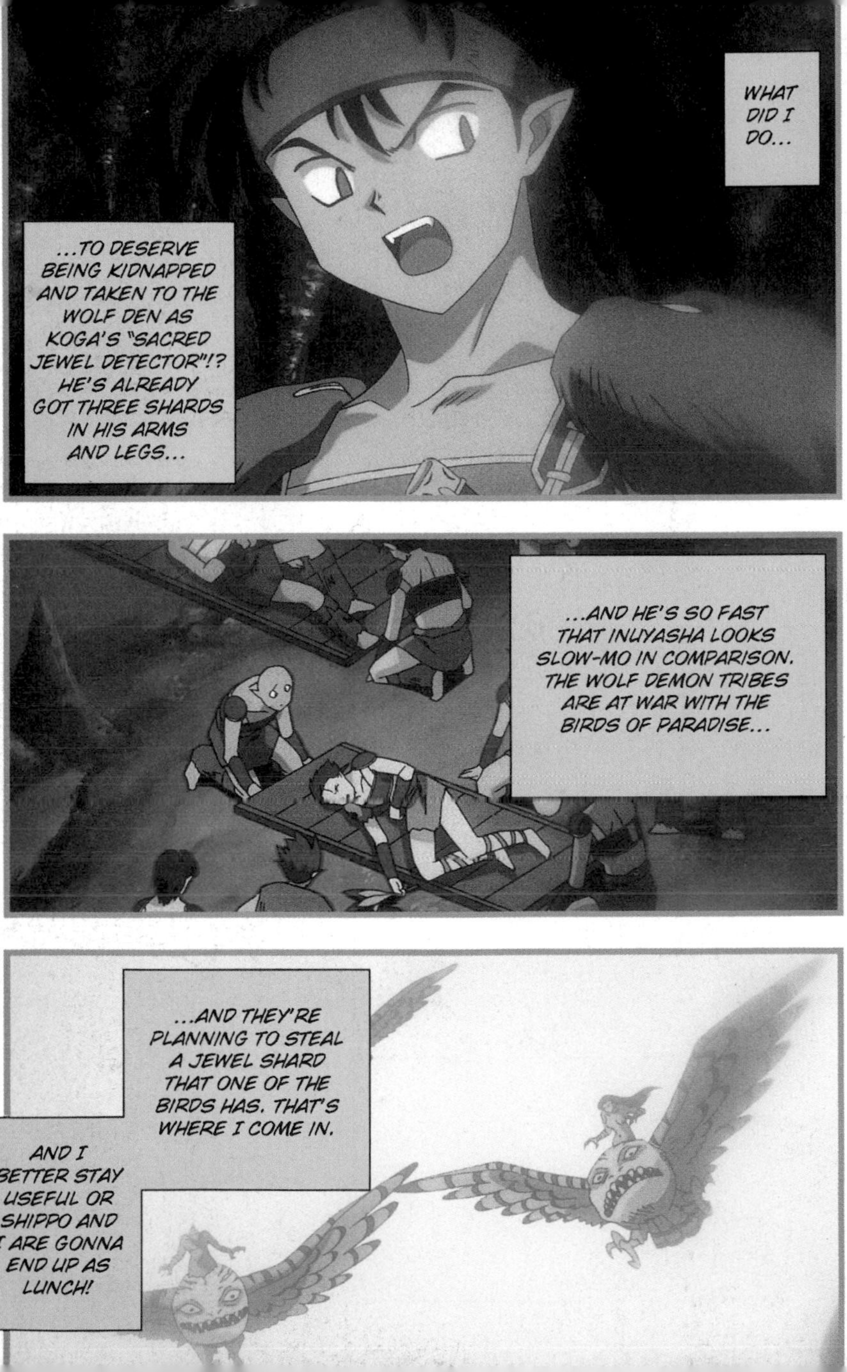
WHAT DID I DO...
...TO DESERVE BEING KIDNAPPED AND TAKEN TO THE WOLF DEN AS KOGA'S "SACRED JEWEL DETECTOR"!? HE'S ALREADY GOT THREE SHARDS IN HIS ARMS AND LEGS...
...AND HE'S SO FAST THAT INUYASHA LOOKS SLOW-MO IN COMPARISON. THE WOLF DEMON TRIBES ARE AT WAR WITH THE BIRDS OF PARADISE...
...AND THEY'RE PLANNING TO STEAL A JEWEL SHARD THAT ONE OF THE BIRDS HAS. THAT'S WHERE I COME IN.
AND I BETTER STAY USEFUL OR SHIPPO AND I ARE GONNA END UP AS LUNCH!

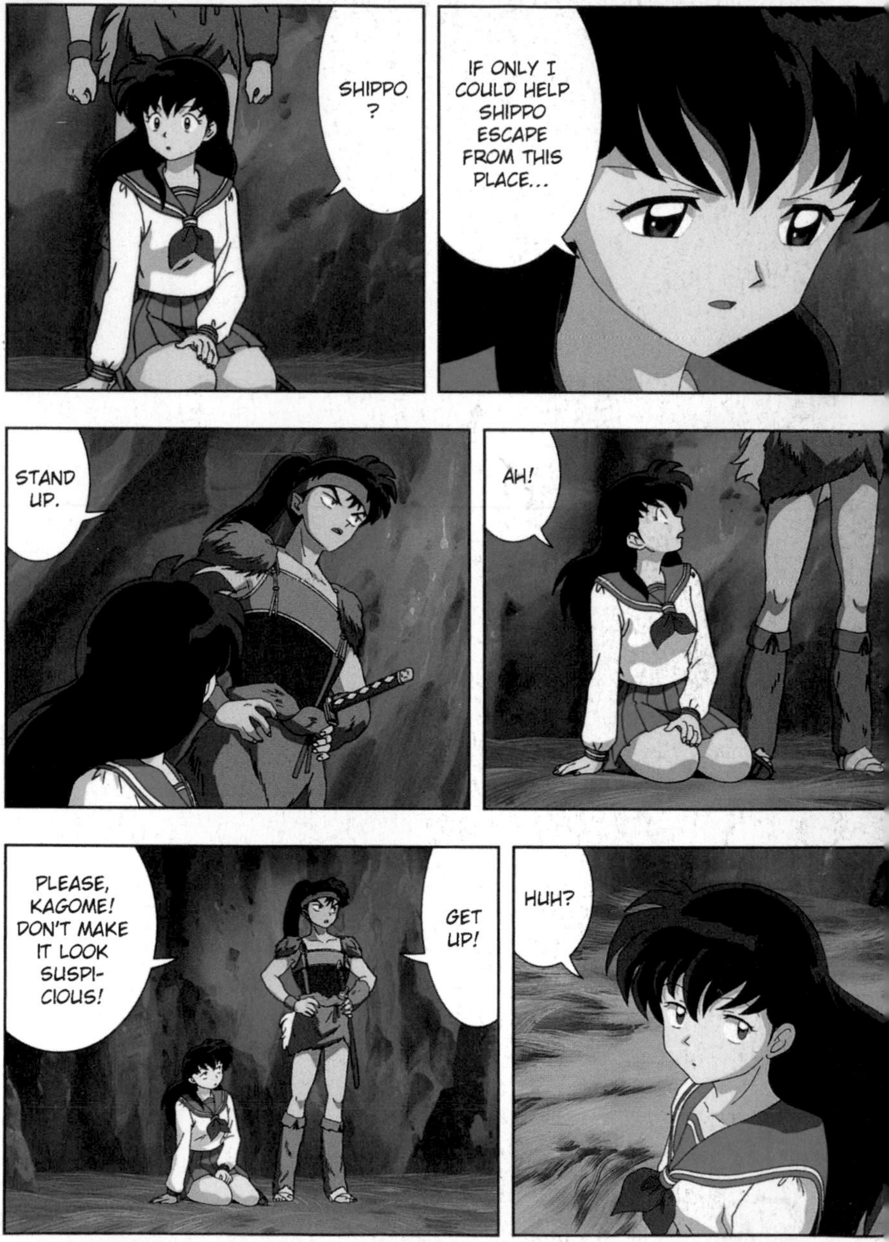
IF ONLY I COULD HELP SHIPPO ESCAPE FROM THIS PLACE...
SHIPPO ?
AH!
STAND UP.
HUH?
GET UP!
PLEASE, KAGOME! DON'T MAKE IT LOOK SUSPI-CIOUS!

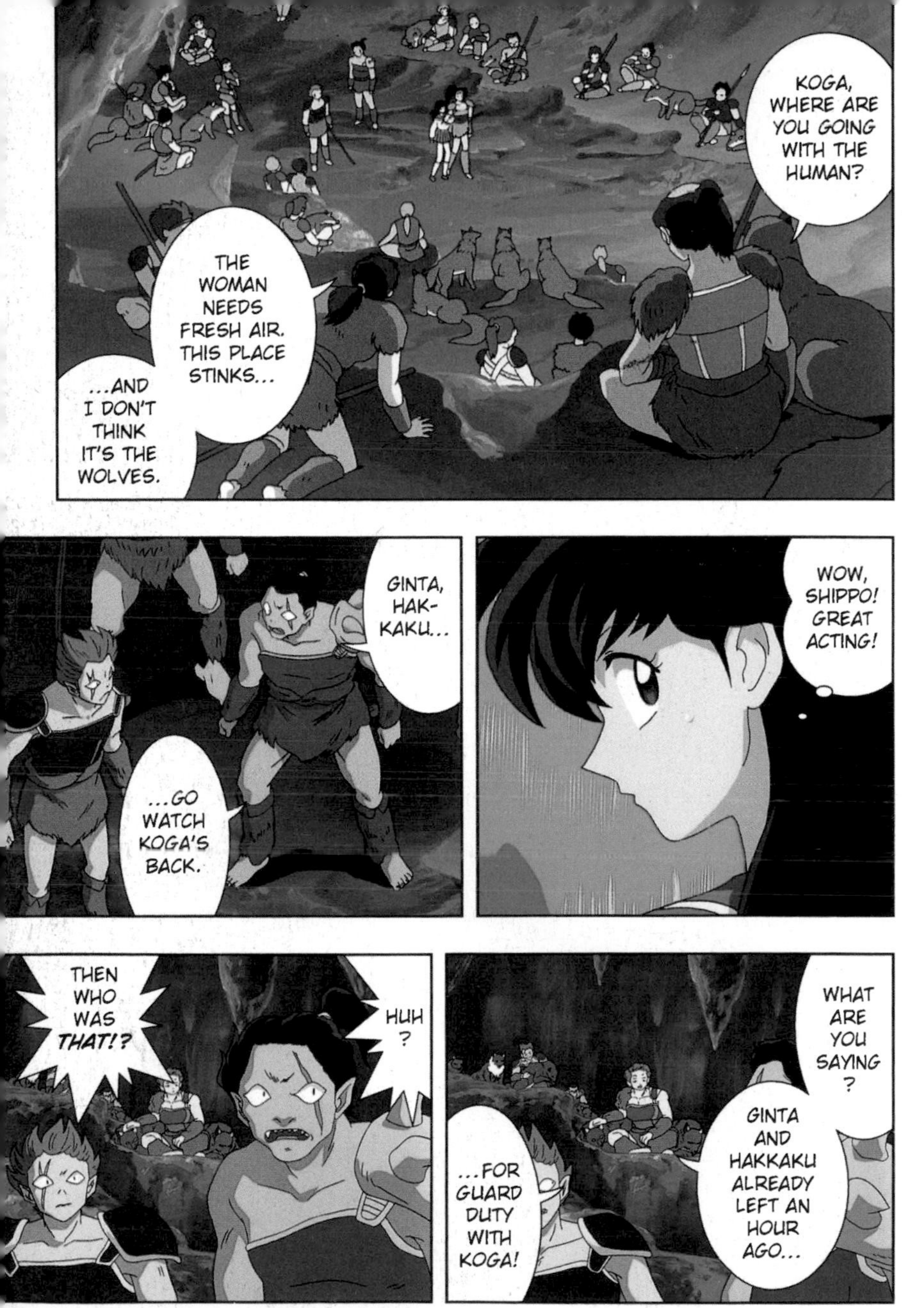
KOGA, WHERE ARE YOU GOING WITH THE HUMAN?
THE WOMAN NEEDS FRESH AIR. THIS PLACE STINKS...
...AND I DON'T THINK IT'S THE WOLVES.
WOW, SHIPPO! GREAT ACTING!
GINTA, HAK-KAKU...
...GO WATCH KOGA'S BACK.
WHAT ARE YOU SAYING?
GINTA AND HAKKAKU ALREADY LEFT AN HOUR AGO...
...FOR GUARD DUTY WITH KOGA!
HUH?
THEN WHO WAS *THAT!?*

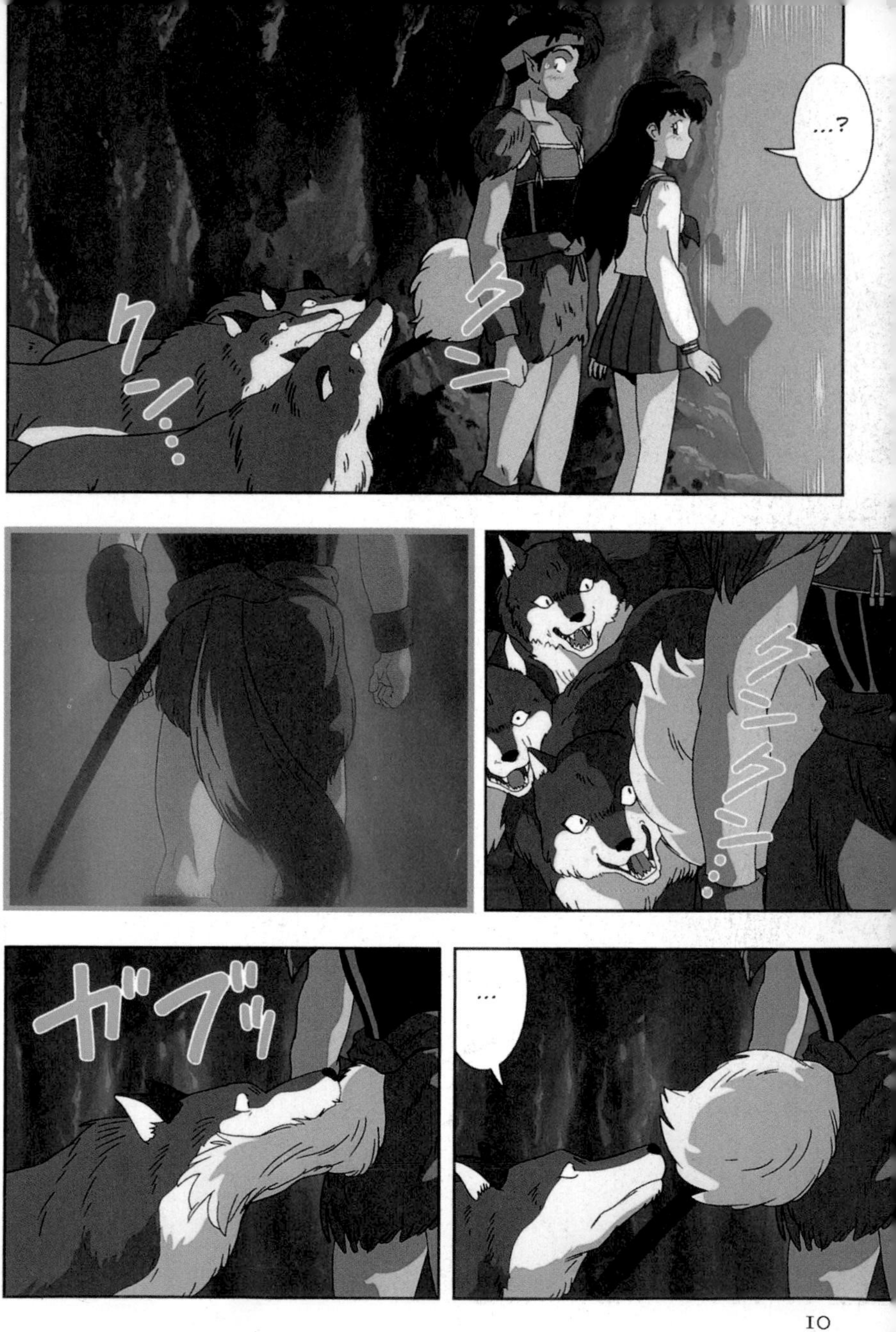
...?
クーン
クーン…
クーンクーン…
...
ガブッ

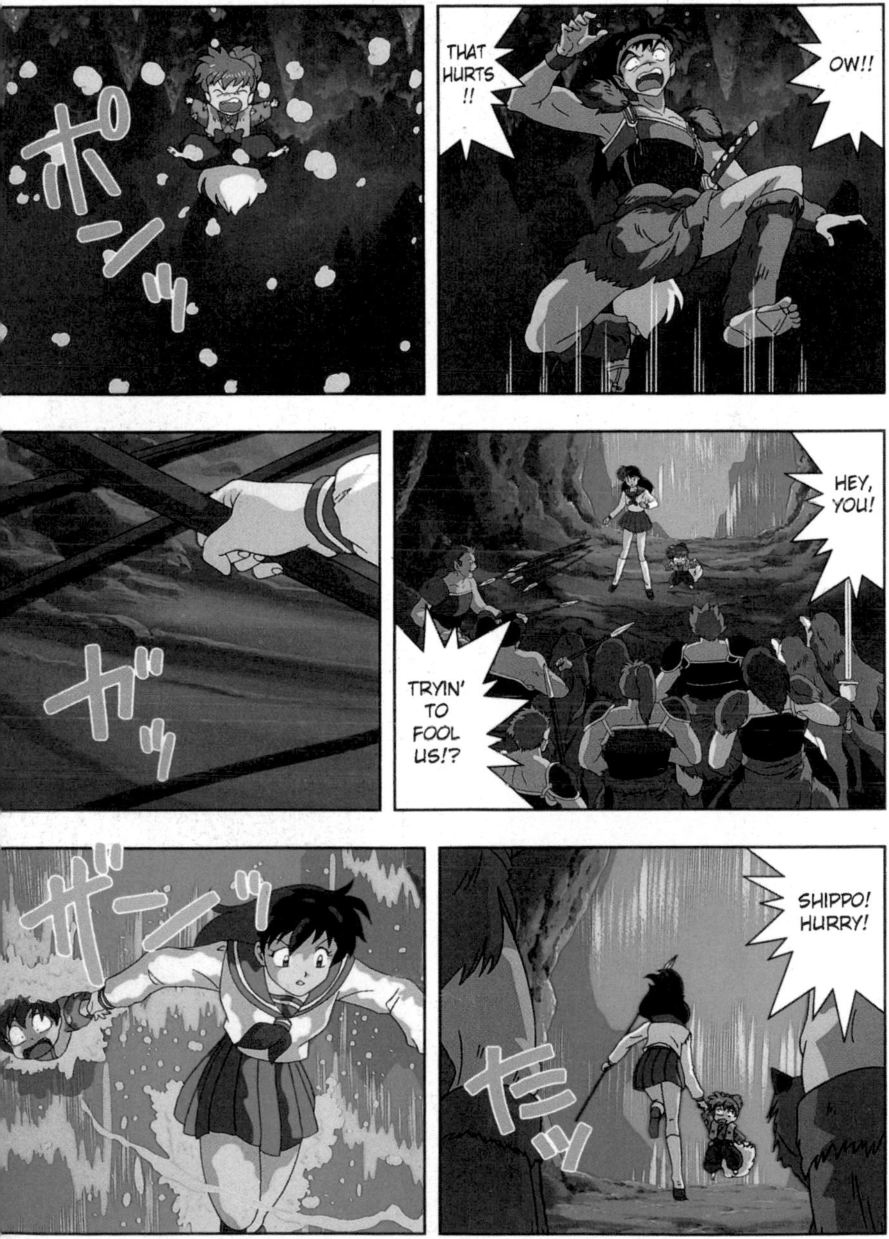
OW!!
THAT HURTS !!
ポンッ
HEY, YOU!
TRYIN' TO FOOL US!?
ガッ
SHIPPO! HURRY!
ダッ

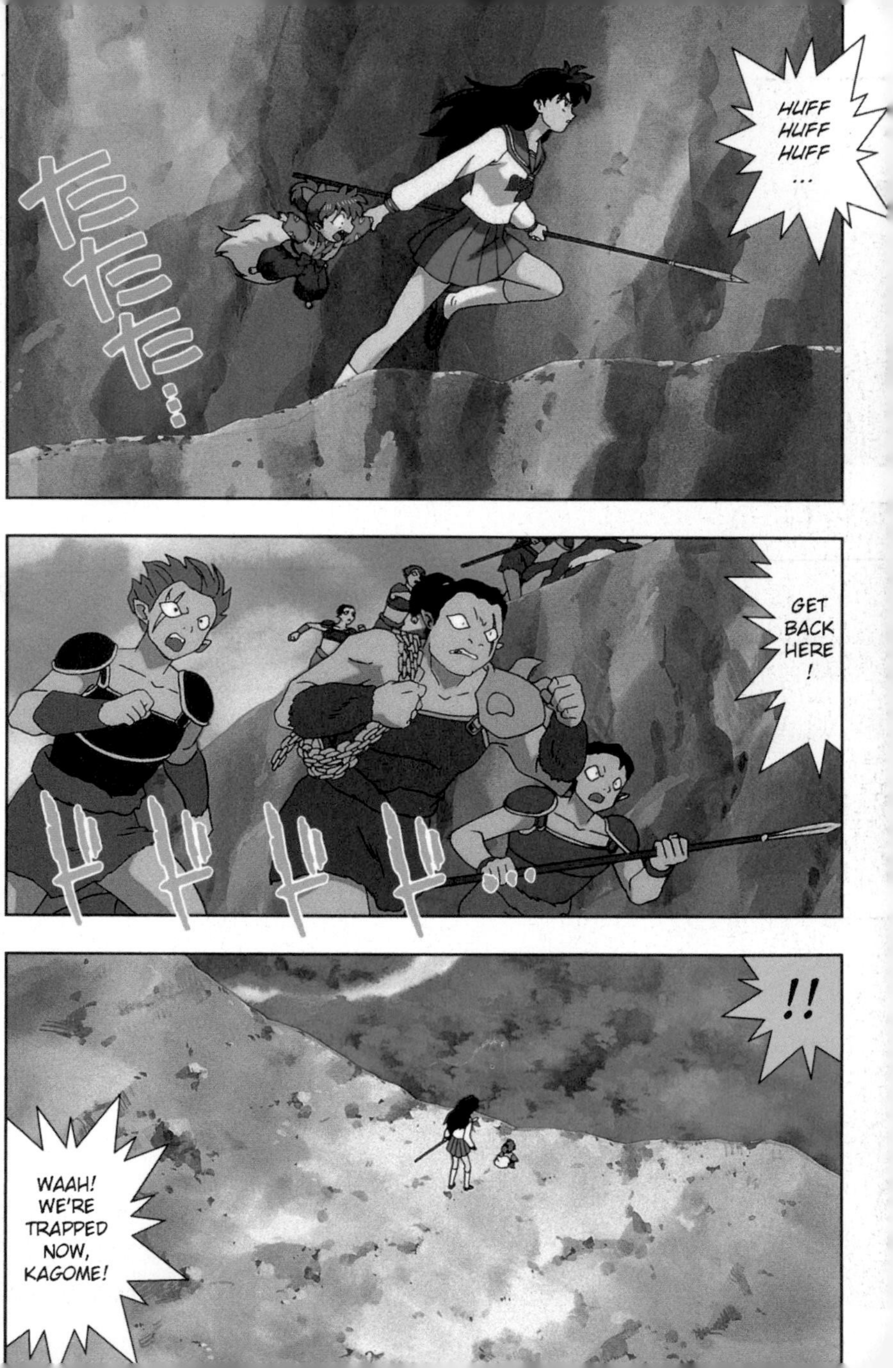
HUFF HUFF HUFF ...
たたた...
GET BACK HERE !
!!
WAAH! WE'RE TRAPPED NOW, KAGOME!

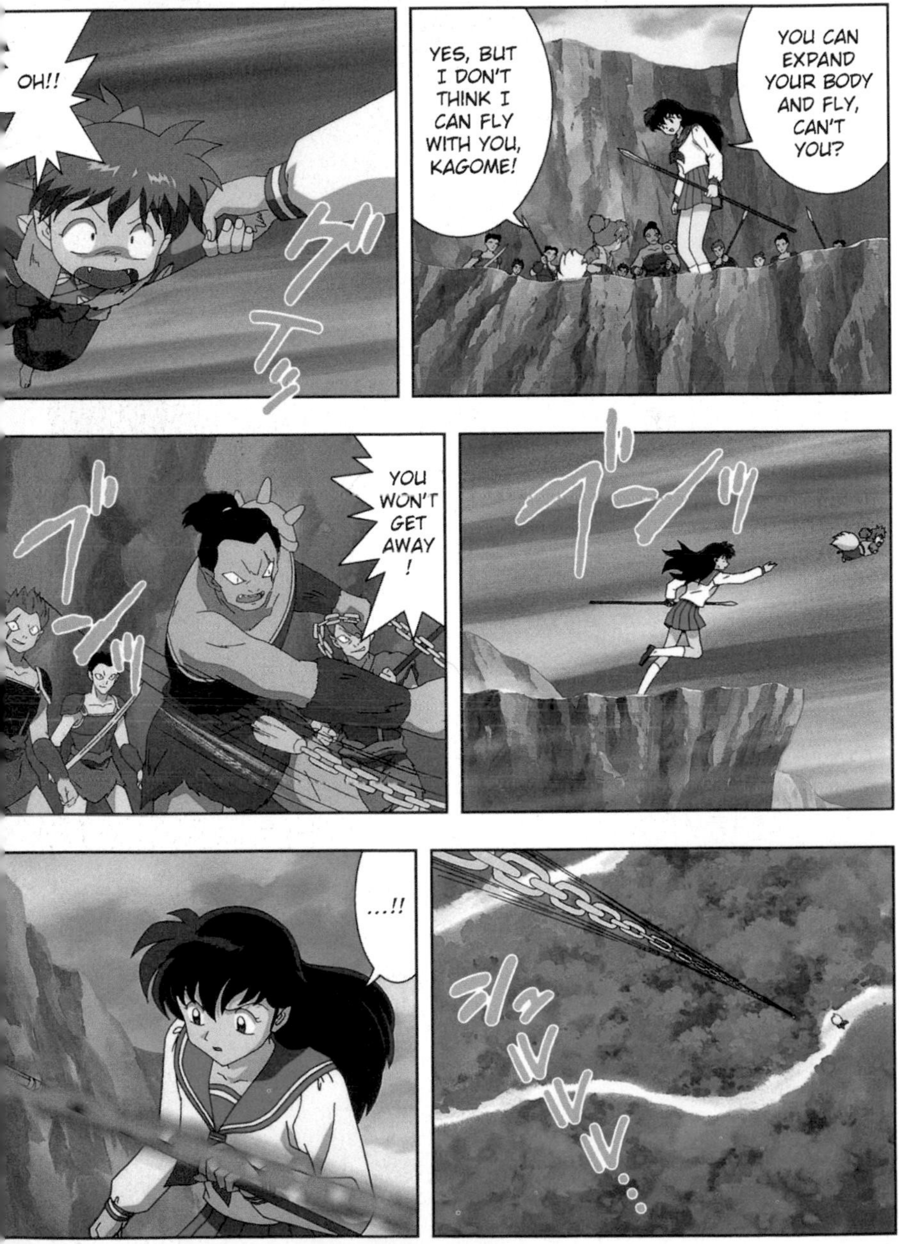
YOU CAN EXPAND YOUR BODY AND FLY, CAN'T YOU?
YES, BUT I DON'T THINK I CAN FLY WITH YOU, KAGOME!
OH!!
YOU WON'T GET AWAY!
...!!

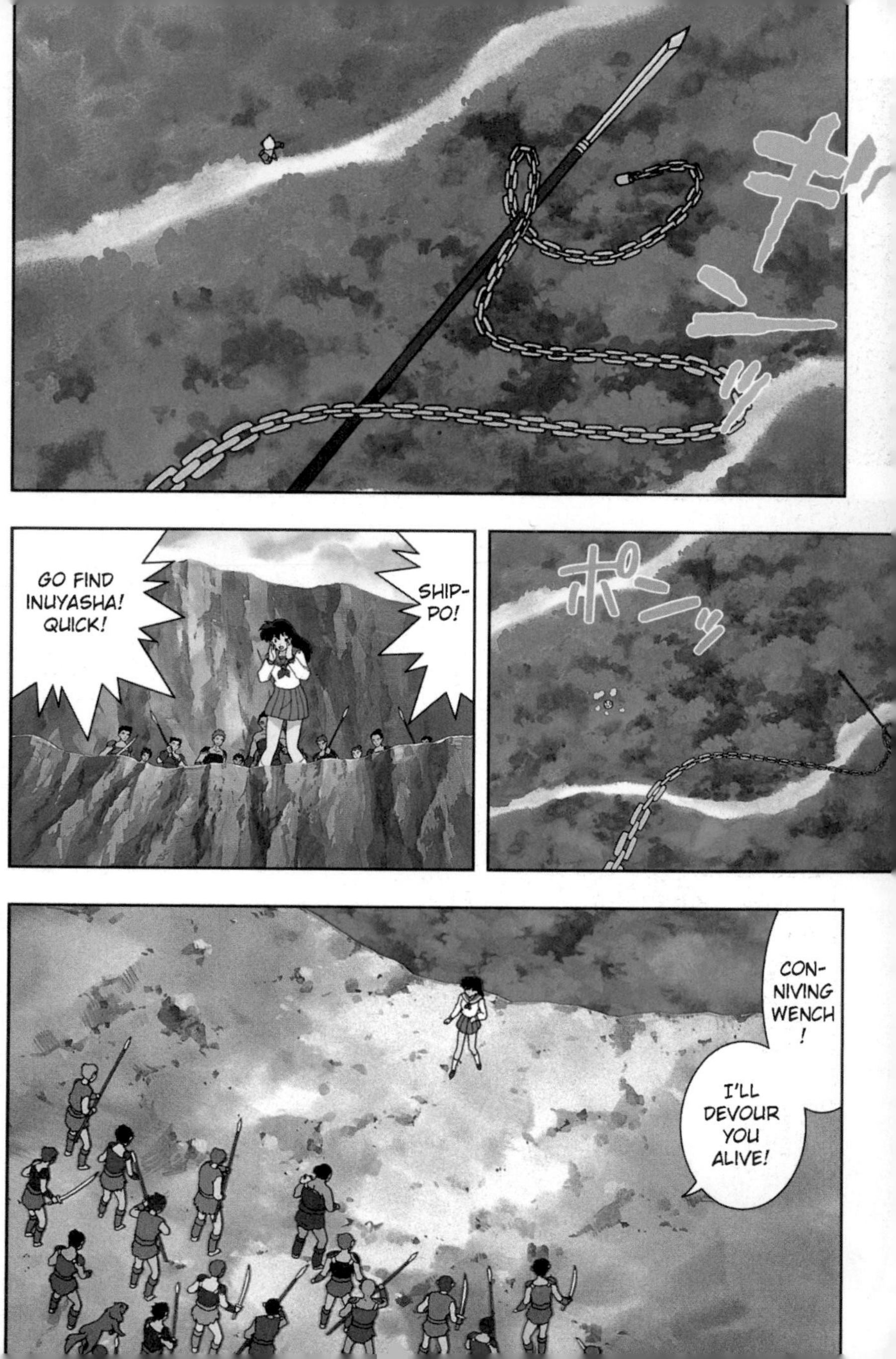
ギンッ
ポンッ
SHIP-PO!
GO FIND INUYASHA! QUICK!
CON-NIVING WENCH!
I'LL DEVOUR YOU ALIVE!

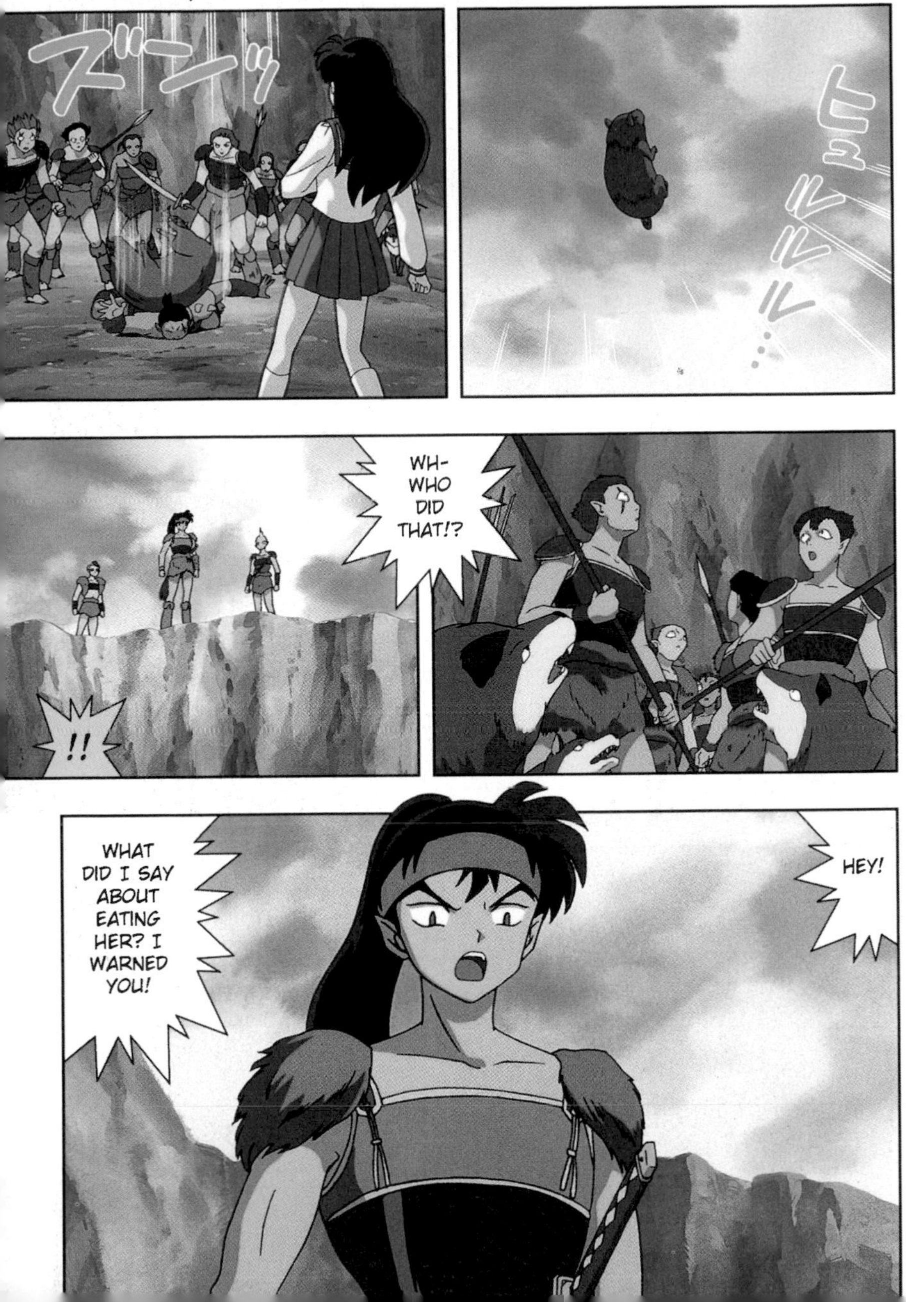
ヒュルルル…
ズーッ
WH- WHO DID THAT!?
!!
HEY!
WHAT DID I SAY ABOUT EATING HER? I WARNED YOU!

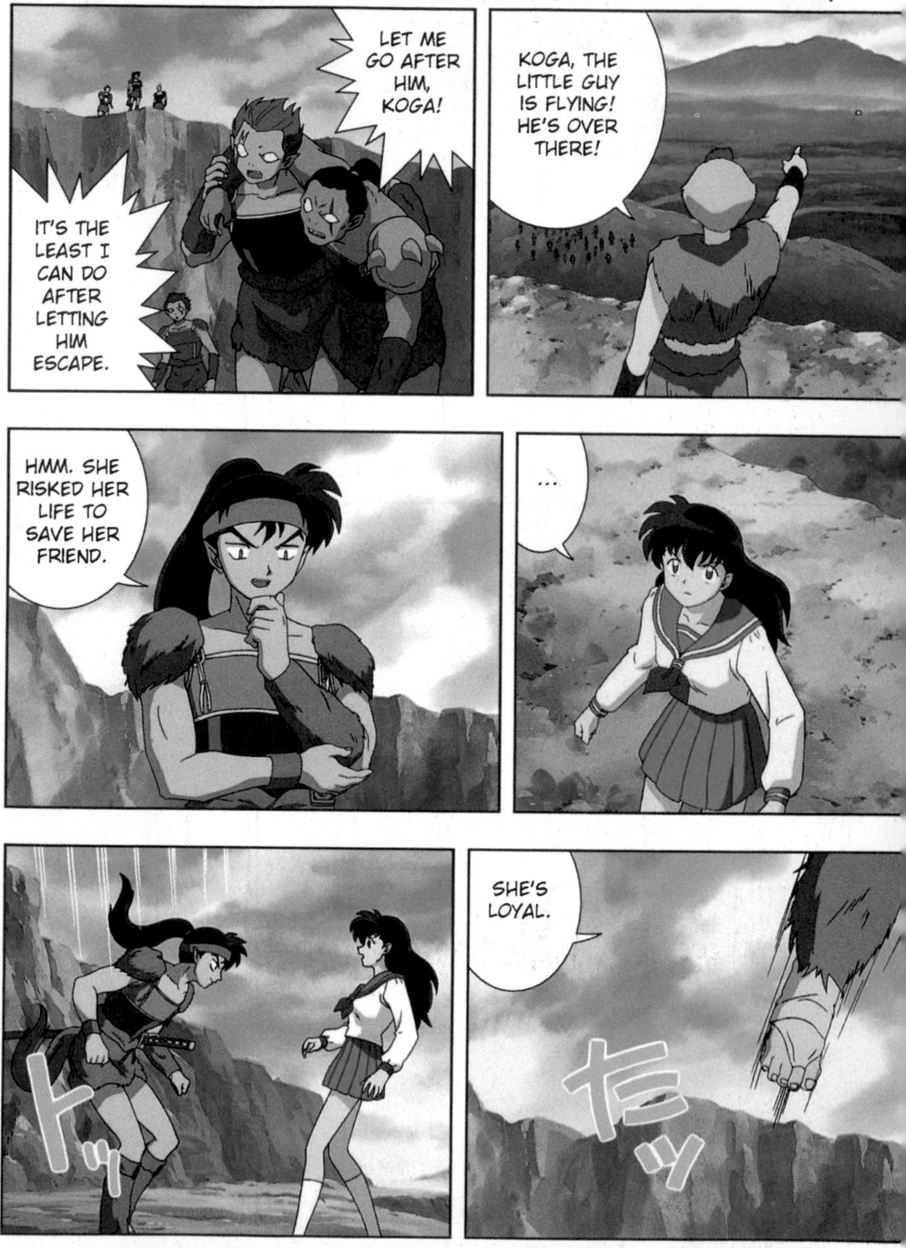
KOGA, THE LITTLE GUY IS FLYING! HE'S OVER THERE!
LET ME GO AFTER HIM, KOGA!
IT'S THE LEAST I CAN DO AFTER LETTING HIM ESCAPE.
...
HMM. SHE RISKED HER LIFE TO SAVE HER FRIEND.
SHE'S LOYAL.
たッ
トッ

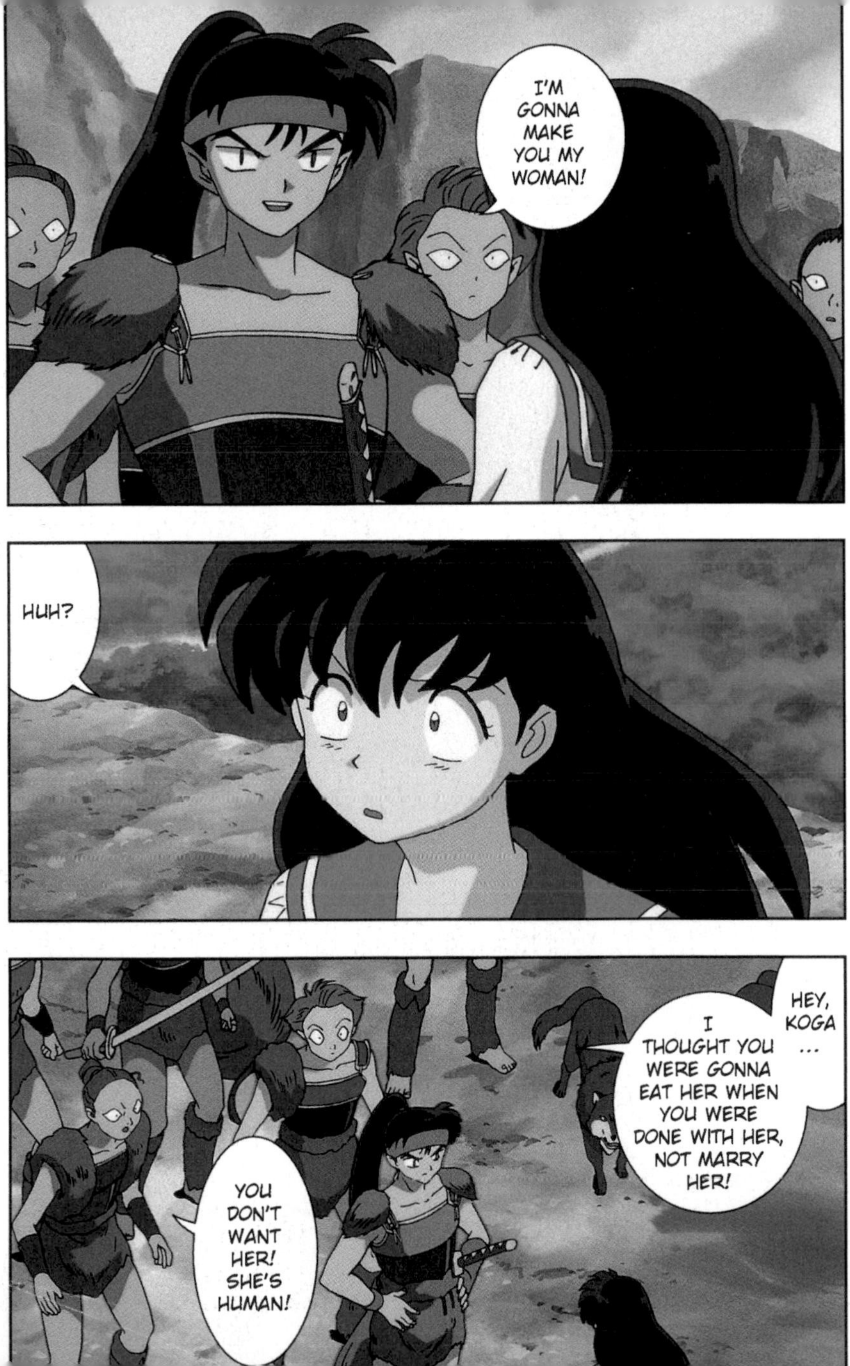
I'M GONNA MAKE YOU MY WOMAN!
HUH?
HEY, KOGA...
I THOUGHT YOU WERE GONNA EAT HER WHEN YOU WERE DONE WITH HER, NOT MARRY HER!
YOU DON'T WANT HER! SHE'S HUMAN!

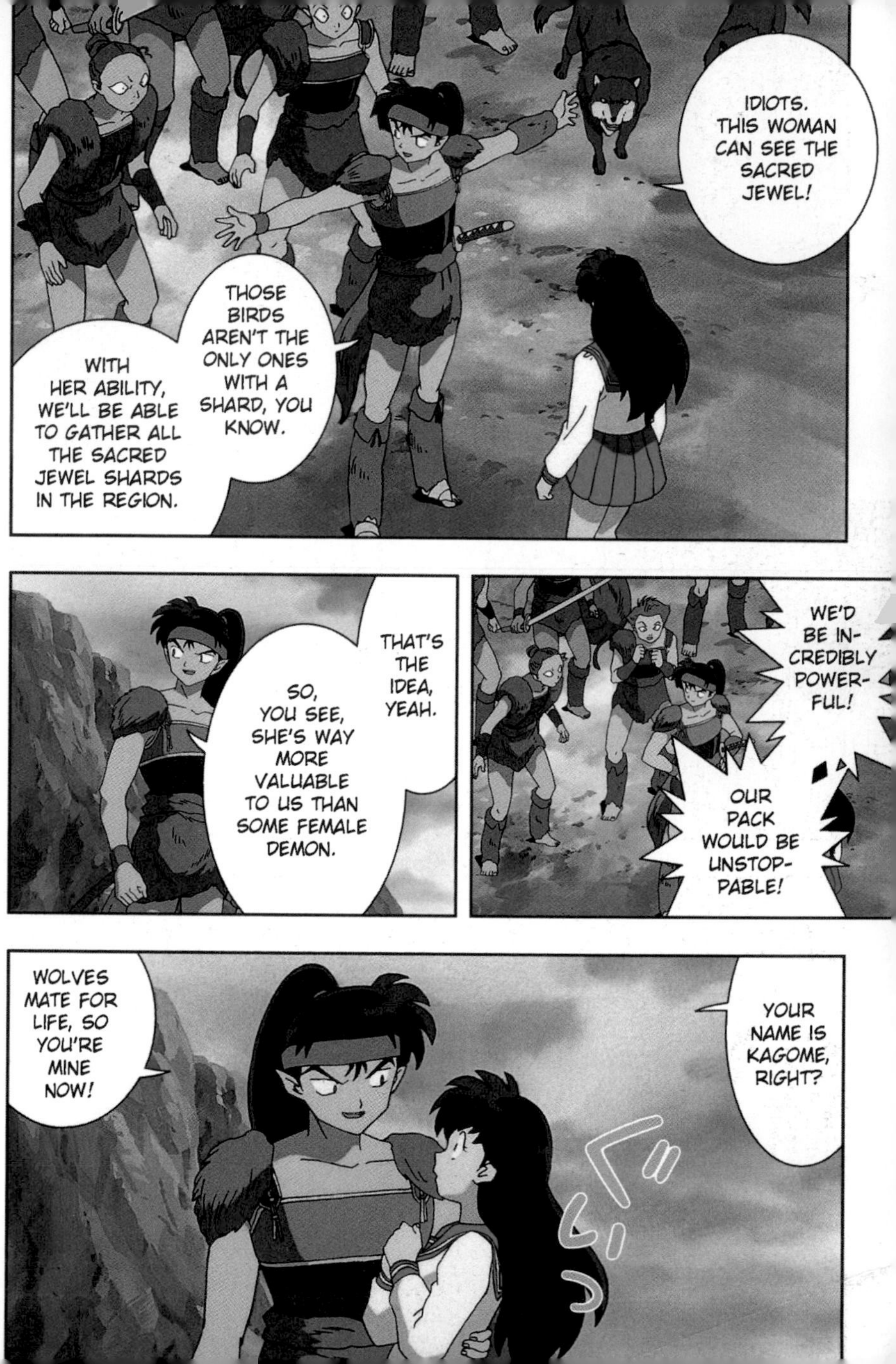
IDIOTS. THIS WOMAN CAN SEE THE SACRED JEWEL!
THOSE BIRDS AREN'T THE ONLY ONES WITH A SHARD, YOU KNOW.
WITH HER ABILITY, WE'LL BE ABLE TO GATHER ALL THE SACRED JEWEL SHARDS IN THE REGION.
WE'D BE INCREDIBLY POWERFUL!
OUR PACK WOULD BE UNSTOPPABLE!
THAT'S THE IDEA, YEAH.
SO, YOU SEE, SHE'S WAY MORE VALUABLE TO US THAN SOME FEMALE DEMON.
YOUR NAME IS KAGOME, RIGHT?
WOLVES MATE FOR LIFE, SO YOU'RE MINE NOW!

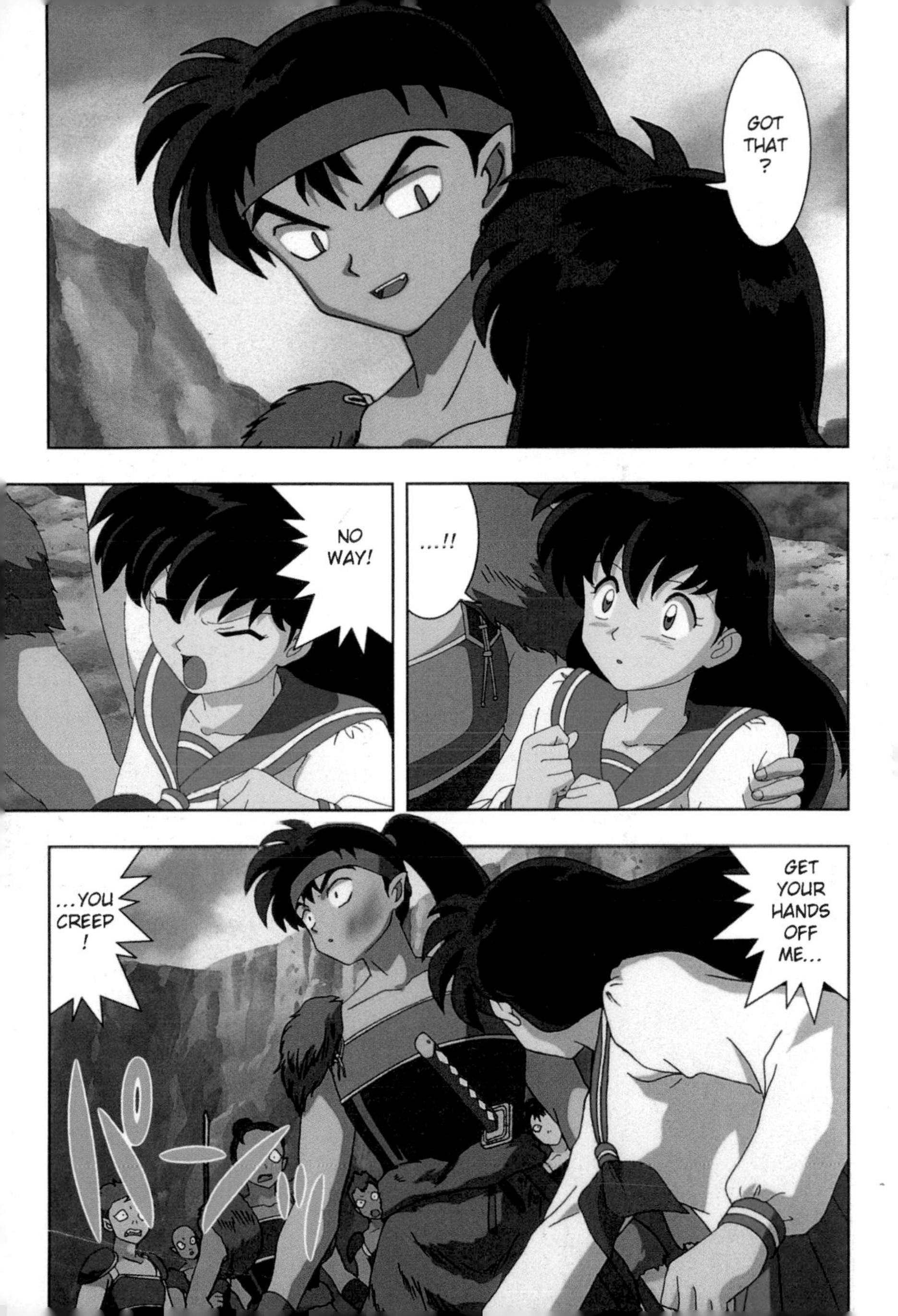
GOT THAT?
...!!
NO WAY!
GET YOUR HANDS OFF ME...
...YOU CREEP!

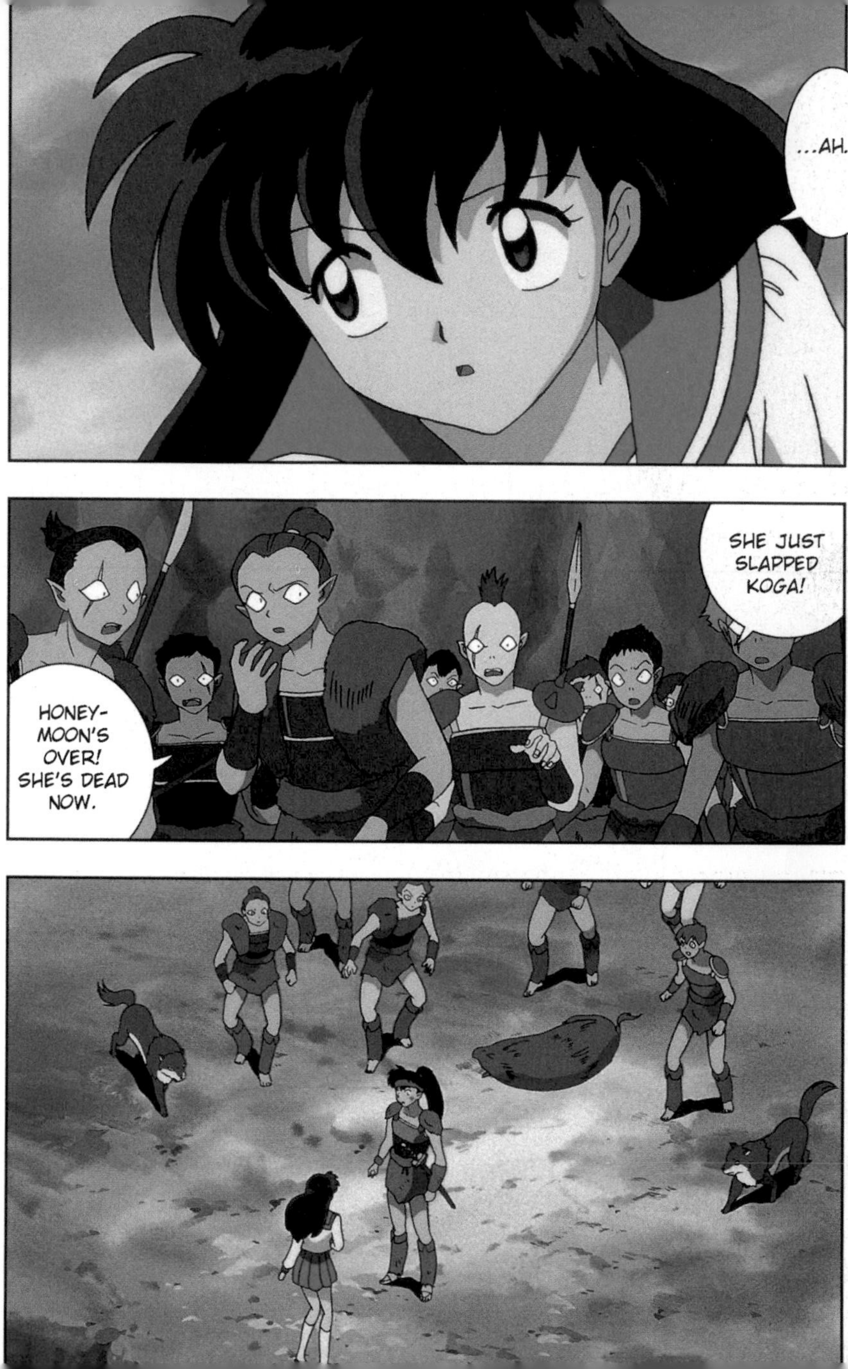
...AH...
SHE JUST SLAPPED KOGA!
HONEY-MOON'S OVER! SHE'S DEAD NOW.

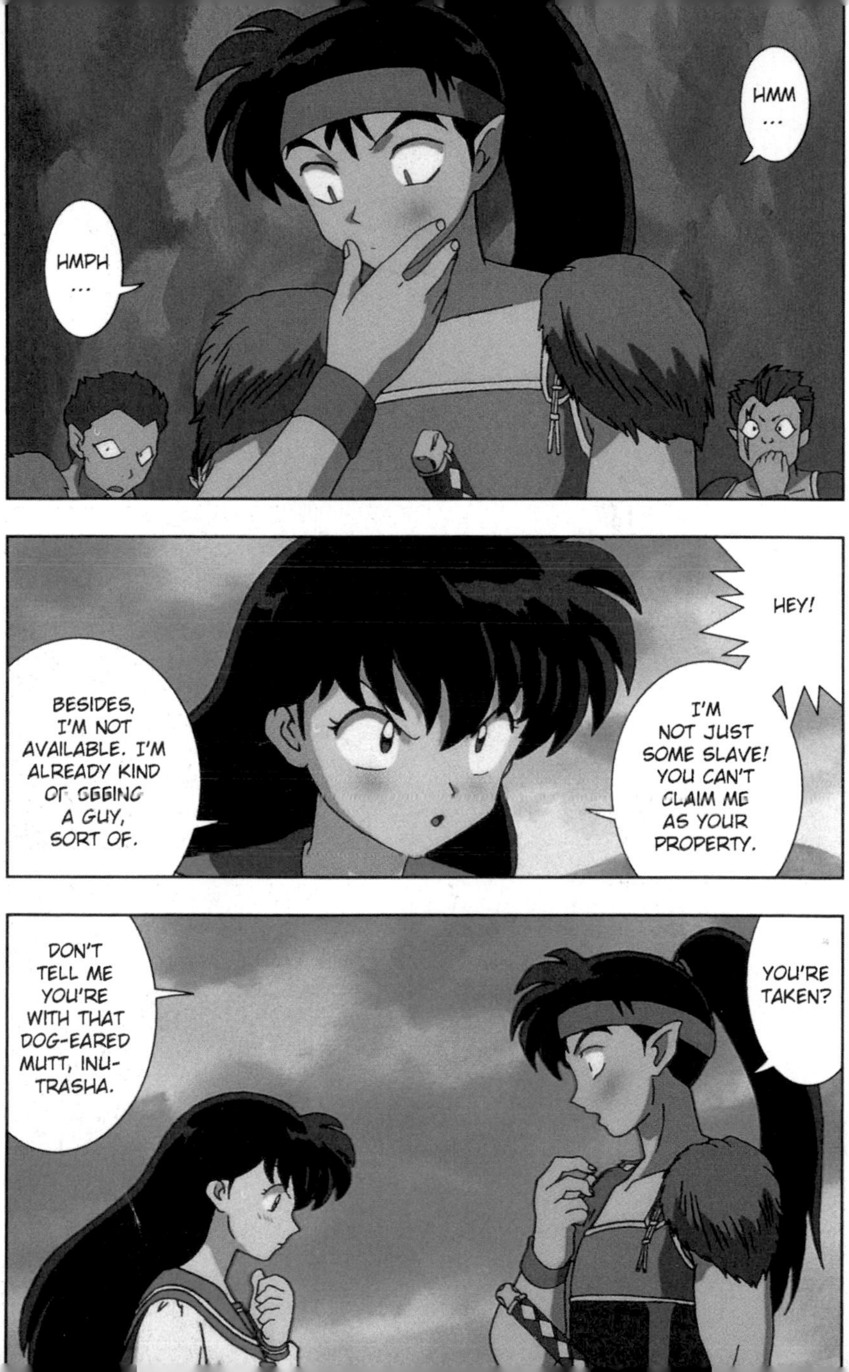
HMM ...
HMPH ...
HEY!
I'M NOT JUST SOME SLAVE! YOU CAN'T CLAIM ME AS YOUR PROPERTY.
BESIDES, I'M NOT AVAILABLE. I'M ALREADY KIND OF SEEING A GUY, SORT OF.
YOU'RE TAKEN?
DON'T TELL ME YOU'RE WITH THAT DOG-EARED MUTT, INU-TRASHA.

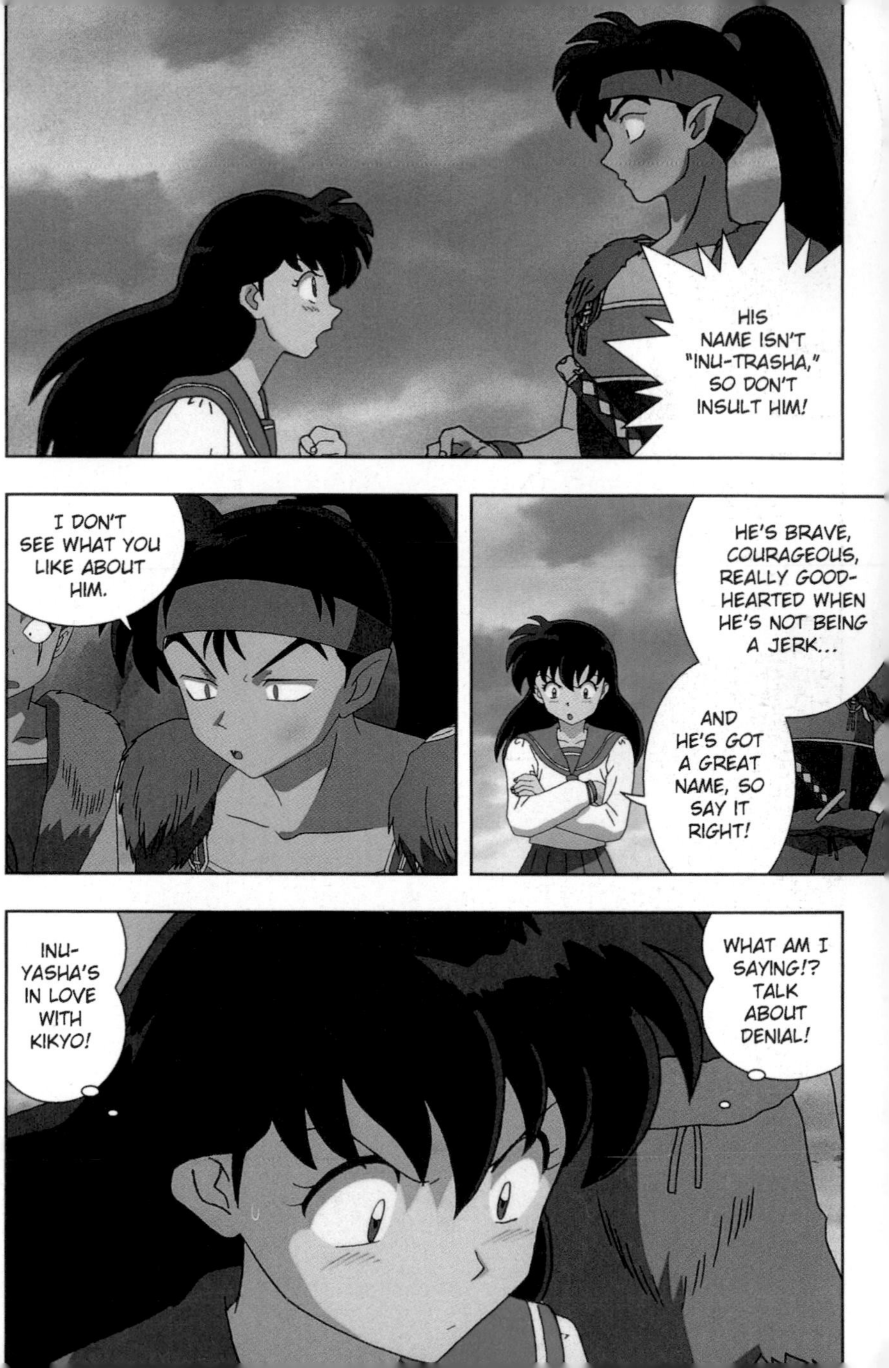
HIS NAME ISN'T "INU-TRASHA," SO DON'T INSULT HIM!
I DON'T SEE WHAT YOU LIKE ABOUT HIM.
HE'S BRAVE, COURAGEOUS, REALLY GOOD-HEARTED WHEN HE'S NOT BEING A JERK...
AND HE'S GOT A GREAT NAME, SO SAY IT RIGHT!
INU-YASHA'S IN LOVE WITH KIKYO!
WHAT AM I SAYING!? TALK ABOUT DENIAL!

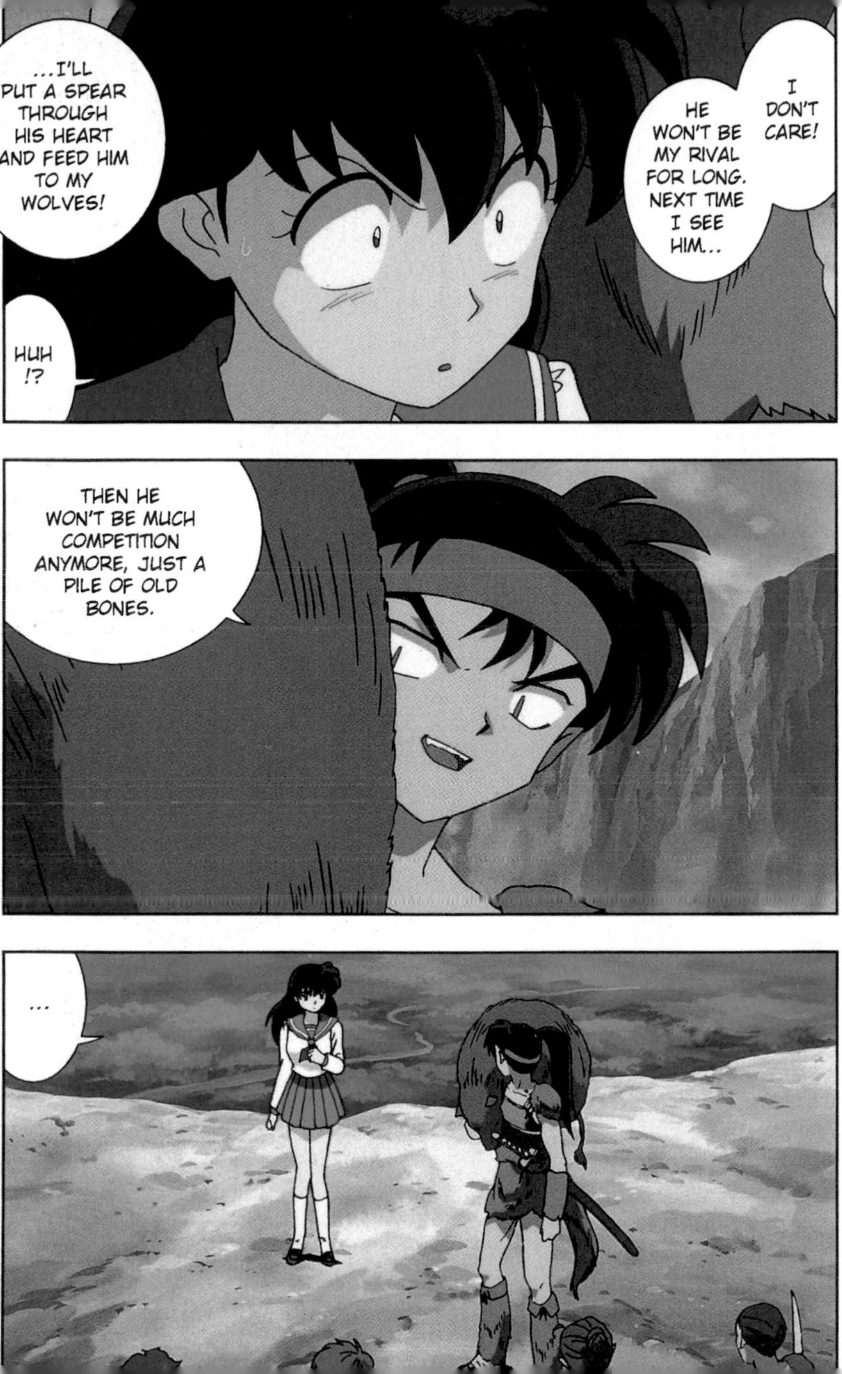
I DON'T CARE!
HE WON'T BE MY RIVAL FOR LONG. NEXT TIME I SEE HIM...
...I'LL PUT A SPEAR THROUGH HIS HEART AND FEED HIM TO MY WOLVES!
HUH !?
THEN HE WON'T BE MUCH COMPETITION ANYMORE, JUST A PILE OF OLD BONES.
...

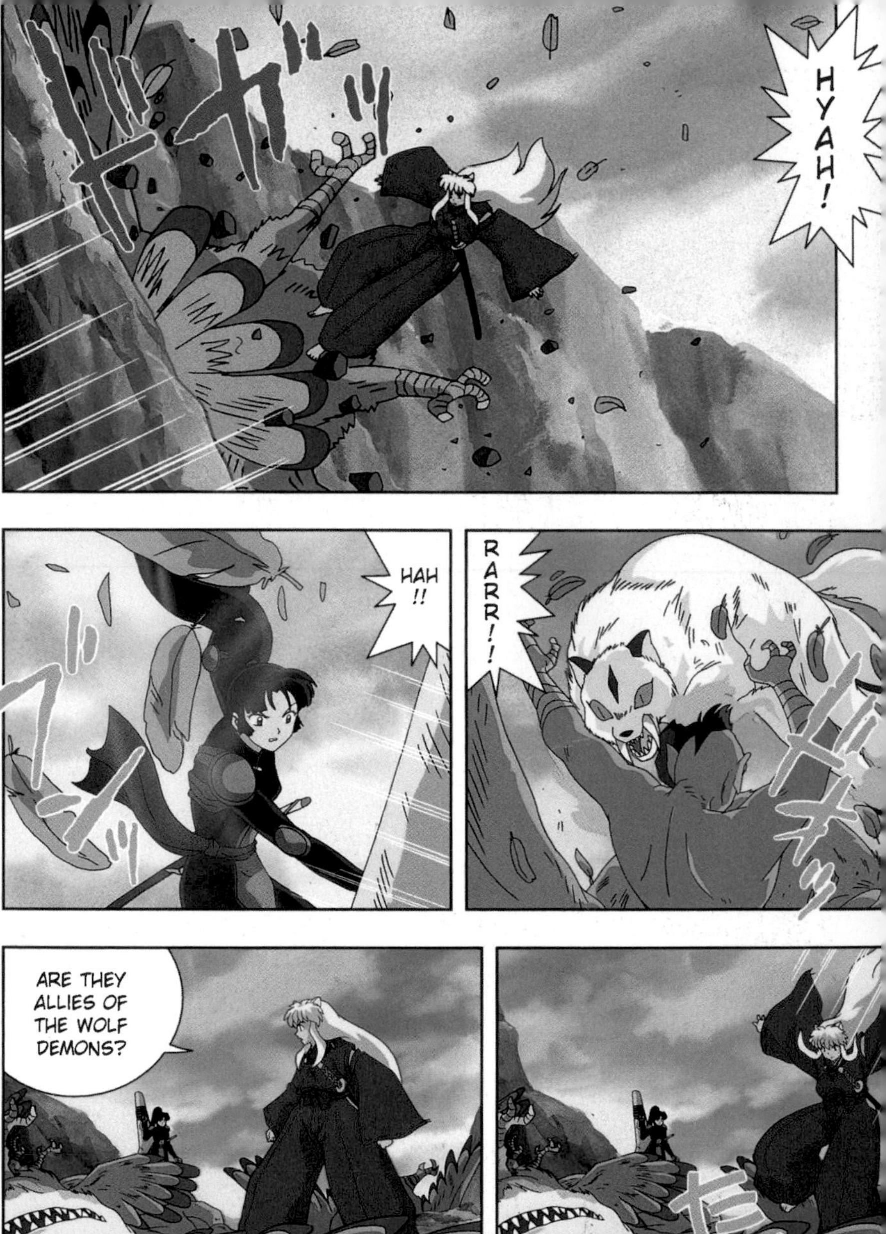
HYAH!
RARR!!
HAH!!
ARE THEY ALLIES OF THE WOLF DEMONS?

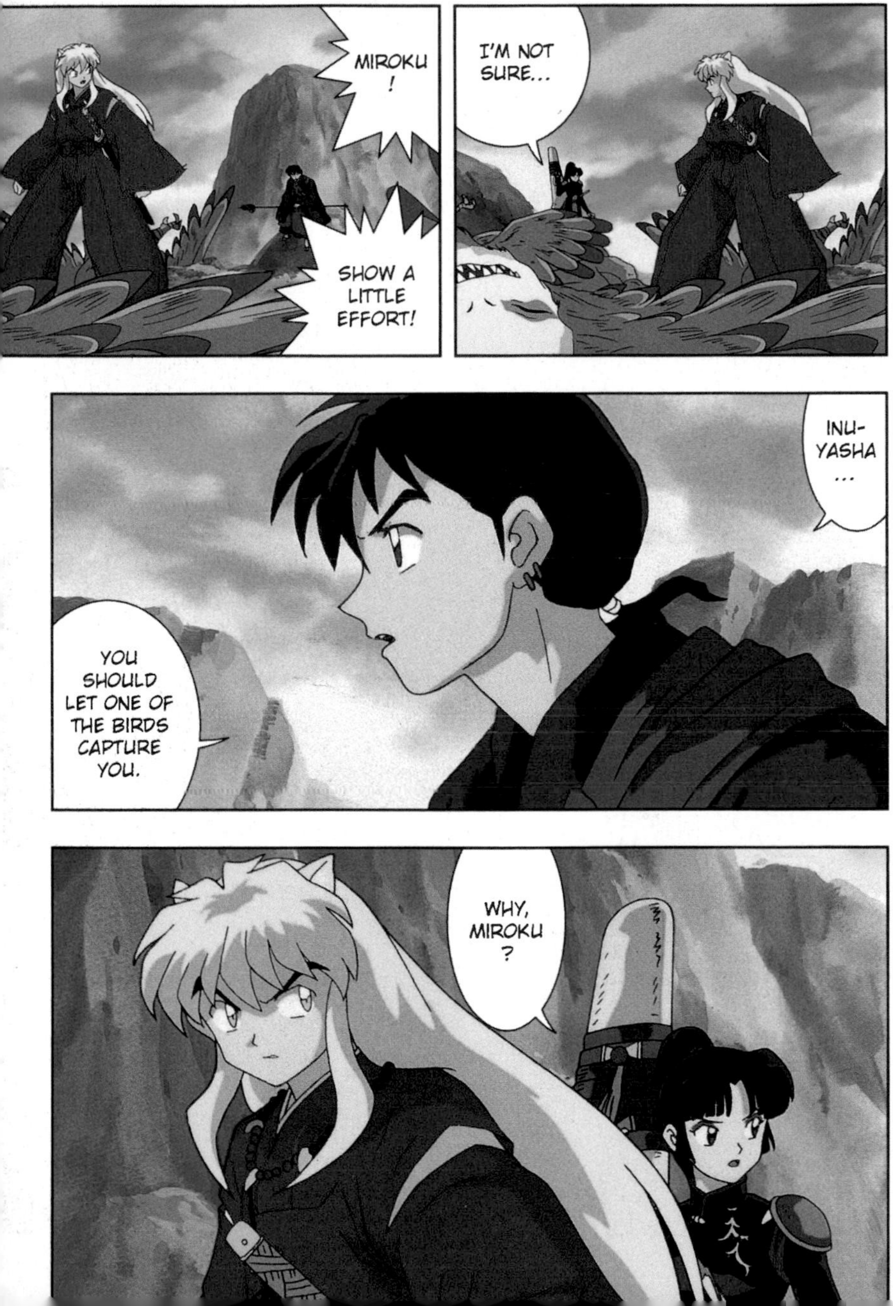
I'M NOT SURE...
MIROKU!
SHOW A LITTLE EFFORT!
INU-YASHA...
YOU SHOULD LET ONE OF THE BIRDS CAPTURE YOU.
WHY, MIROKU?

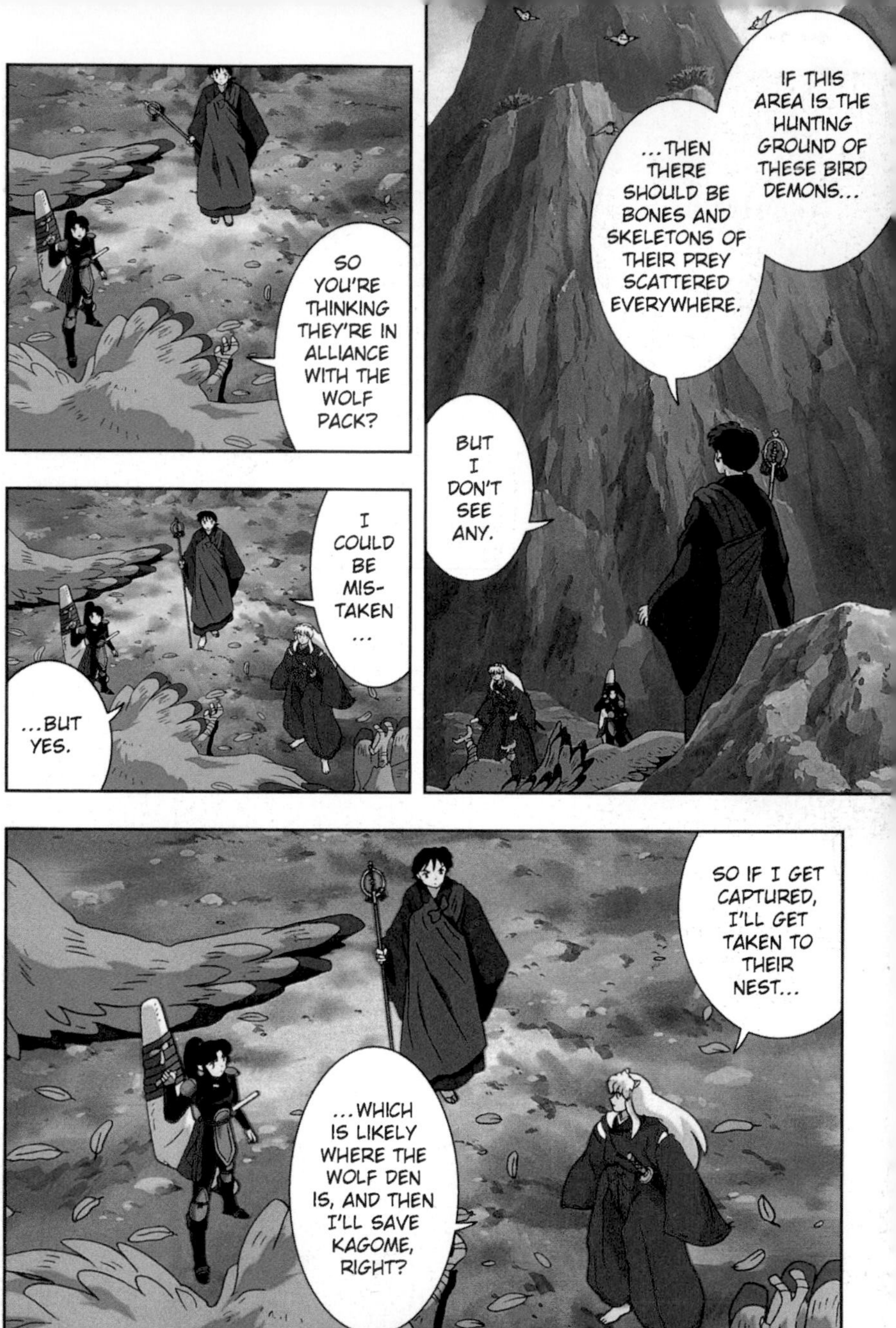
IF THIS AREA IS THE HUNTING GROUND OF THESE BIRD DEMONS...
...THEN THERE SHOULD BE BONES AND SKELETONS OF THEIR PREY SCATTERED EVERYWHERE.
BUT I DON'T SEE ANY.
SO YOU'RE THINKING THEY'RE IN ALLIANCE WITH THE WOLF PACK?
I COULD BE MIS-TAKEN...
...BUT YES.
SO IF I GET CAPTURED, I'LL GET TAKEN TO THEIR NEST...
...WHICH IS LIKELY WHERE THE WOLF DEN IS, AND THEN I'LL SAVE KAGOME, RIGHT?

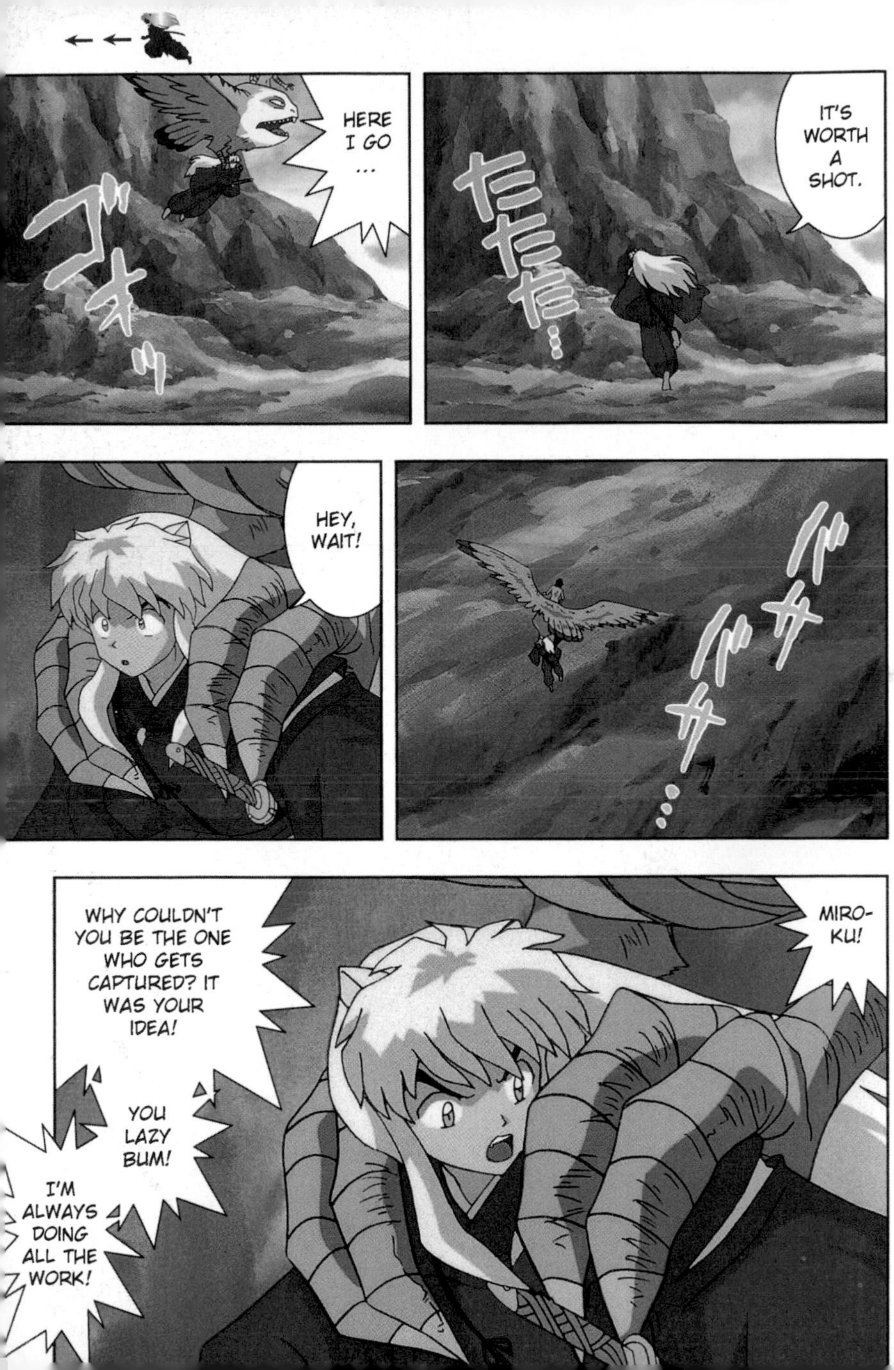
IT'S WORTH A SHOT.
たたた…
HERE I GO…
ゴォォッ
バサバサ…
HEY, WAIT!
MIRO-KU!
WHY COULDN'T YOU BE THE ONE WHO GETS CAPTURED? IT WAS YOUR IDEA!
YOU LAZY BUM!
I'M ALWAYS DOING ALL THE WORK!

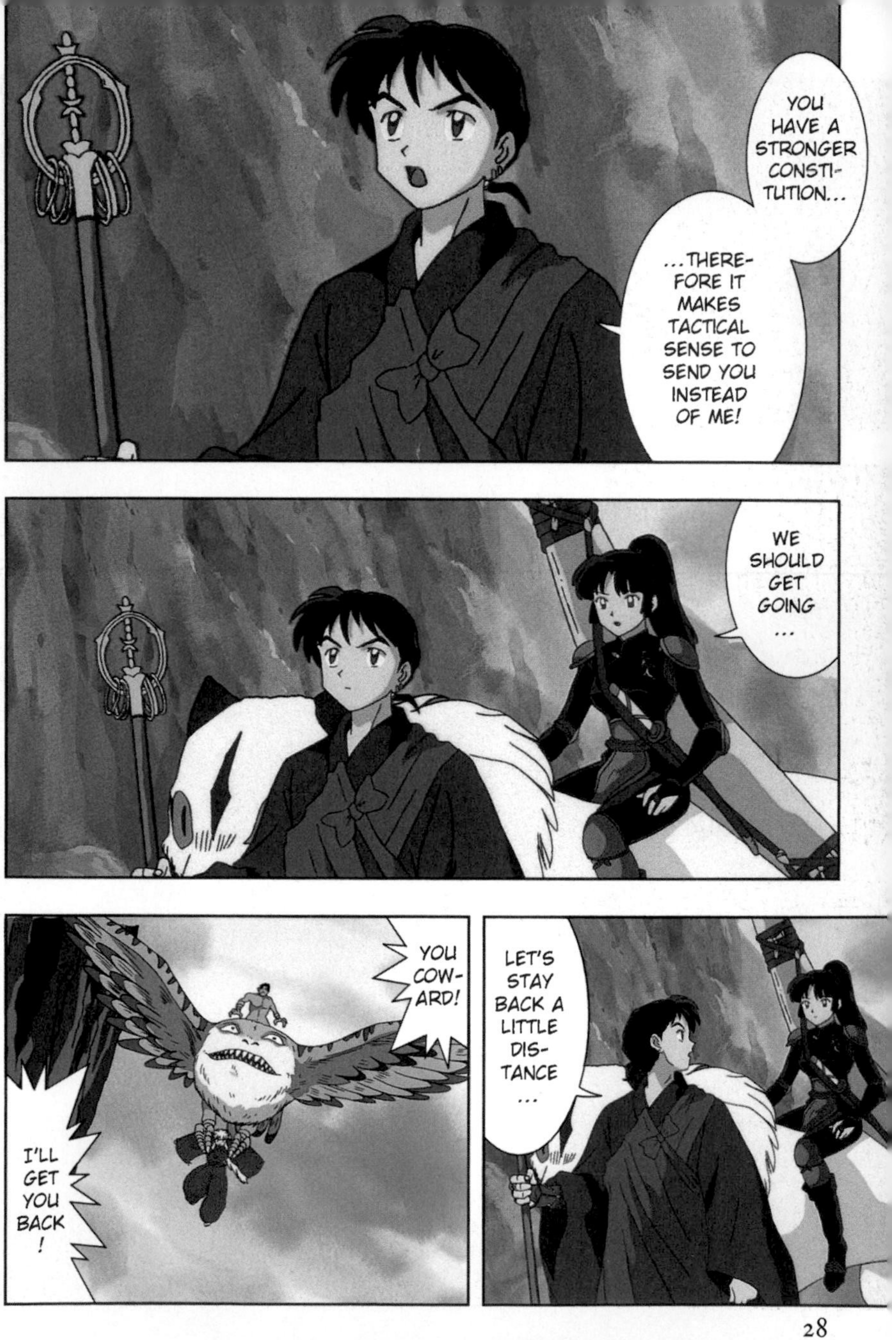
YOU HAVE A STRONGER CONSTI-TUTION...
...THERE-FORE IT MAKES TACTICAL SENSE TO SEND YOU INSTEAD OF ME!
WE SHOULD GET GOING ...
LET'S STAY BACK A LITTLE DIS-TANCE ...
YOU COW-ARD!
I'LL GET YOU BACK !

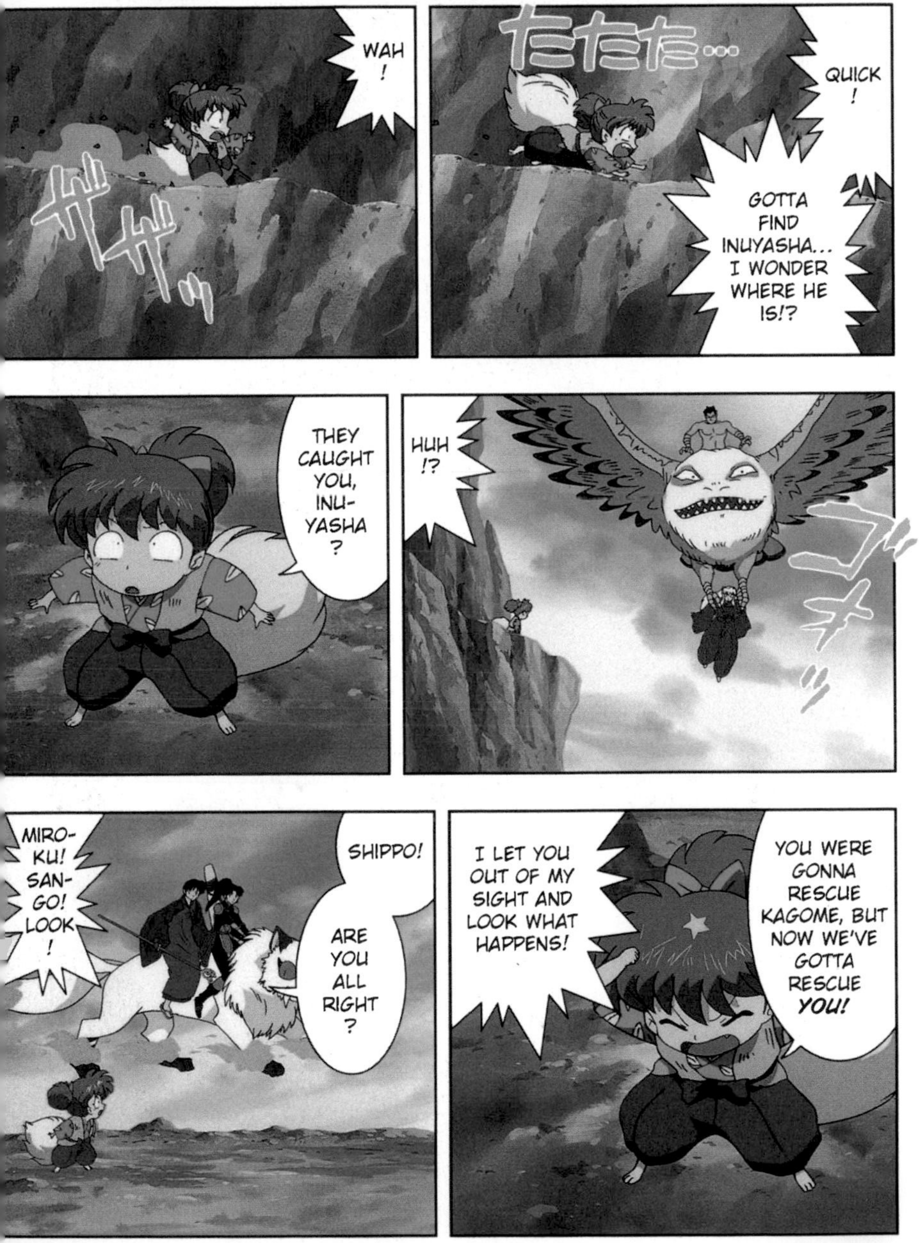
たたたた…
QUICK!
GOTTA FIND INUYASHA... I WONDER WHERE HE IS!?
WAH!
ザザッ
HUH!?
ゴォッ
THEY CAUGHT YOU, INU-YASHA?
YOU WERE GONNA RESCUE KAGOME, BUT NOW WE'VE GOTTA RESCUE ***YOU!***
I LET YOU OUT OF MY SIGHT AND LOOK WHAT HAPPENS!
SHIPPO!
MIRO-KU! SAN-GO! LOOK!
ARE YOU ALL RIGHT?

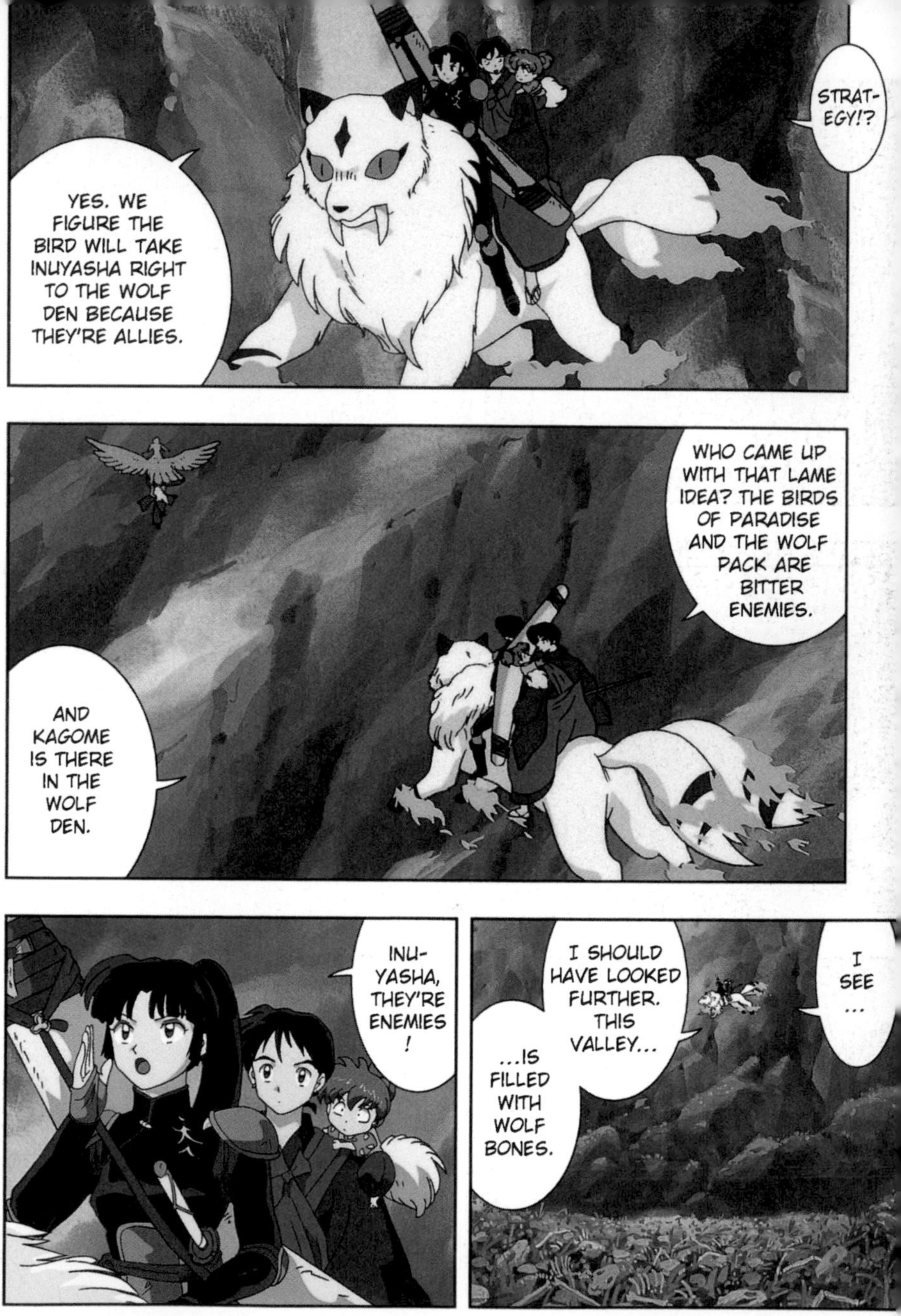
STRATEGY!?
YES. WE FIGURE THE BIRD WILL TAKE INUYASHA RIGHT TO THE WOLF DEN BECAUSE THEY'RE ALLIES.
WHO CAME UP WITH THAT LAME IDEA? THE BIRDS OF PARADISE AND THE WOLF PACK ARE BITTER ENEMIES.
AND KAGOME IS THERE IN THE WOLF DEN.
I SEE...
I SHOULD HAVE LOOKED FURTHER. THIS VALLEY...
...IS FILLED WITH WOLF BONES.
INUYASHA, THEY'RE ENEMIES!

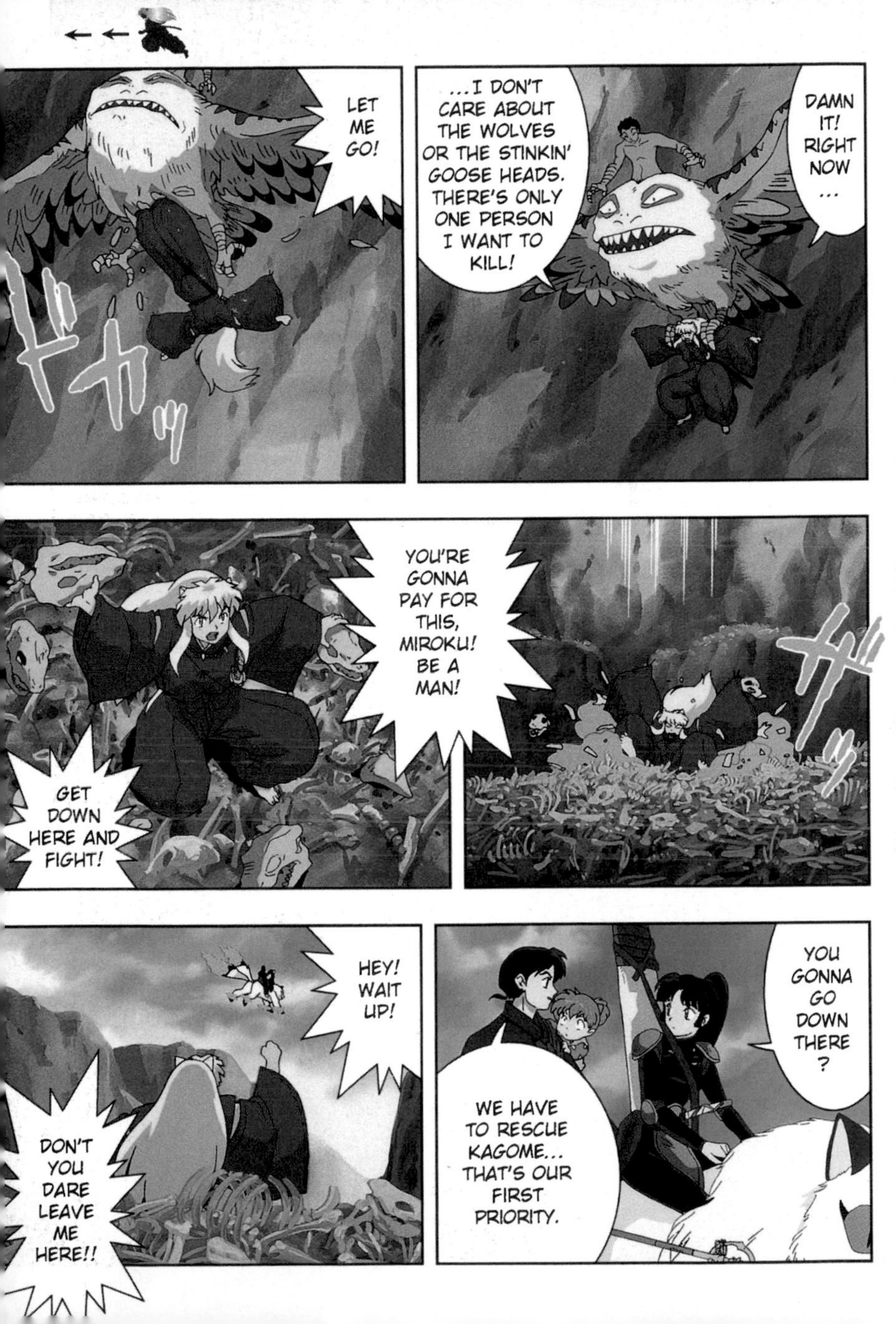
DAMN IT! RIGHT NOW ...
...I DON'T CARE ABOUT THE WOLVES OR THE STINKIN' GOOSE HEADS. THERE'S ONLY ONE PERSON I WANT TO KILL!
LET ME GO!
ドカッ
ザッ
YOU'RE GONNA PAY FOR THIS, MIROKU! BE A MAN!
GET DOWN HERE AND FIGHT!
YOU GONNA GO DOWN THERE?
WE HAVE TO RESCUE KAGOME... THAT'S OUR FIRST PRIORITY.
HEY! WAIT UP!
DON'T YOU DARE LEAVE ME HERE!!

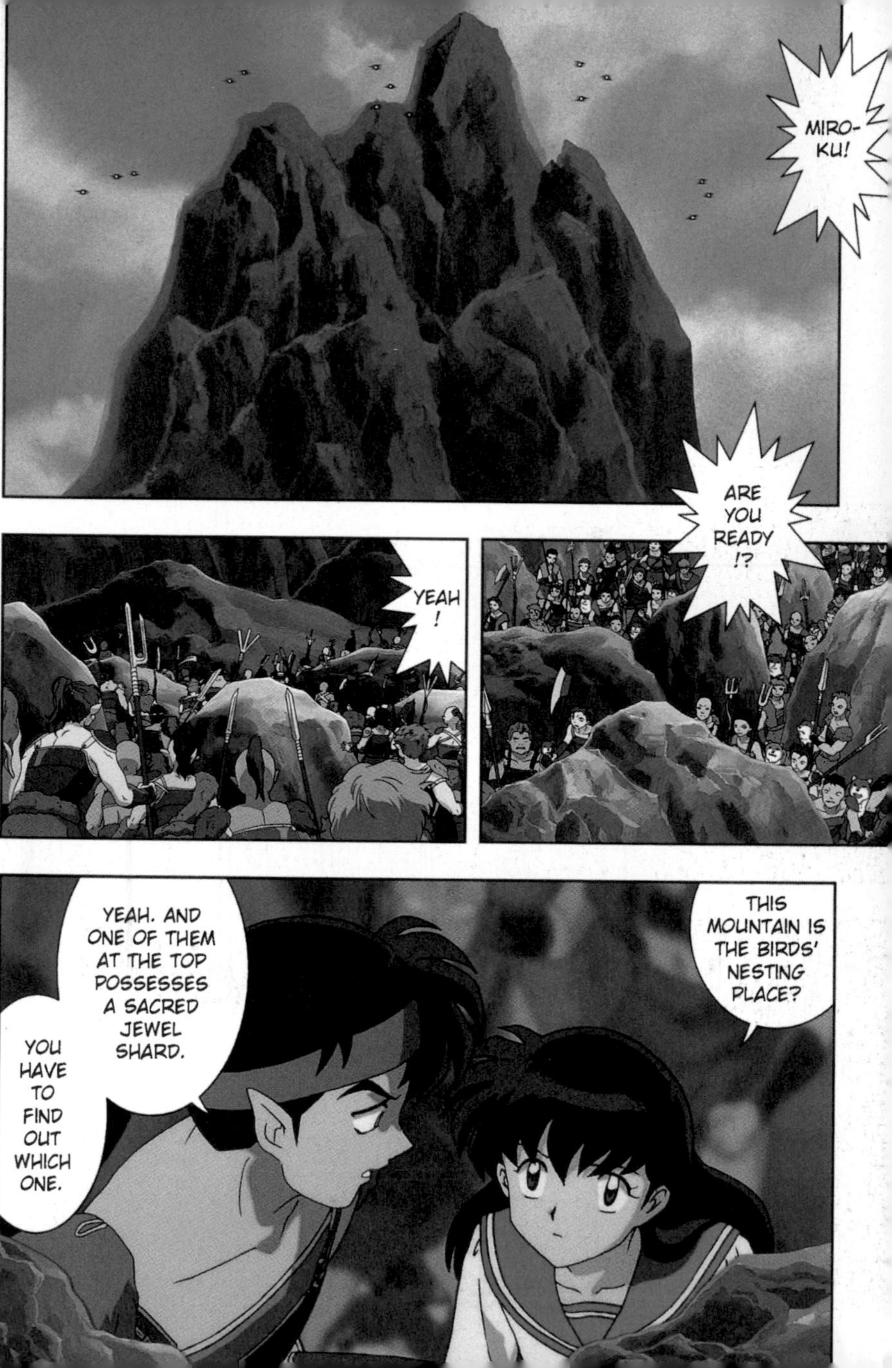
MIRO-KU!
ARE YOU READY !?
YEAH !
THIS MOUNTAIN IS THE BIRDS' NESTING PLACE?
YEAH. AND ONE OF THEM AT THE TOP POSSESSES A SACRED JEWEL SHARD.
YOU HAVE TO FIND OUT WHICH ONE.

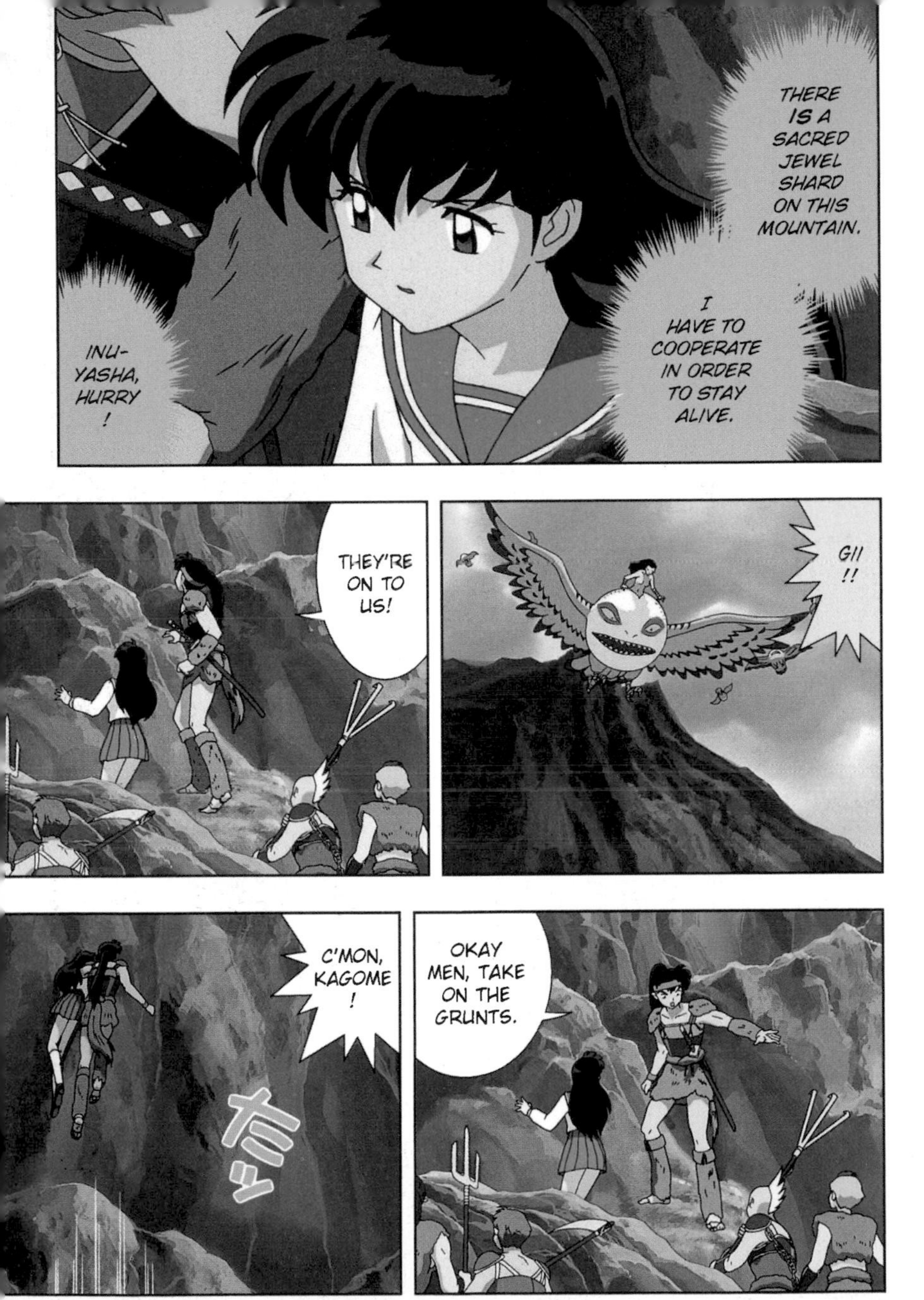
THERE IS A SACRED JEWEL SHARD ON THIS MOUNTAIN.
I HAVE TO COOPERATE IN ORDER TO STAY ALIVE.
INU-YASHA, HURRY!
GII!!
THEY'RE ON TO US!
OKAY MEN, TAKE ON THE GRUNTS.
C'MON, KAGOME!
タッ

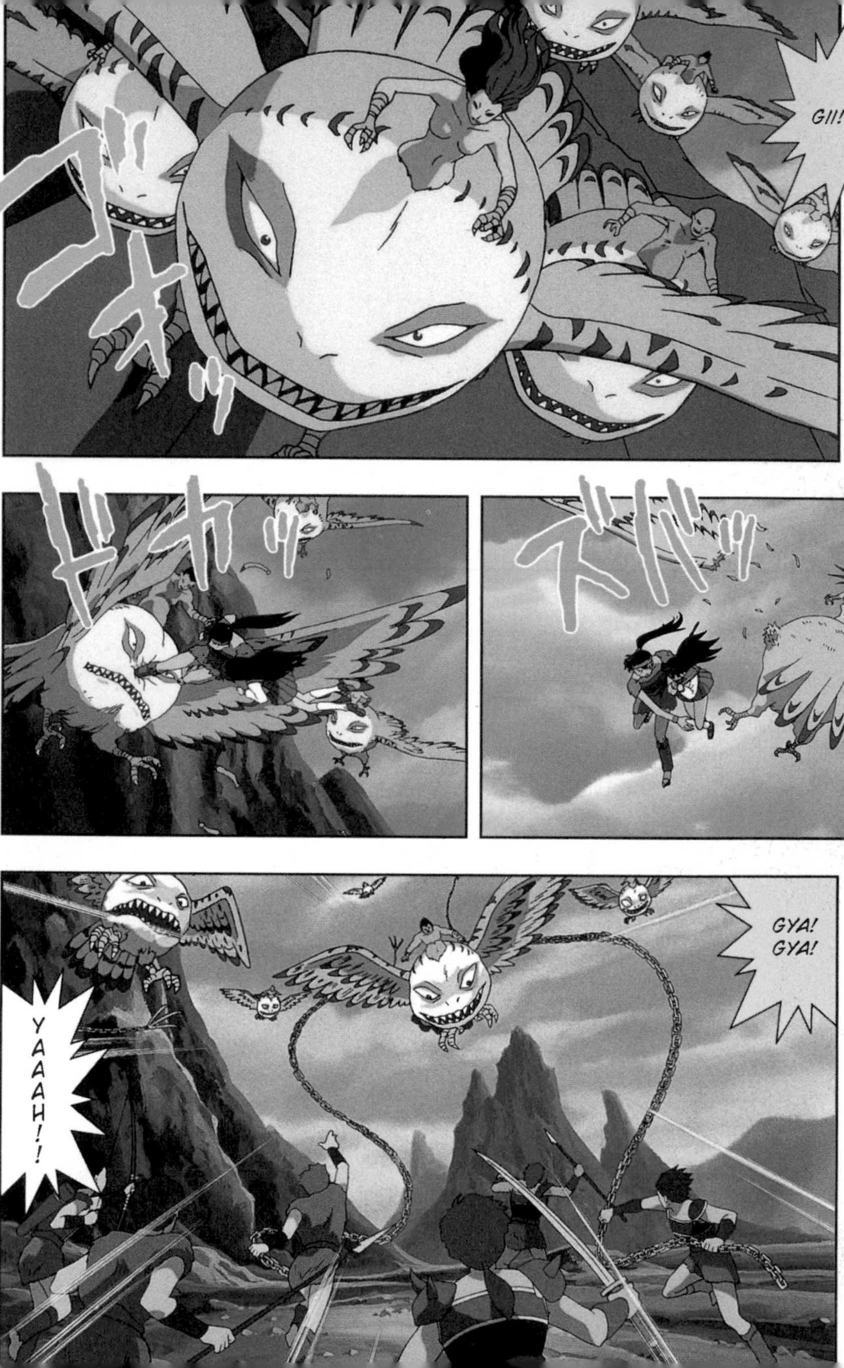
GII!!
ゴオッ
ズバッ
ドカッ
GYA! GYA!
YAAAAH!!

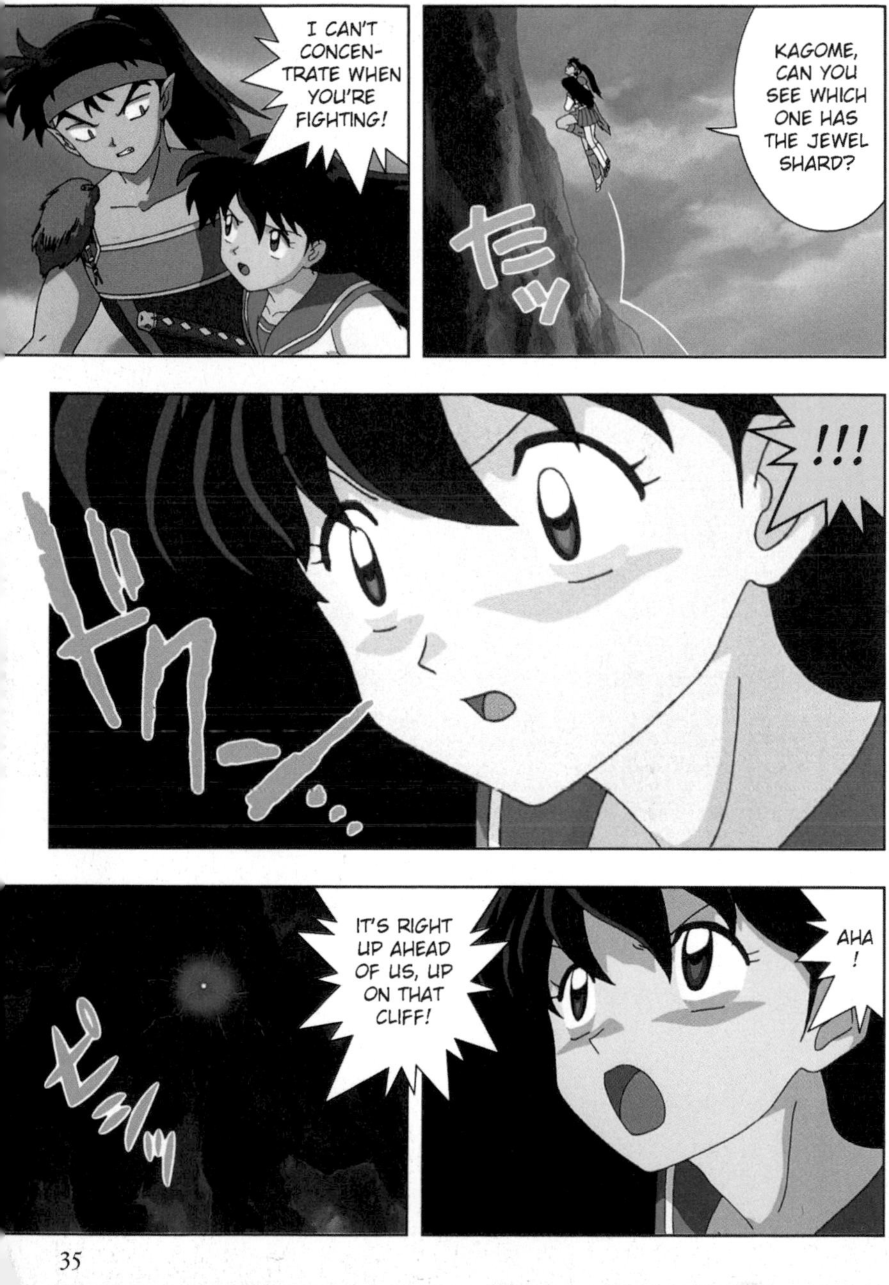
KAGOME, CAN YOU SEE WHICH ONE HAS THE JEWEL SHARD?
I CAN'T CONCEN-TRATE WHEN YOU'RE FIGHTING!
!!!
AHA!
IT'S RIGHT UP AHEAD OF US, UP ON THAT CLIFF!

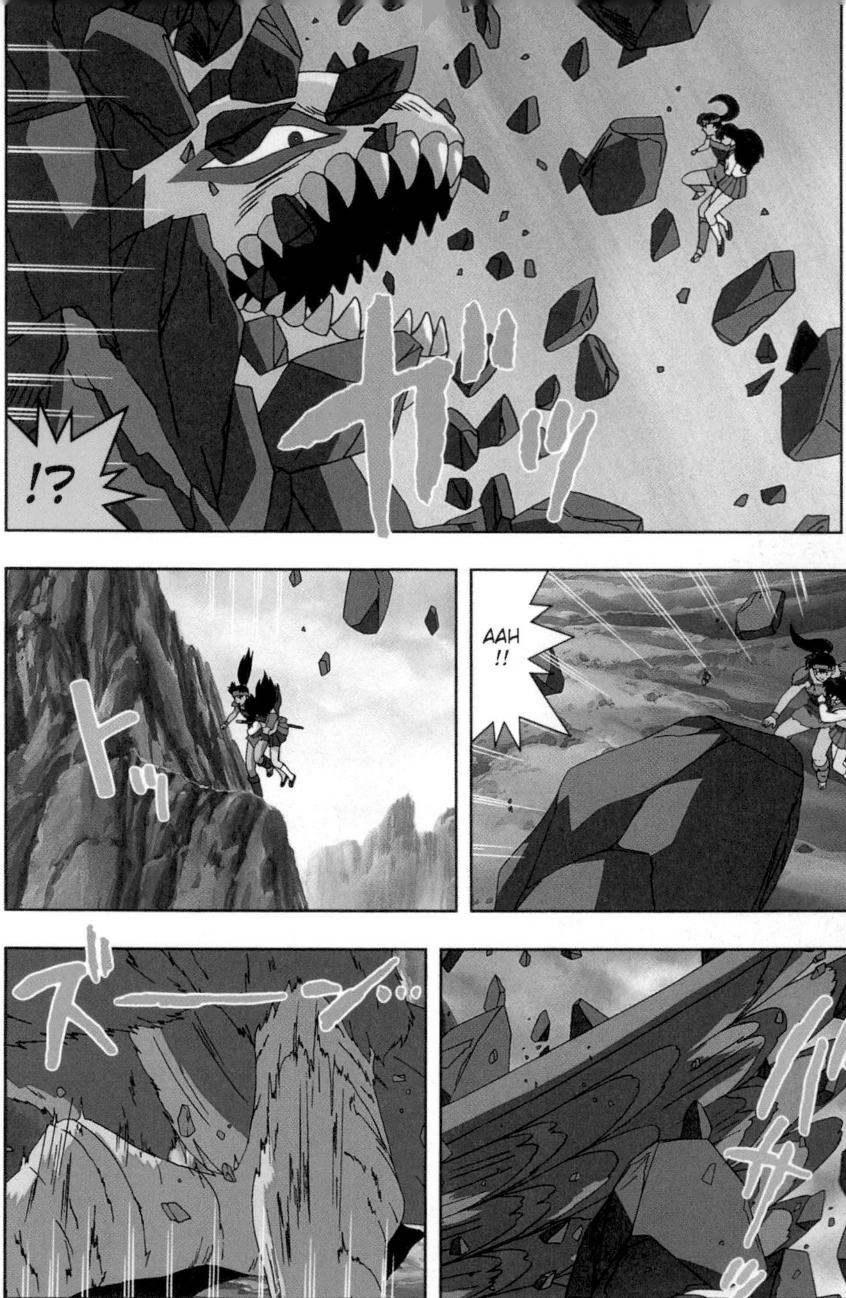
ガッ
!?
AAH !!
トッ
ガサッ
ズーーン…

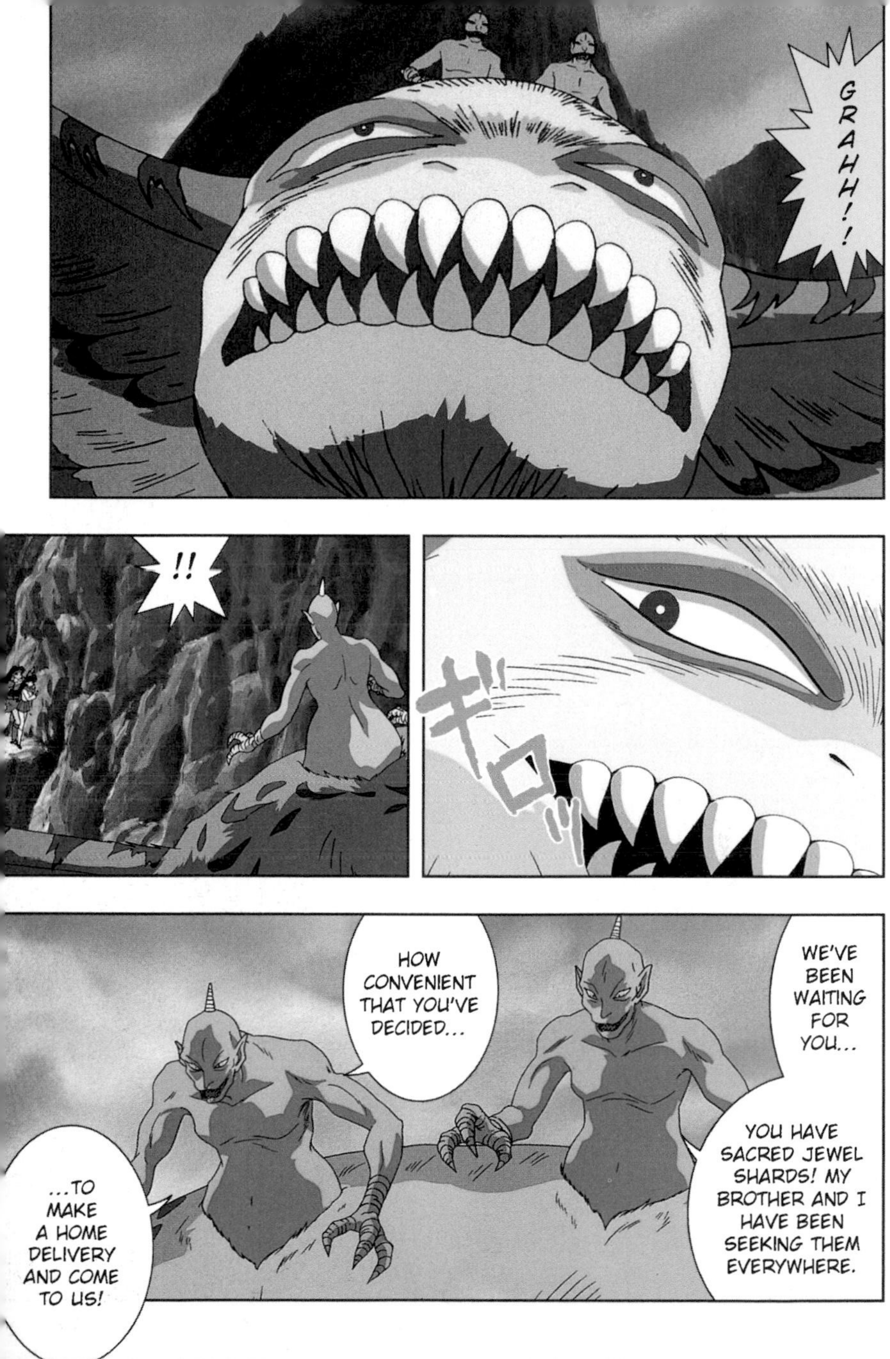
GRAHH!!
ギロッ
!!
WE'VE BEEN WAITING FOR YOU...
HOW CONVENIENT THAT YOU'VE DECIDED...
YOU HAVE SACRED JEWEL SHARDS! MY BROTHER AND I HAVE BEEN SEEKING THEM EVERYWHERE.
...TO MAKE A HOME DELIVERY AND COME TO US!

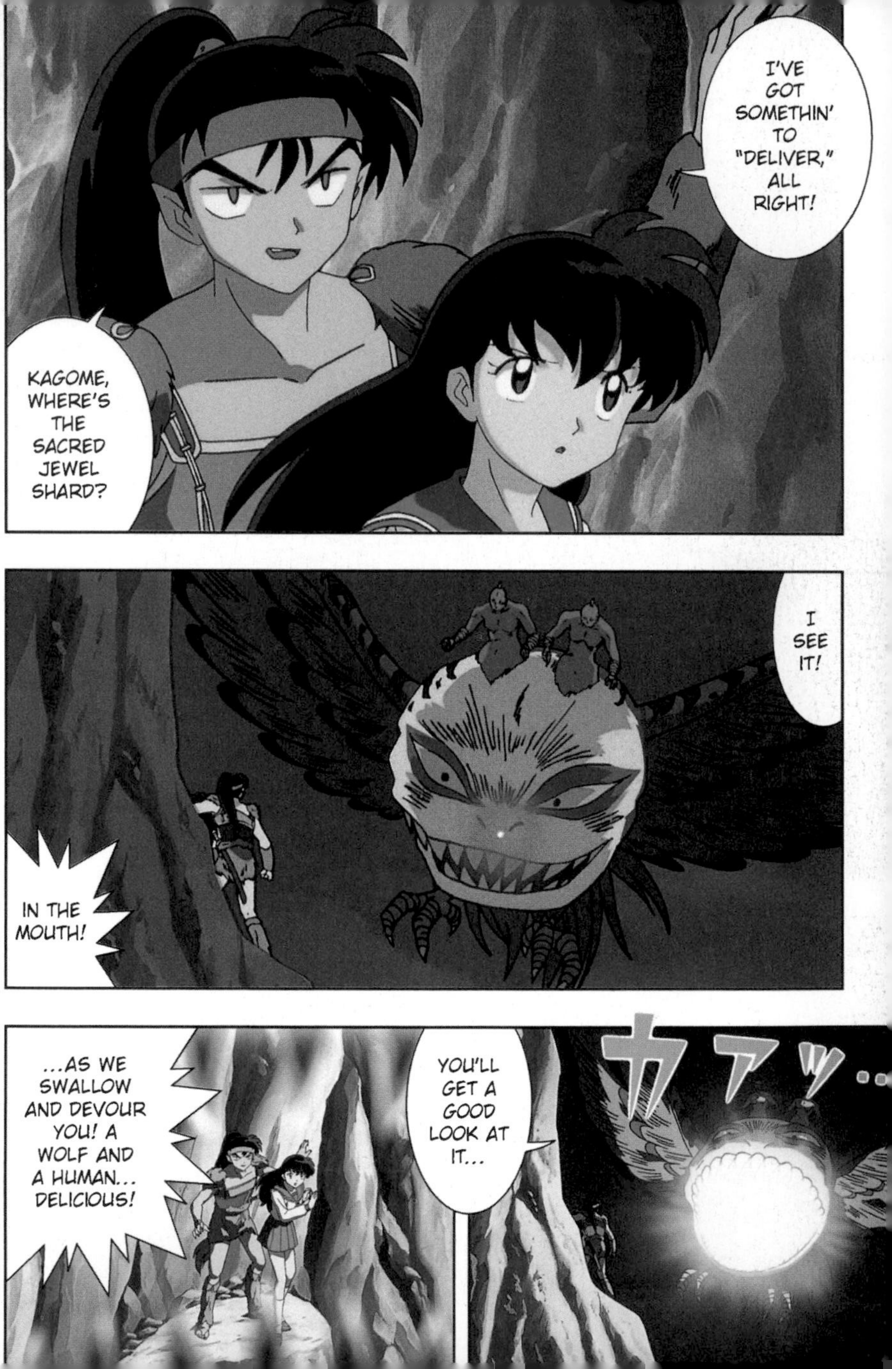
I'VE GOT SOMETHIN' TO "DELIVER," ALL RIGHT!
KAGOME, WHERE'S THE SACRED JEWEL SHARD?
I SEE IT!
IN THE MOUTH!
カァッ..
YOU'LL GET A GOOD LOOK AT IT...
...AS WE SWALLOW AND DEVOUR YOU! A WOLF AND A HUMAN... DELICIOUS!

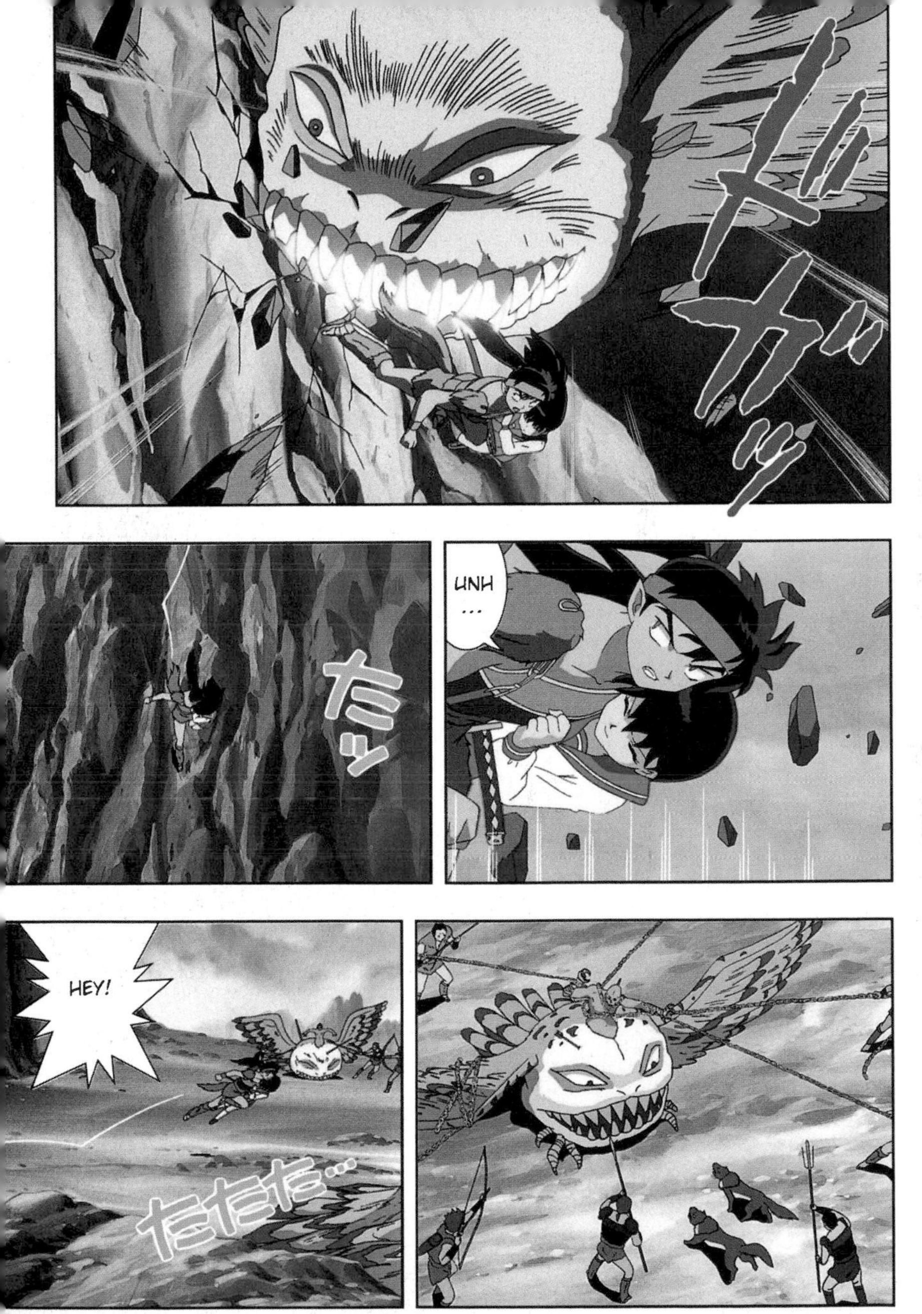
ドガッ
UNH ...
たッ
HEY!
たたた…

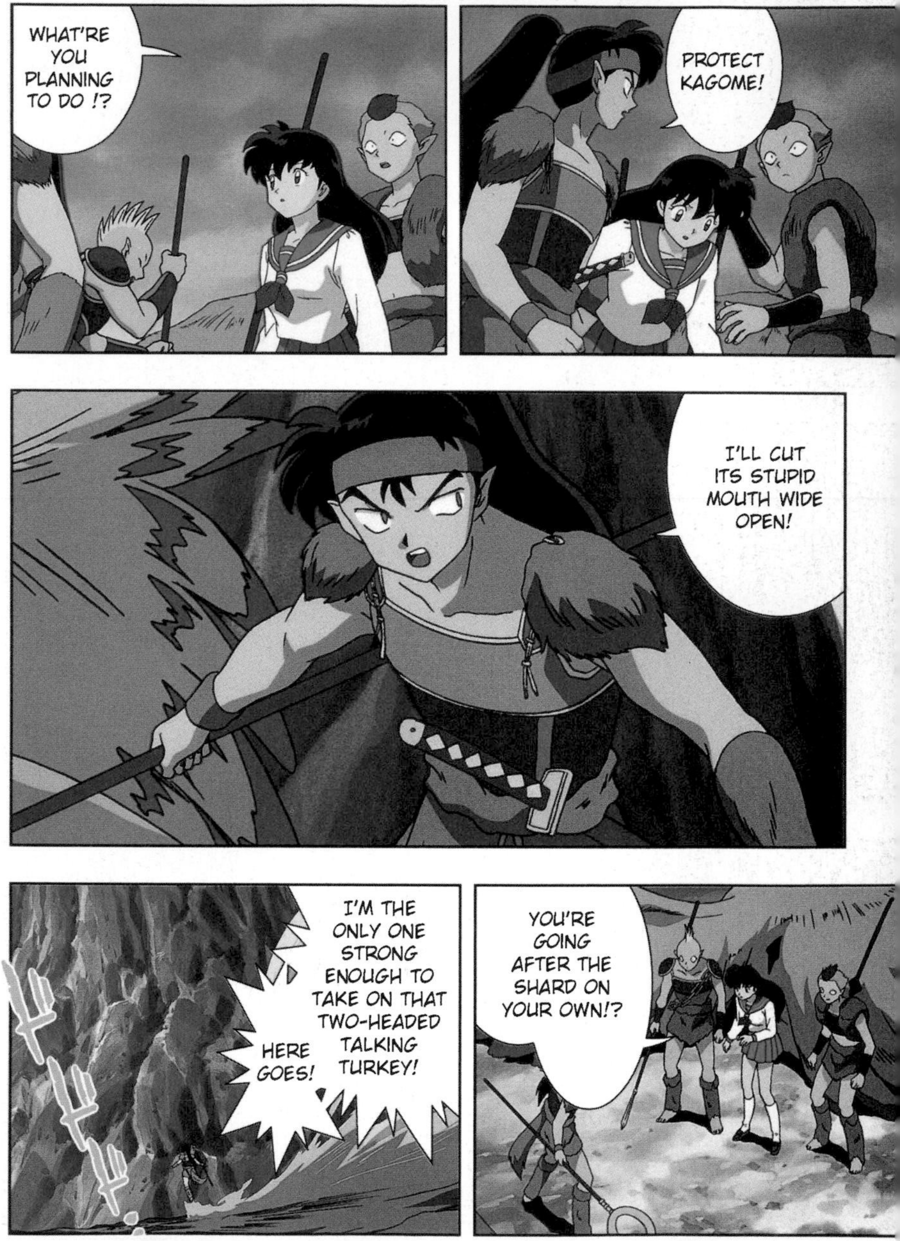
PROTECT KAGOME!
WHAT'RE YOU PLANNING TO DO !?
I'LL CUT ITS STUPID MOUTH WIDE OPEN!
YOU'RE GOING AFTER THE SHARD ON YOUR OWN!?
I'M THE ONLY ONE STRONG ENOUGH TO TAKE ON THAT TWO-HEADED TALKING TURKEY!
HERE GOES!

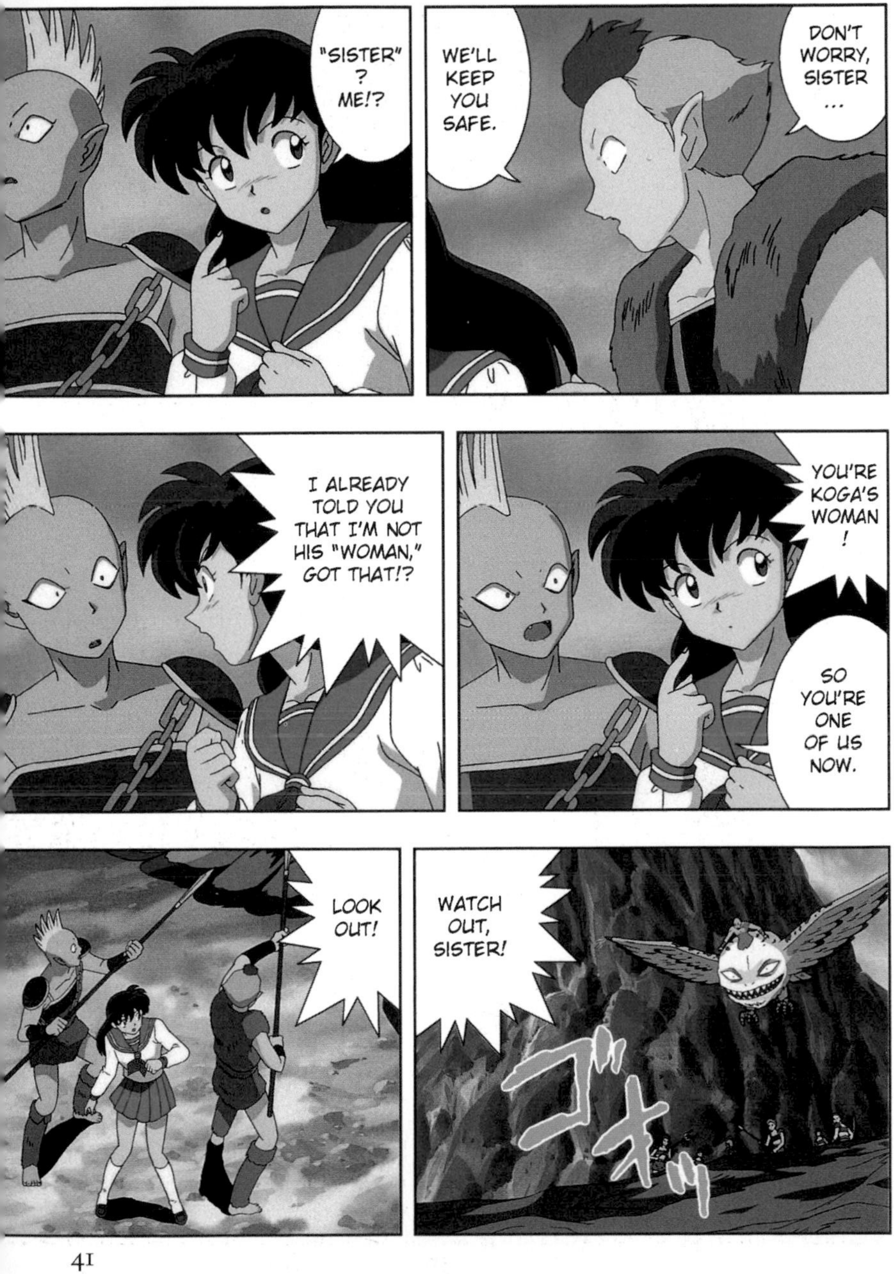
DON'T WORRY, SISTER ...
WE'LL KEEP YOU SAFE.
"SISTER"? ME!?
YOU'RE KOGA'S WOMAN!
SO YOU'RE ONE OF US NOW.
I ALREADY TOLD YOU THAT I'M NOT HIS "WOMAN," GOT THAT!?
WATCH OUT, SISTER!
LOOK OUT!

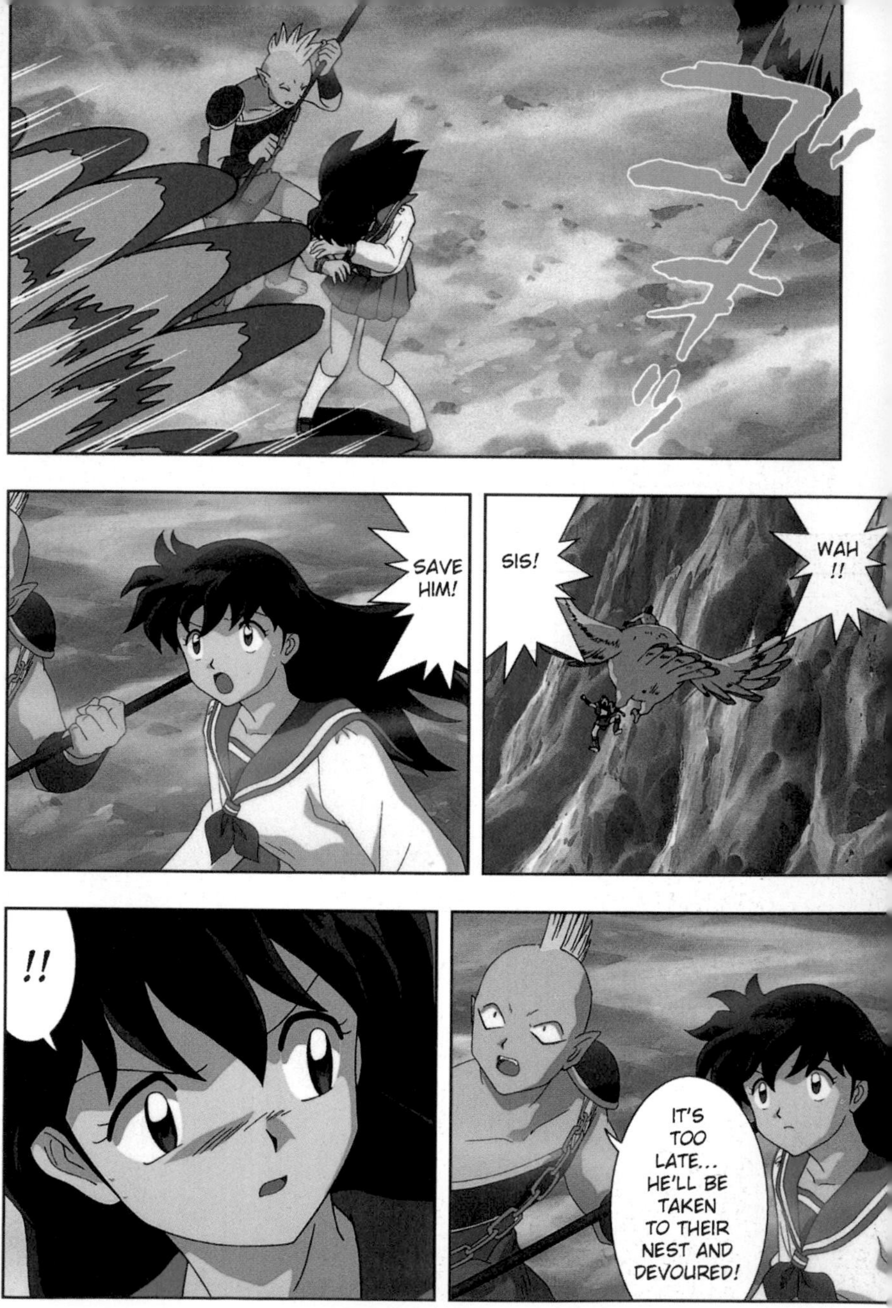
WAH !!
SIS!
SAVE HIM!
IT'S TOO LATE... HE'LL BE TAKEN TO THEIR NEST AND DEVOURED!
!!

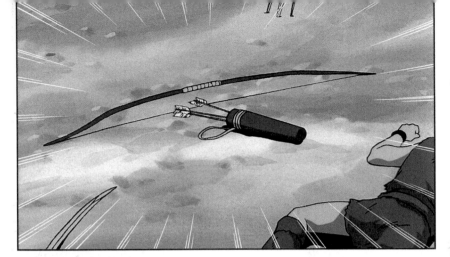

HIT THE MARK!

STAY BACK, SIS!

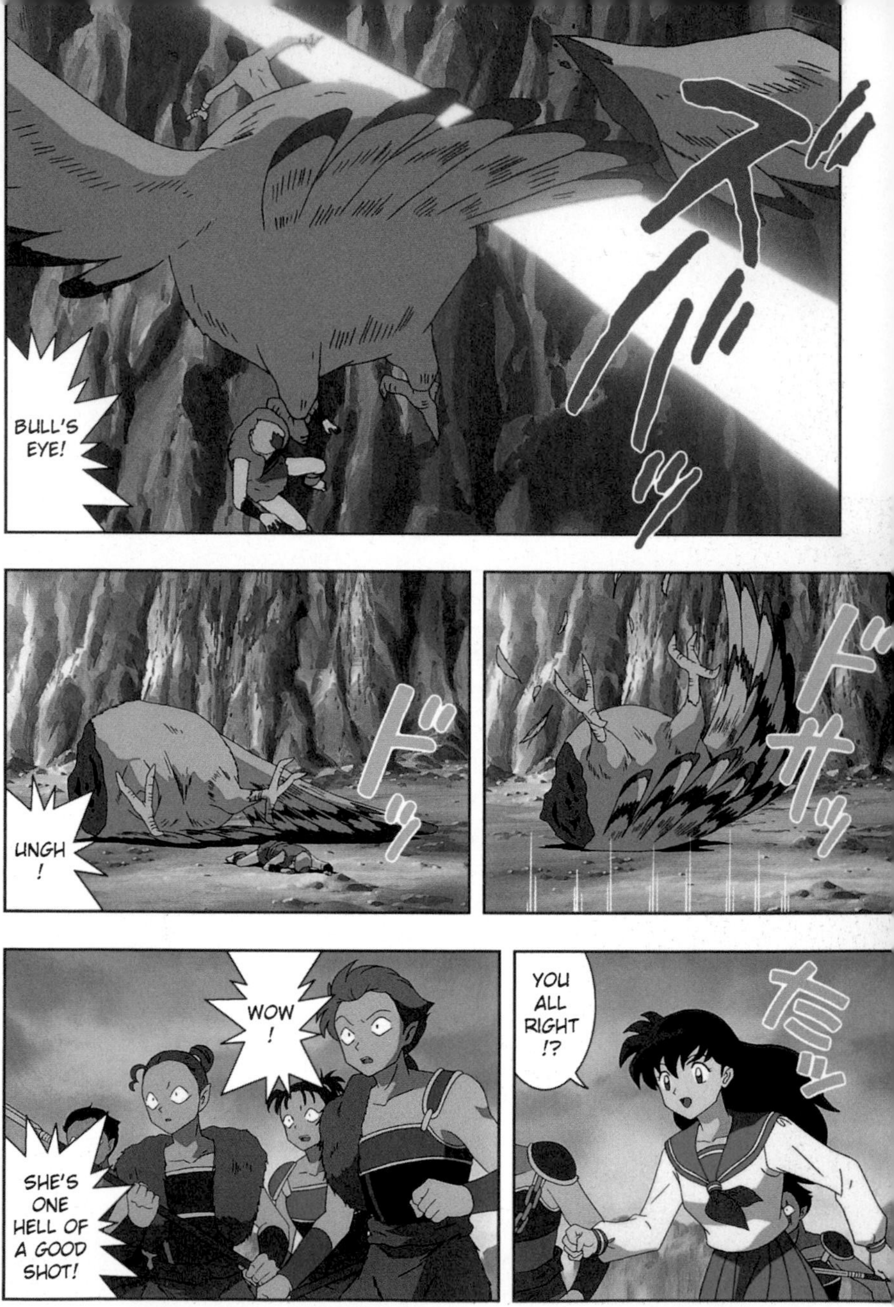

ズドッ
BULL'S EYE!
ドサッ
ドッ
UNGH!
たッ
YOU ALL RIGHT!?
WOW!
SHE'S ONE HELL OF A GOOD SHOT!

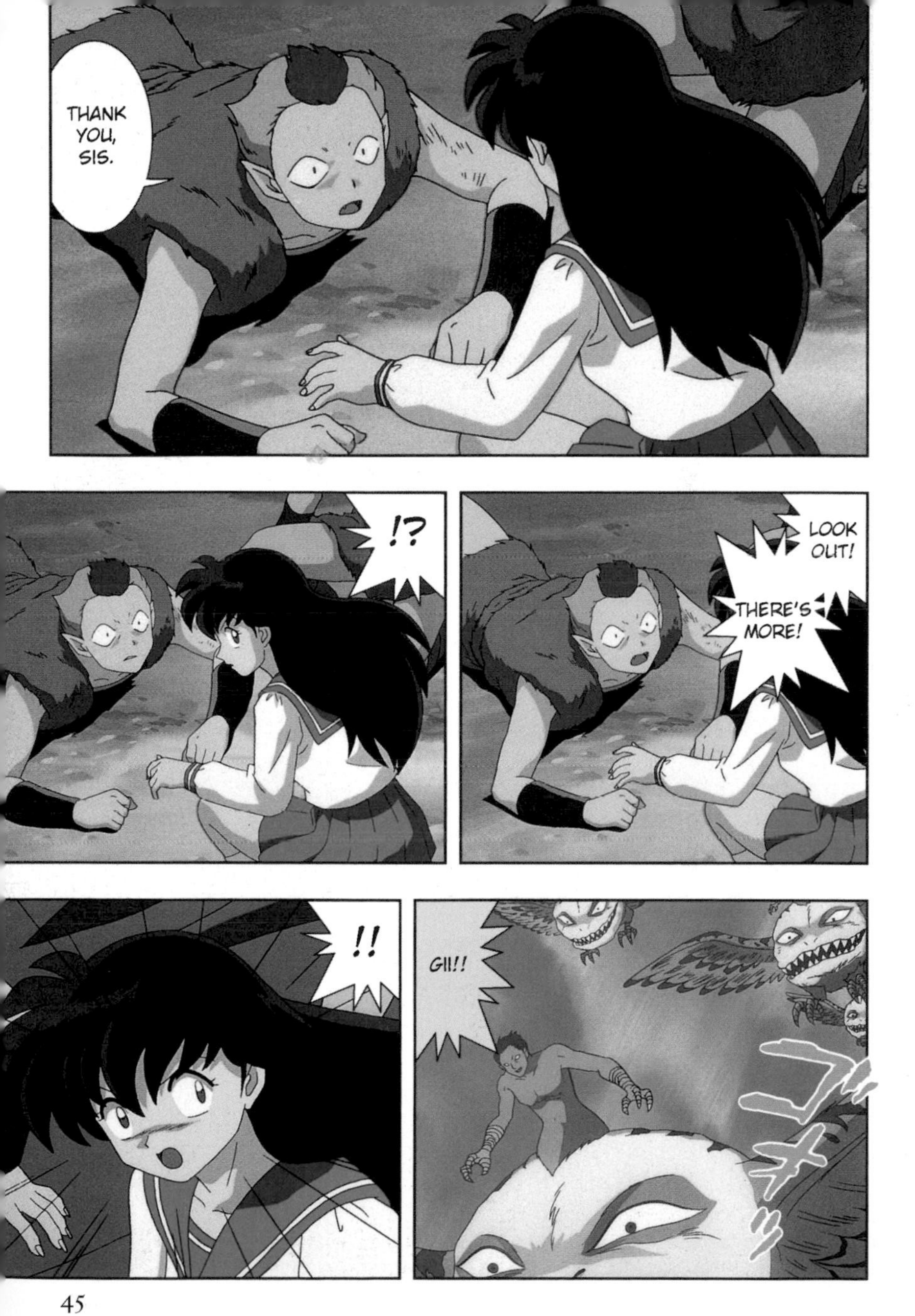
THANK YOU, SIS.
LOOK OUT!
THERE'S MORE!
!?
GII!!
ゴォッ
!!

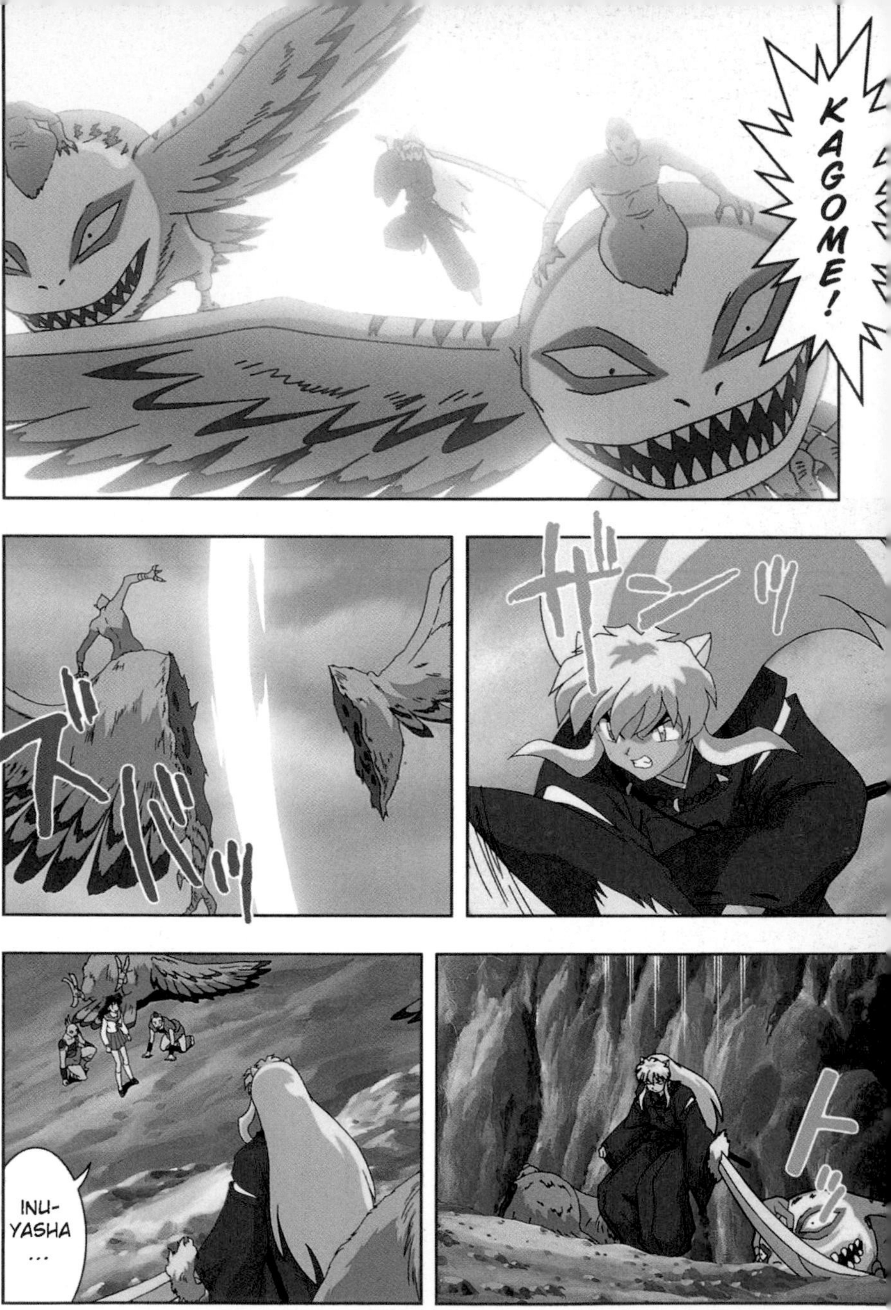
KAGOME!
トッ
INU-YASHA ...

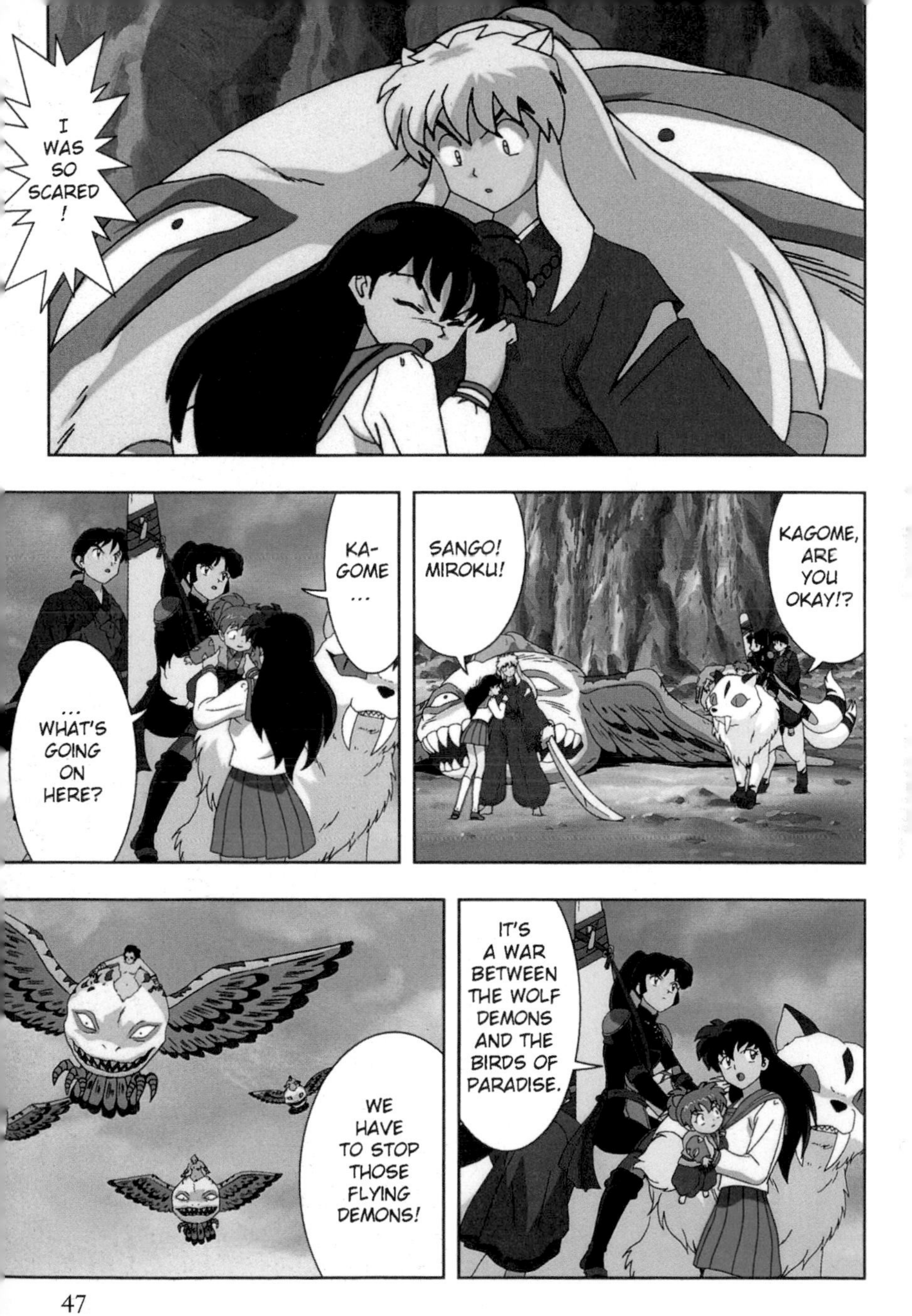
I WAS SO SCARED!
KAGOME, ARE YOU OKAY!?
SANGO! MIROKU!
KA-GOME...
...WHAT'S GOING ON HERE?
IT'S A WAR BETWEEN THE WOLF DEMONS AND THE BIRDS OF PARADISE.
WE HAVE TO STOP THOSE FLYING DEMONS!

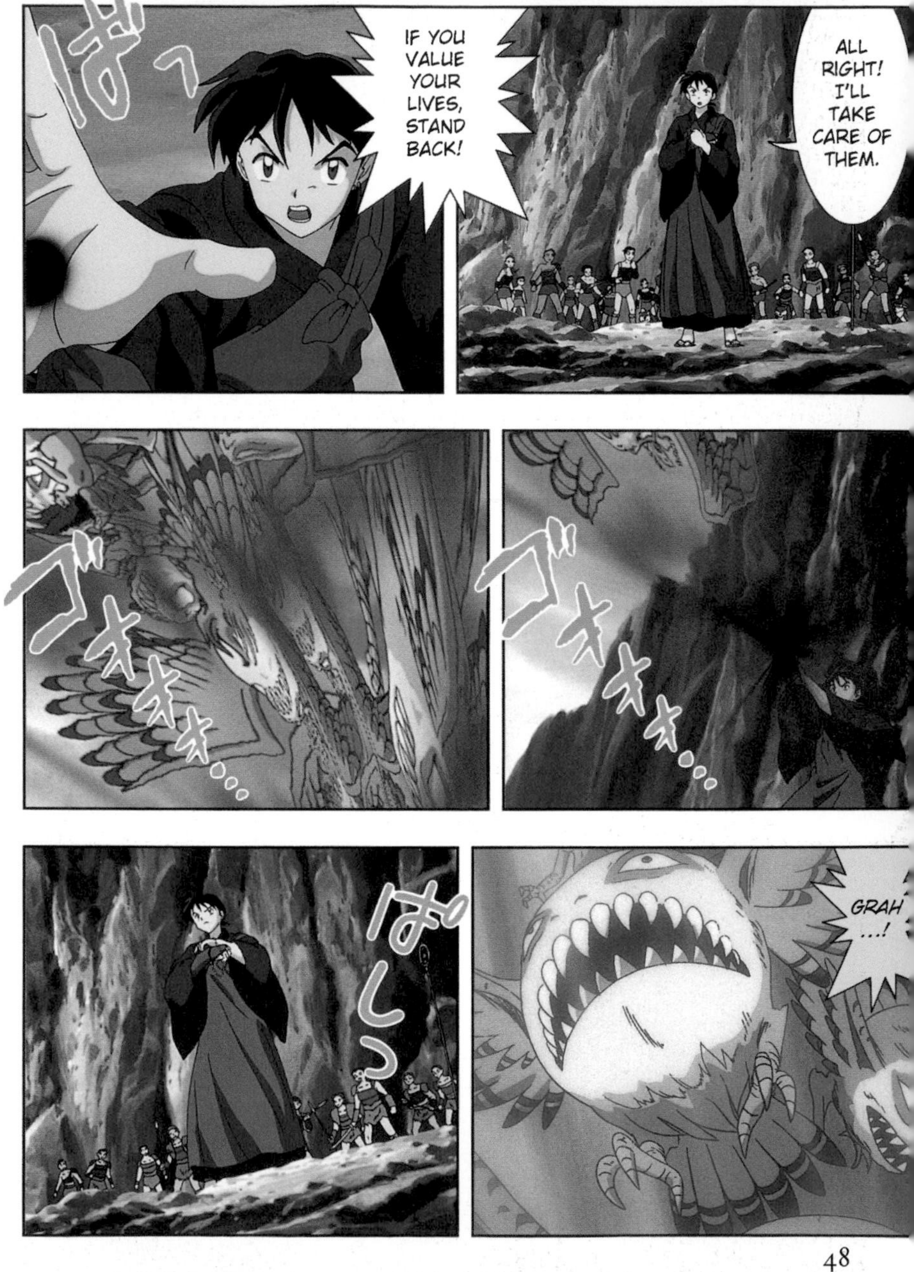
ALL RIGHT! I'LL TAKE CARE OF THEM.
IF YOU VALUE YOUR LIVES, STAND BACK!
ばっ
ゴォォォ…
ゴォォォォ…
GRAH ...!
ばしっ

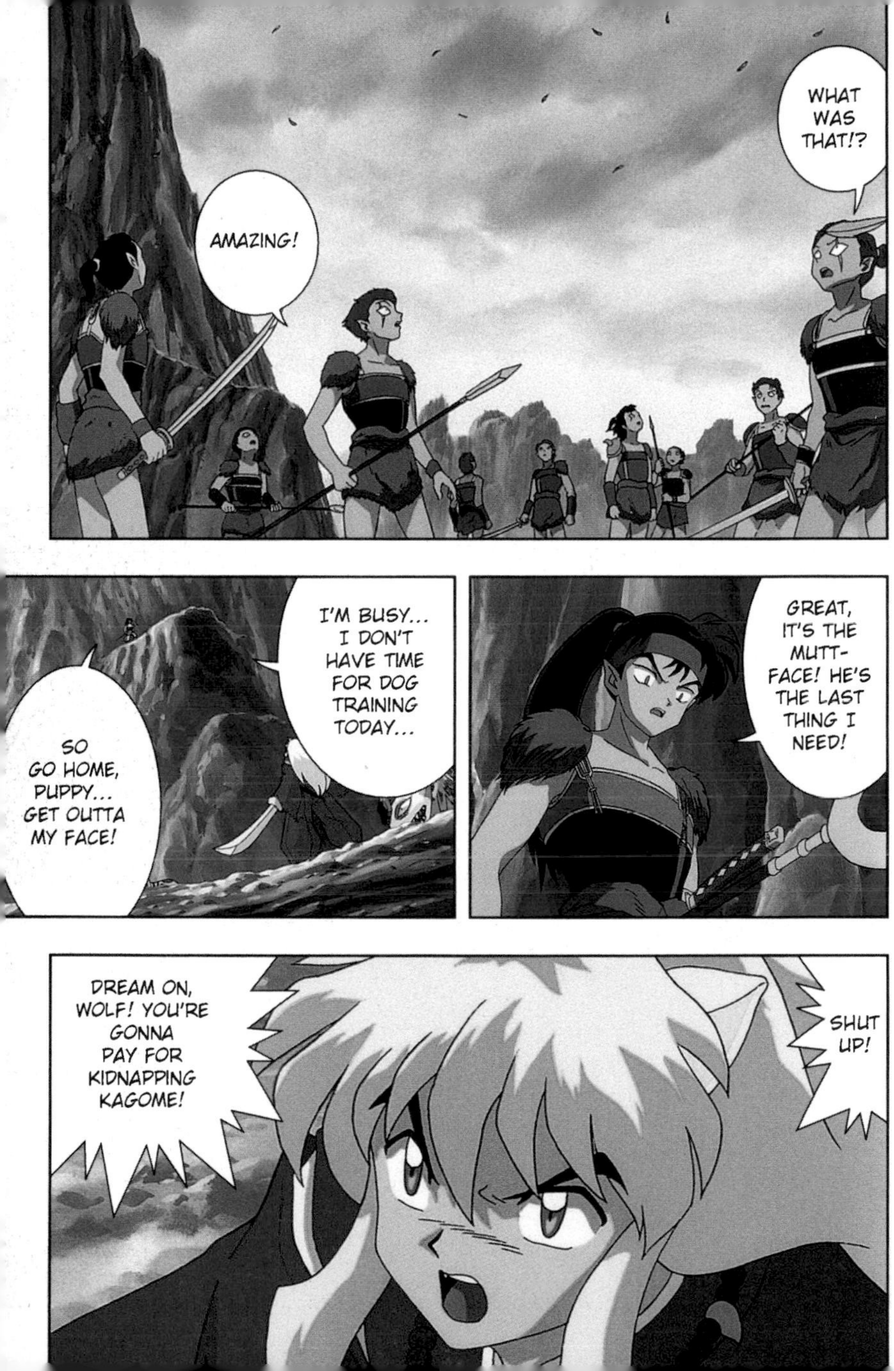
WHAT WAS THAT!?
AMAZING!
GREAT, IT'S THE MUTT-FACE! HE'S THE LAST THING I NEED!
I'M BUSY... I DON'T HAVE TIME FOR DOG TRAINING TODAY...
SO GO HOME, PUPPY... GET OUTTA MY FACE!
SHUT UP!
DREAM ON, WOLF! YOU'RE GONNA PAY FOR KIDNAPPING KAGOME!

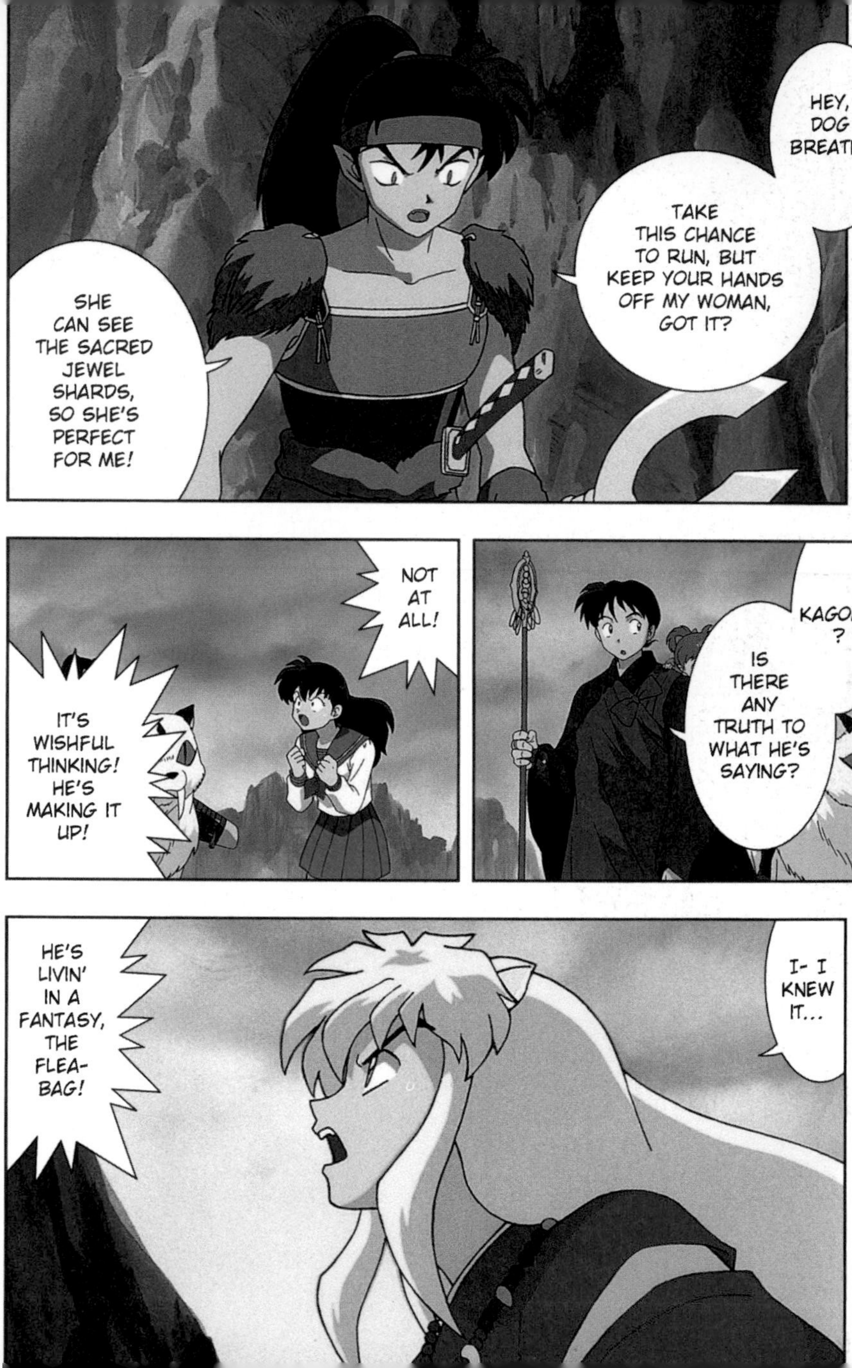
HEY, DOG BREATH!
TAKE THIS CHANCE TO RUN, BUT KEEP YOUR HANDS OFF MY WOMAN, GOT IT?
SHE CAN SEE THE SACRED JEWEL SHARDS, SO SHE'S PERFECT FOR ME!
KAGOME?
IS THERE ANY TRUTH TO WHAT HE'S SAYING?
NOT AT ALL!
IT'S WISHFUL THINKING! HE'S MAKING IT UP!
I- I KNEW IT...
HE'S LIVIN' IN A FANTASY, THE FLEA-BAG!

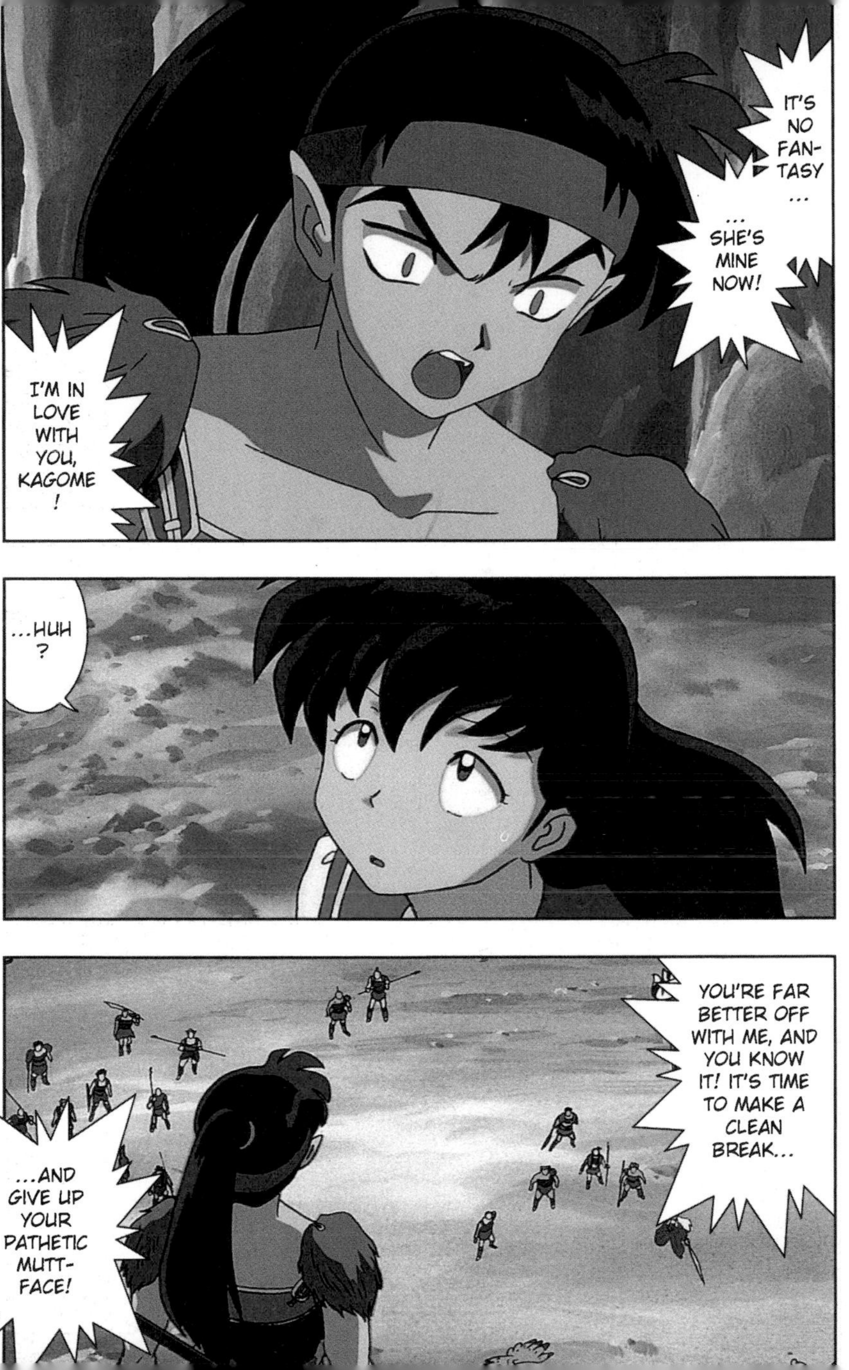
IT'S NO FAN-TASY ...
... SHE'S MINE NOW!
I'M IN LOVE WITH YOU, KAGOME!
...HUH?
YOU'RE FAR BETTER OFF WITH ME, AND YOU KNOW IT! IT'S TIME TO MAKE A CLEAN BREAK...
...AND GIVE UP YOUR PATHETIC MUTT-FACE!

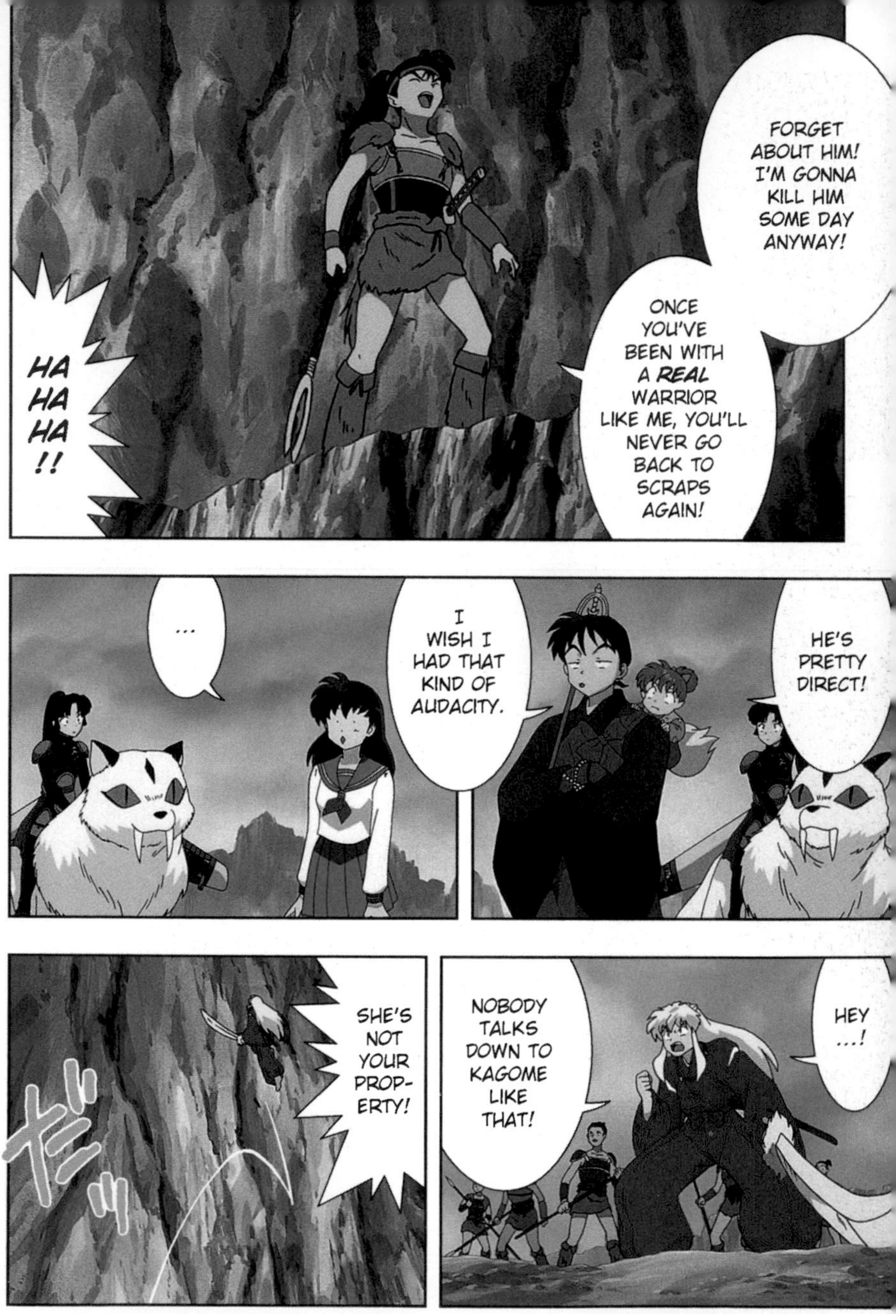
FORGET ABOUT HIM! I'M GONNA KILL HIM SOME DAY ANYWAY!
ONCE YOU'VE BEEN WITH A ***REAL*** WARRIOR LIKE ME, YOU'LL NEVER GO BACK TO SCRAPS AGAIN!
HA HA HA!!
HE'S PRETTY DIRECT!
I WISH I HAD THAT KIND OF AUDACITY.
...
HEY ...!
NOBODY TALKS DOWN TO KAGOME LIKE THAT!
SHE'S NOT YOUR PROP-ERTY!

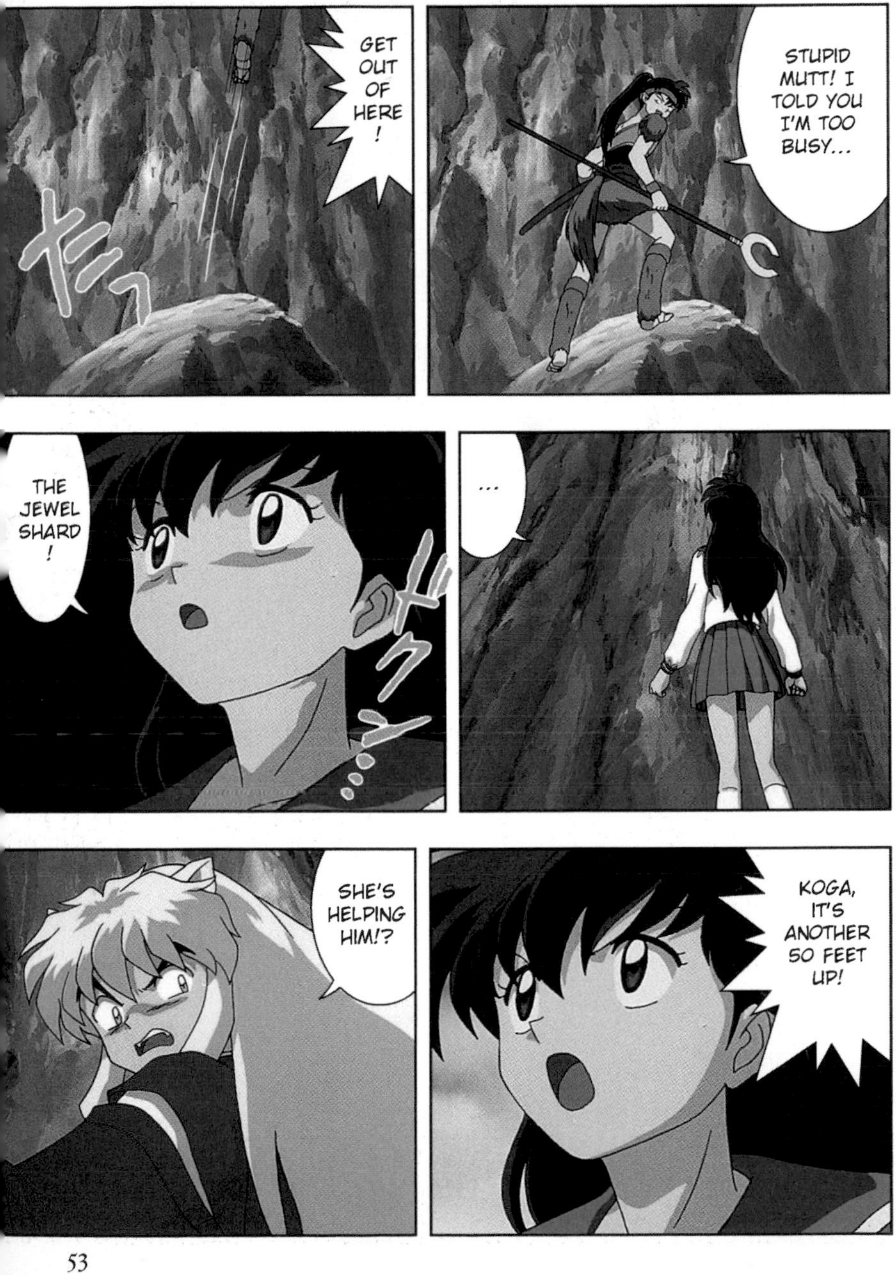
STUPID MUTT! I TOLD YOU I'M TOO BUSY...
GET OUT OF HERE!
...
THE JEWEL SHARD!
KOGA, IT'S ANOTHER 50 FEET UP!
SHE'S HELPING HIM!?

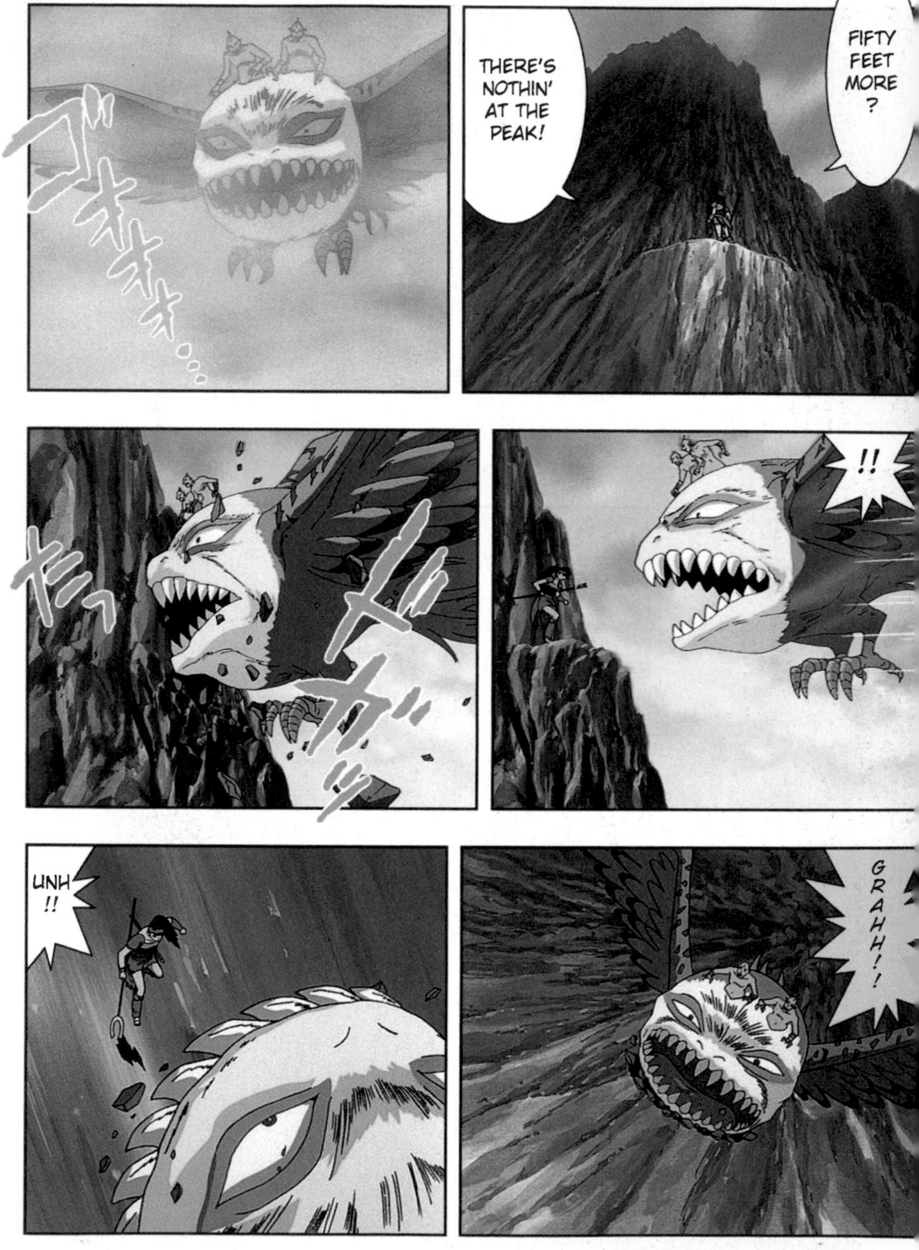
FIFTY FEET MORE ?
THERE'S NOTHIN' AT THE PEAK!
!!
GRAHH!!
UNH !!

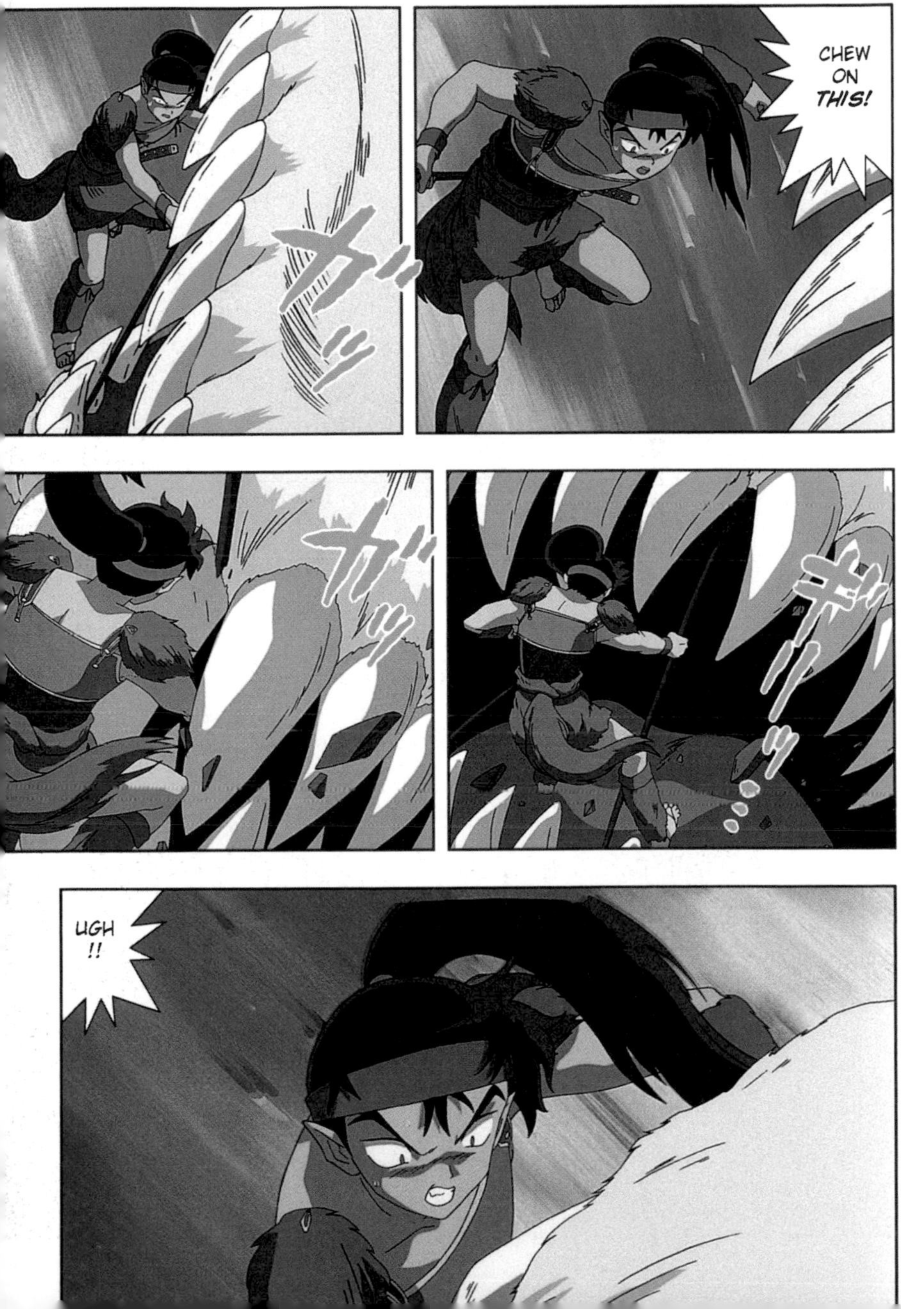
CHEW ON THIS!
ガッ
ガッ
UGH!!

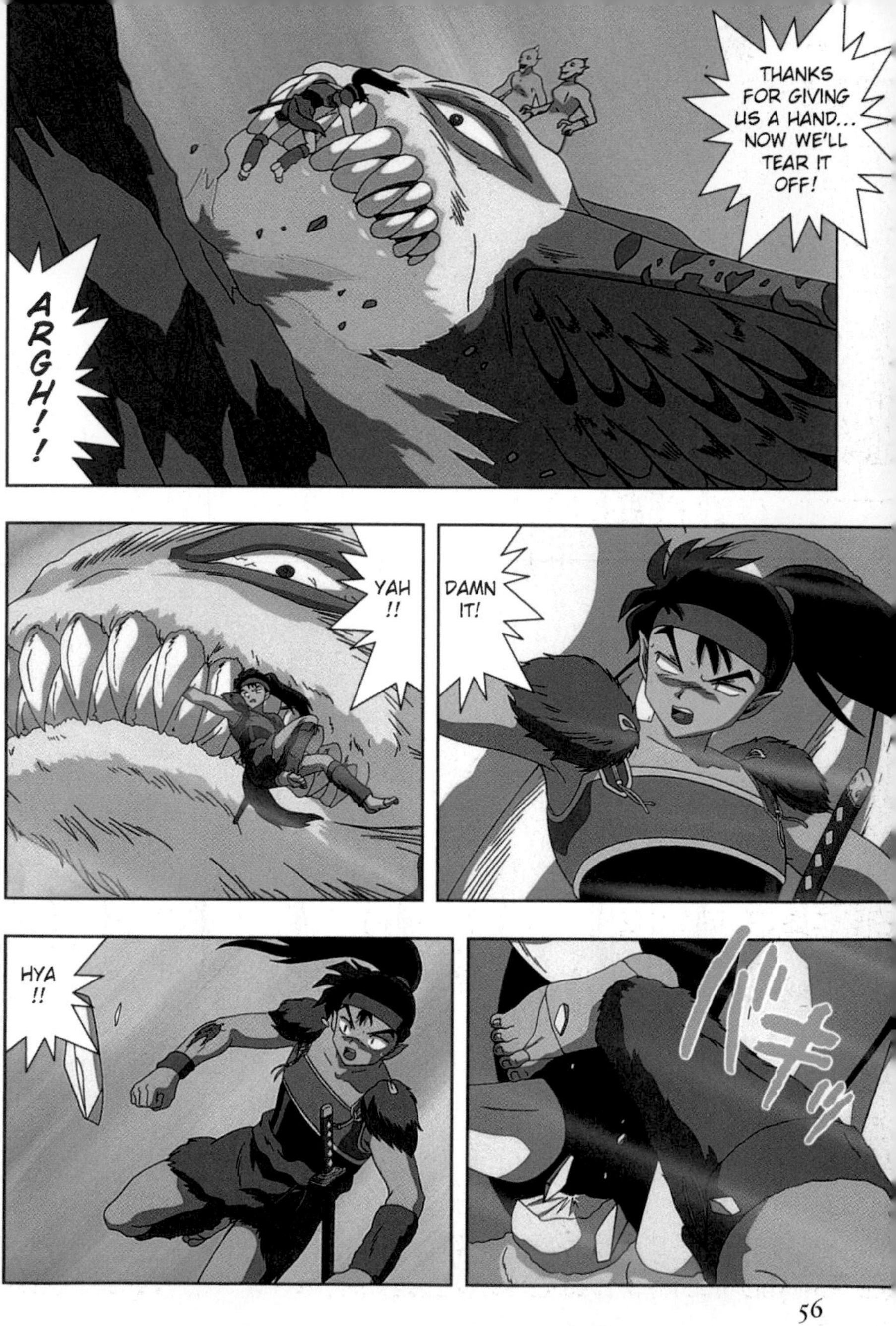
THANKS FOR GIVING US A HAND... NOW WE'LL TEAR IT OFF!
ARGH!!
DAMN IT!
YAH !!
バキッ
HYA !!

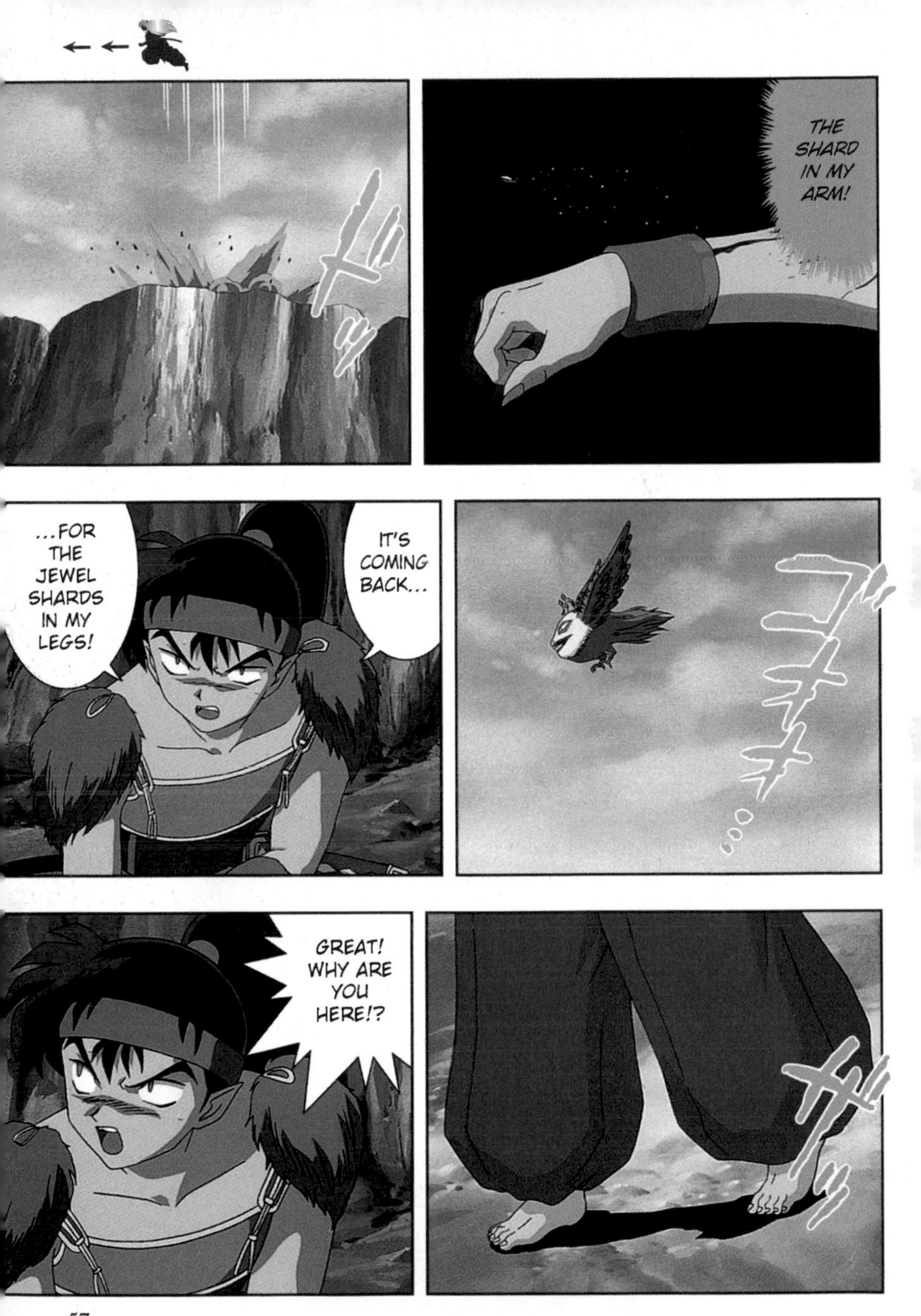
THE SHARD IN MY ARM!
IT'S COMING BACK...
...FOR THE JEWEL SHARDS IN MY LEGS!
GREAT! WHY ARE YOU HERE!?

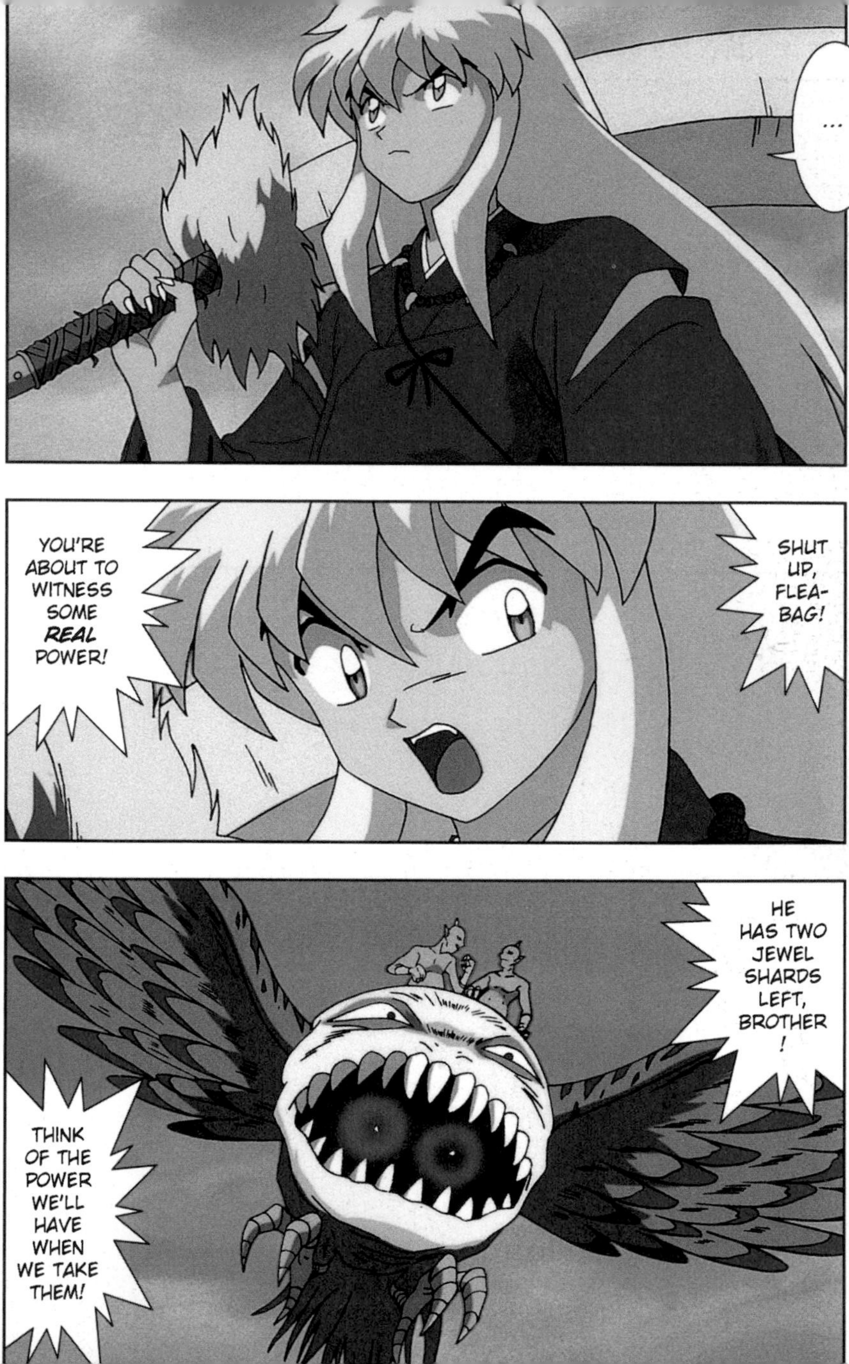
...
SHUT UP, FLEA-BAG!
YOU'RE ABOUT TO WITNESS SOME REAL POWER!
HE HAS TWO JEWEL SHARDS LEFT, BROTHER!
THINK OF THE POWER WE'LL HAVE WHEN WE TAKE THEM!

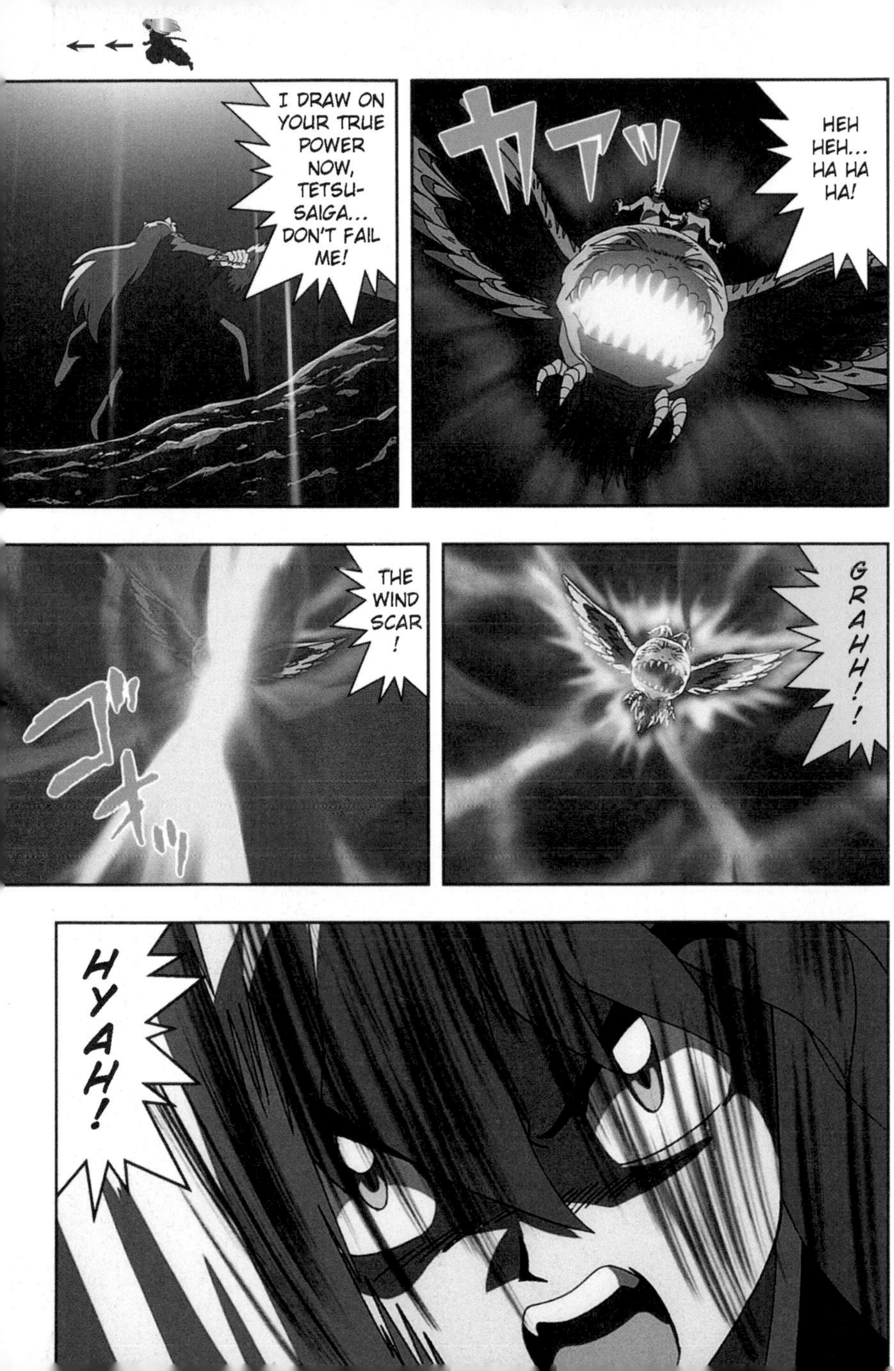
カァッ
HEH HEH... HA HA HA!
I DRAW ON YOUR TRUE POWER NOW, TETSU-SAIGA... DON'T FAIL ME!
GRAHH!!
THE WIND SCAR!
ゴォッ
HYAH!

ゴオッ
ザーンッ
ゴオオオオ…

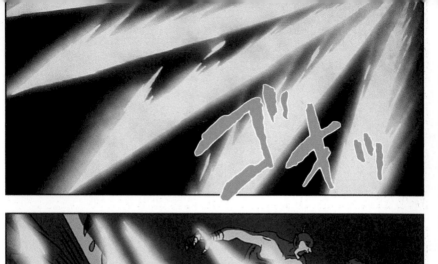

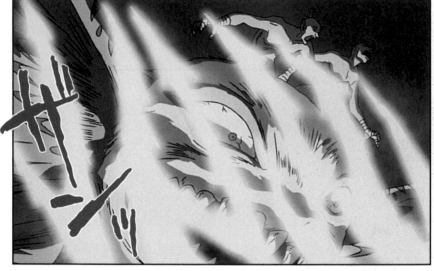

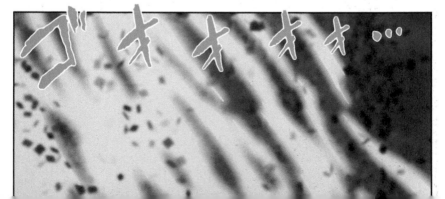

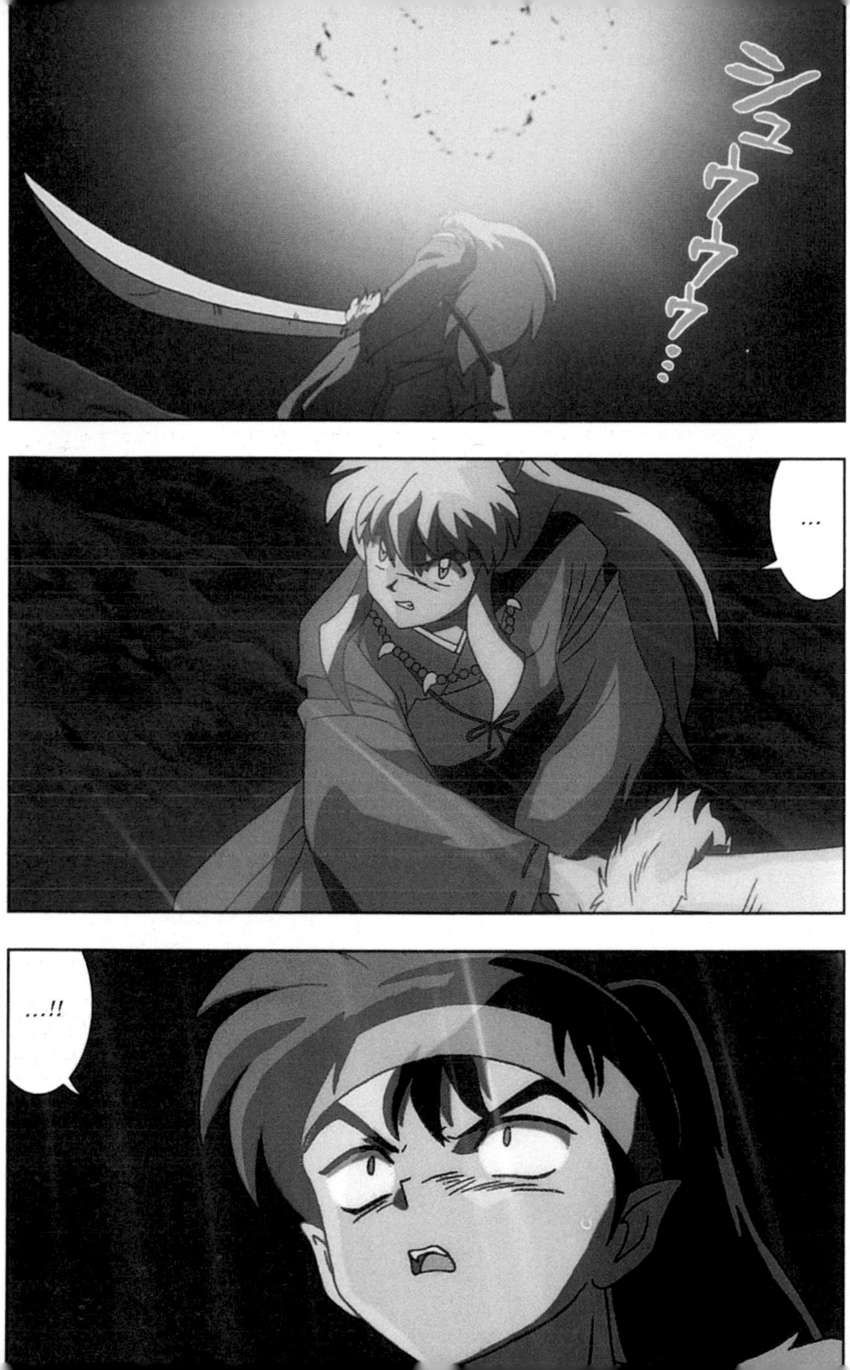
シュウウウ…
...
...!!

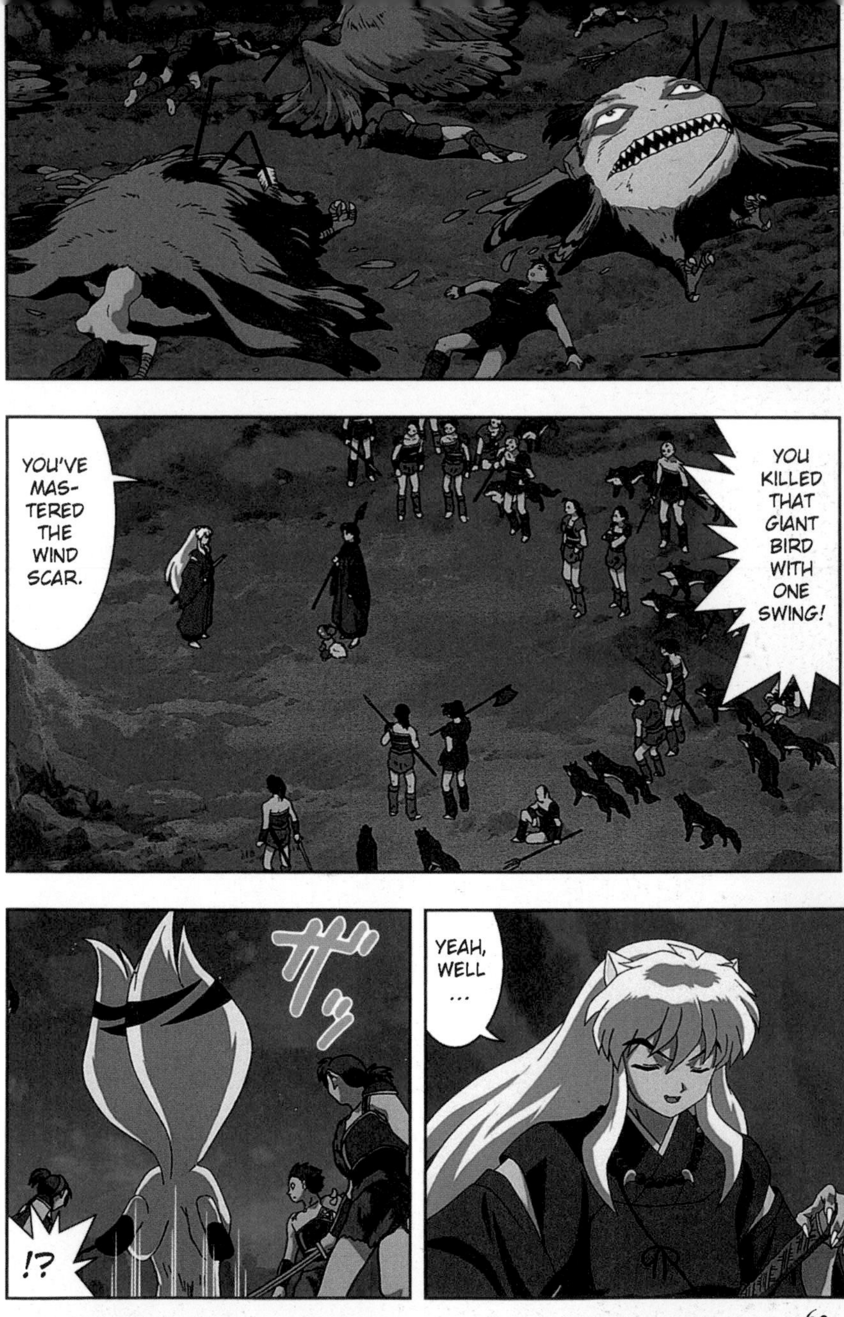
YOU KILLED THAT GIANT BIRD WITH ONE SWING!
YOU'VE MAS-TERED THE WIND SCAR.
YEAH, WELL ...
ザッ
!?

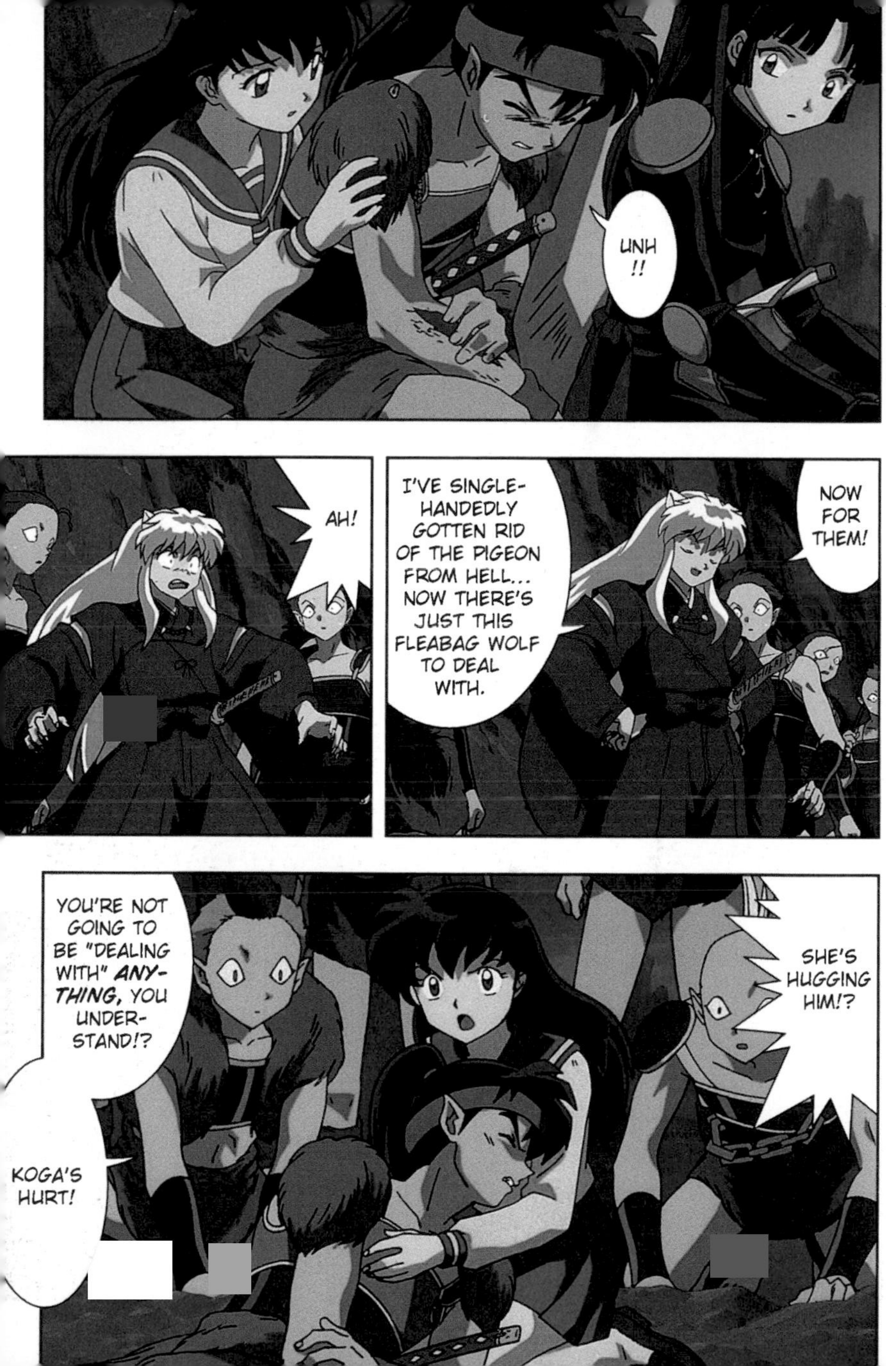
UNH !!
NOW FOR THEM!
I'VE SINGLE-HANDEDLY GOTTEN RID OF THE PIGEON FROM HELL... NOW THERE'S JUST THIS FLEABAG WOLF TO DEAL WITH.
AH!
SHE'S HUGGING HIM!?
YOU'RE NOT GOING TO BE "DEALING WITH" *ANYTHING,* YOU UNDERSTAND!?
KOGA'S HURT!

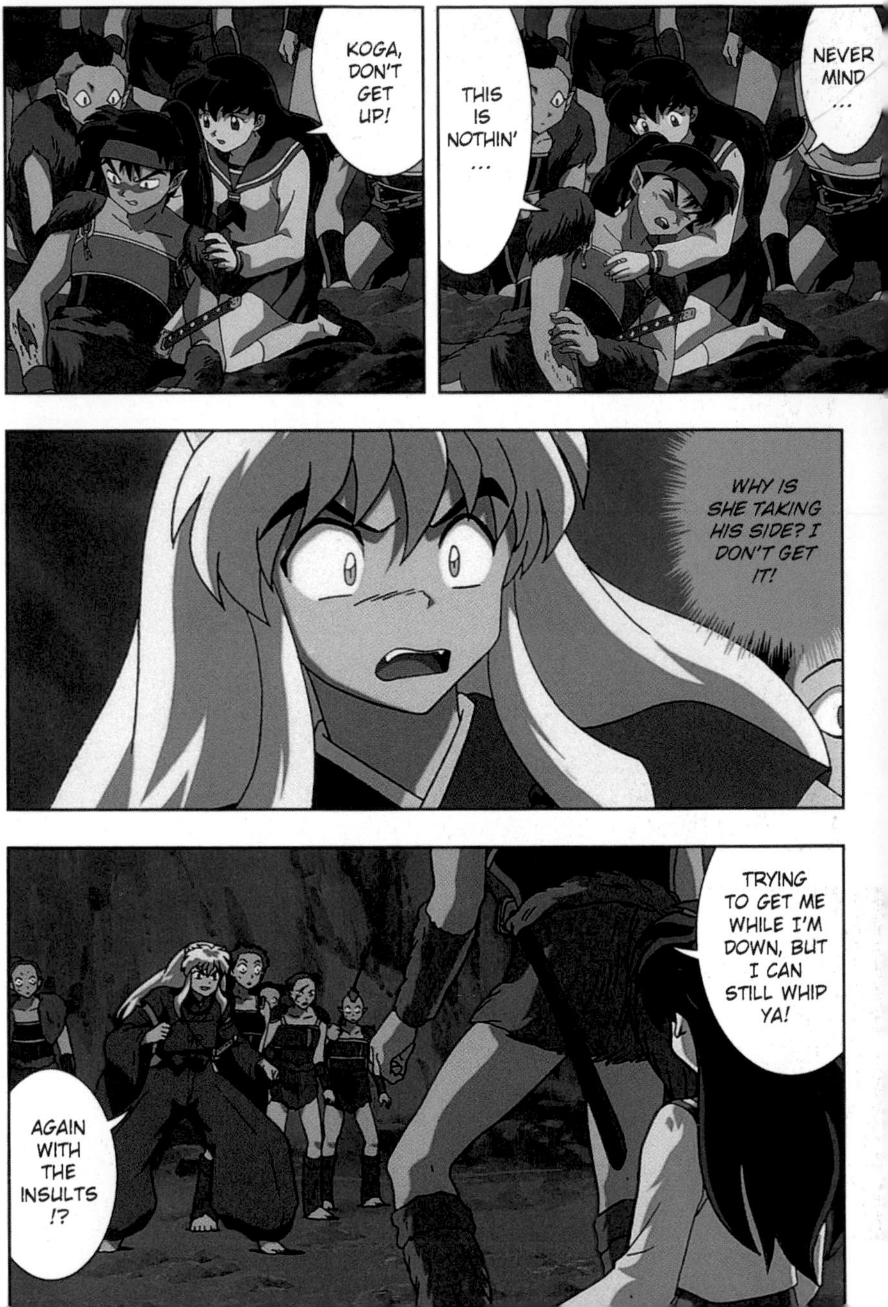
NEVER MIND ...
THIS IS NOTHIN' ...
KOGA, DON'T GET UP!
WHY IS SHE TAKING HIS SIDE? I DON'T GET IT!
TRYING TO GET ME WHILE I'M DOWN, BUT I CAN STILL WHIP YA!
AGAIN WITH THE INSULTS !?

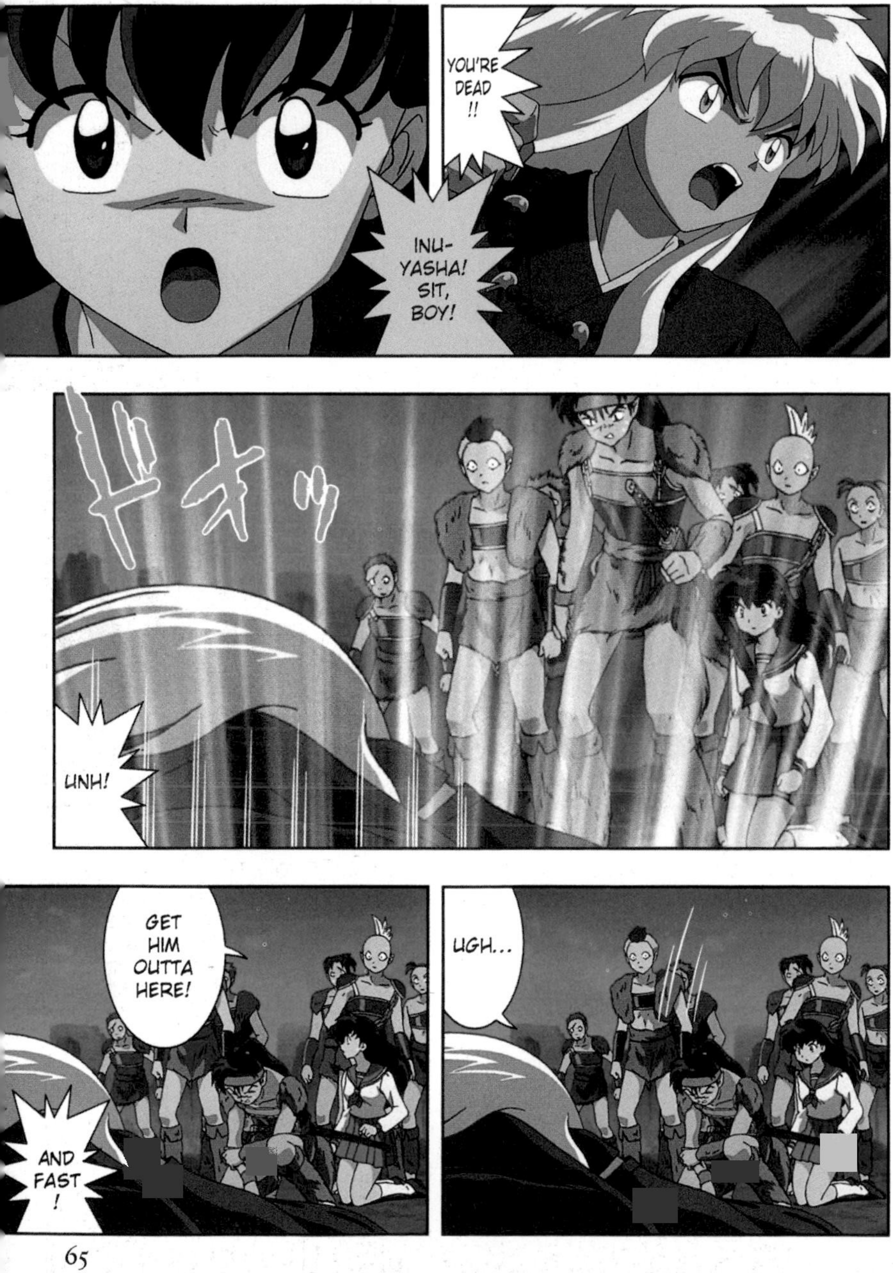
YOU'RE DEAD !!
INU-YASHA! SIT, BOY!
ドオッ
UNH!
UGH...
GET HIM OUTTA HERE!
AND FAST !

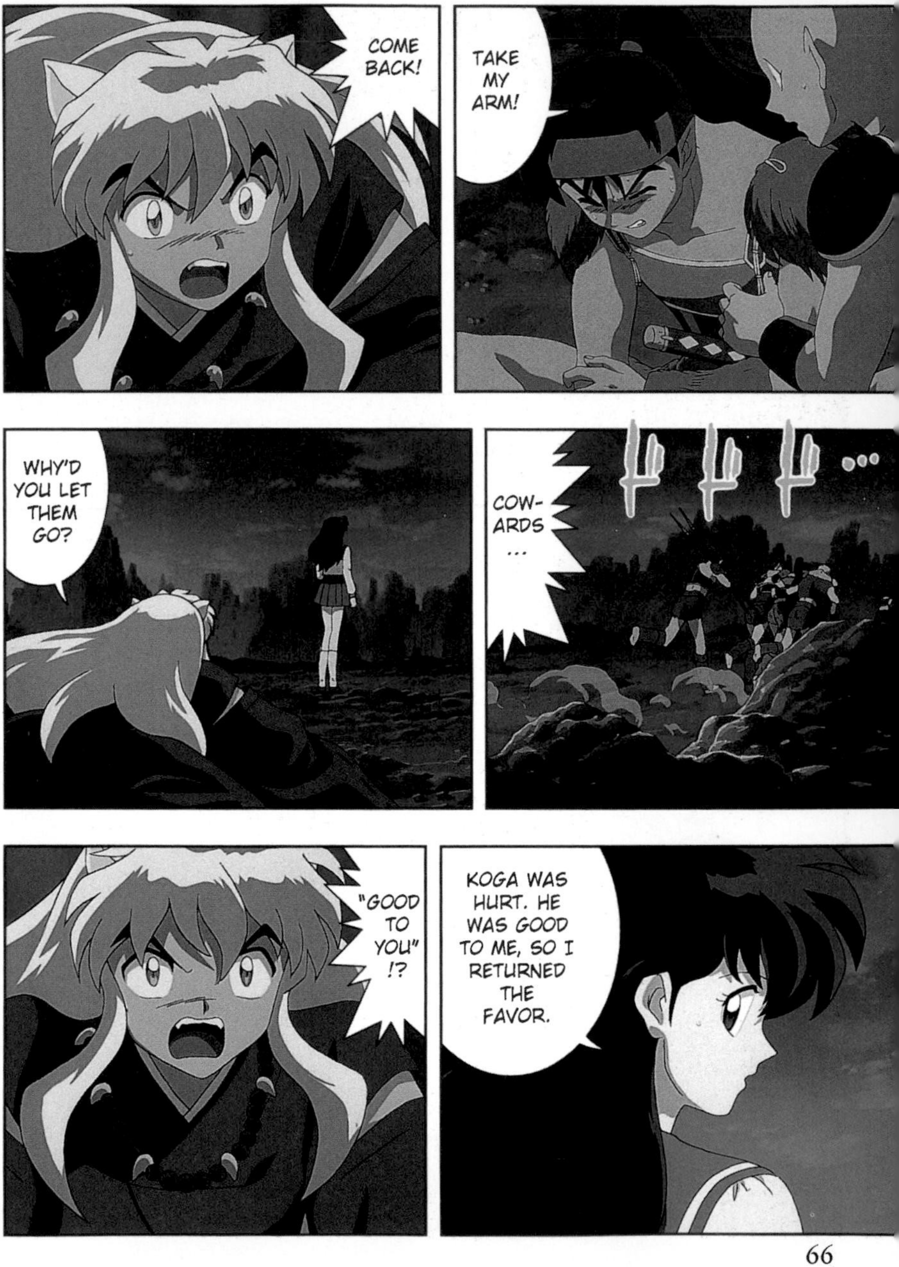
TAKE MY ARM!
COME BACK!
COW-ARDS...
WHY'D YOU LET THEM GO?
KOGA WAS HURT. HE WAS GOOD TO ME, SO I RETURNED THE FAVOR.
"GOOD TO YOU"!?

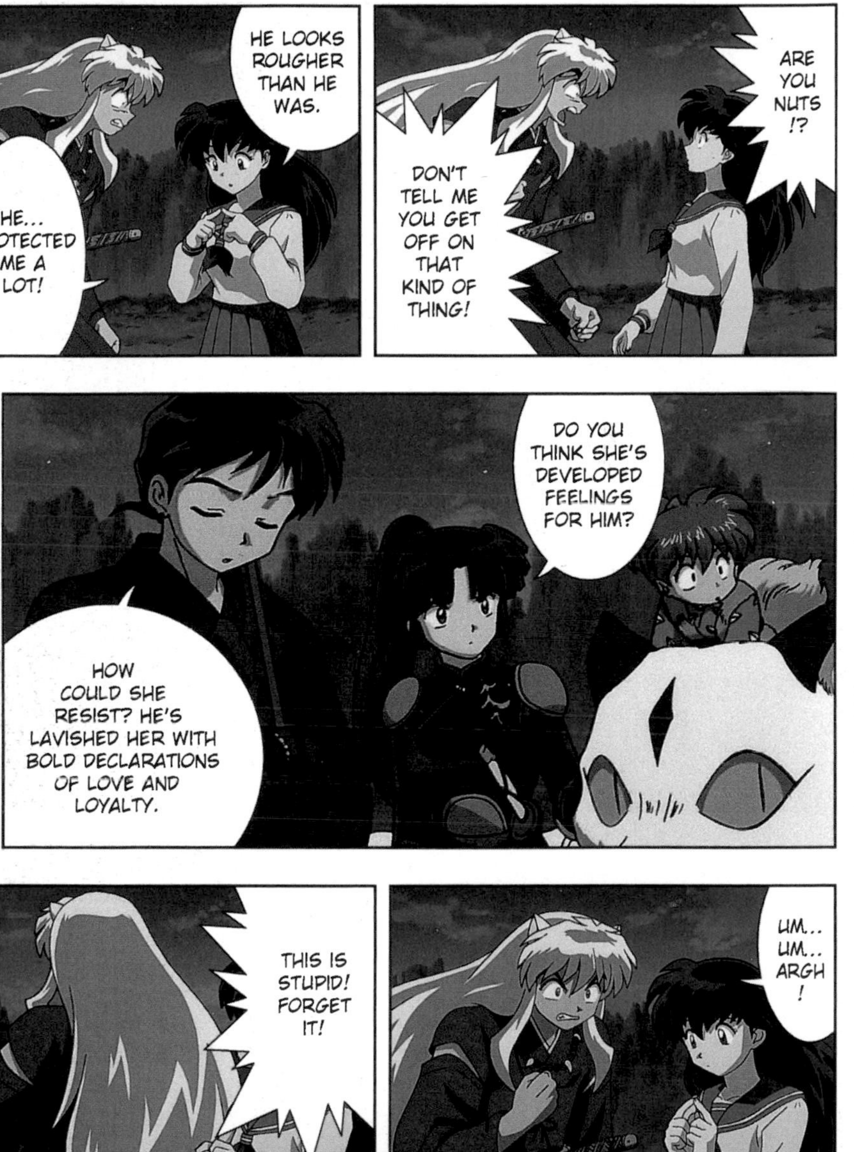
HE LOOKS ROUGHER THAN HE WAS.
HE... PROTECTED ME A LOT!
ARE YOU NUTS!?
DON'T TELL ME YOU GET OFF ON THAT KIND OF THING!
DO YOU THINK SHE'S DEVELOPED FEELINGS FOR HIM?
HOW COULD SHE RESIST? HE'S LAVISHED HER WITH BOLD DECLARATIONS OF LOVE AND LOYALTY.
THIS IS STUPID! FORGET IT!
UM... UM... ARGH!

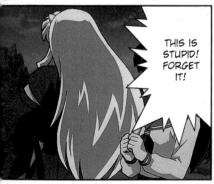

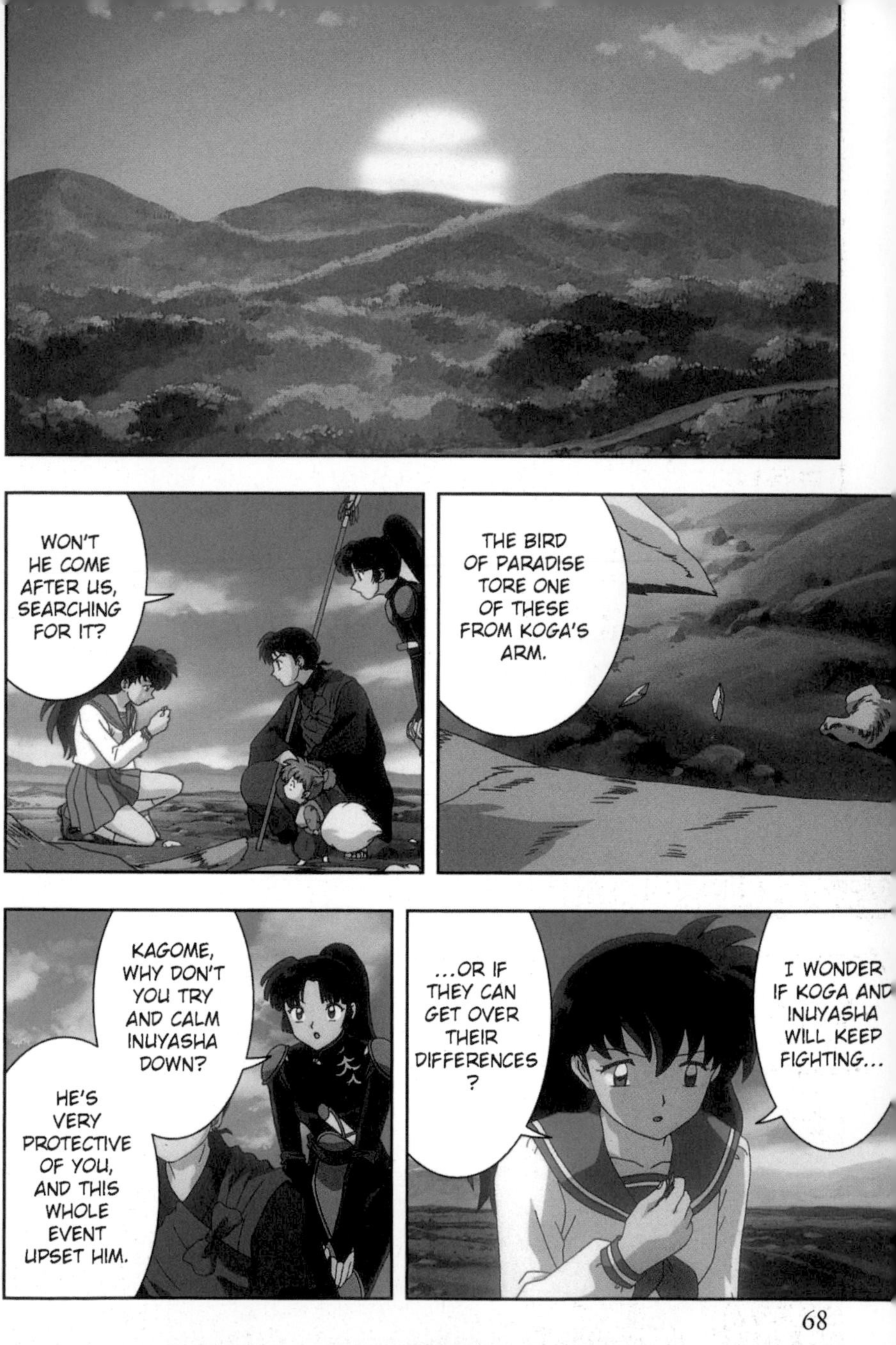
THE BIRD OF PARADISE TORE ONE OF THESE FROM KOGA'S ARM.
WON'T HE COME AFTER US, SEARCHING FOR IT?
I WONDER IF KOGA AND INUYASHA WILL KEEP FIGHTING...
...OR IF THEY CAN GET OVER THEIR DIFFERENCES?
KAGOME, WHY DON'T YOU TRY AND CALM INUYASHA DOWN?
HE'S VERY PROTECTIVE OF YOU, AND THIS WHOLE EVENT UPSET HIM.

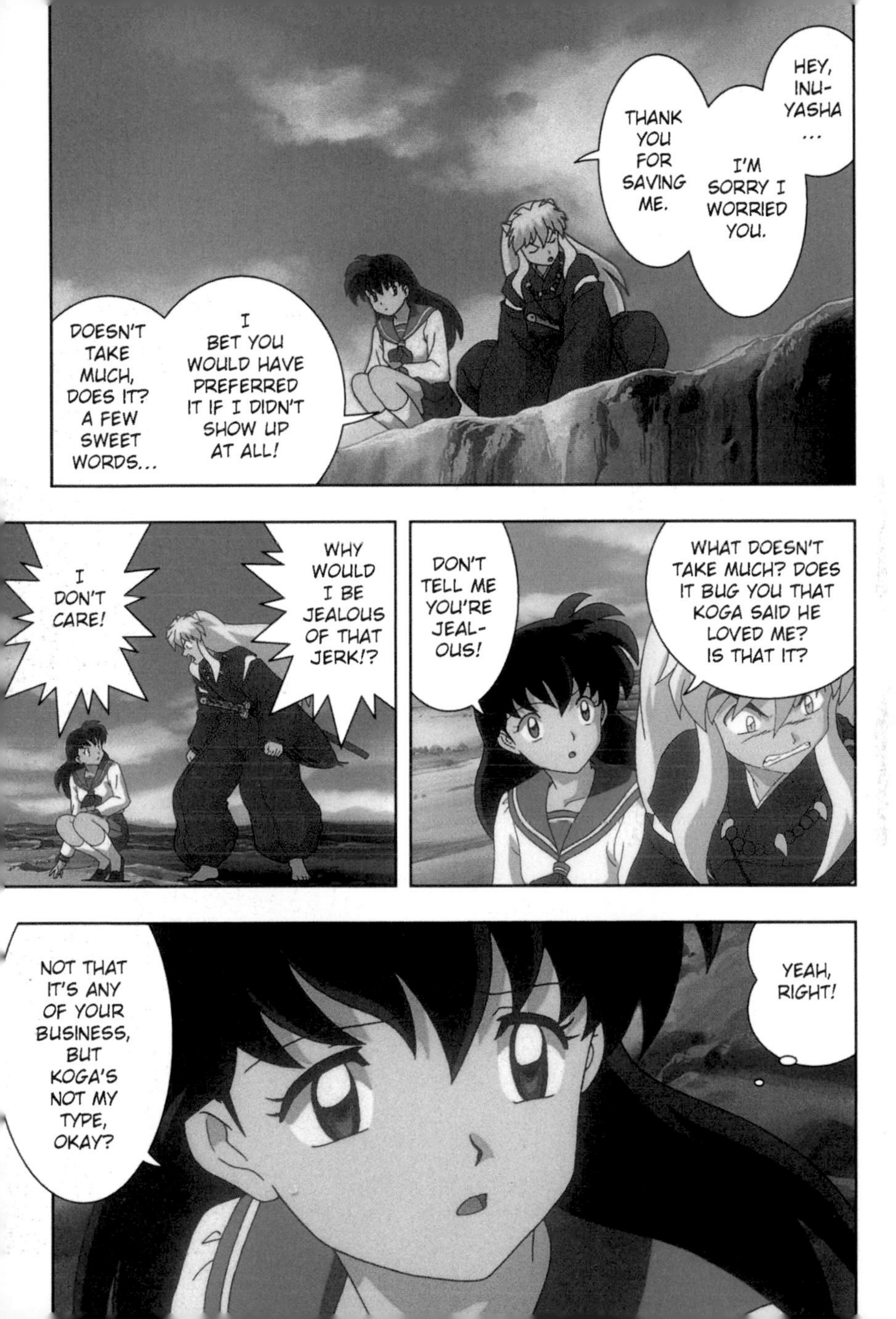
HEY, INU-YASHA... I'M SORRY I WORRIED YOU.
THANK YOU FOR SAVING ME.
I BET YOU WOULD HAVE PREFERRED IT IF I DIDN'T SHOW UP AT ALL!
DOESN'T TAKE MUCH, DOES IT? A FEW SWEET WORDS...
WHAT DOESN'T TAKE MUCH? DOES IT BUG YOU THAT KOGA SAID HE LOVED ME? IS THAT IT?
DON'T TELL ME YOU'RE JEAL-OUS!
WHY WOULD I BE JEALOUS OF THAT JERK!?
I DON'T CARE!
YEAH, RIGHT!
NOT THAT IT'S ANY OF YOUR BUSINESS, BUT KOGA'S NOT MY TYPE, OKAY?

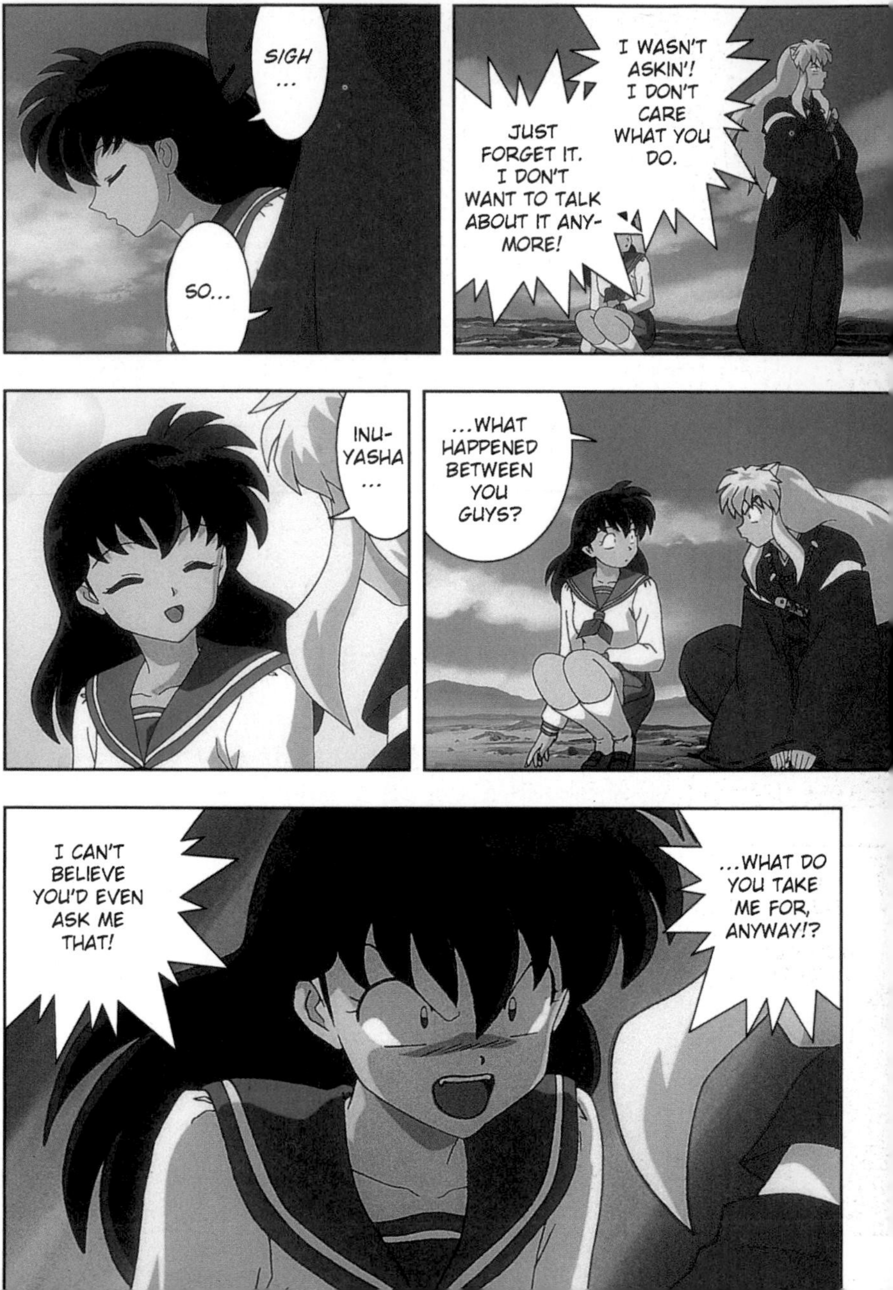
I WASN'T ASKIN'! I DON'T CARE WHAT YOU DO.
JUST FORGET IT. I DON'T WANT TO TALK ABOUT IT ANYMORE!
SIGH...
SO...
...WHAT HAPPENED BETWEEN YOU GUYS?
INU-YASHA...
...WHAT DO YOU TAKE ME FOR, ANYWAY!?
I CAN'T BELIEVE YOU'D EVEN ASK ME THAT!

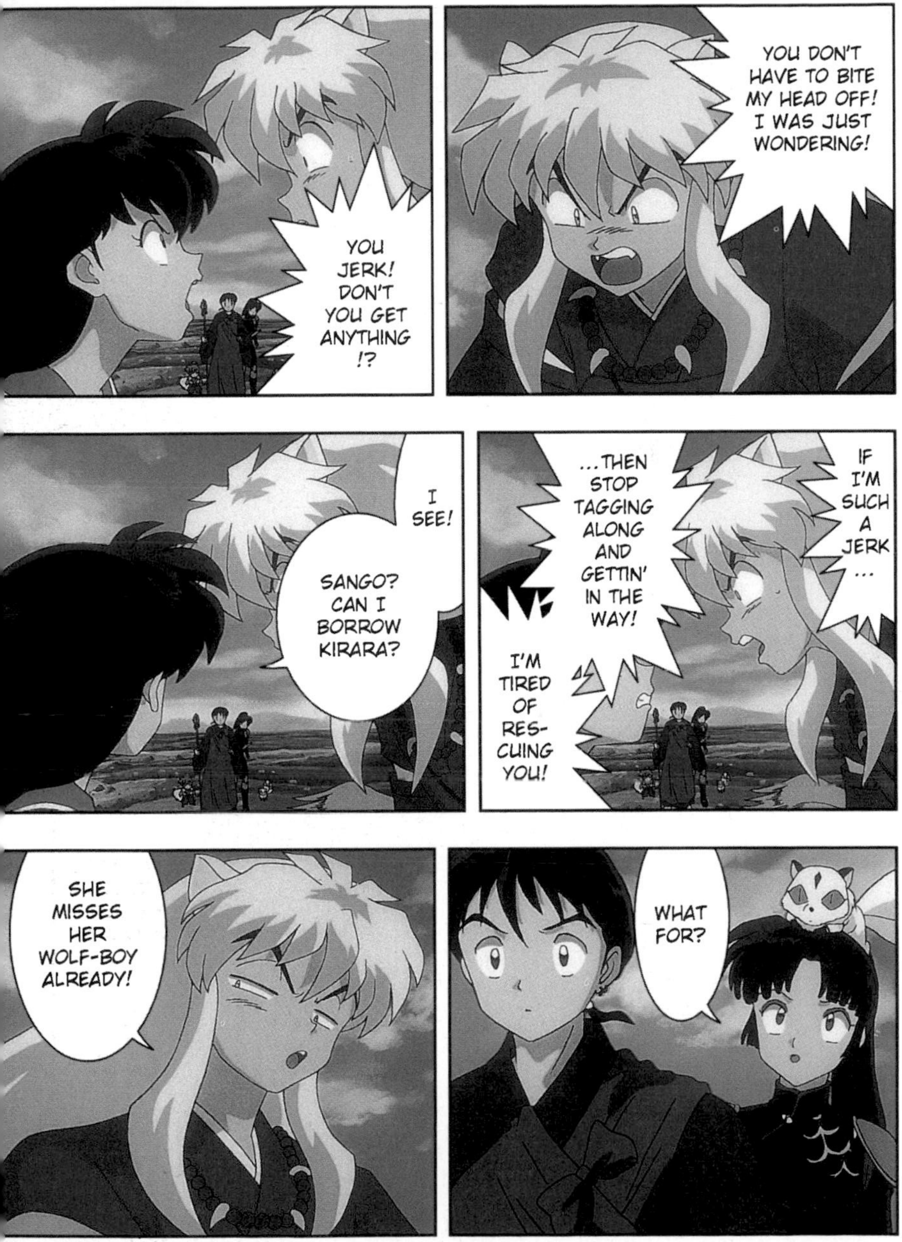
YOU DON'T HAVE TO BITE MY HEAD OFF! I WAS JUST WONDERING!
YOU JERK! DON'T YOU GET ANYTHING !?
IF I'M SUCH A JERK ...
...THEN STOP TAGGING ALONG AND GETTIN' IN THE WAY!
I'M TIRED OF RES-CUING YOU!
I SEE!
SANGO? CAN I BORROW KIRARA?
WHAT FOR?
SHE MISSES HER WOLF-BOY ALREADY!

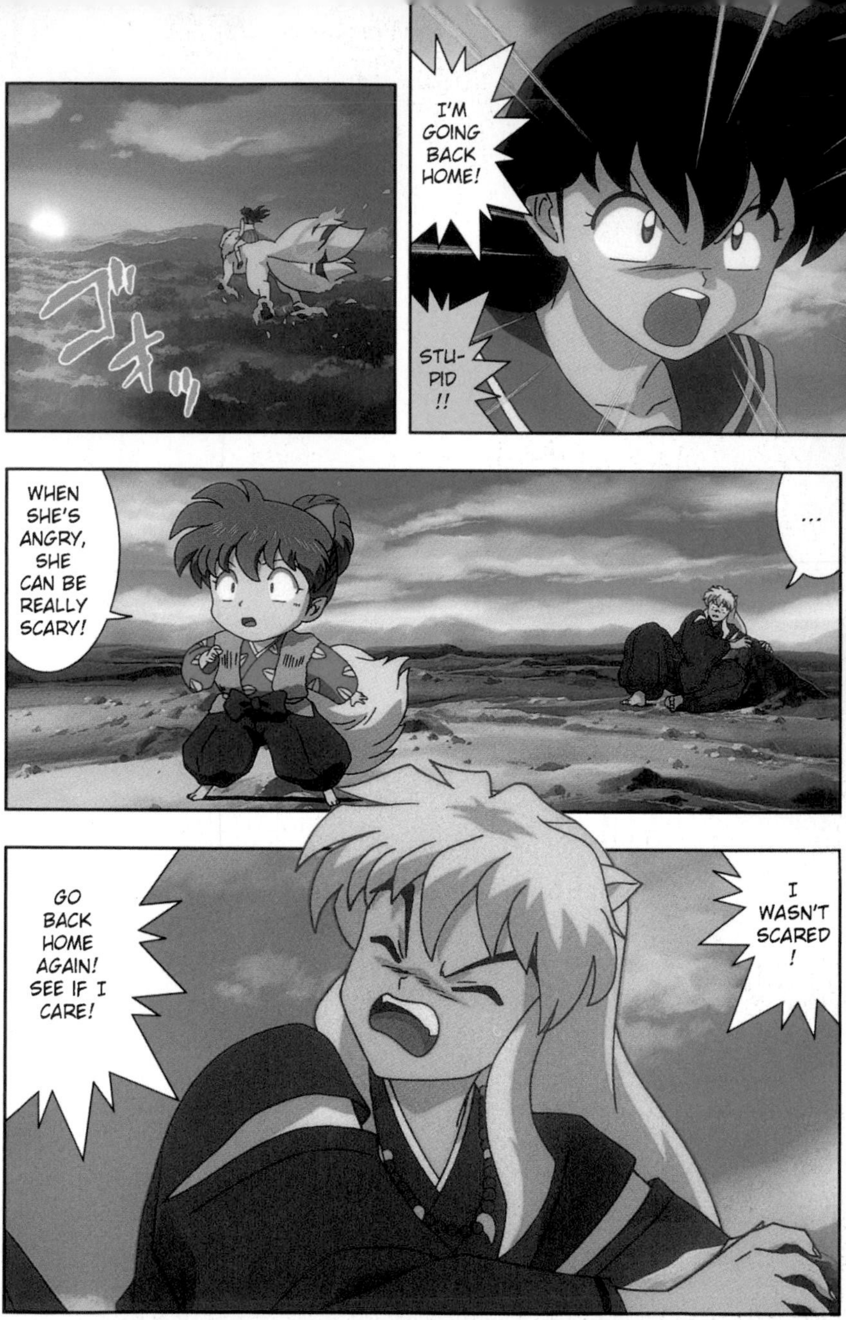
I'M GOING BACK HOME!
STU-PID !!
ゴォッ
...
WHEN SHE'S ANGRY, SHE CAN BE REALLY SCARY!
I WASN'T SCARED!
GO BACK HOME AGAIN! SEE IF I CARE!

38
Two Hearts, One Mind

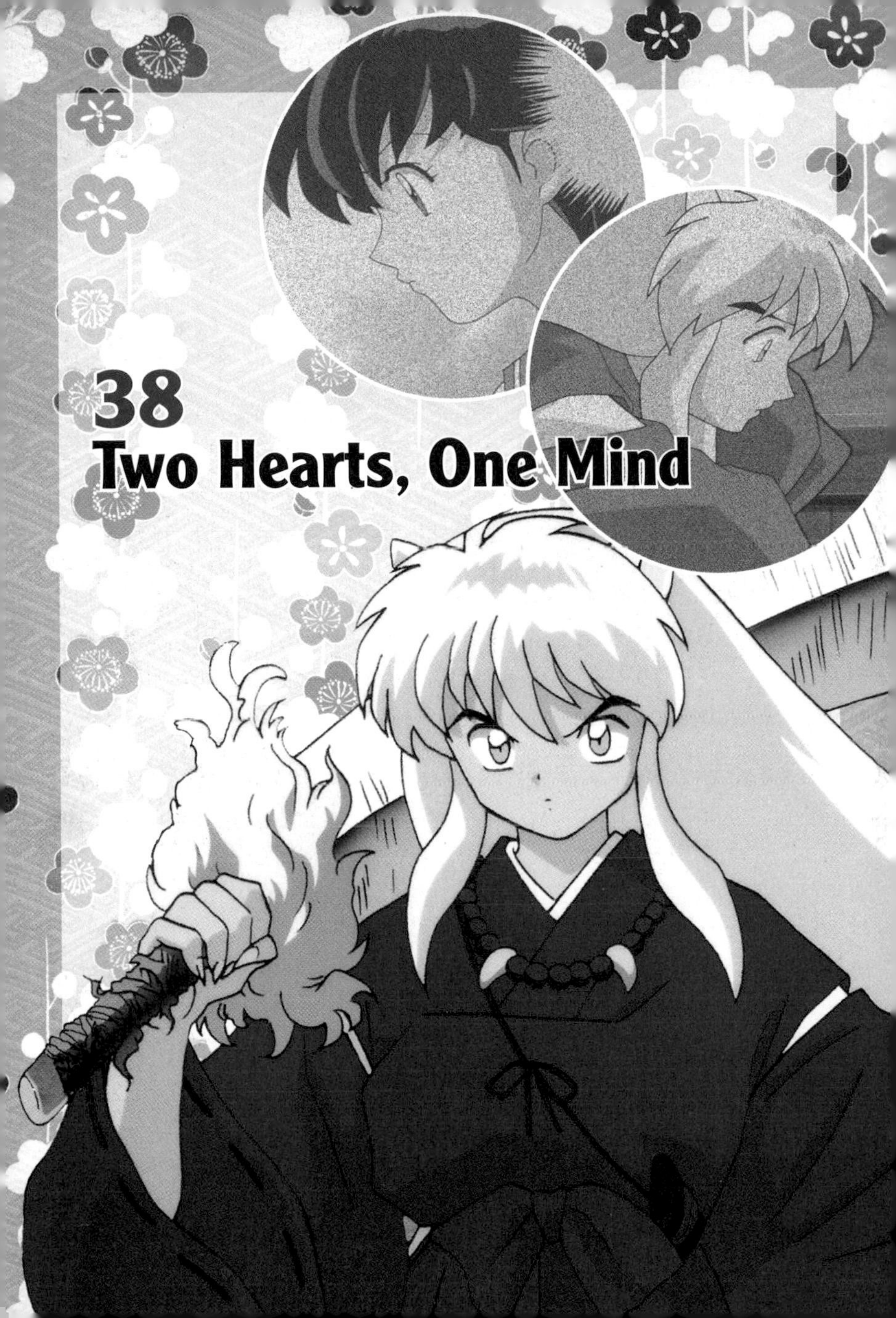

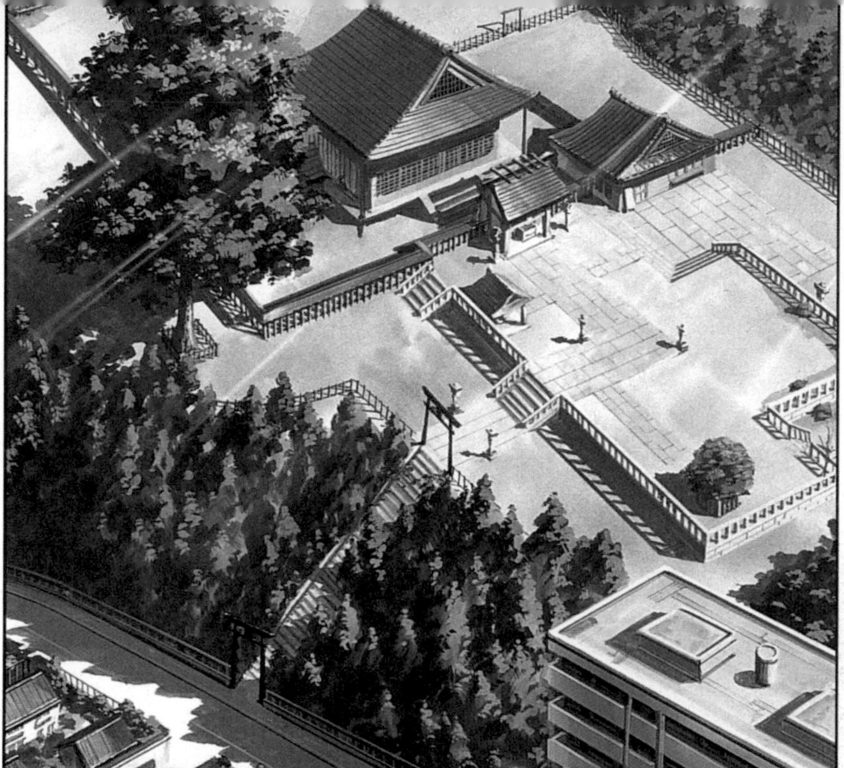
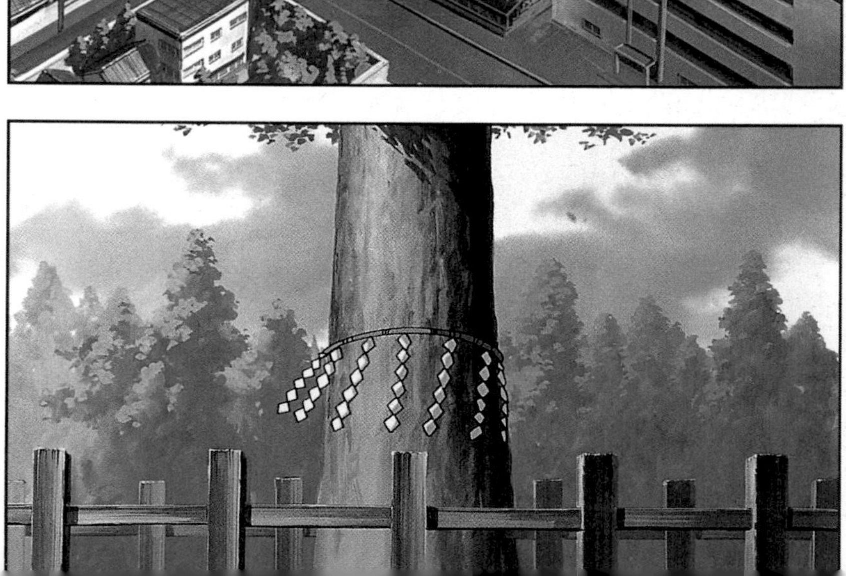

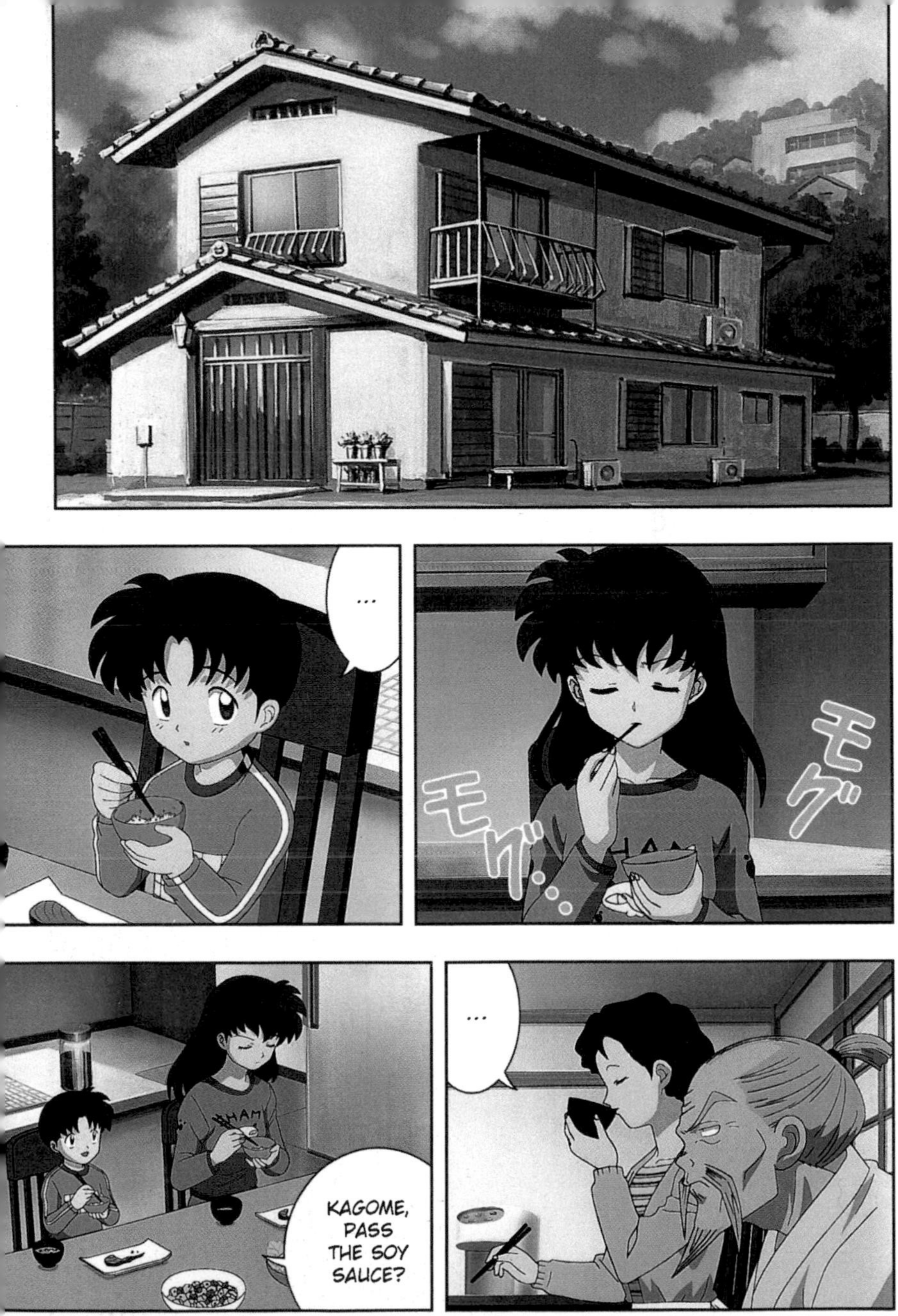
モグ
モグ...
...
...
KAGOME, PASS THE SOY SAUCE?

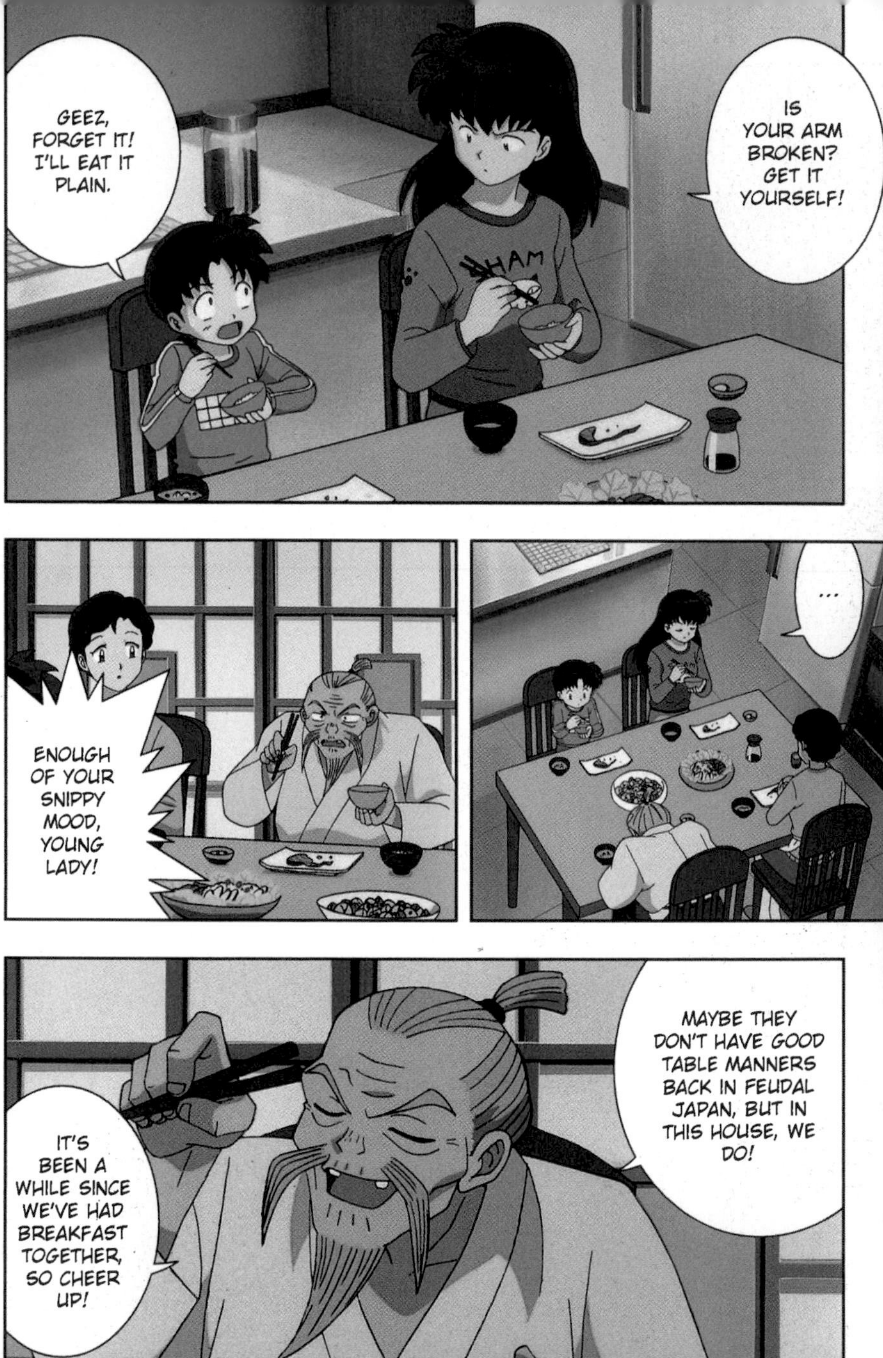
IS YOUR ARM BROKEN? GET IT YOURSELF!
GEEZ, FORGET IT! I'LL EAT IT PLAIN.
...
ENOUGH OF YOUR SNIPPY MOOD, YOUNG LADY!
MAYBE THEY DON'T HAVE GOOD TABLE MANNERS BACK IN FEUDAL JAPAN, BUT IN THIS HOUSE, WE DO!
IT'S BEEN A WHILE SINCE WE'VE HAD BREAKFAST TOGETHER, SO CHEER UP!

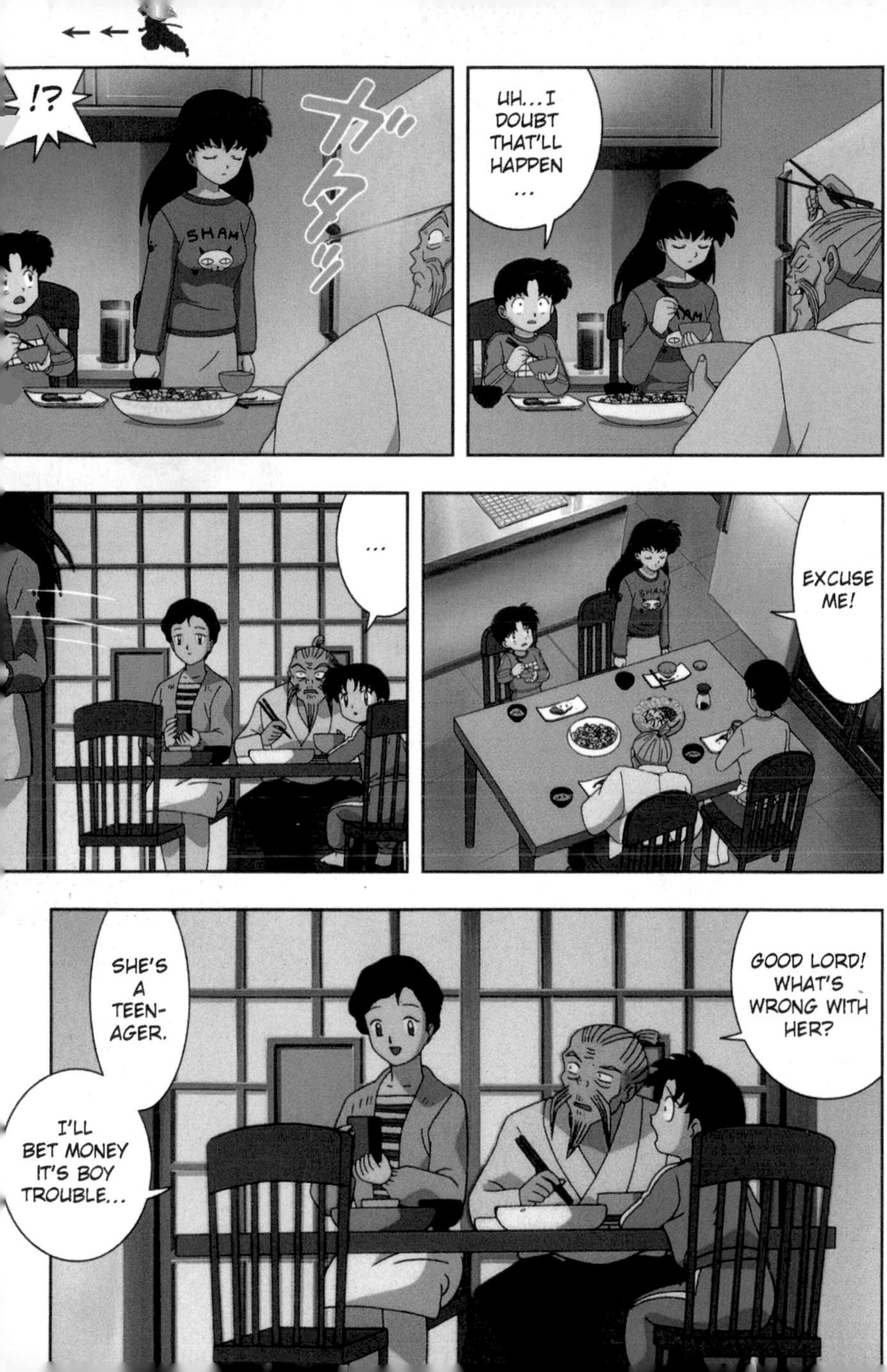
UH...I DOUBT THAT'LL HAPPEN ...
!?
ガタッ
EXCUSE ME!
...
GOOD LORD! WHAT'S WRONG WITH HER?
SHE'S A TEEN-AGER.
I'LL BET MONEY IT'S BOY TROUBLE...

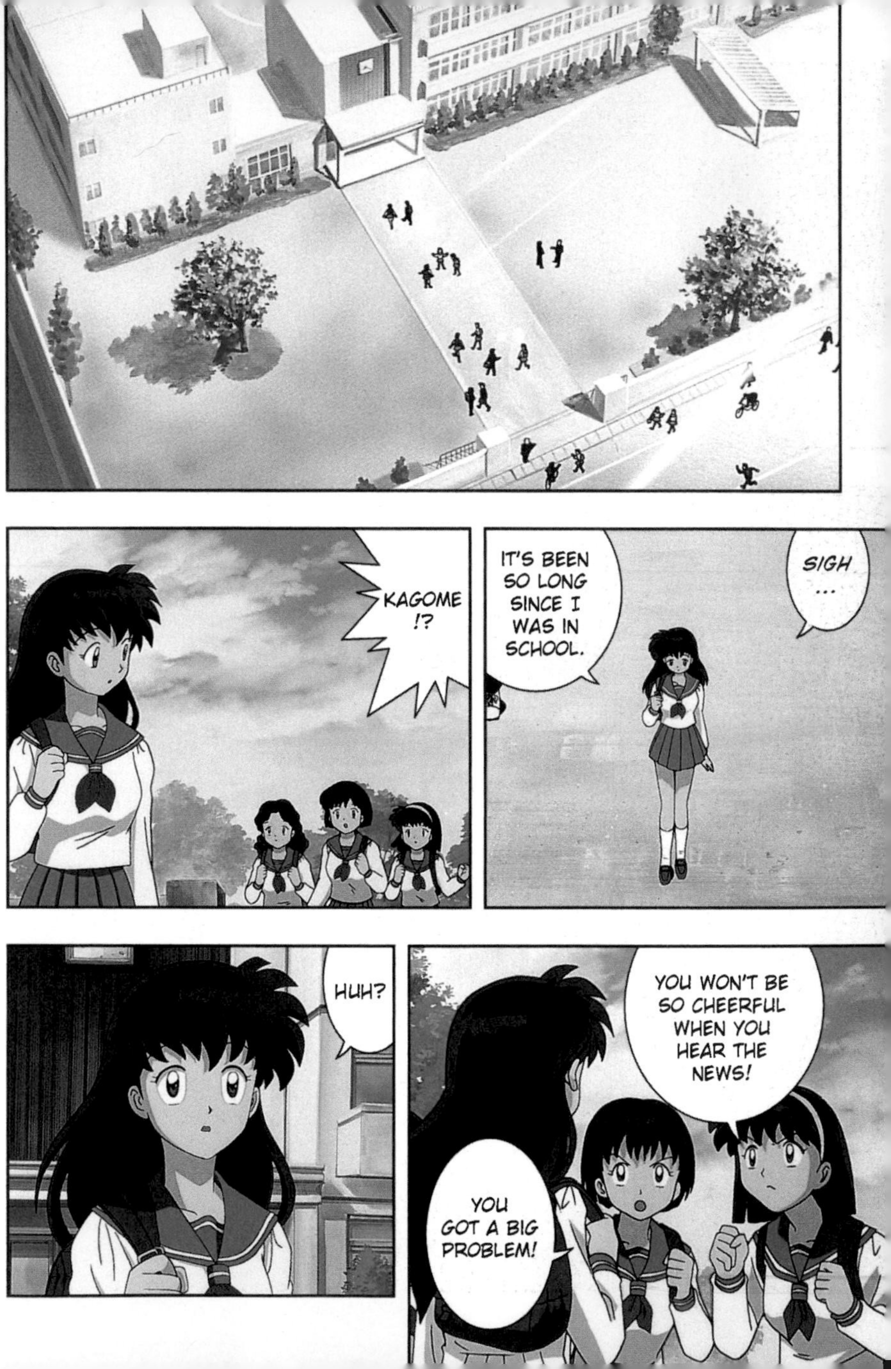
SIGH ...
IT'S BEEN SO LONG SINCE I WAS IN SCHOOL.
KAGOME !?
YOU WON'T BE SO CHEERFUL WHEN YOU HEAR THE NEWS!
YOU GOT A BIG PROBLEM!
HUH?

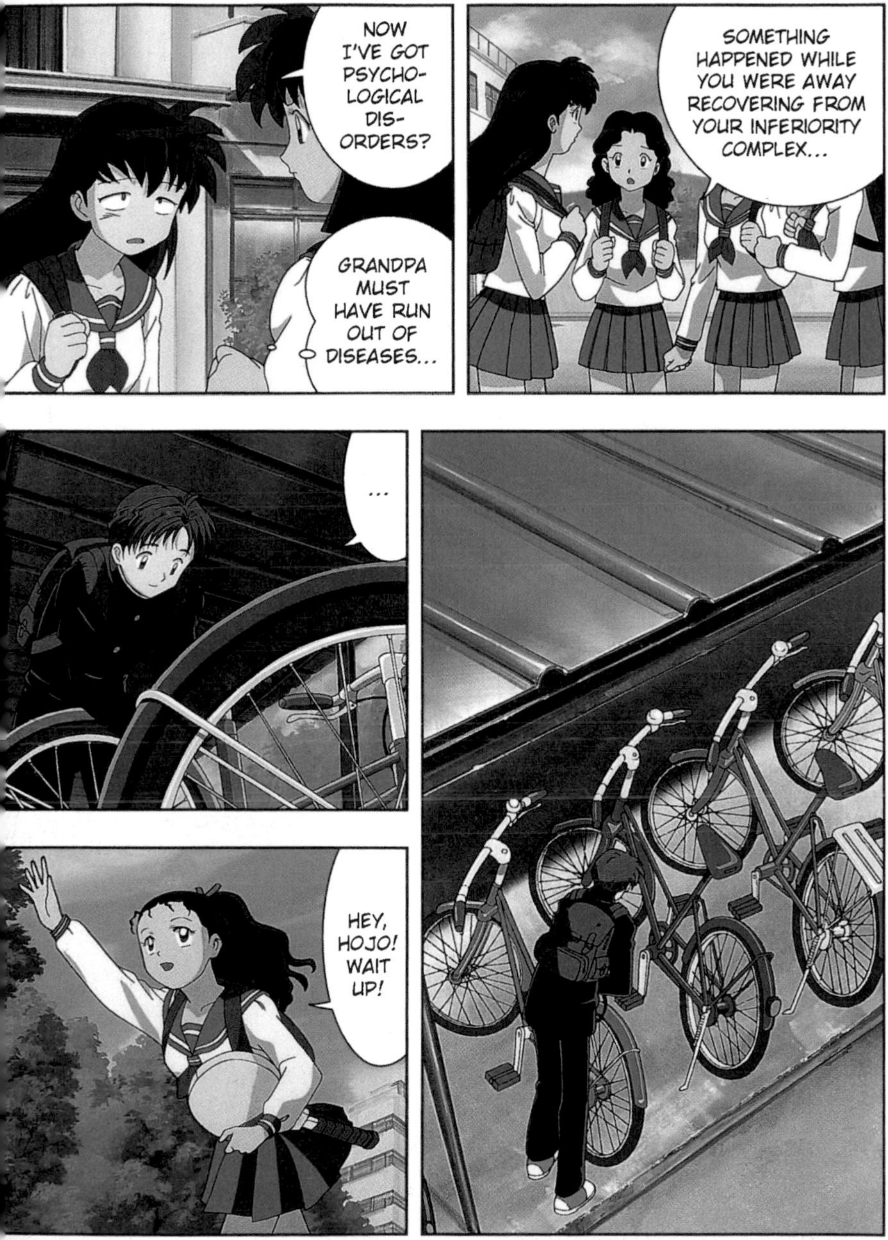
SOMETHING HAPPENED WHILE YOU WERE AWAY RECOVERING FROM YOUR INFERIORITY COMPLEX...
NOW I'VE GOT PSYCHO-LOGICAL DIS-ORDERS?
GRANDPA MUST HAVE RUN OUT OF DISEASES...
...
HEY, HOJO! WAIT UP!

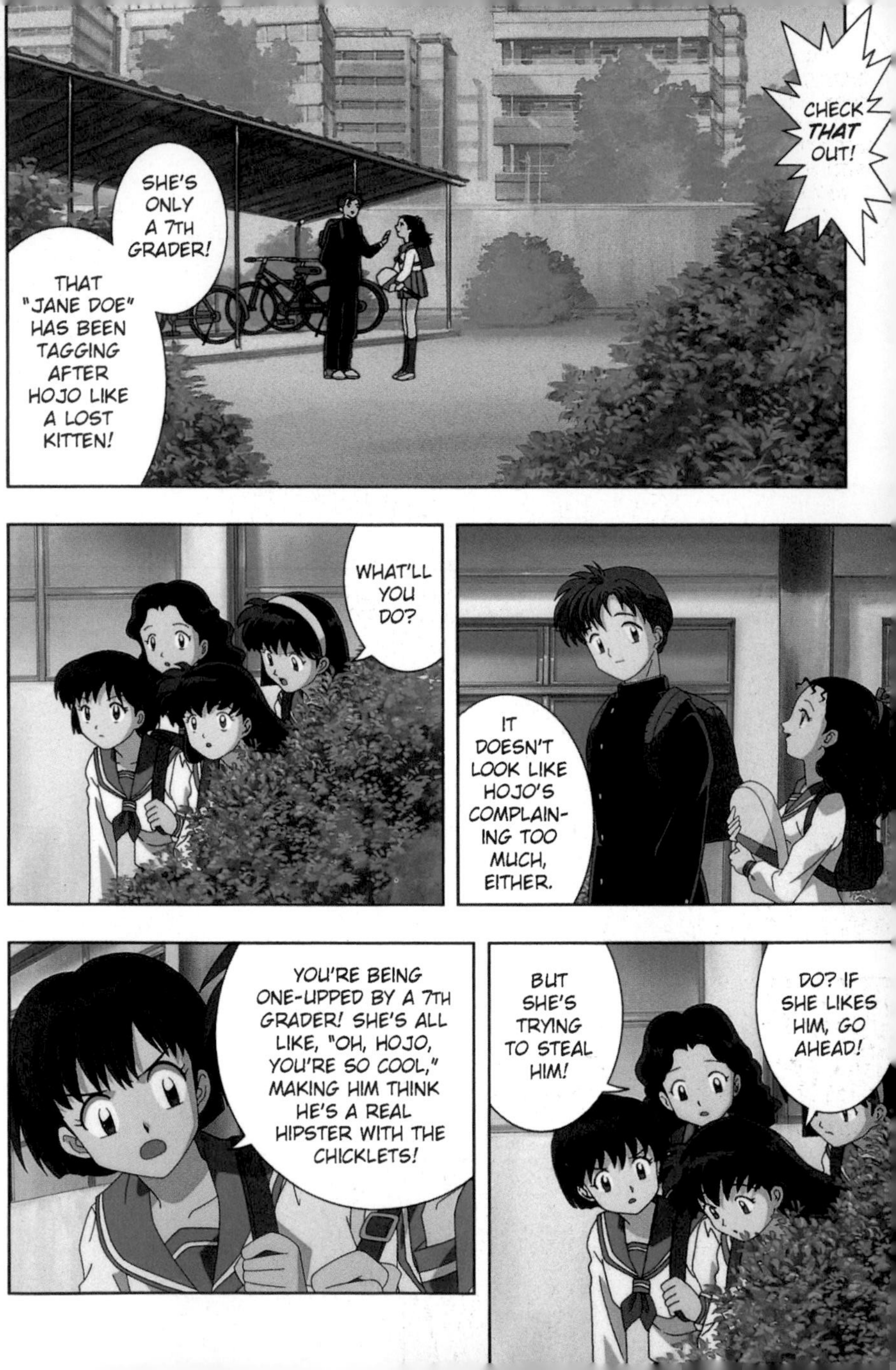
CHECK THAT OUT!
SHE'S ONLY A 7TH GRADER!
THAT "JANE DOE" HAS BEEN TAGGING AFTER HOJO LIKE A LOST KITTEN!
IT DOESN'T LOOK LIKE HOJO'S COMPLAIN-ING TOO MUCH, EITHER.
WHAT'LL YOU DO?
DO? IF SHE LIKES HIM, GO AHEAD!
BUT SHE'S TRYING TO STEAL HIM!
YOU'RE BEING ONE-UPPED BY A 7TH GRADER! SHE'S ALL LIKE, "OH, HOJO, YOU'RE SO COOL," MAKING HIM THINK HE'S A REAL HIPSTER WITH THE CHICKLETS!

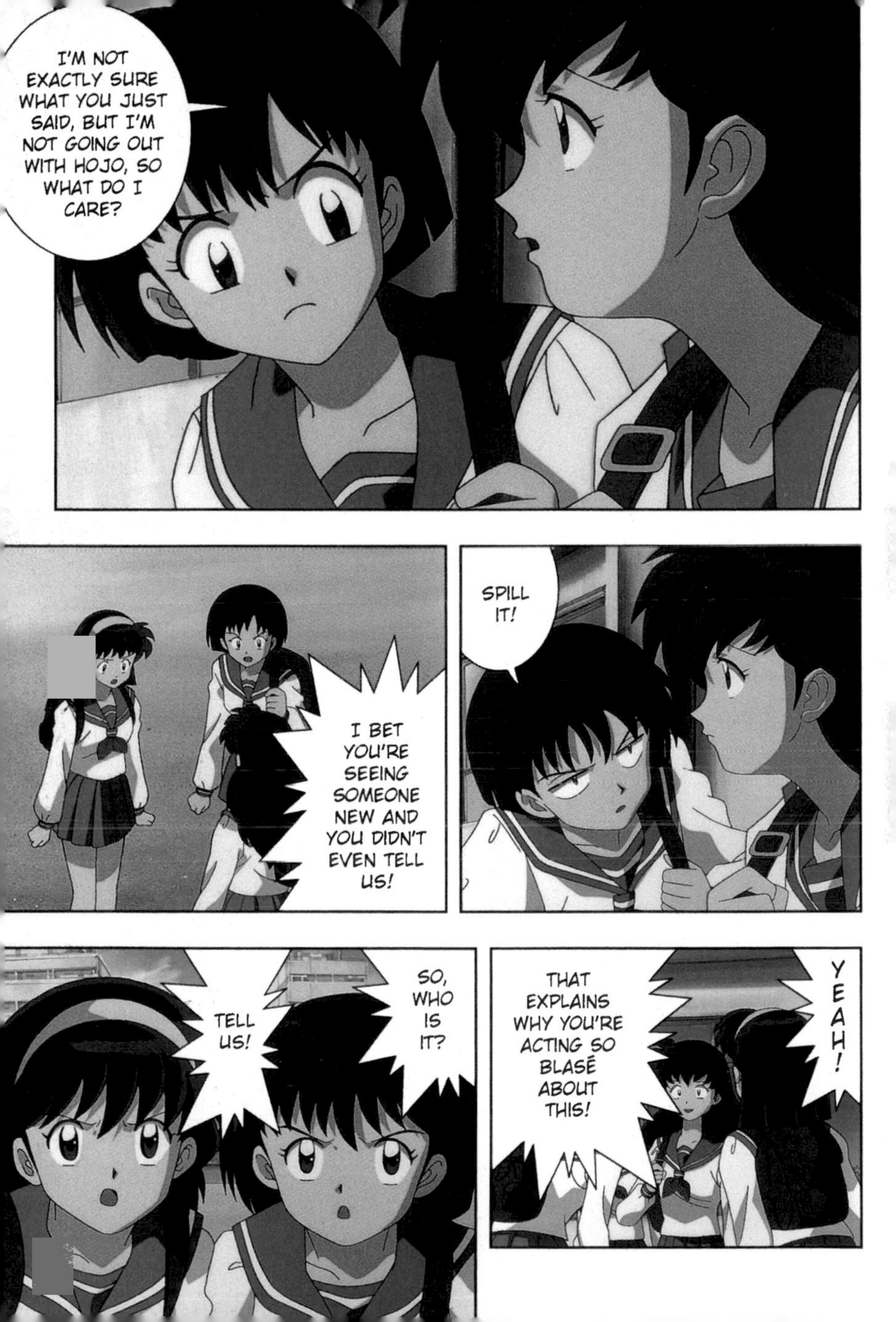
I'M NOT EXACTLY SURE WHAT YOU JUST SAID, BUT I'M NOT GOING OUT WITH HOJO, SO WHAT DO I CARE?
SPILL IT!
I BET YOU'RE SEEING SOMEONE NEW AND YOU DIDN'T EVEN TELL US!
YEAH!
THAT EXPLAINS WHY YOU'RE ACTING SO BLASÉ ABOUT THIS!
SO, WHO IS IT?
TELL US!

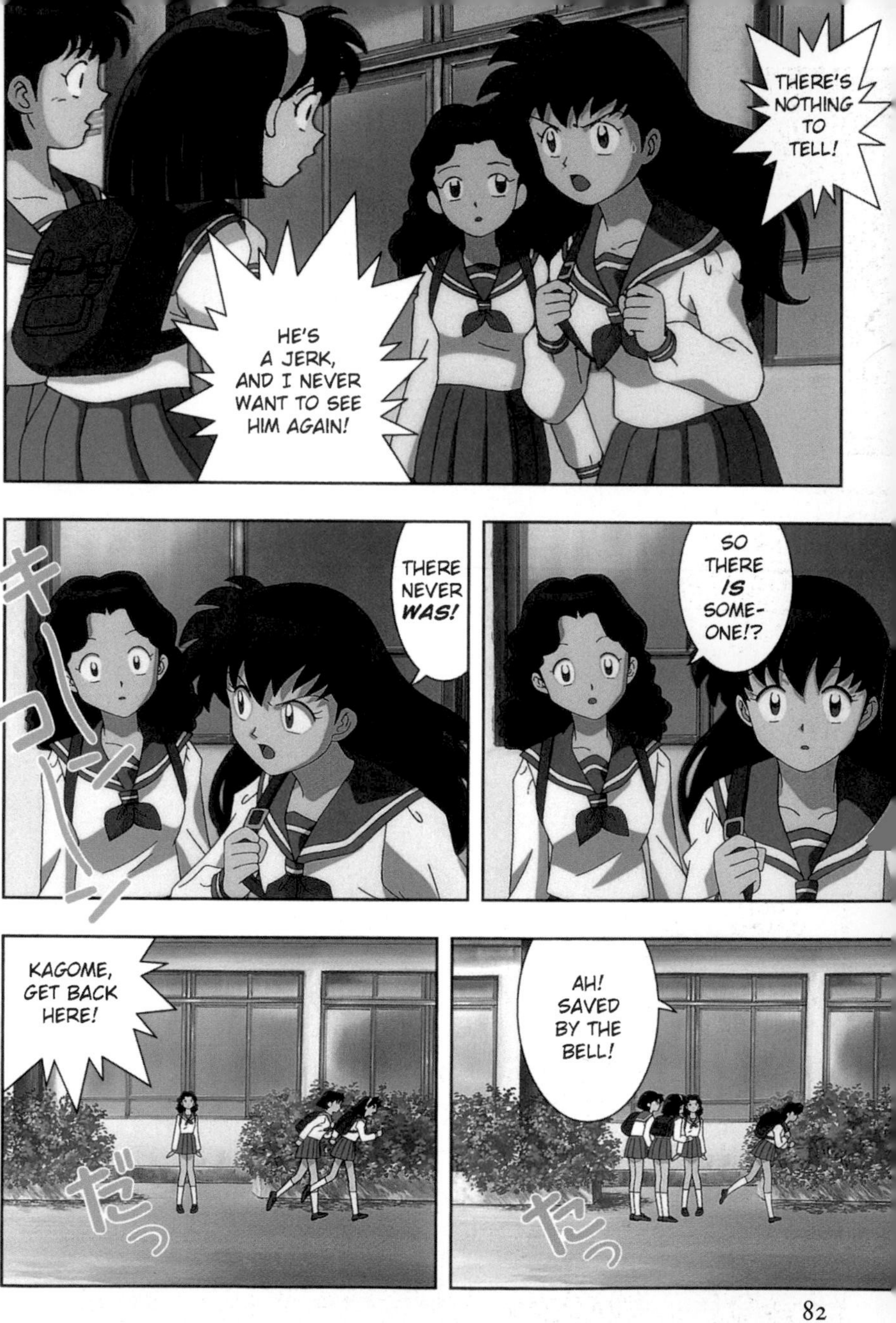
THERE'S NOTHING TO TELL!
HE'S A JERK, AND I NEVER WANT TO SEE HIM AGAIN!
SO THERE *IS* SOME-ONE!?
THERE NEVER ***WAS!***
キーンコーン
AH! SAVED BY THE BELL!
だっ
KAGOME, GET BACK HERE!
だっ

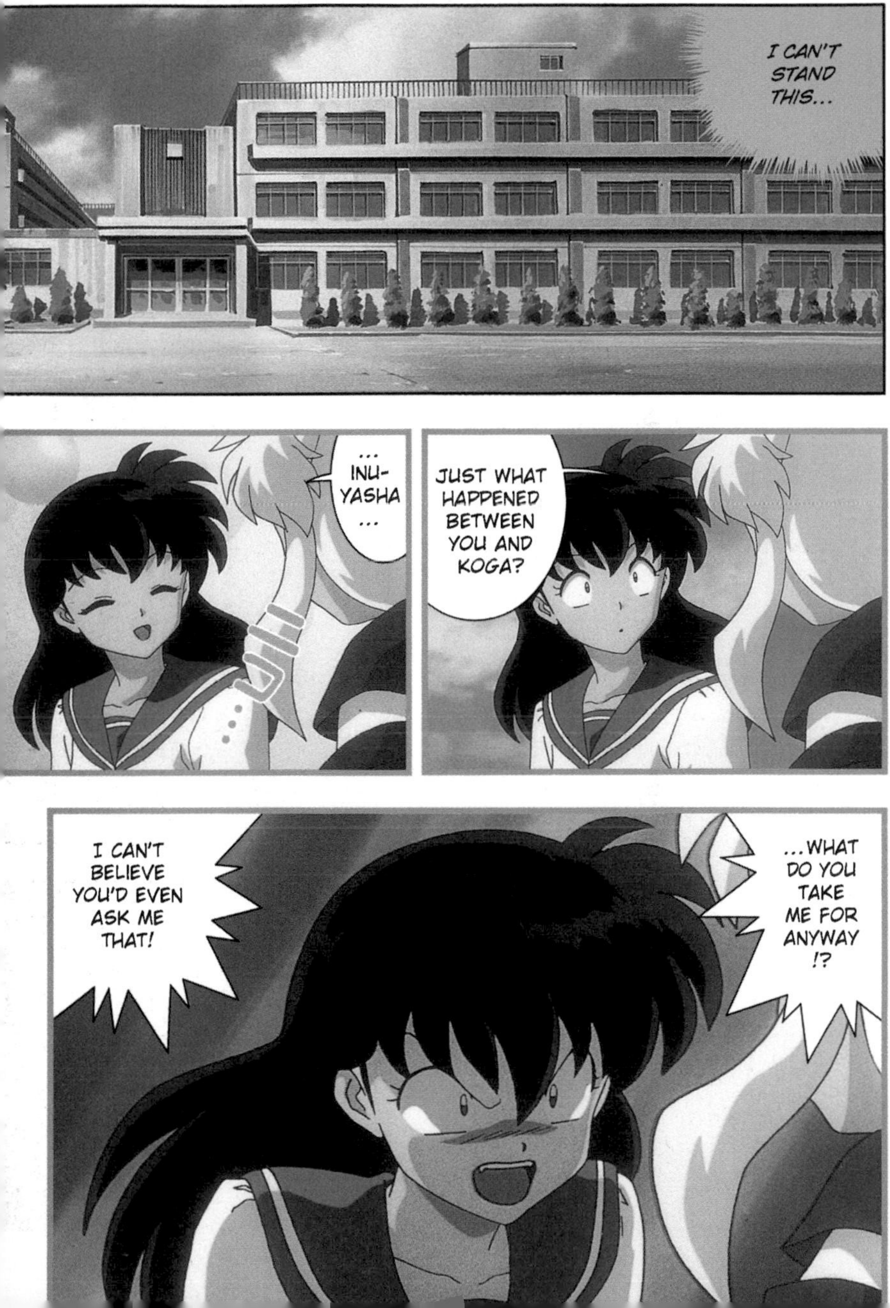
I CAN'T STAND THIS...
JUST WHAT HAPPENED BETWEEN YOU AND KOGA?
... INU-YASHA ...
...WHAT DO YOU TAKE ME FOR ANYWAY !?
I CAN'T BELIEVE YOU'D EVEN ASK ME THAT!

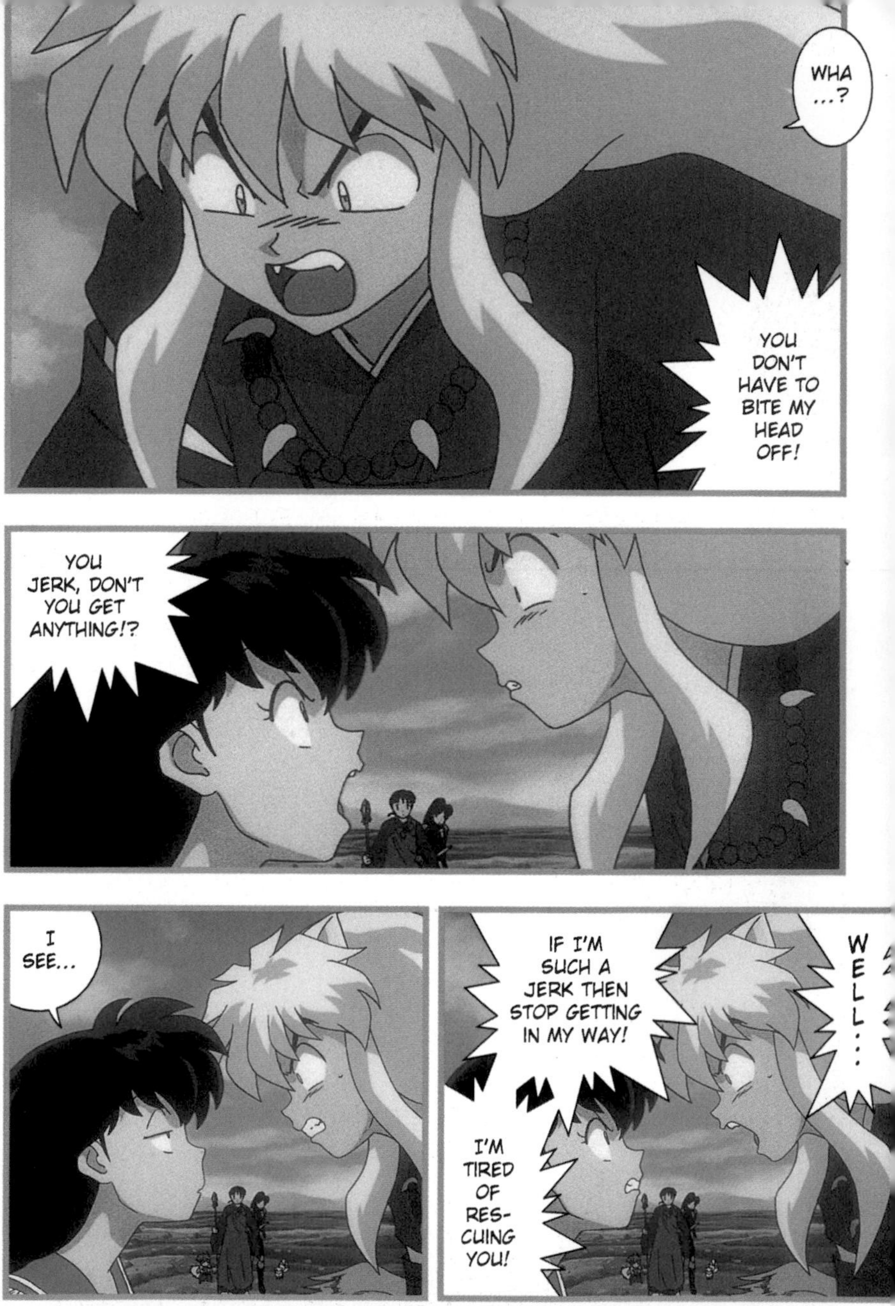
WHA ...?
YOU DON'T HAVE TO BITE MY HEAD OFF!
YOU JERK, DON'T YOU GET ANYTHING!?
WELL...
IF I'M SUCH A JERK THEN STOP GETTING IN MY WAY!
I'M TIRED OF RES-CUING YOU!
I SEE...

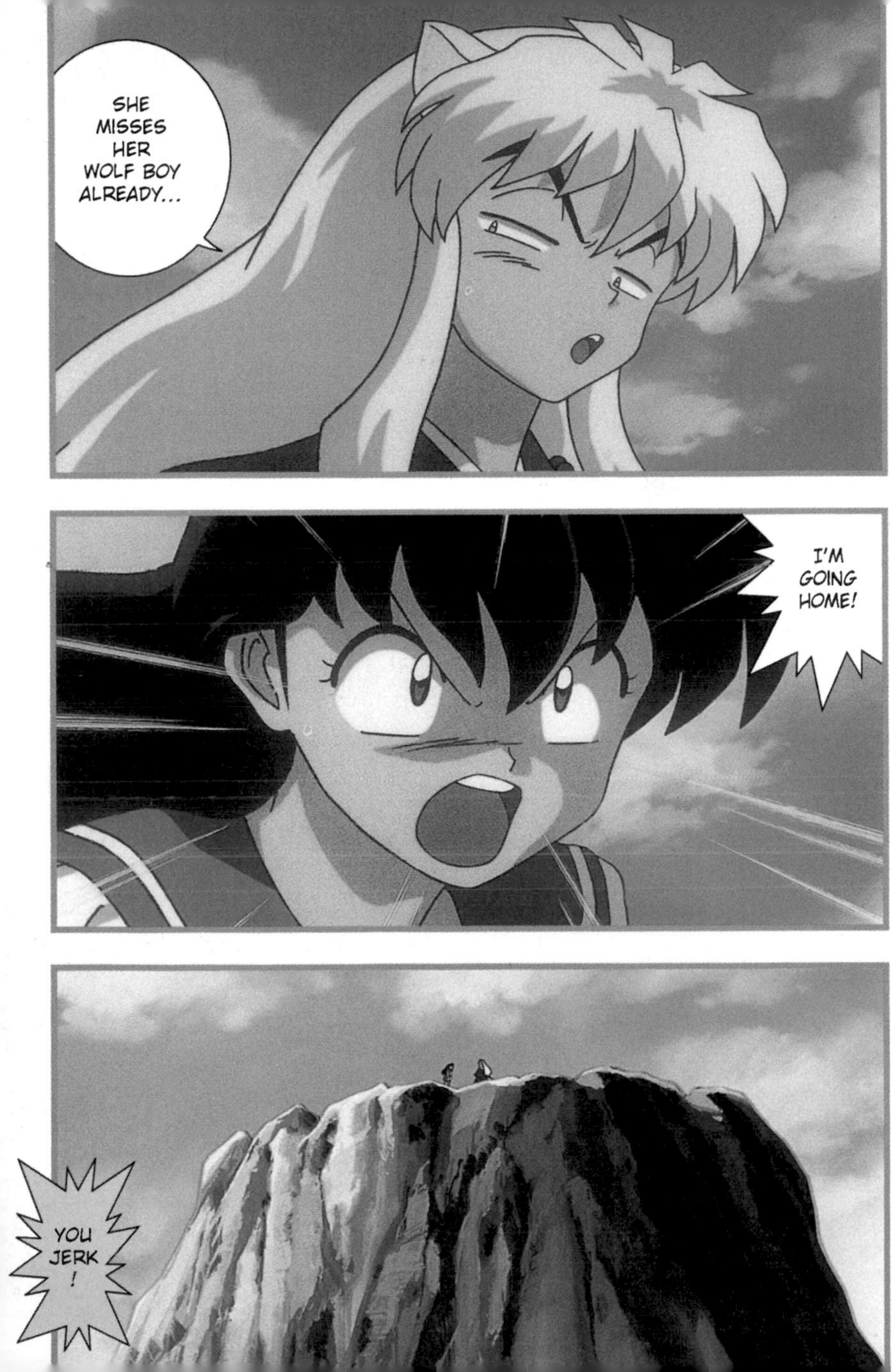
SHE MISSES HER WOLF BOY ALREADY...
I'M GOING HOME!
YOU JERK!

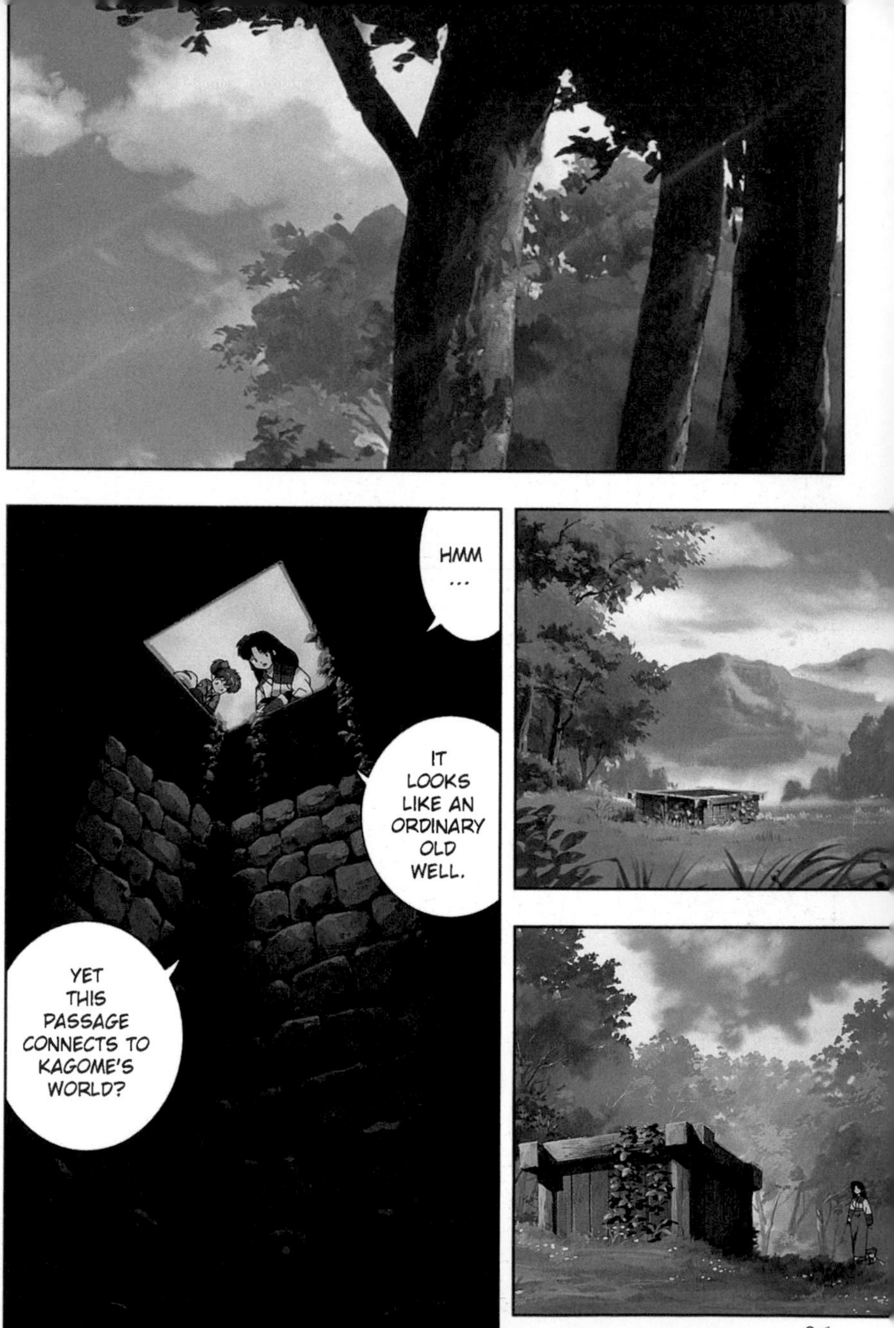
HMM ...
IT LOOKS LIKE AN ORDINARY OLD WELL.
YET THIS PASSAGE CONNECTS TO KAGOME'S WORLD?

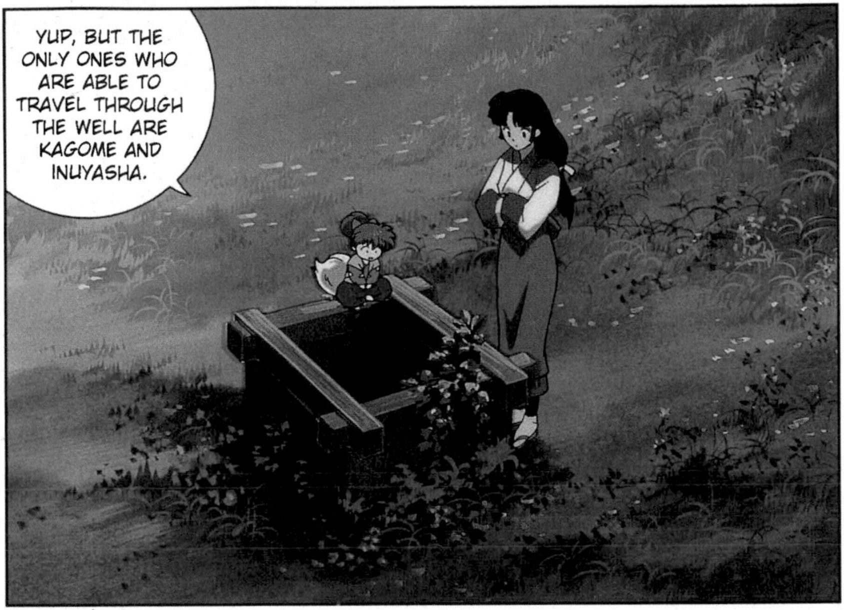
YUP, BUT THE ONLY ONES WHO ARE ABLE TO TRAVEL THROUGH THE WELL ARE KAGOME AND INUYASHA.

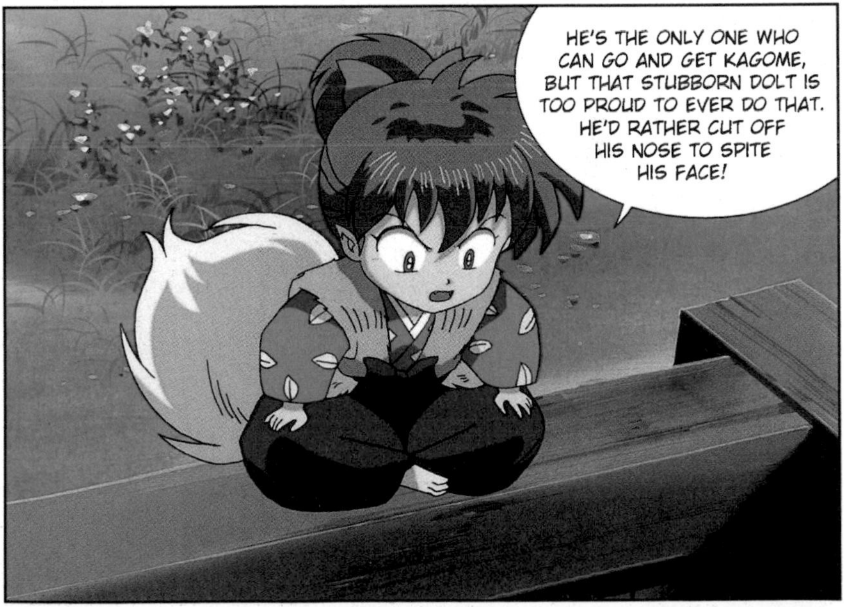
HE'S THE ONLY ONE WHO CAN GO AND GET KAGOME, BUT THAT STUBBORN DOLT IS TOO PROUD TO EVER DO THAT. HE'D RATHER CUT OFF HIS NOSE TO SPITE HIS FACE!

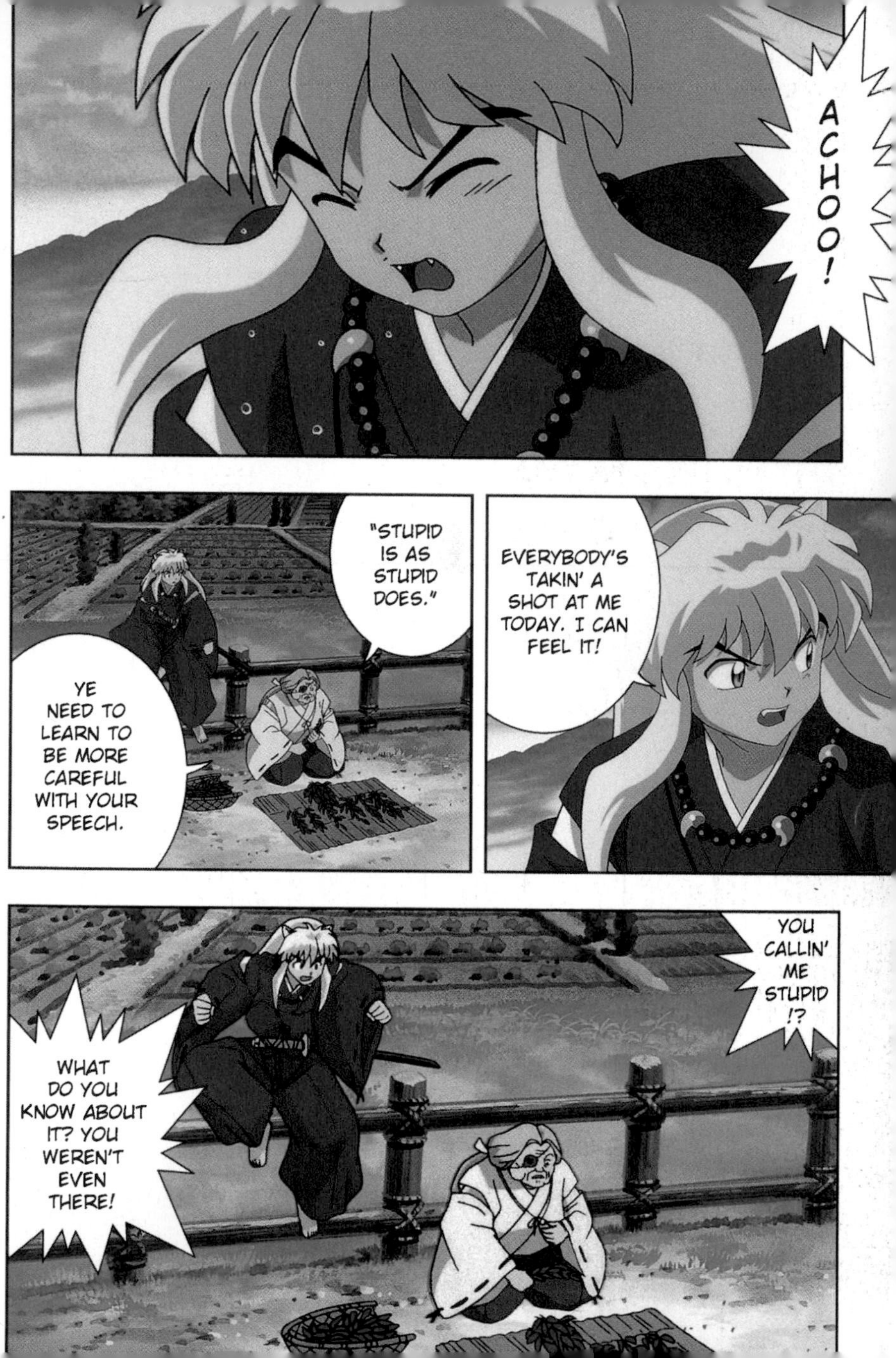
ACHOO!
EVERYBODY'S TAKIN' A SHOT AT ME TODAY. I CAN FEEL IT!
"STUPID IS AS STUPID DOES."
YE NEED TO LEARN TO BE MORE CAREFUL WITH YOUR SPEECH.
YOU CALLIN' ME STUPID !?
WHAT DO YOU KNOW ABOUT IT? YOU WEREN'T EVEN THERE!

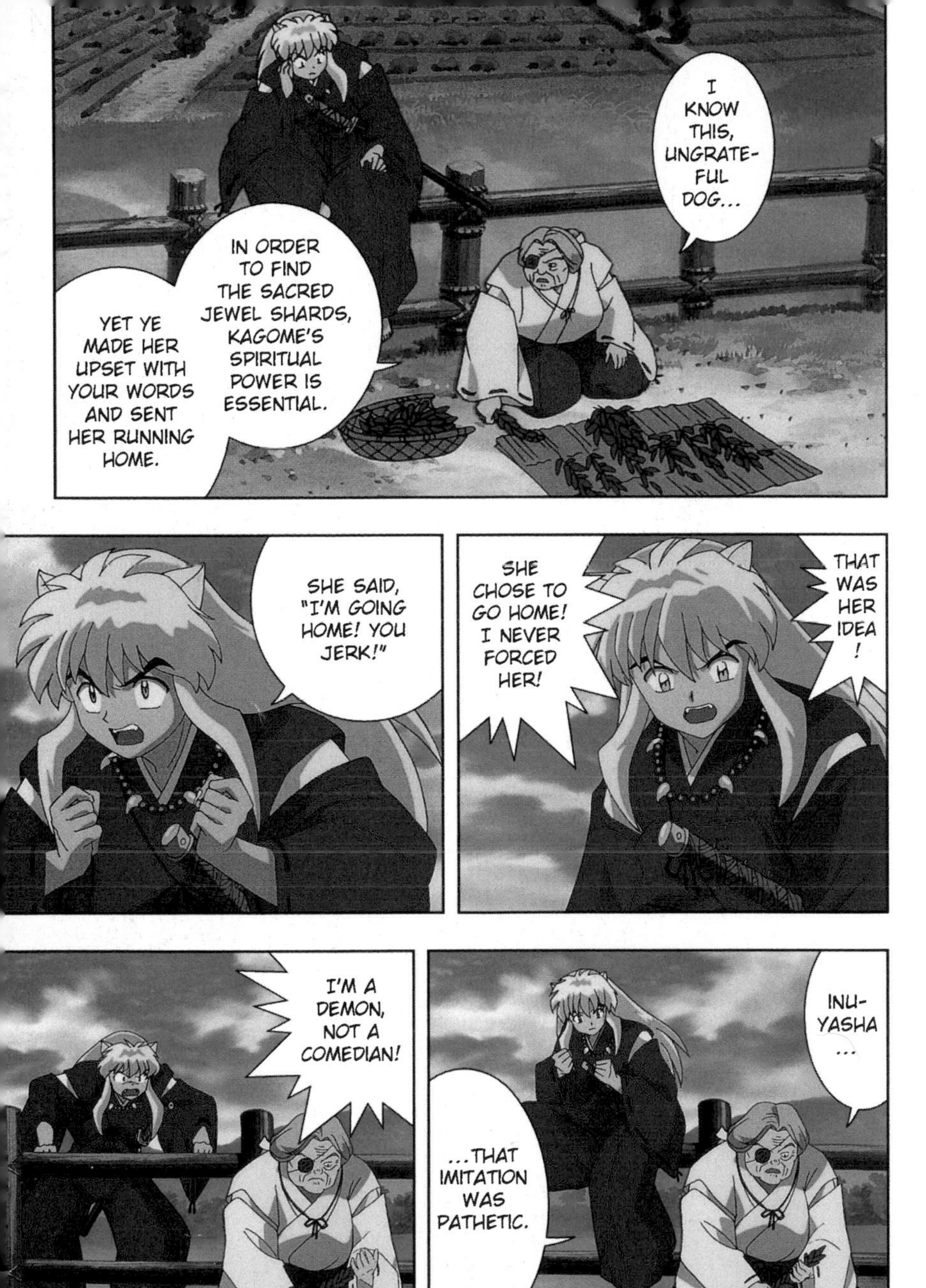
I KNOW THIS, UNGRATEFUL DOG...
IN ORDER TO FIND THE SACRED JEWEL SHARDS, KAGOME'S SPIRITUAL POWER IS ESSENTIAL.
YET YE MADE HER UPSET WITH YOUR WORDS AND SENT HER RUNNING HOME.
THAT WAS HER IDEA!
SHE CHOSE TO GO HOME! I NEVER FORCED HER!
SHE SAID, "I'M GOING HOME! YOU JERK!"
INU-YASHA...
...THAT IMITATION WAS PATHETIC.
I'M A DEMON, NOT A COMEDIAN!

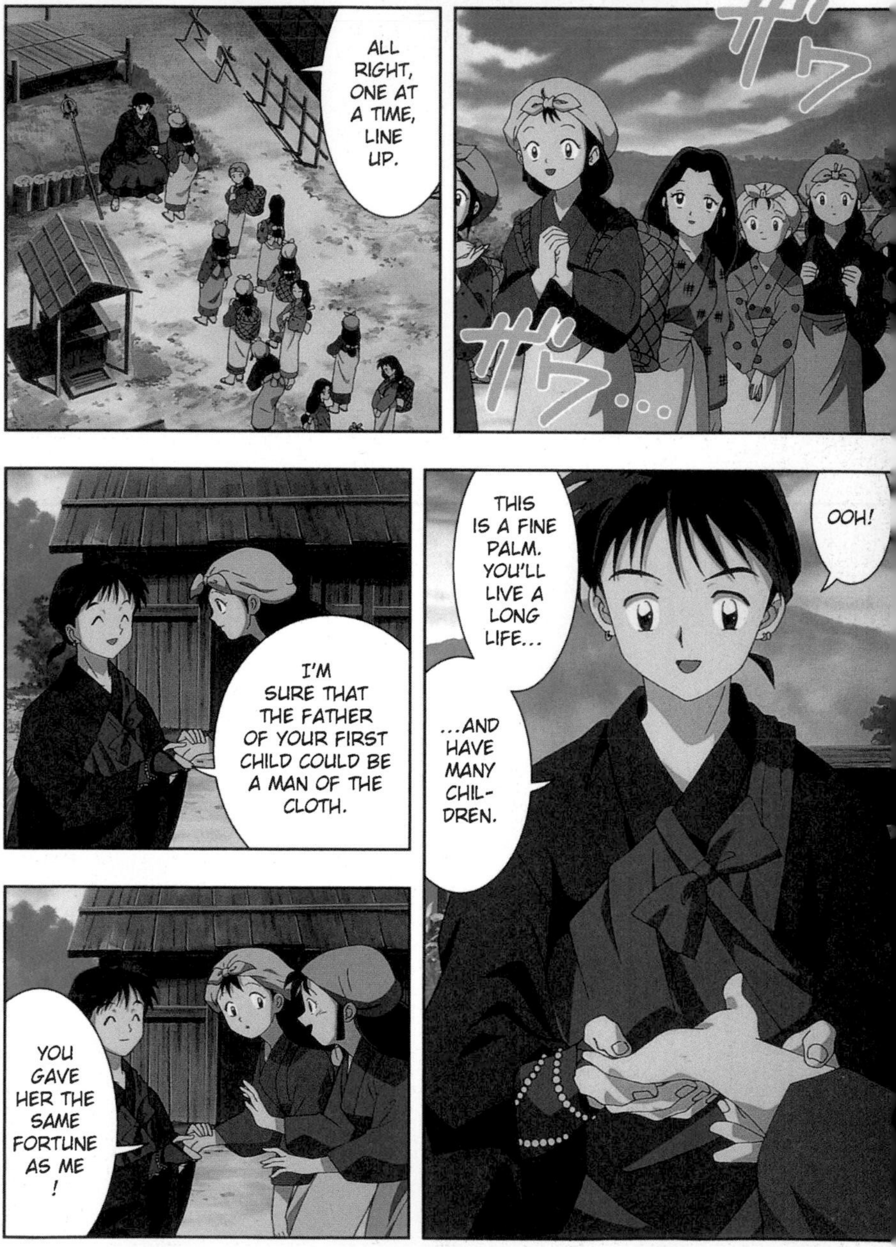

ザワ
ザワ...
ALL RIGHT, ONE AT A TIME, LINE UP.
OOH!
THIS IS A FINE PALM. YOU'LL LIVE A LONG LIFE...
...AND HAVE MANY CHIL-DREN.
I'M SURE THAT THE FATHER OF YOUR FIRST CHILD COULD BE A MAN OF THE CLOTH.
YOU GAVE HER THE SAME FORTUNE AS ME!

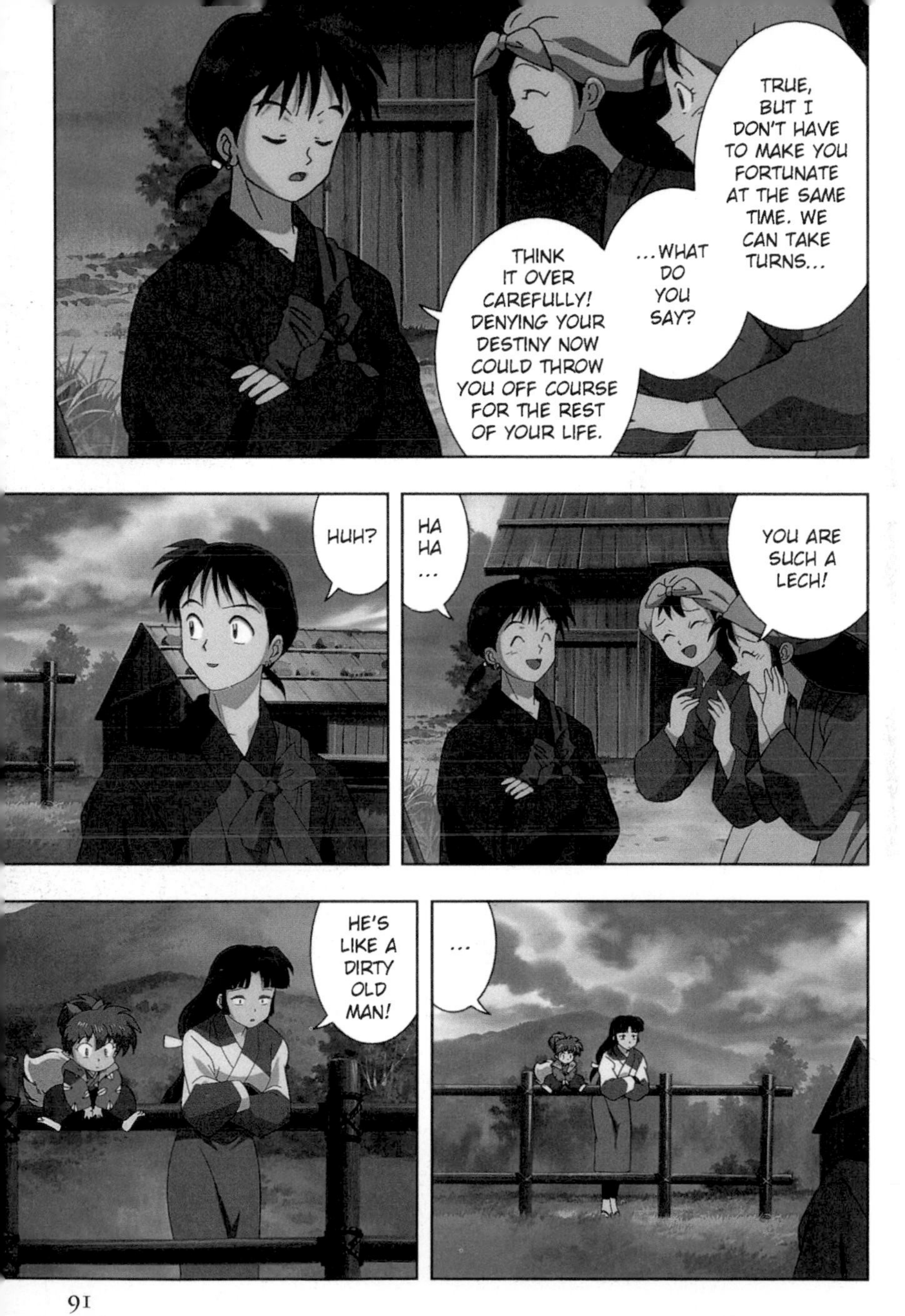
THINK IT OVER CAREFULLY! DENYING YOUR DESTINY NOW COULD THROW YOU OFF COURSE FOR THE REST OF YOUR LIFE.
...WHAT DO YOU SAY?
TRUE, BUT I DON'T HAVE TO MAKE YOU FORTUNATE AT THE SAME TIME. WE CAN TAKE TURNS...
HUH?
HA HA ...
YOU ARE SUCH A LECH!
HE'S LIKE A DIRTY OLD MAN!
...

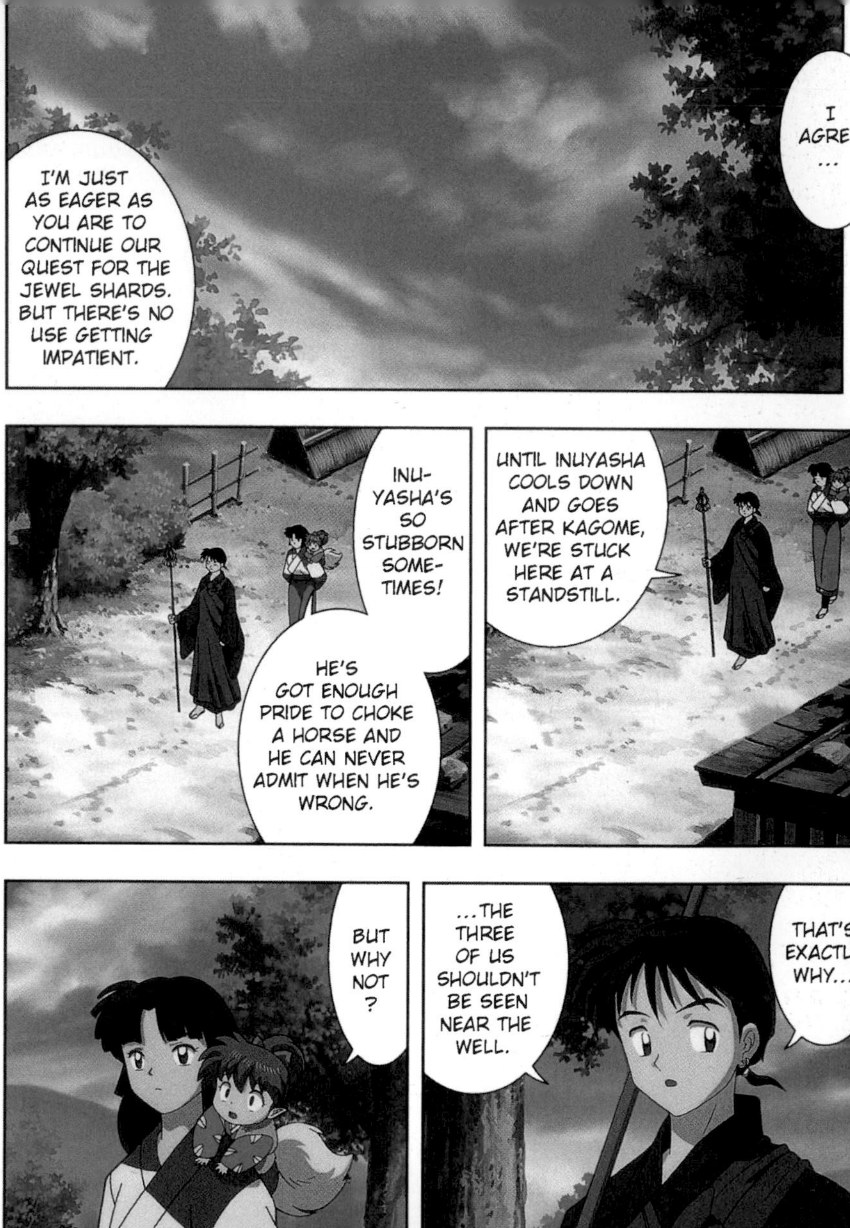
I AGREE ...
I'M JUST AS EAGER AS YOU ARE TO CONTINUE OUR QUEST FOR THE JEWEL SHARDS. BUT THERE'S NO USE GETTING IMPATIENT.
UNTIL INUYASHA COOLS DOWN AND GOES AFTER KAGOME, WE'RE STUCK HERE AT A STANDSTILL.
INU-YASHA'S SO STUBBORN SOME-TIMES!
HE'S GOT ENOUGH PRIDE TO CHOKE A HORSE AND HE CAN NEVER ADMIT WHEN HE'S WRONG.
THAT'S EXACTLY WHY...
...THE THREE OF US SHOULDN'T BE SEEN NEAR THE WELL.
BUT WHY NOT ?

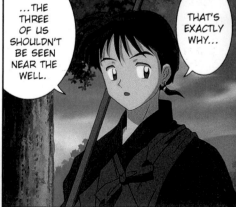

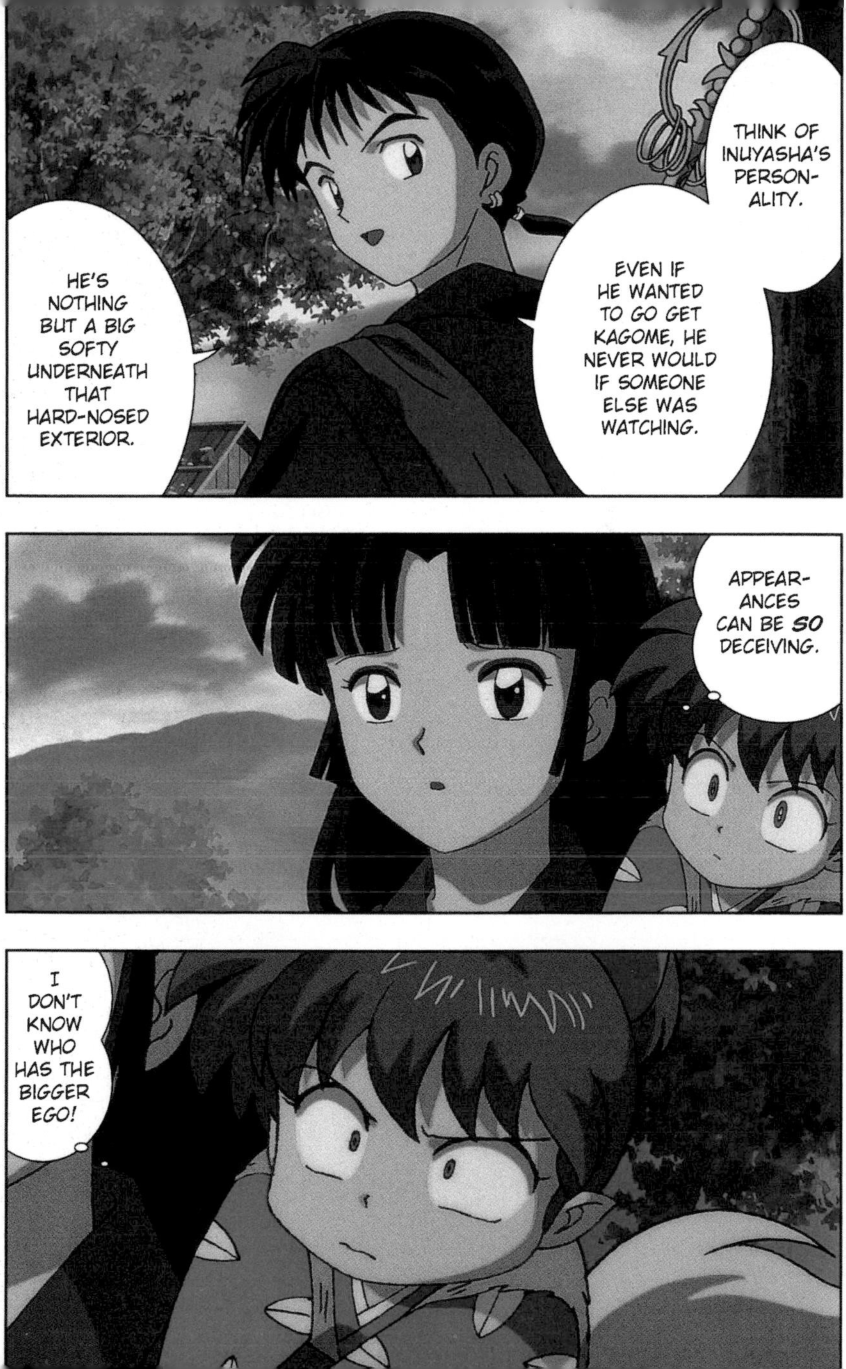
THINK OF INUYASHA'S PERSON-ALITY.
EVEN IF HE WANTED TO GO GET KAGOME, HE NEVER WOULD IF SOMEONE ELSE WAS WATCHING.
HE'S NOTHING BUT A BIG SOFTY UNDERNEATH THAT HARD-NOSED EXTERIOR.
APPEAR-ANCES CAN BE *SO* DECEIVING.
I DON'T KNOW WHO HAS THE BIGGER EGO!

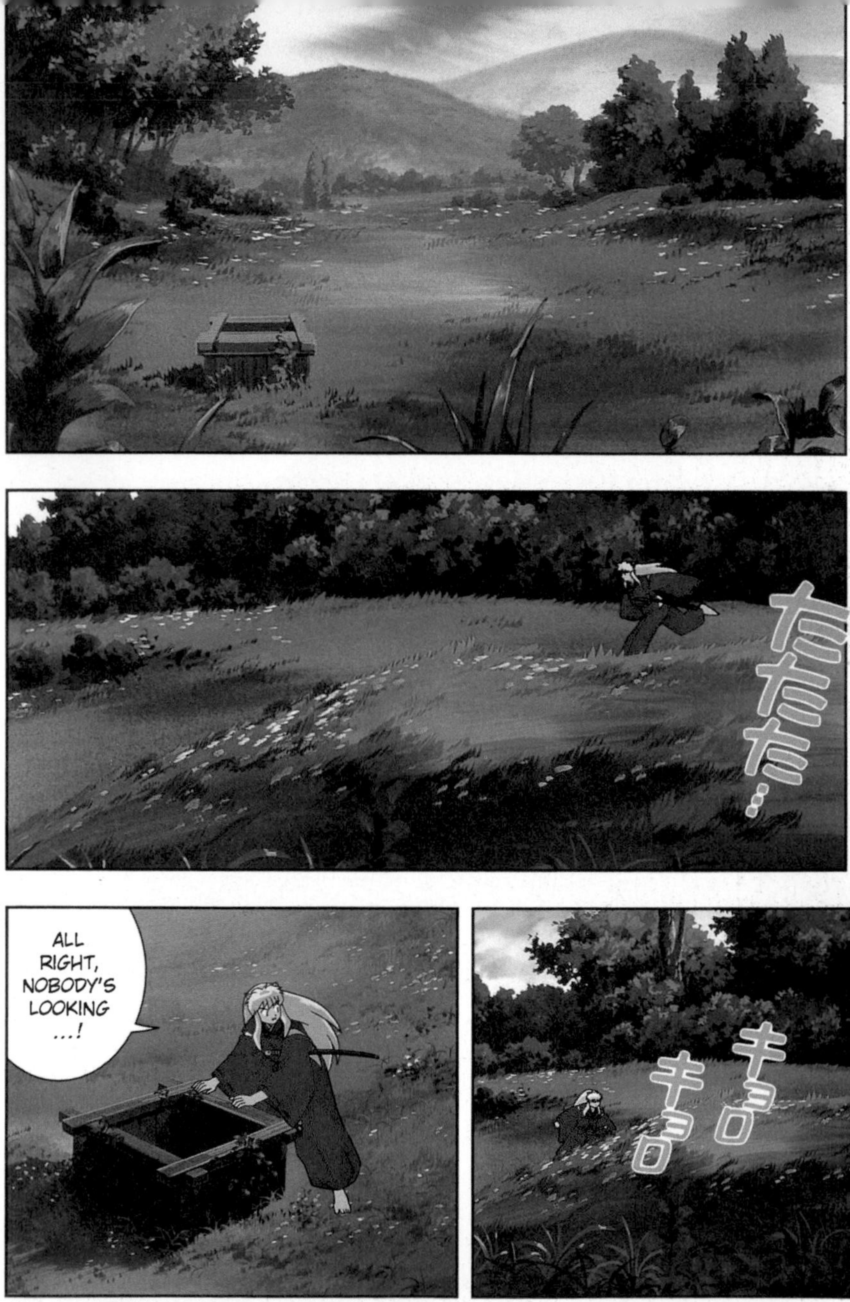
たたた…
キョロキョロ
ALL RIGHT, NOBODY'S LOOKING ...!

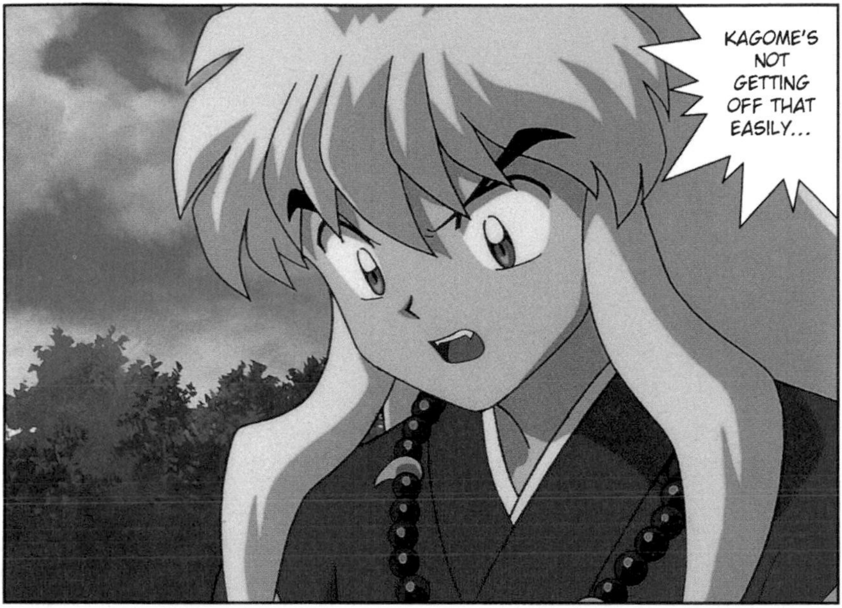
KAGOME'S NOT GETTING OFF THAT EASILY...

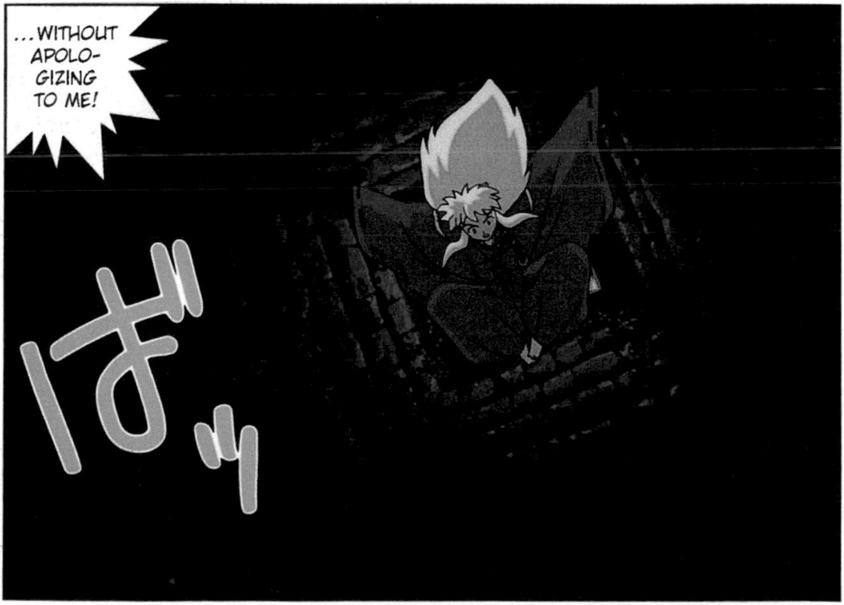
...WITHOUT APOLO-GIZING TO ME!
ばッ

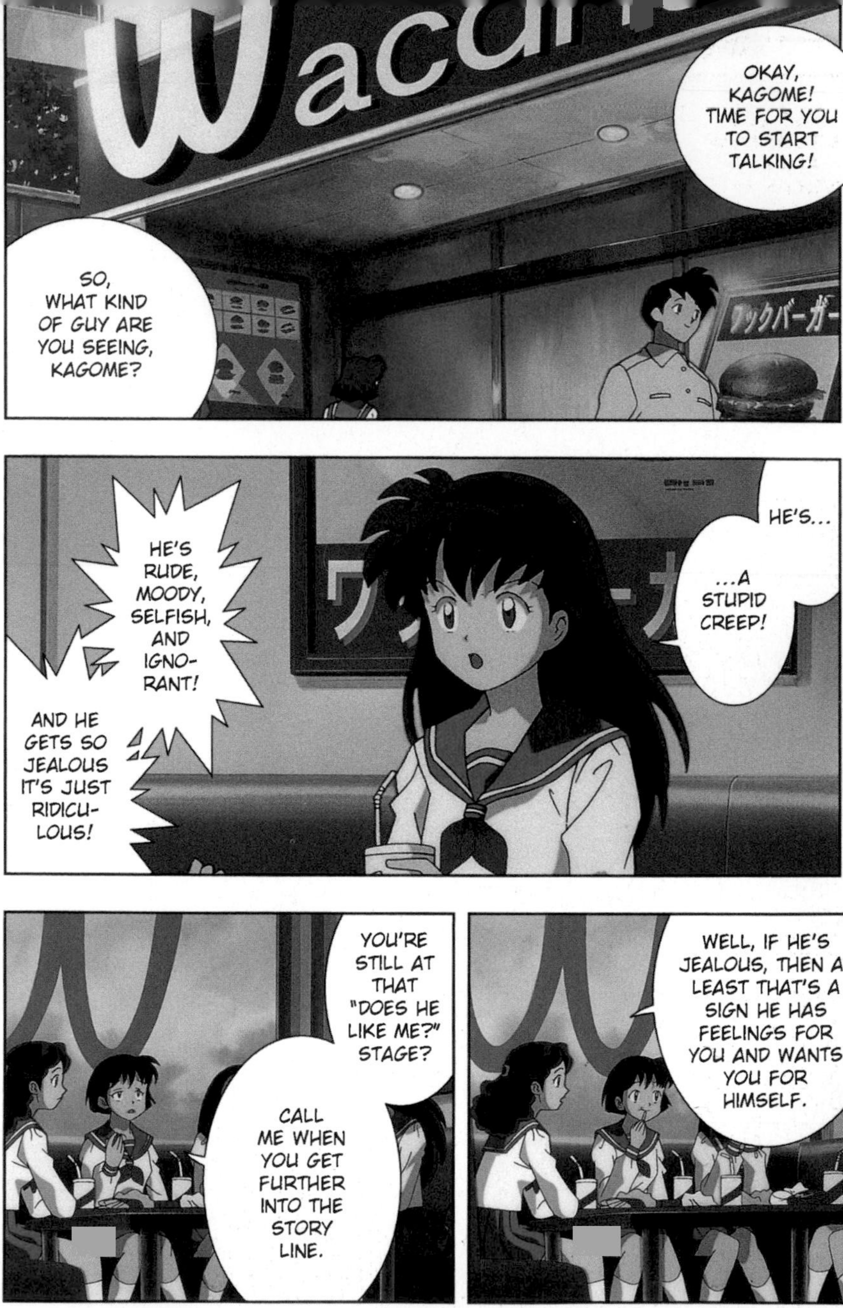
OKAY, KAGOME! TIME FOR YOU TO START TALKING!
SO, WHAT KIND OF GUY ARE YOU SEEING, KAGOME?
HE'S...
...A STUPID CREEP!
HE'S RUDE, MOODY, SELFISH, AND IGNORANT!
AND HE GETS SO JEALOUS IT'S JUST RIDICULOUS!
WELL, IF HE'S JEALOUS, THEN AT LEAST THAT'S A SIGN HE HAS FEELINGS FOR YOU AND WANTS YOU FOR HIMSELF.
YOU'RE STILL AT THAT "DOES HE LIKE ME?" STAGE?
CALL ME WHEN YOU GET FURTHER INTO THE STORY LINE.

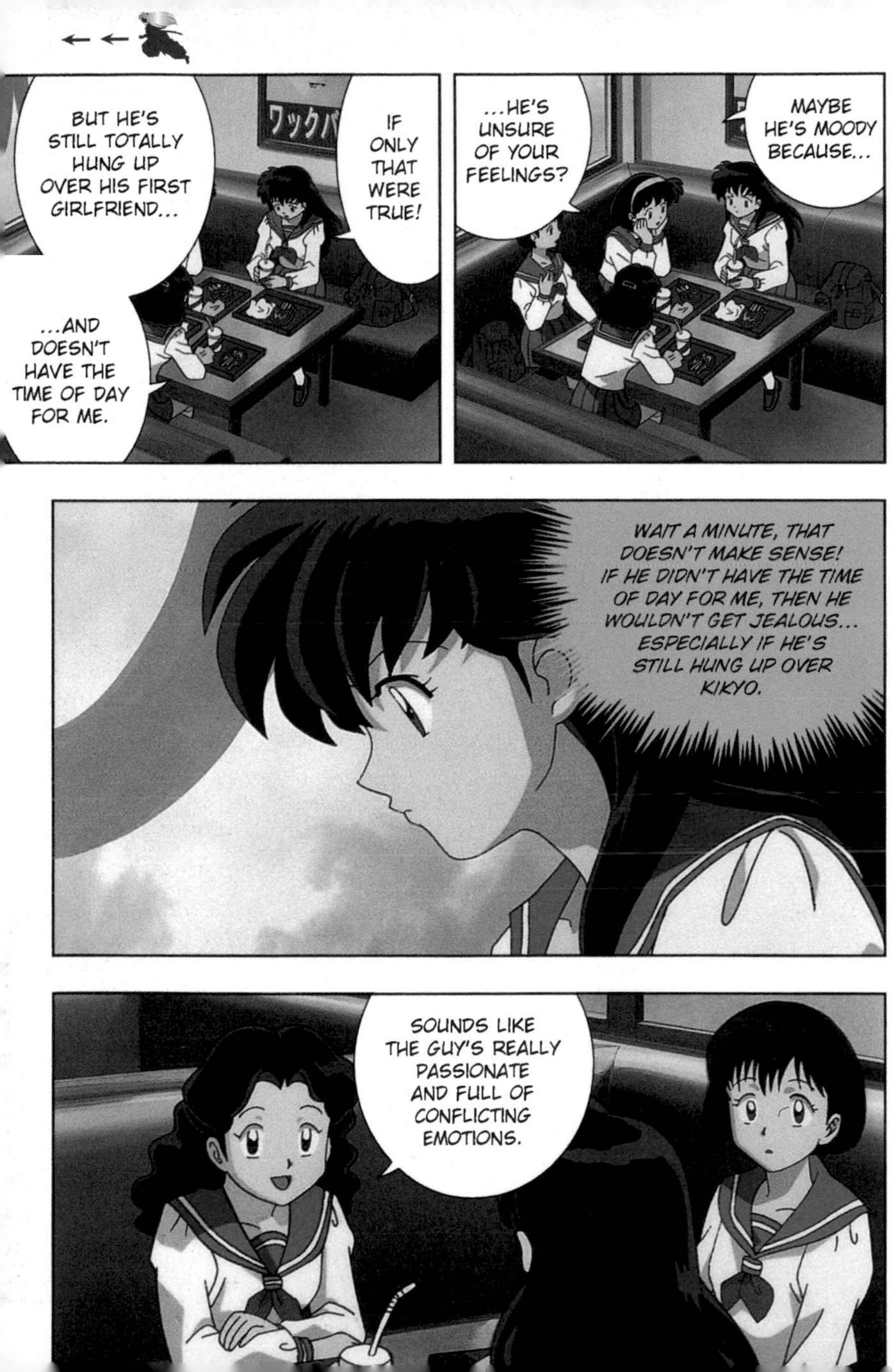
MAYBE HE'S MOODY BECAUSE...
...HE'S UNSURE OF YOUR FEELINGS?
IF ONLY THAT WERE TRUE!
BUT HE'S STILL TOTALLY HUNG UP OVER HIS FIRST GIRLFRIEND...
...AND DOESN'T HAVE THE TIME OF DAY FOR ME.
WAIT A MINUTE, THAT DOESN'T MAKE SENSE! IF HE DIDN'T HAVE THE TIME OF DAY FOR ME, THEN HE WOULDN'T GET JEALOUS... ESPECIALLY IF HE'S STILL HUNG UP OVER KIKYO.
SOUNDS LIKE THE GUY'S REALLY PASSIONATE AND FULL OF CONFLICTING EMOTIONS.

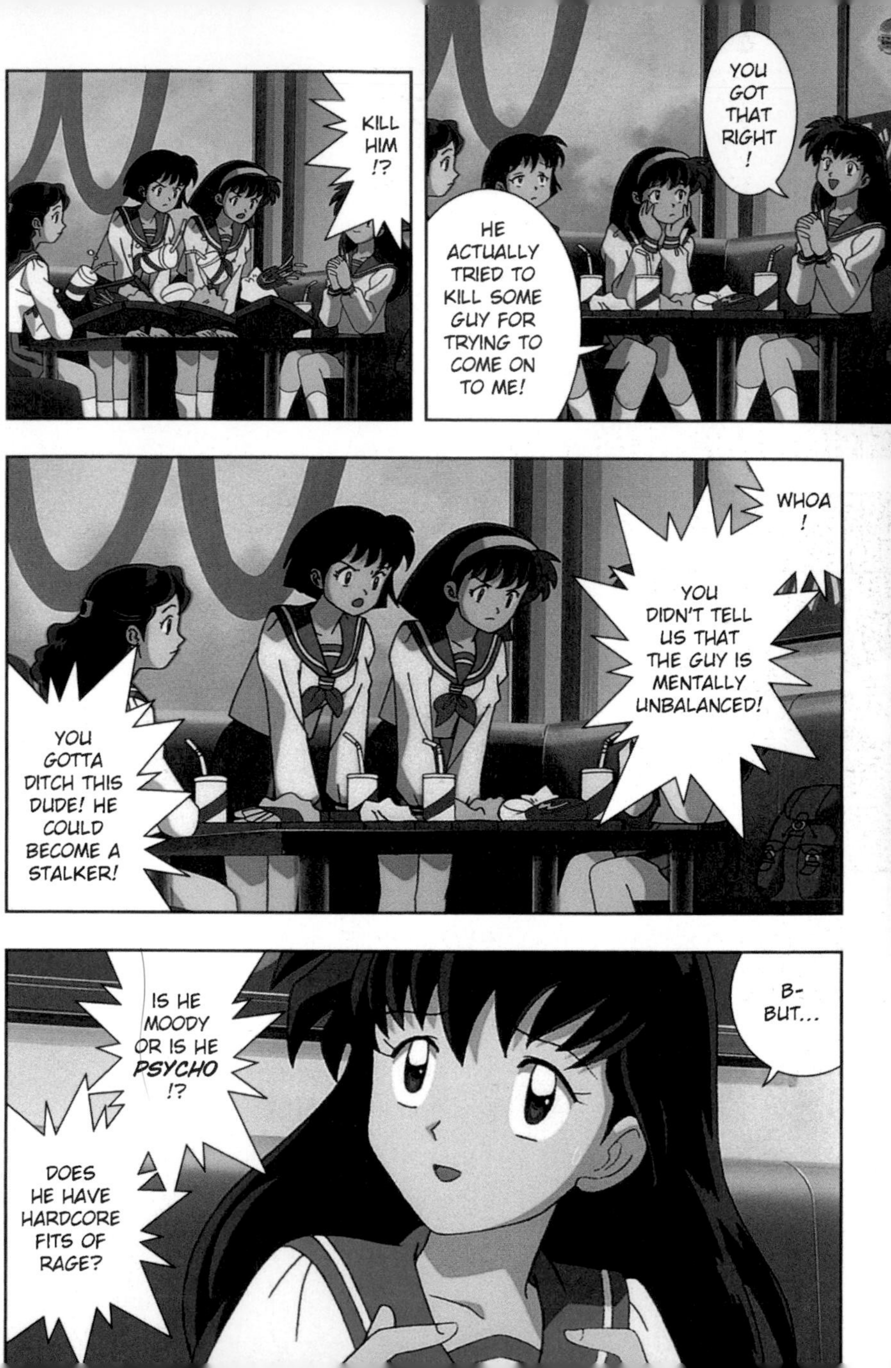
YOU GOT THAT RIGHT!
HE ACTUALLY TRIED TO KILL SOME GUY FOR TRYING TO COME ON TO ME!
KILL HIM!?
WHOA!
YOU DIDN'T TELL US THAT THE GUY IS MENTALLY UNBALANCED!
YOU GOTTA DITCH THIS DUDE! HE COULD BECOME A STALKER!
B-BUT...
IS HE MOODY OR IS HE PSYCHO!?
DOES HE HAVE HARDCORE FITS OF RAGE?

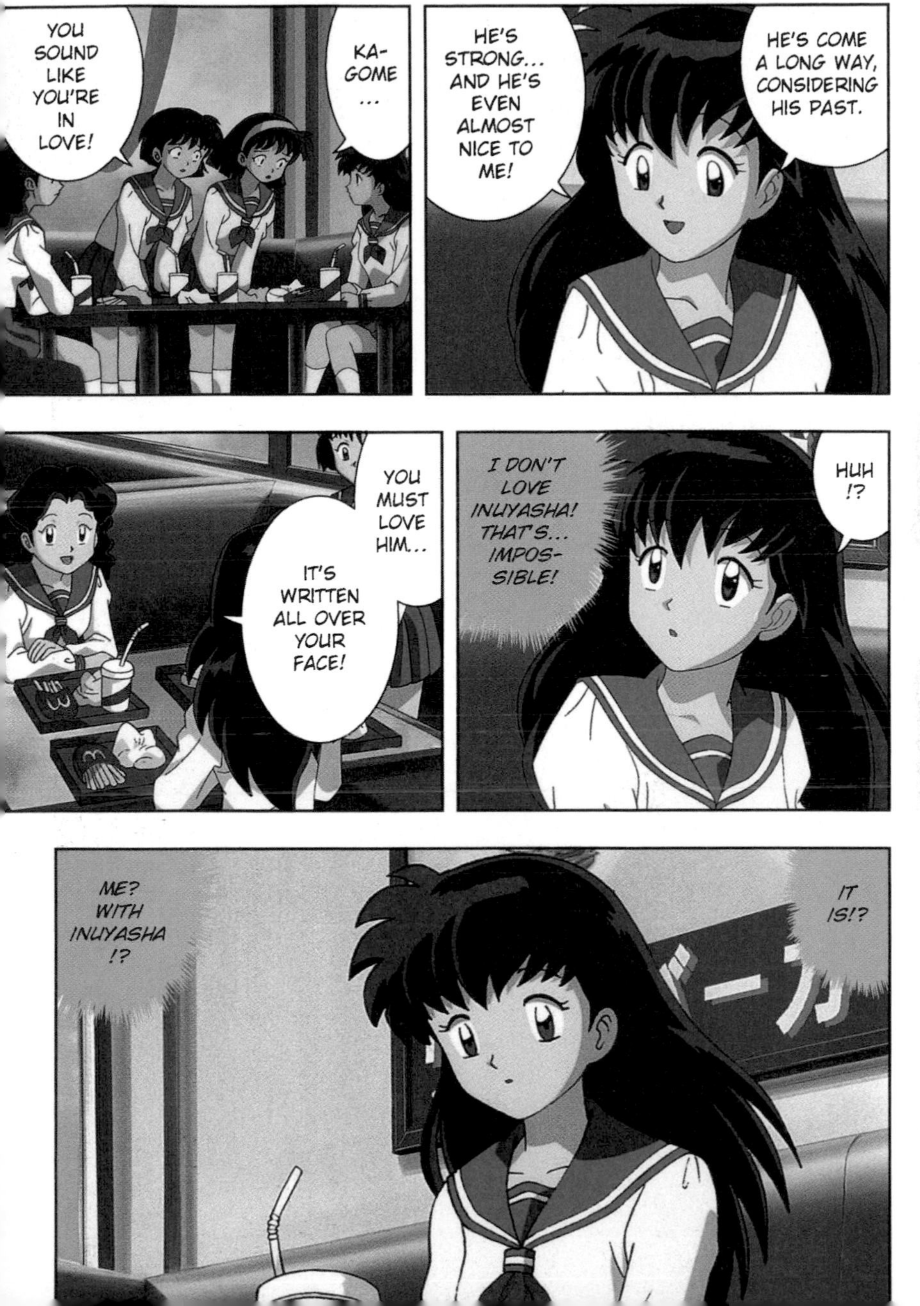
HE'S COME A LONG WAY, CONSIDERING HIS PAST.
HE'S STRONG... AND HE'S EVEN ALMOST NICE TO ME!
KA-GOME...
YOU SOUND LIKE YOU'RE IN LOVE!
HUH!?
I DON'T LOVE INUYASHA! THAT'S... IMPOSSIBLE!
YOU MUST LOVE HIM...
IT'S WRITTEN ALL OVER YOUR FACE!
IT IS!?
ME? WITH INUYASHA!?

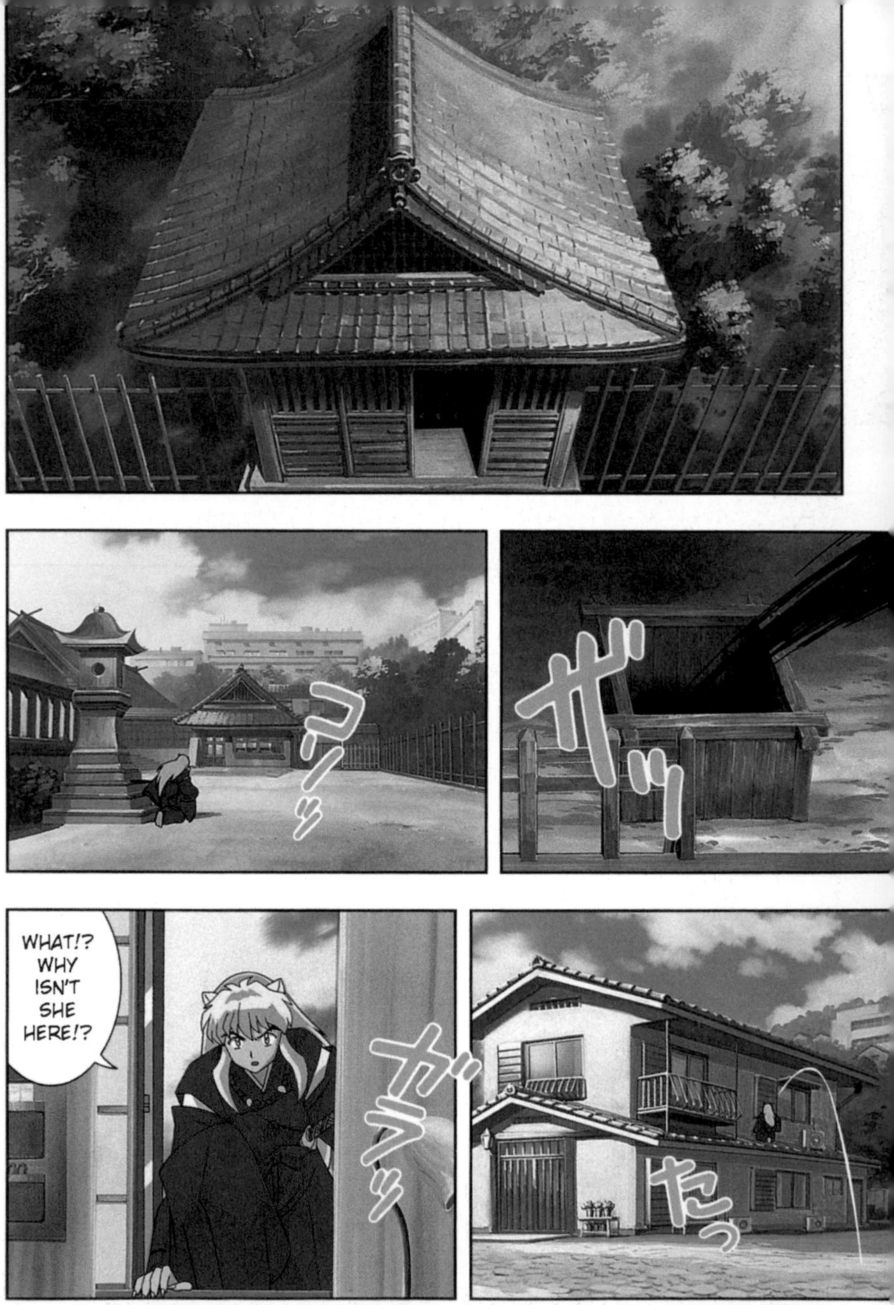
ザッ
コンッ
たっ
ガラッ
WHAT!? WHY ISN'T SHE HERE!?

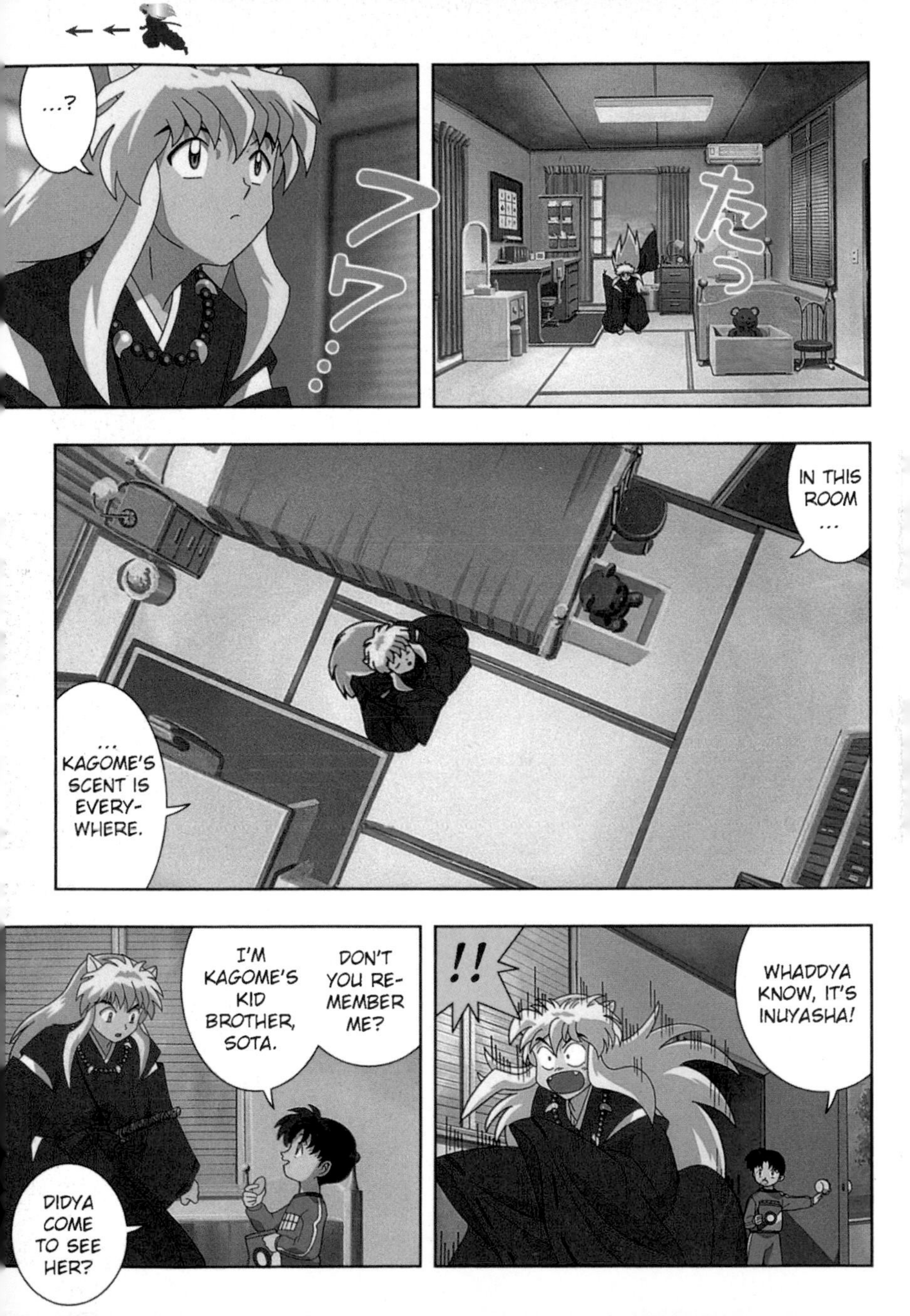
たっ
...?
フワ
IN THIS ROOM ...
... KAGOME'S SCENT IS EVERY-WHERE.
!!
WHADDYA KNOW, IT'S INUYASHA!
DON'T YOU RE-MEMBER ME?
I'M KAGOME'S KID BROTHER, SOTA.
DIDYA COME TO SEE HER?

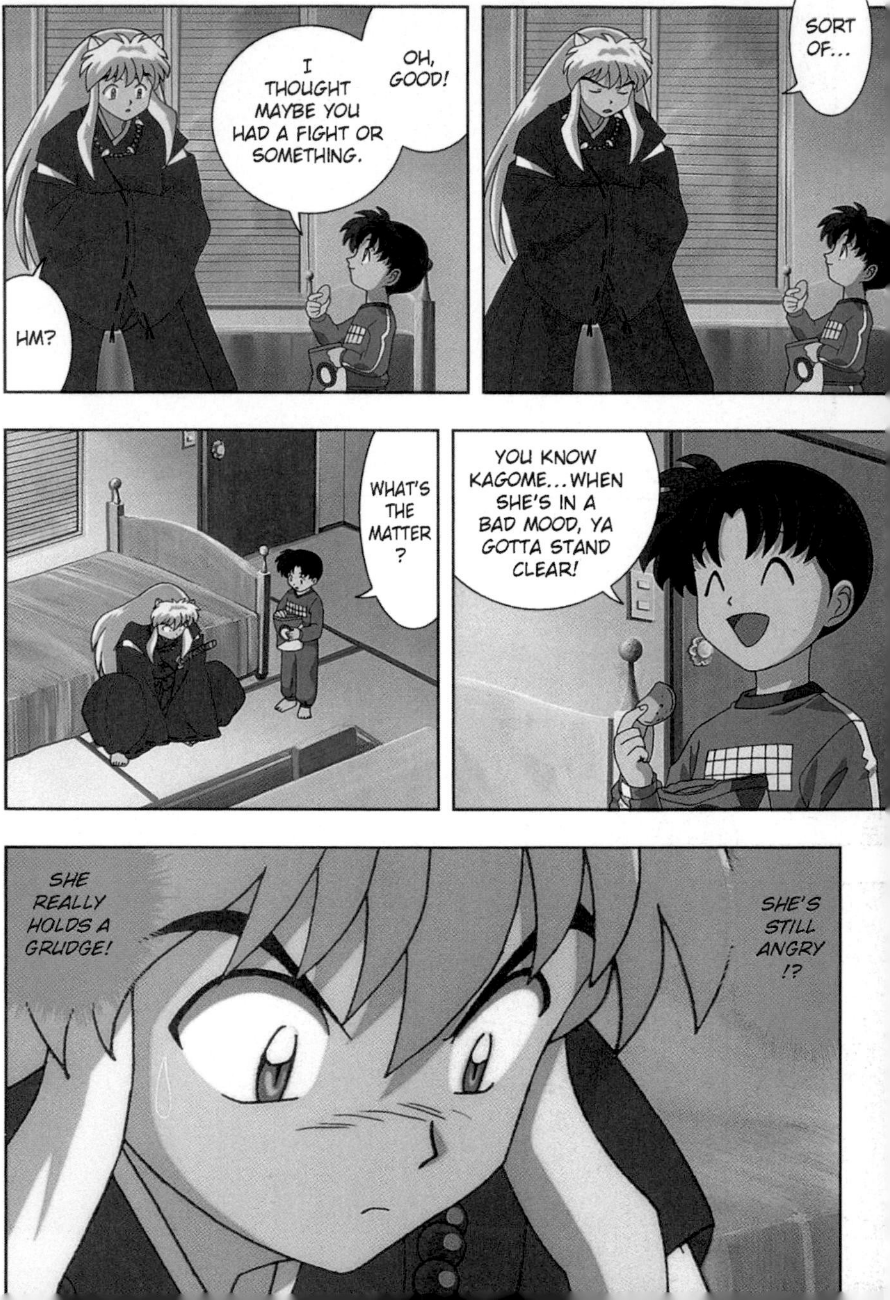
OH, GOOD!
I THOUGHT MAYBE YOU HAD A FIGHT OR SOMETHING.
HM?
SORT OF...
WHAT'S THE MATTER?
YOU KNOW KAGOME...WHEN SHE'S IN A BAD MOOD, YA GOTTA STAND CLEAR!
SHE'S STILL ANGRY!?
SHE REALLY HOLDS A GRUDGE!

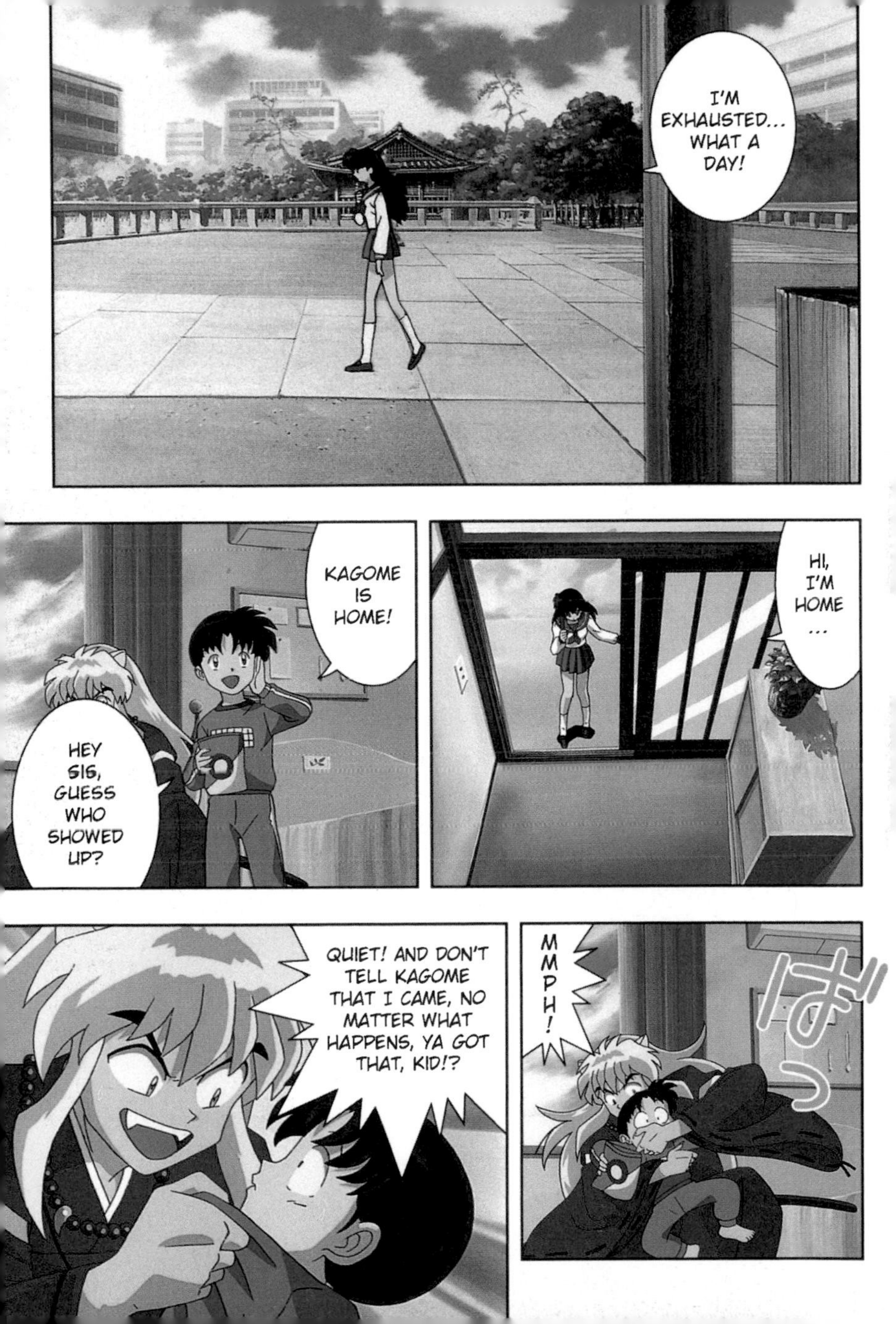
I'M EXHAUSTED... WHAT A DAY!
HI, I'M HOME...
KAGOME IS HOME!
HEY SIS, GUESS WHO SHOWED UP?
MMPH!
はっ
QUIET! AND DON'T TELL KAGOME THAT I CAME, NO MATTER WHAT HAPPENS, YA GOT THAT, KID!?

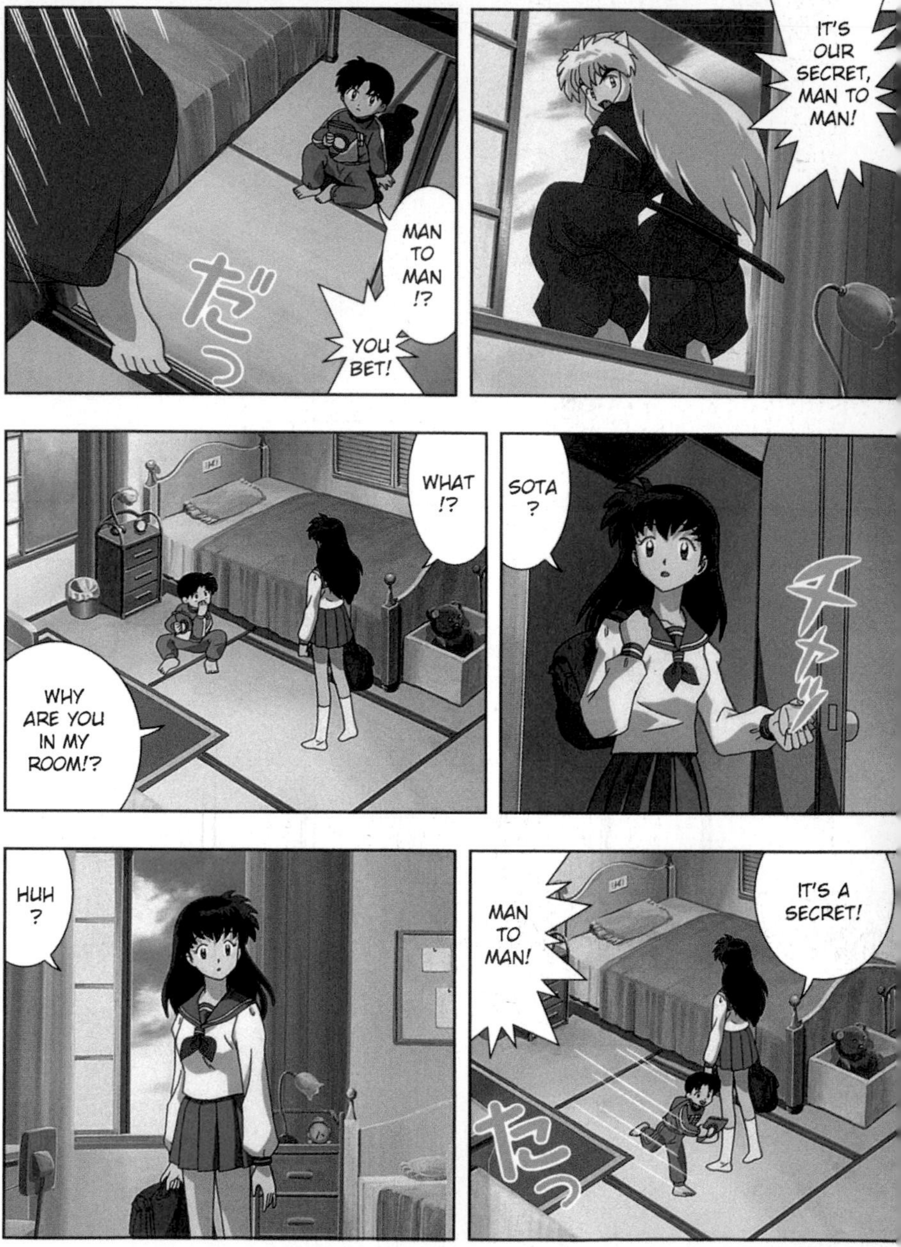
IT'S OUR SECRET, MAN TO MAN!
MAN TO MAN!?
YOU BET!
だっ
SOTA?
チャッ
WHAT!?
WHY ARE YOU IN MY ROOM!?
IT'S A SECRET!
MAN TO MAN!
たっ
HUH?

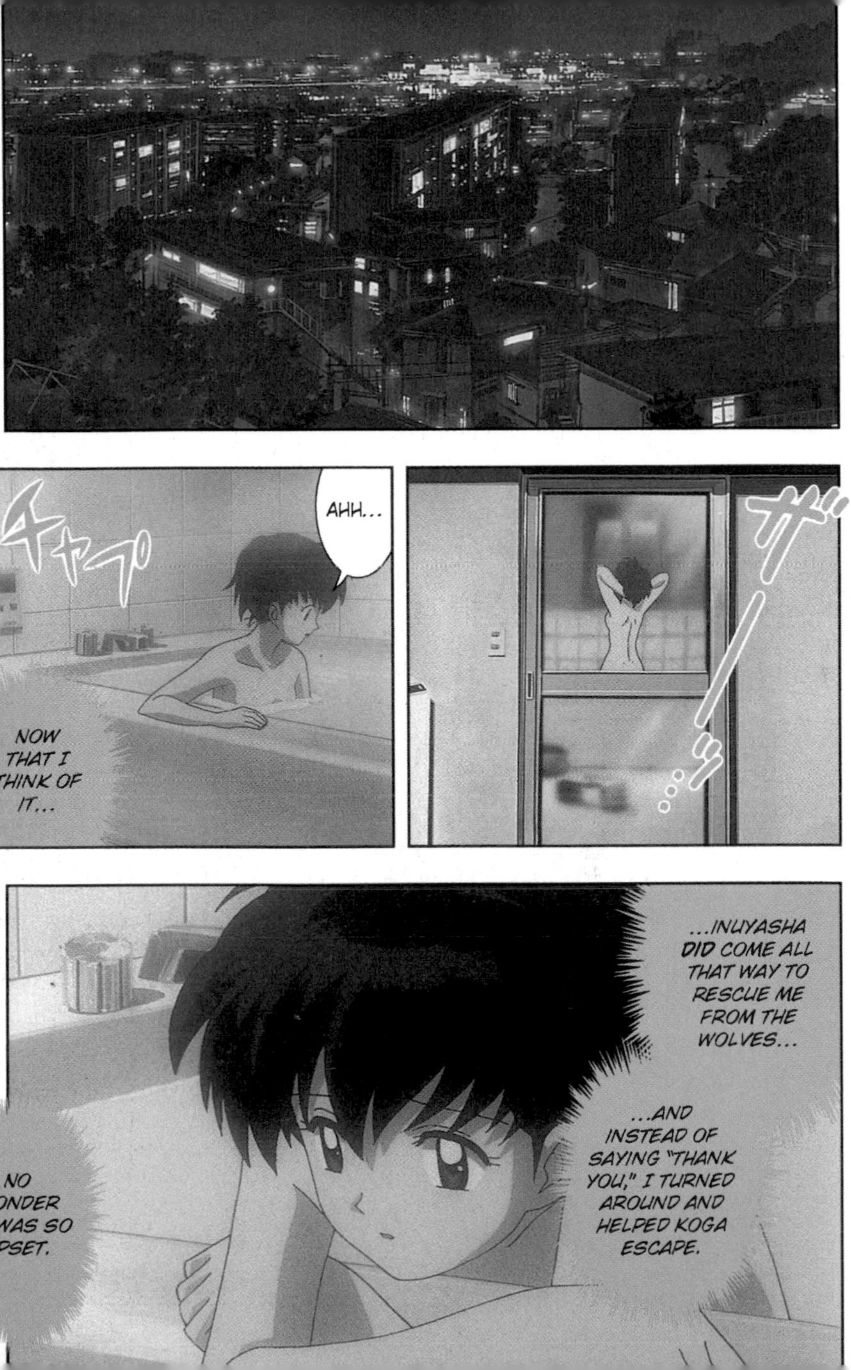
ザーッ…
チャプ
AHH...
NOW THAT I THINK OF IT...
...INUYASHA DID COME ALL THAT WAY TO RESCUE ME FROM THE WOLVES...
...AND INSTEAD OF SAYING "THANK YOU," I TURNED AROUND AND HELPED KOGA ESCAPE.
NO WONDER HE WAS SO UPSET.

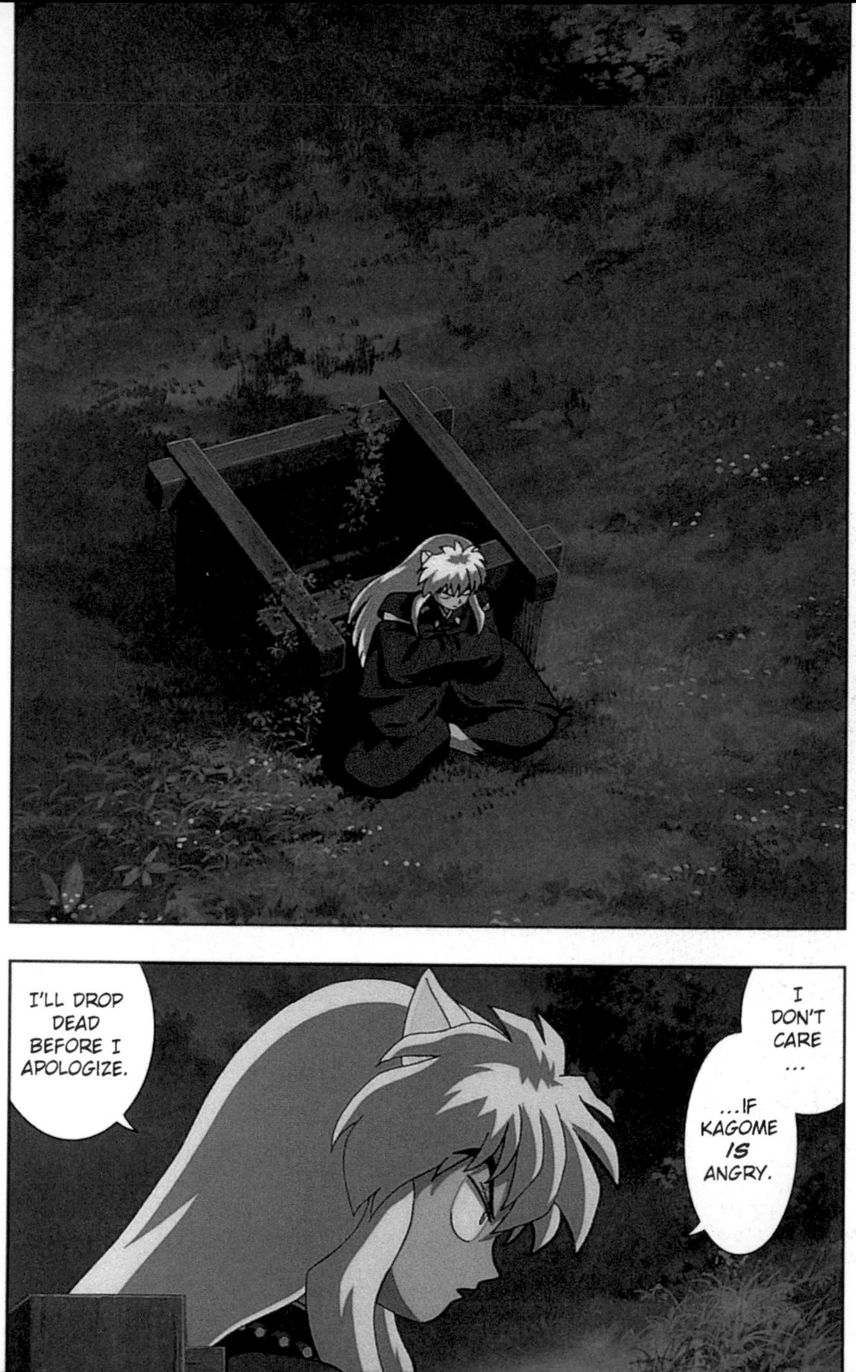
I DON'T CARE ...
...IF KAGOME IS ANGRY.
I'LL DROP DEAD BEFORE I APOLOGIZE.

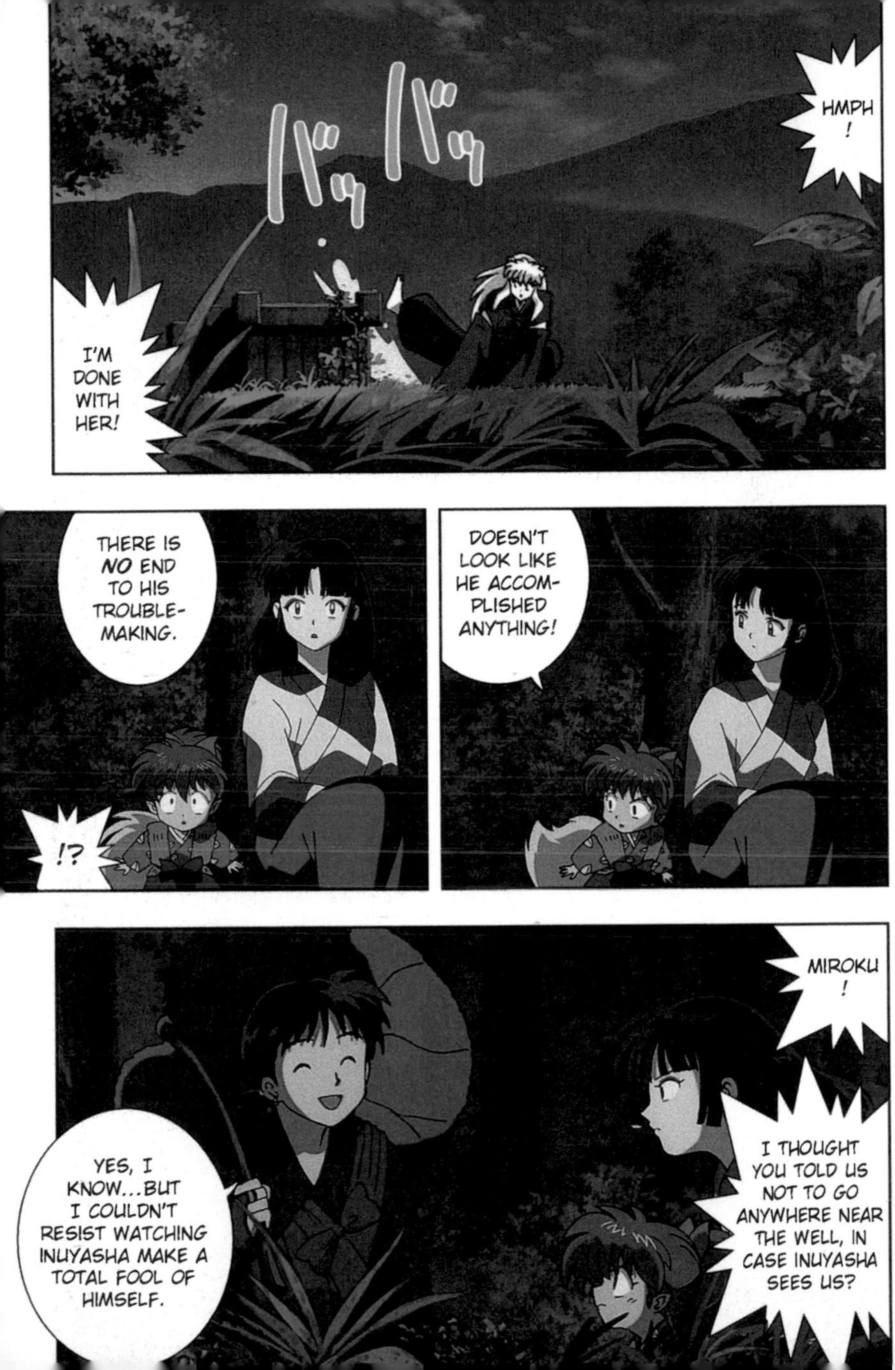
HMPH!
バッ バッ
I'M DONE WITH HER!
DOESN'T LOOK LIKE HE ACCOM-PLISHED ANYTHING!
THERE IS **NO** END TO HIS TROUBLE-MAKING.
!?
MIROKU!
I THOUGHT YOU TOLD US NOT TO GO ANYWHERE NEAR THE WELL, IN CASE INUYASHA SEES US?
YES, I KNOW...BUT I COULDN'T RESIST WATCHING INUYASHA MAKE A TOTAL FOOL OF HIMSELF.

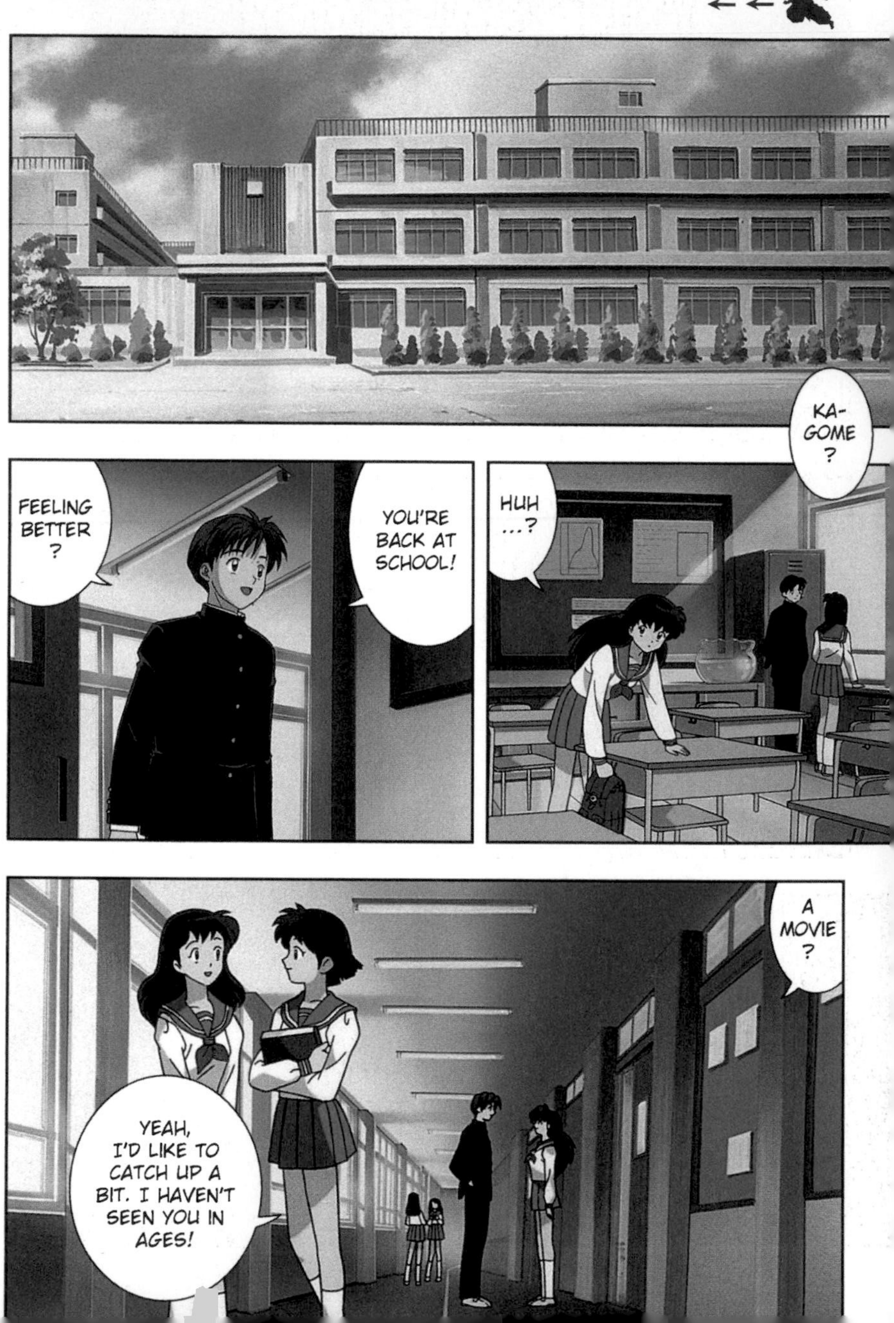
KA-GOME?
HUH...?
YOU'RE BACK AT SCHOOL!
FEELING BETTER?
A MOVIE?
YEAH, I'D LIKE TO CATCH UP A BIT. I HAVEN'T SEEN YOU IN AGES!

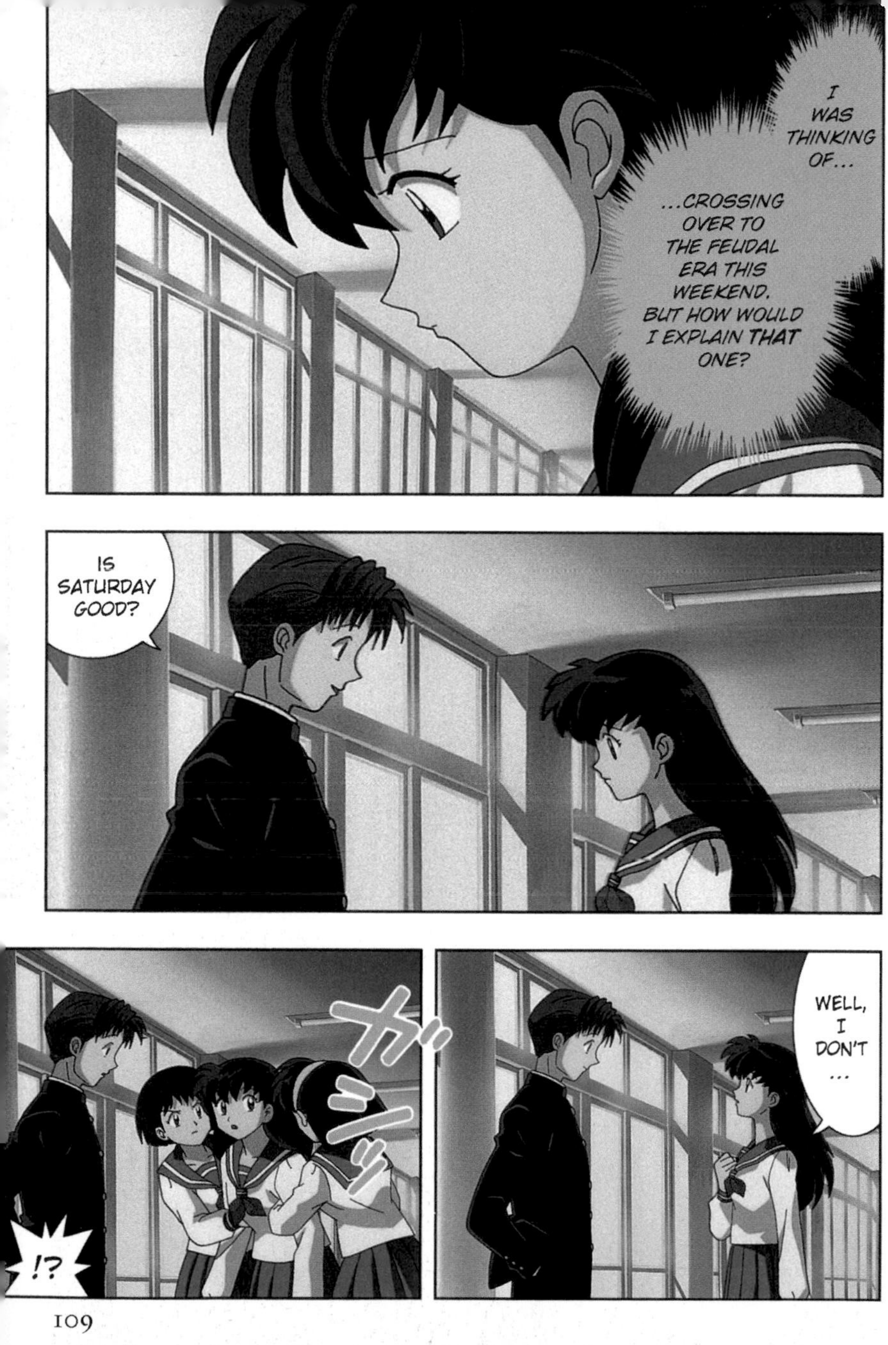
I WAS THINKING OF...
...CROSSING OVER TO THE FEUDAL ERA THIS WEEKEND. BUT HOW WOULD I EXPLAIN THAT ONE?
IS SATURDAY GOOD?
WELL, I DON'T ...
ガシッ
!?

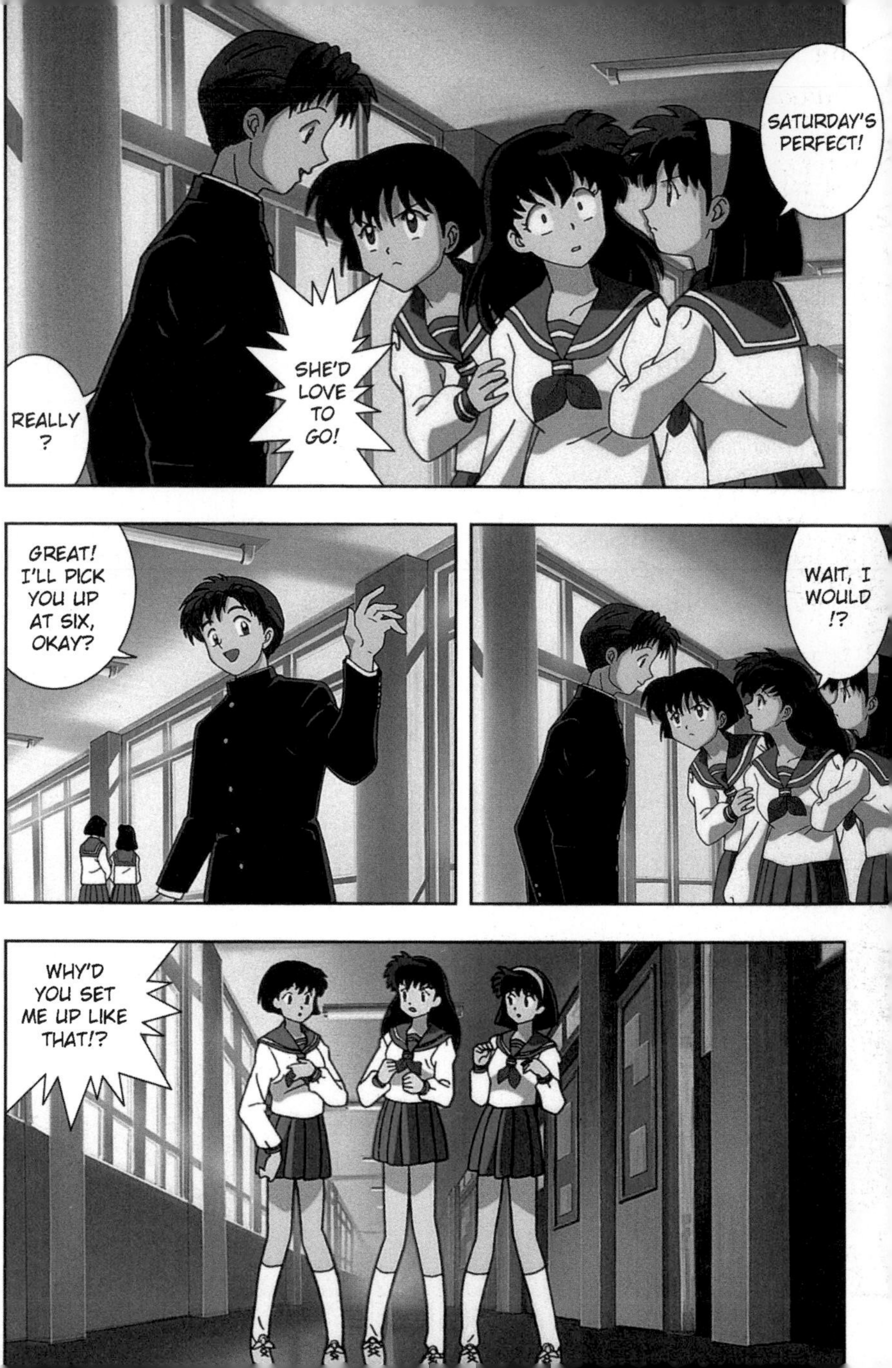
SATURDAY'S PERFECT!
SHE'D LOVE TO GO!
REALLY?
WAIT, I WOULD!?
GREAT! I'LL PICK YOU UP AT SIX, OKAY?
WHY'D YOU SET ME UP LIKE THAT!?

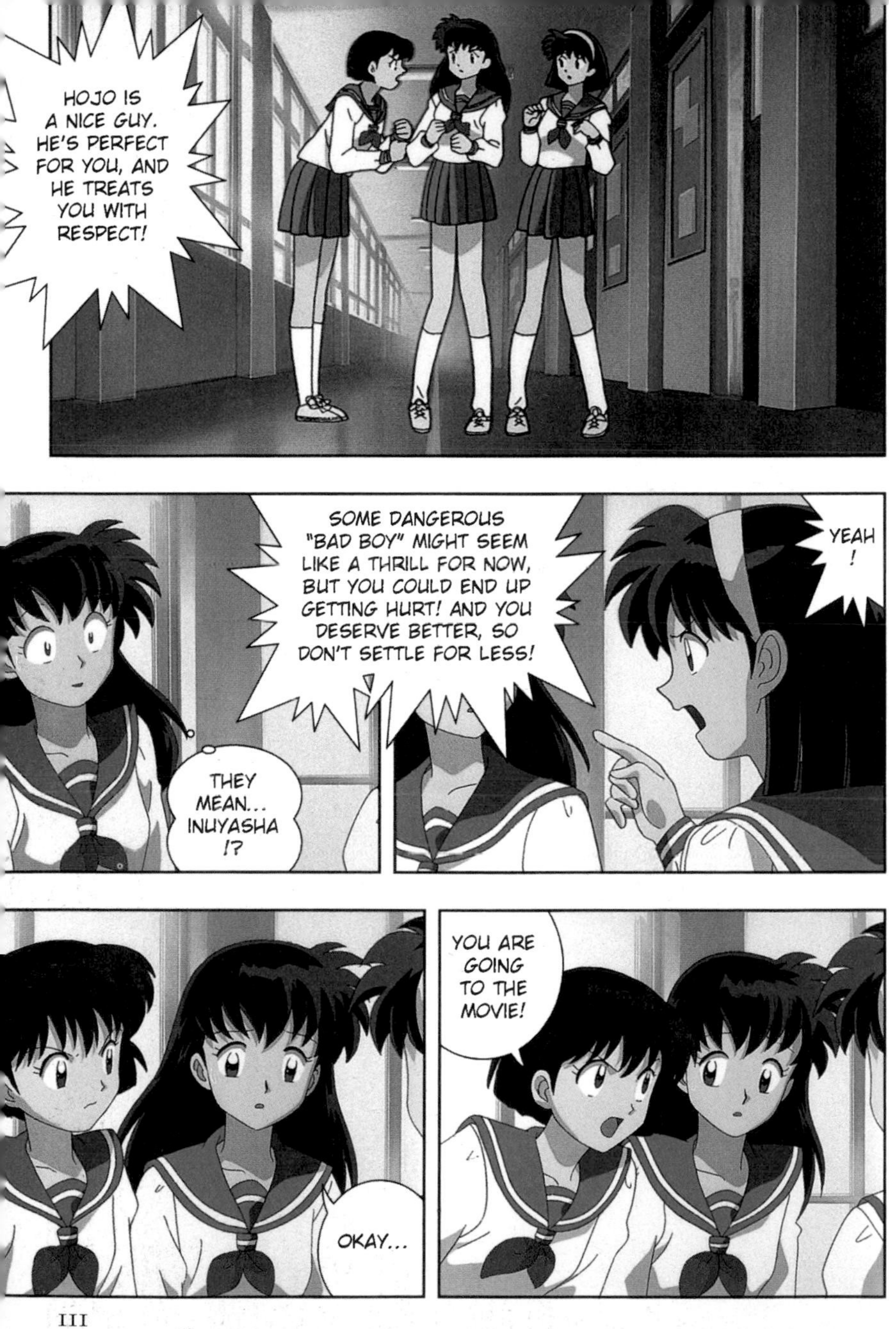
HOJO IS A NICE GUY. HE'S PERFECT FOR YOU, AND HE TREATS YOU WITH RESPECT!
SOME DANGEROUS "BAD BOY" MIGHT SEEM LIKE A THRILL FOR NOW, BUT YOU COULD END UP GETTING HURT! AND YOU DESERVE BETTER, SO DON'T SETTLE FOR LESS!
YEAH!
THEY MEAN... INUYASHA!?
YOU ARE GOING TO THE MOVIE!
OKAY...

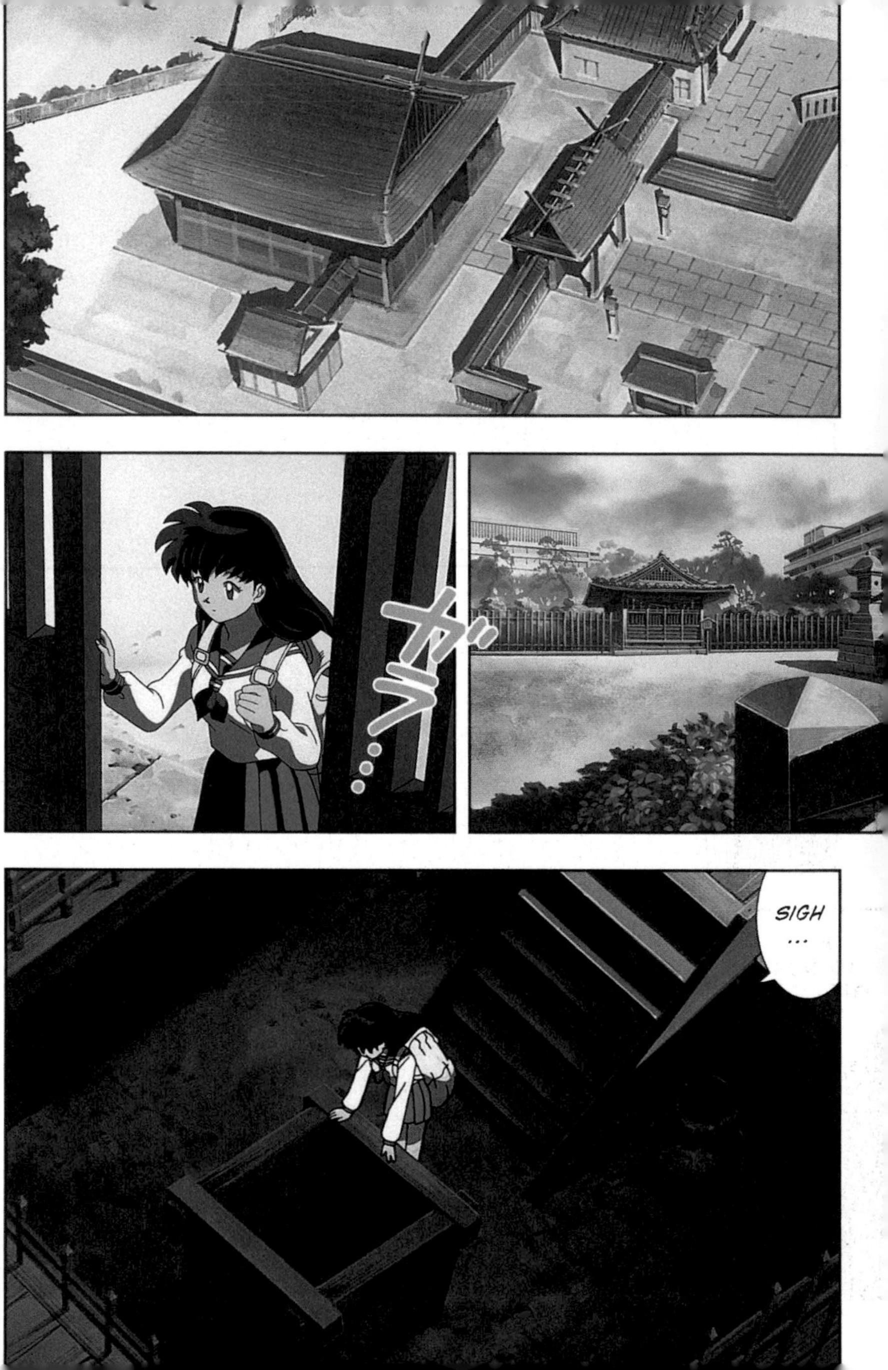
ガラ...
SIGH ...

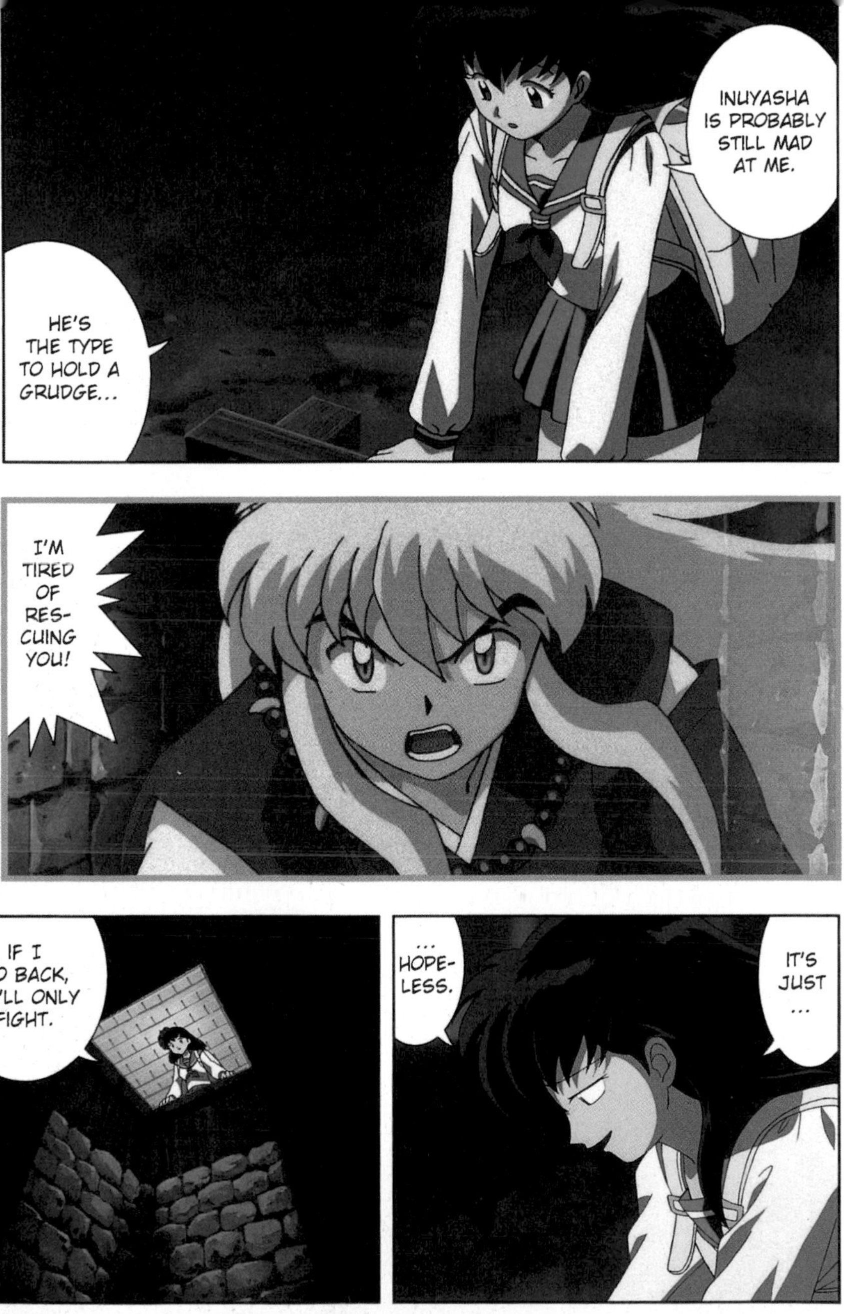
INUYASHA IS PROBABLY STILL MAD AT ME.
HE'S THE TYPE TO HOLD A GRUDGE...
I'M TIRED OF RES-CUING YOU!
IT'S JUST ...
... HOPE-LESS.
IF I GO BACK, WE'LL ONLY FIGHT.

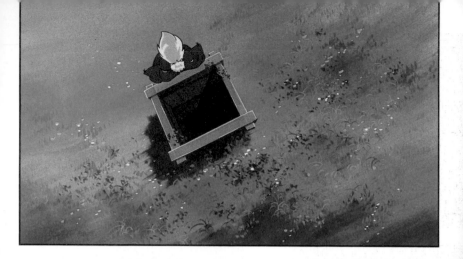

YOU KNOW KAGOME! WHEN SHE'S IN A BAD MOOD, YA GOTTA STAND CLEAR!

...

SIGH ...

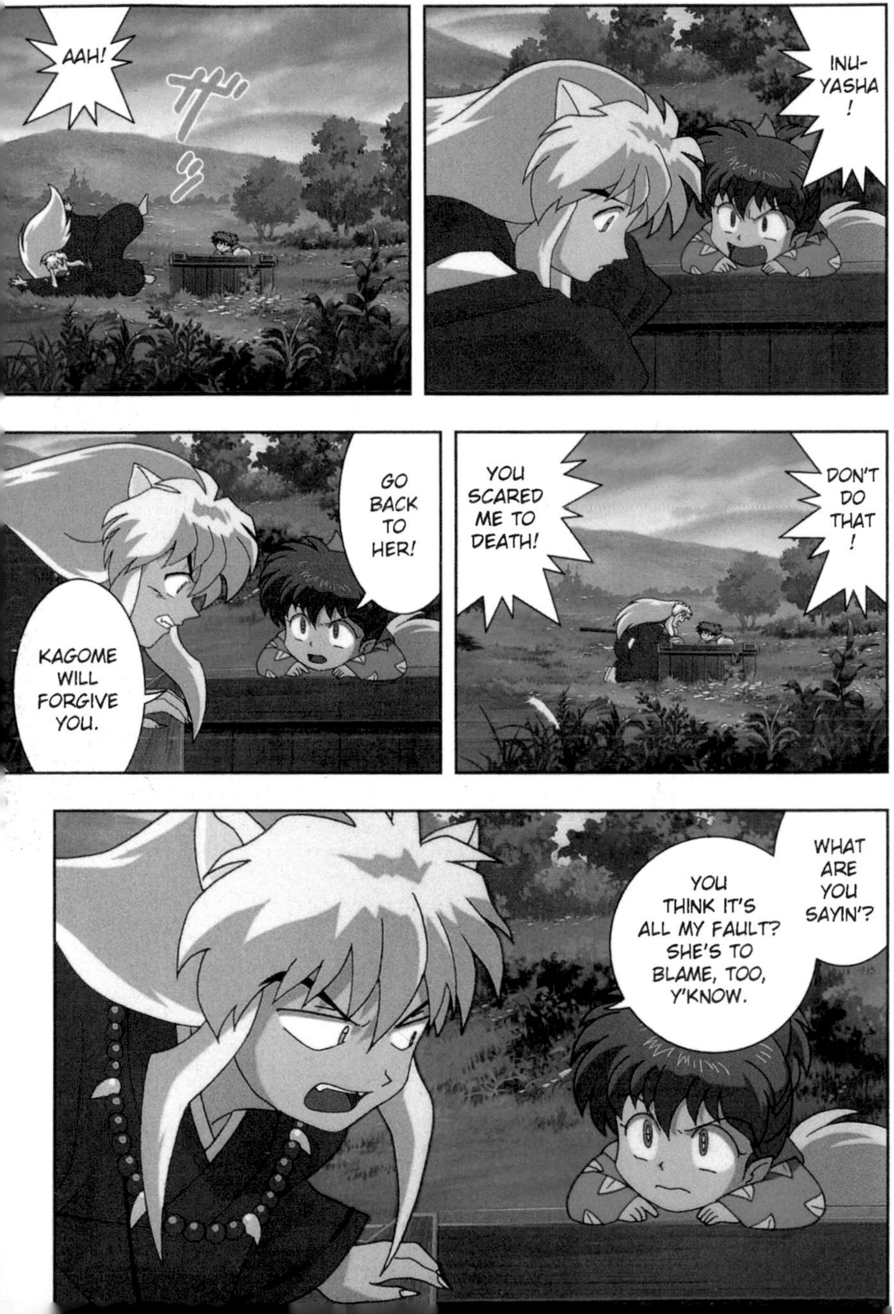
INU-YASHA!
AAH!
ザッ
DON'T DO THAT!
YOU SCARED ME TO DEATH!
GO BACK TO HER!
KAGOME WILL FORGIVE YOU.
WHAT ARE YOU SAYIN'?
YOU THINK IT'S ALL MY FAULT? SHE'S TO BLAME, TOO, Y'KNOW.

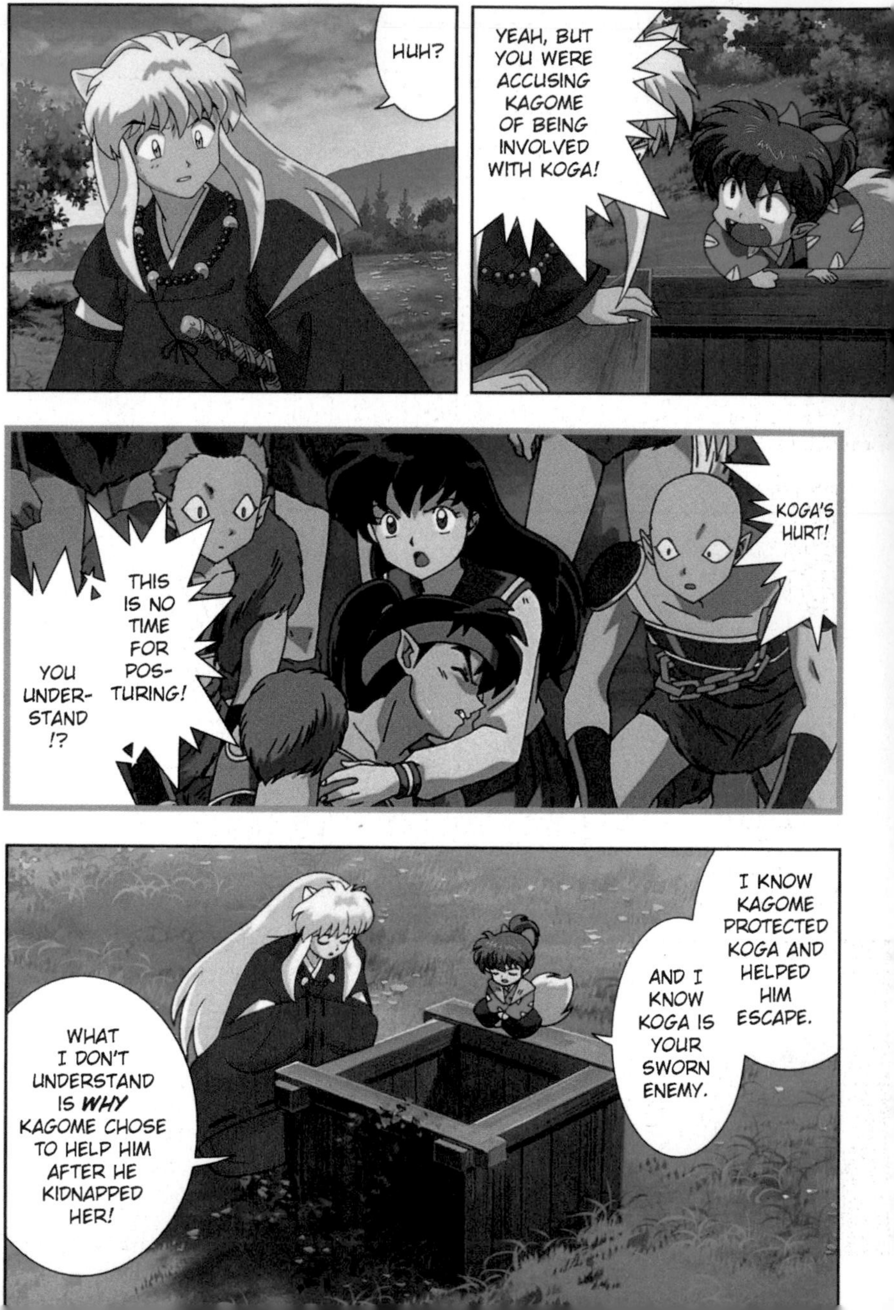
YEAH, BUT YOU WERE ACCUSING KAGOME OF BEING INVOLVED WITH KOGA!
HUH?
KOGA'S HURT!
THIS IS NO TIME FOR POS-TURING!
YOU UNDER-STAND !?
I KNOW KAGOME PROTECTED KOGA AND HELPED HIM ESCAPE.
AND I KNOW KOGA IS YOUR SWORN ENEMY.
WHAT I DON'T UNDERSTAND IS *WHY* KAGOME CHOSE TO HELP HIM AFTER HE KIDNAPPED HER!

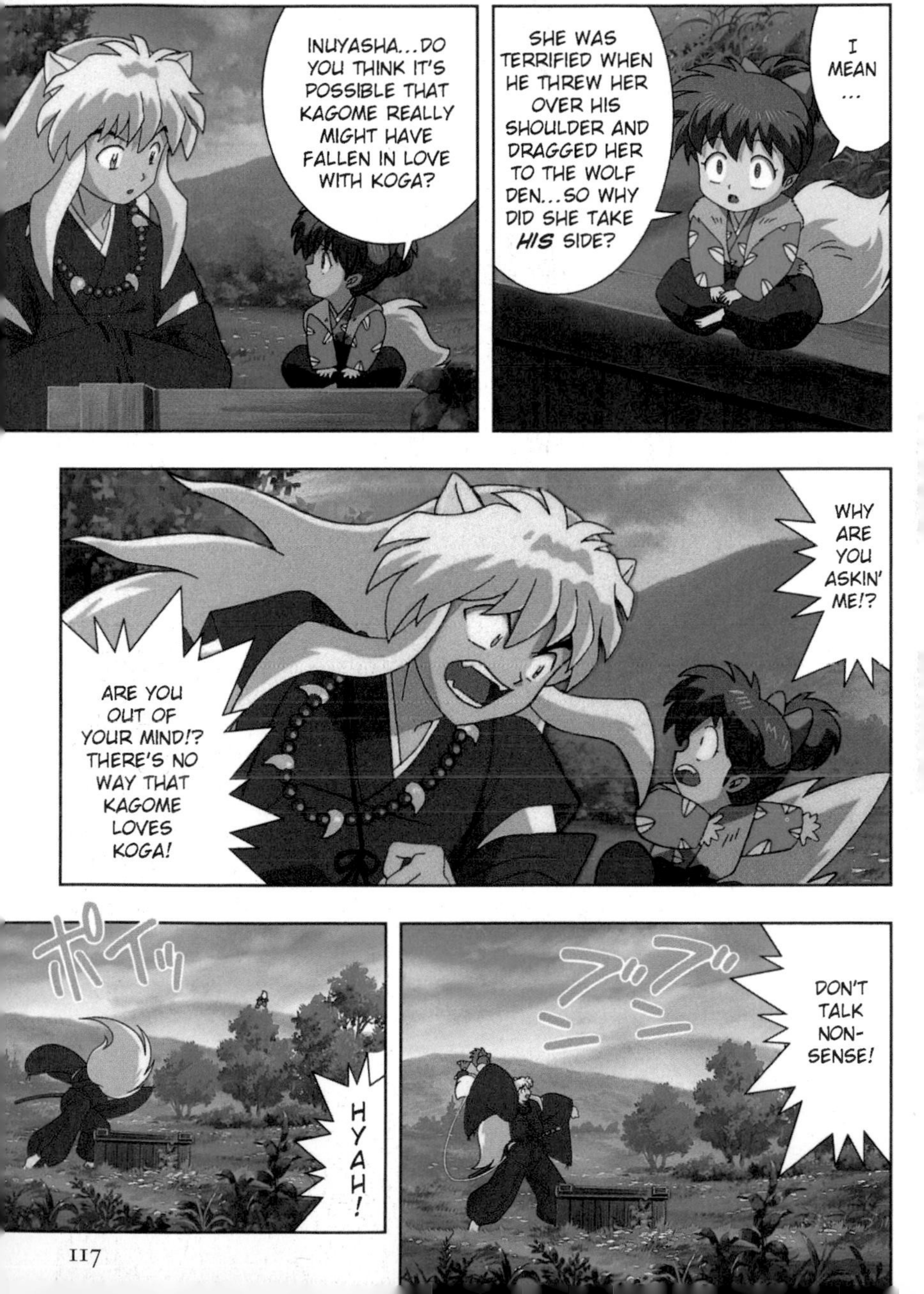
I MEAN ...
SHE WAS TERRIFIED WHEN HE THREW HER OVER HIS SHOULDER AND DRAGGED HER TO THE WOLF DEN...SO WHY DID SHE TAKE ***HIS*** SIDE?
INUYASHA...DO YOU THINK IT'S POSSIBLE THAT KAGOME REALLY MIGHT HAVE FALLEN IN LOVE WITH KOGA?
WHY ARE YOU ASKIN' ME!?
ARE YOU OUT OF YOUR MIND!? THERE'S NO WAY THAT KAGOME LOVES KOGA!
DON'T TALK NON-SENSE!
ポイッ
HYAH!

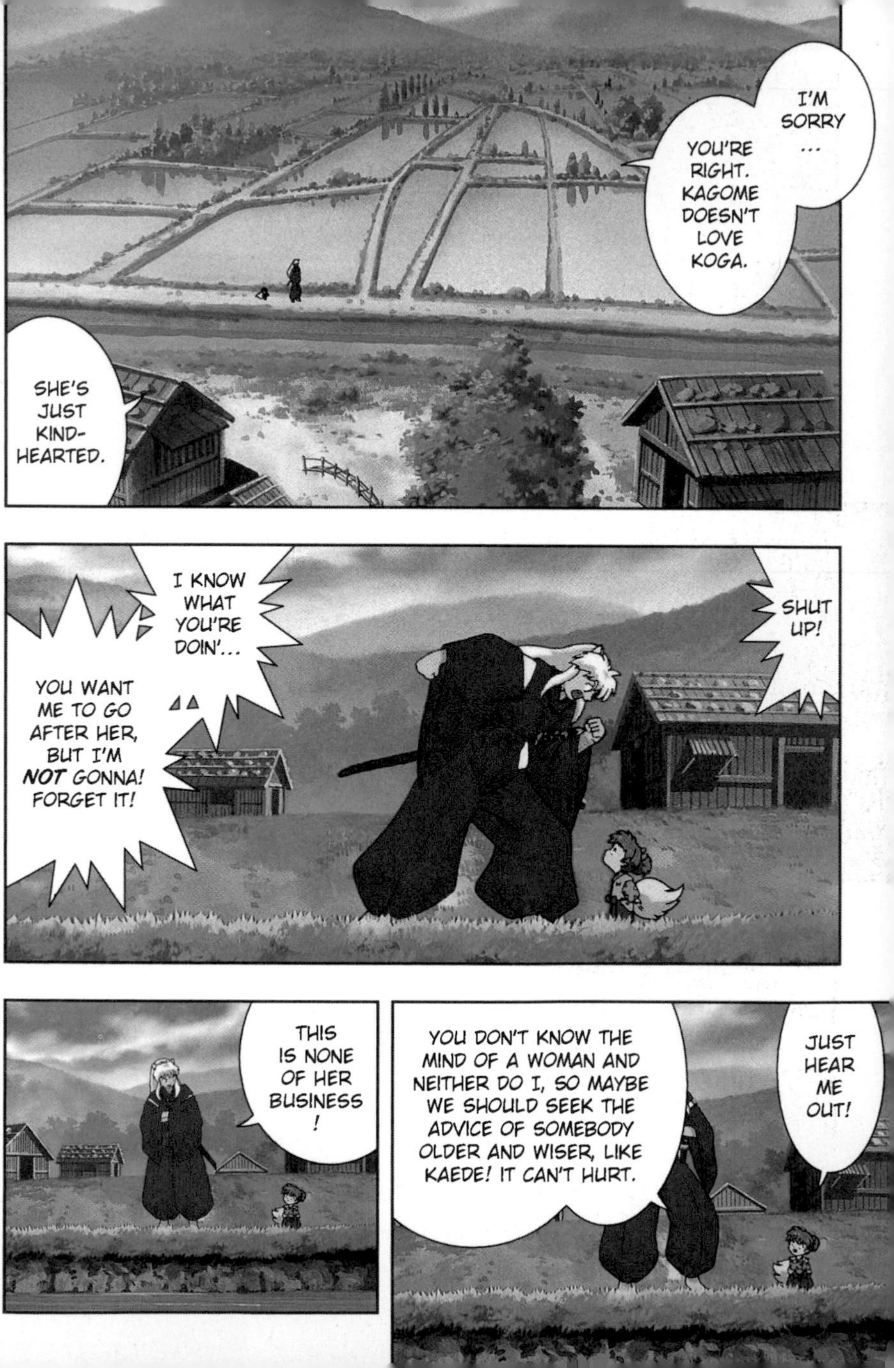
I'M SORRY ...
YOU'RE RIGHT. KAGOME DOESN'T LOVE KOGA.
SHE'S JUST KIND-HEARTED.
SHUT UP!
I KNOW WHAT YOU'RE DOIN'...
YOU WANT ME TO GO AFTER HER, BUT I'M **NOT** GONNA! FORGET IT!
JUST HEAR ME OUT!
YOU DON'T KNOW THE MIND OF A WOMAN AND NEITHER DO I, SO MAYBE WE SHOULD SEEK THE ADVICE OF SOMEBODY OLDER AND WISER, LIKE KAEDE! IT CAN'T HURT.
THIS IS NONE OF HER BUSINESS!

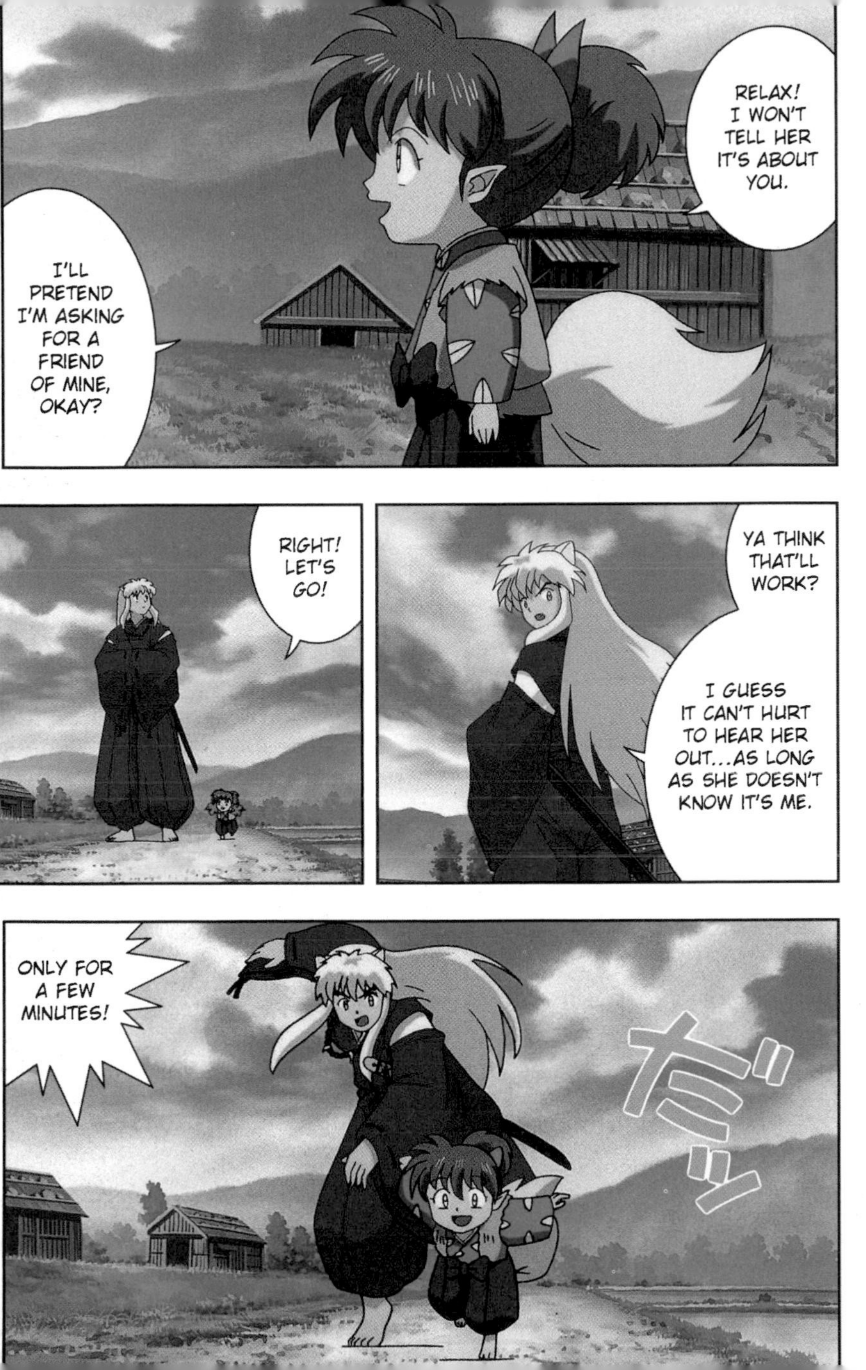
RELAX! I WON'T TELL HER IT'S ABOUT YOU.
I'LL PRETEND I'M ASKING FOR A FRIEND OF MINE, OKAY?
YA THINK THAT'LL WORK?
I GUESS IT CAN'T HURT TO HEAR HER OUT...AS LONG AS SHE DOESN'T KNOW IT'S ME.
RIGHT! LET'S GO!
ONLY FOR A FEW MINUTES!
ダッ

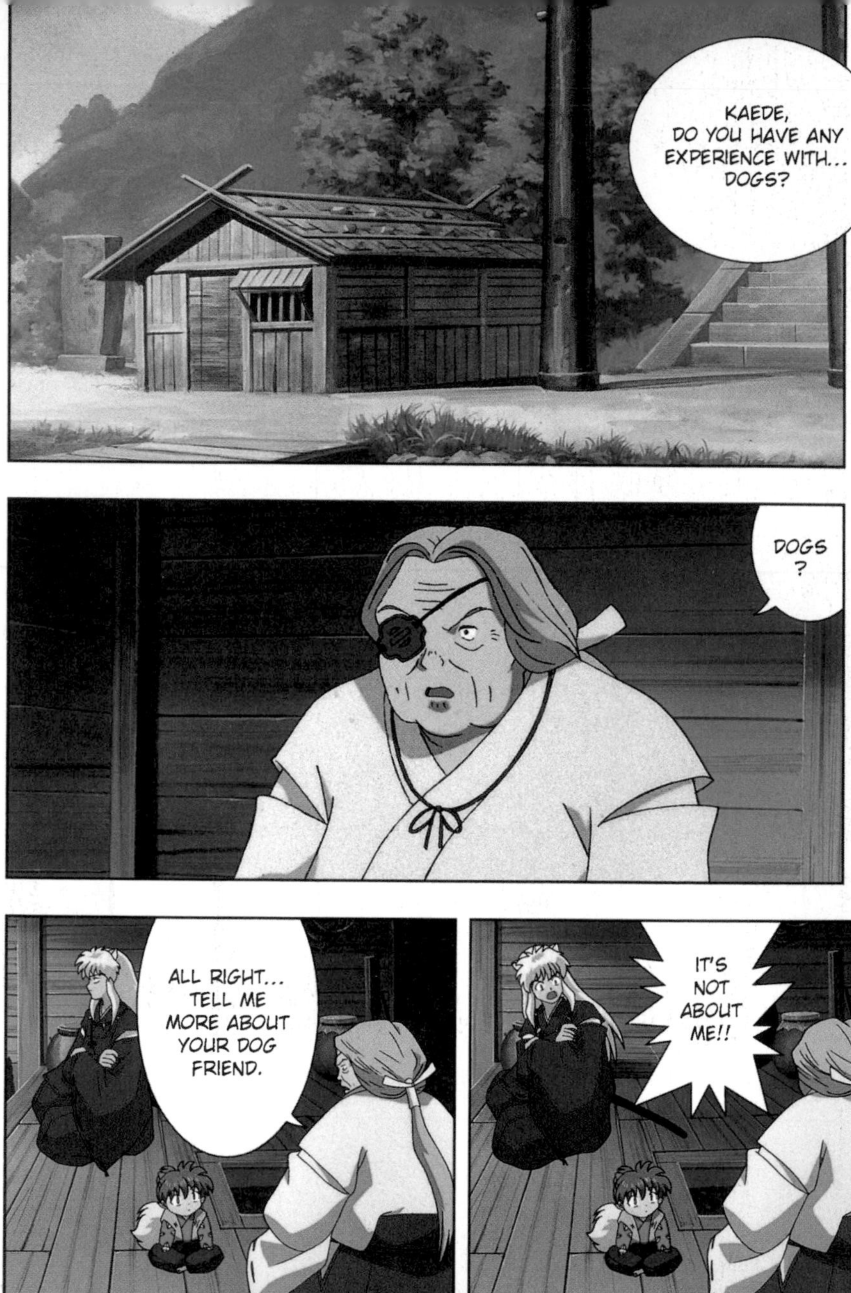
KAEDE, DO YOU HAVE ANY EXPERIENCE WITH... DOGS?
DOGS ?
ALL RIGHT... TELL ME MORE ABOUT YOUR DOG FRIEND.
IT'S NOT ABOUT ME!!

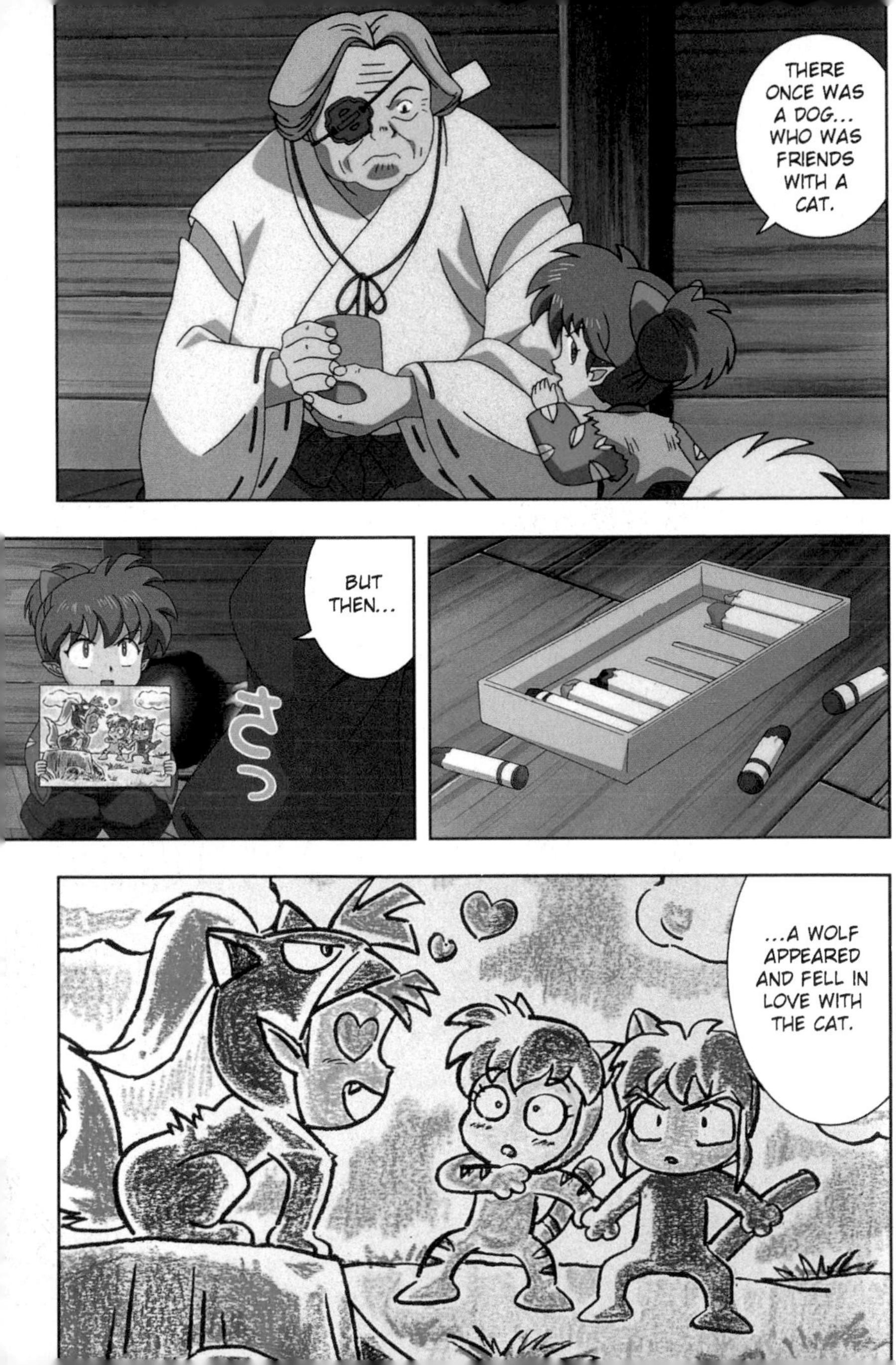
THERE ONCE WAS A DOG... WHO WAS FRIENDS WITH A CAT.
BUT THEN...
さっ
...A WOLF APPEARED AND FELL IN LOVE WITH THE CAT.

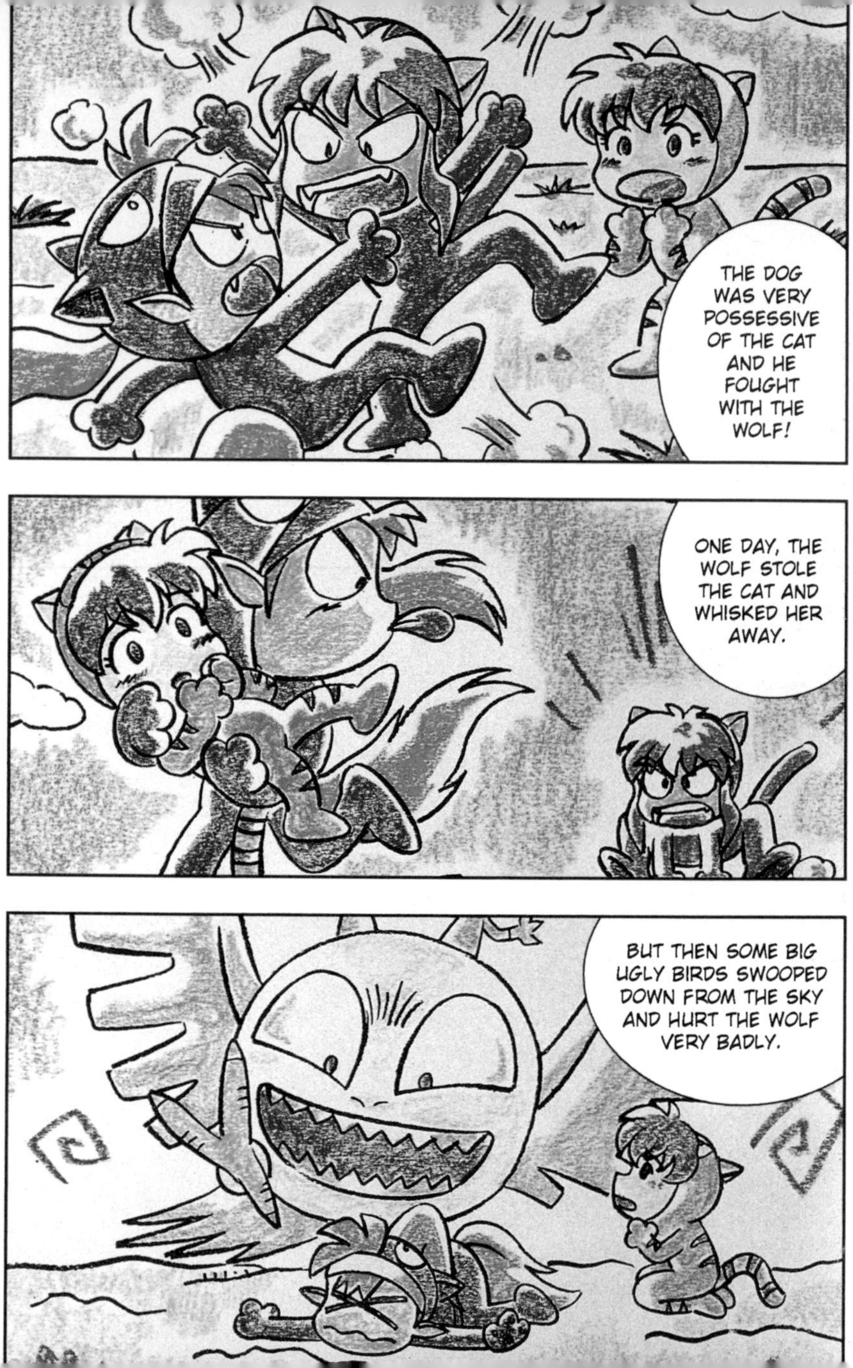
THE DOG WAS VERY POSSESSIVE OF THE CAT AND HE FOUGHT WITH THE WOLF!
ONE DAY, THE WOLF STOLE THE CAT AND WHISKED HER AWAY.
BUT THEN SOME BIG UGLY BIRDS SWOOPED DOWN FROM THE SKY AND HURT THE WOLF VERY BADLY.

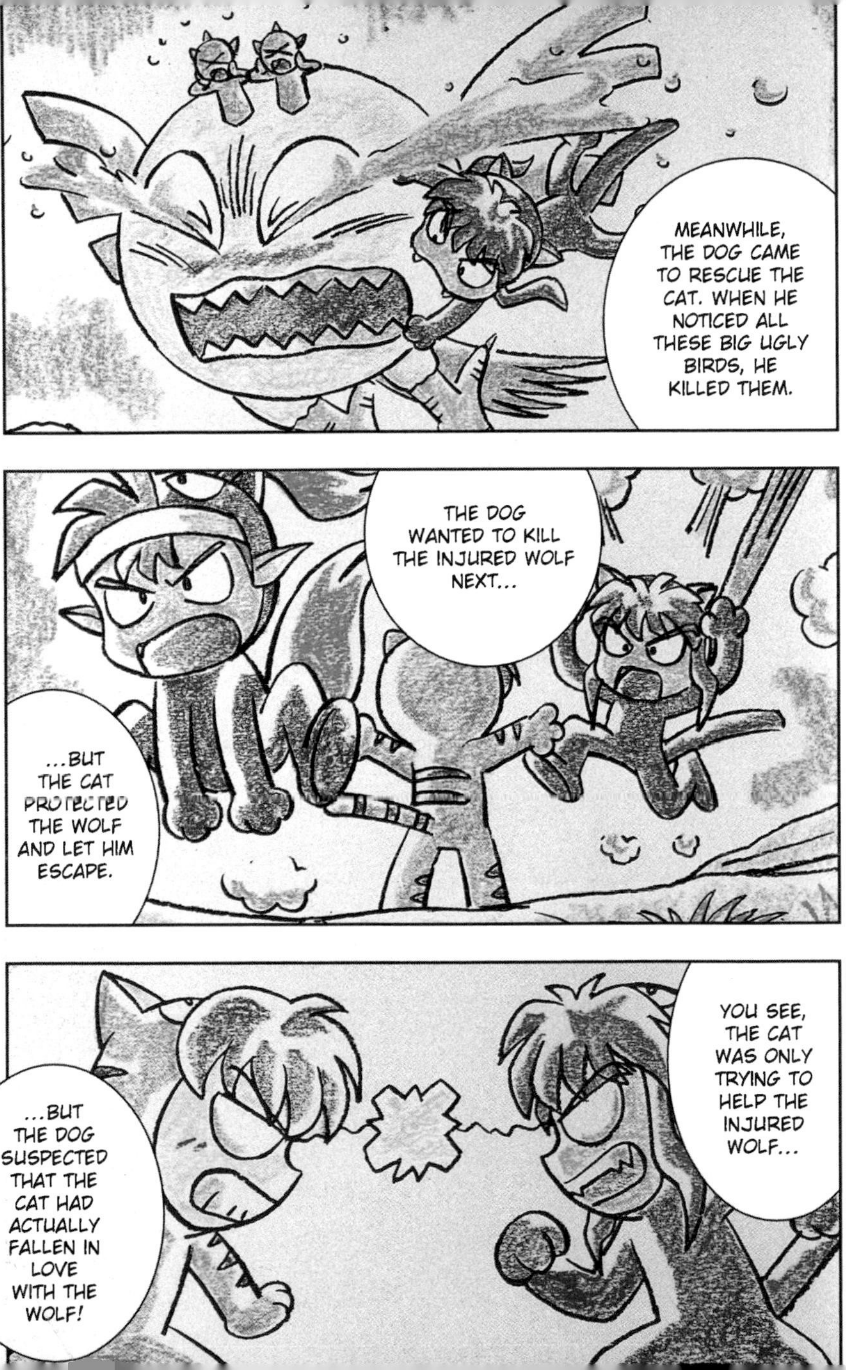
MEANWHILE, THE DOG CAME TO RESCUE THE CAT. WHEN HE NOTICED ALL THESE BIG UGLY BIRDS, HE KILLED THEM.
THE DOG WANTED TO KILL THE INJURED WOLF NEXT...
...BUT THE CAT PROTECTED THE WOLF AND LET HIM ESCAPE.
YOU SEE, THE CAT WAS ONLY TRYING TO HELP THE INJURED WOLF...
...BUT THE DOG SUSPECTED THAT THE CAT HAD ACTUALLY FALLEN IN LOVE WITH THE WOLF!

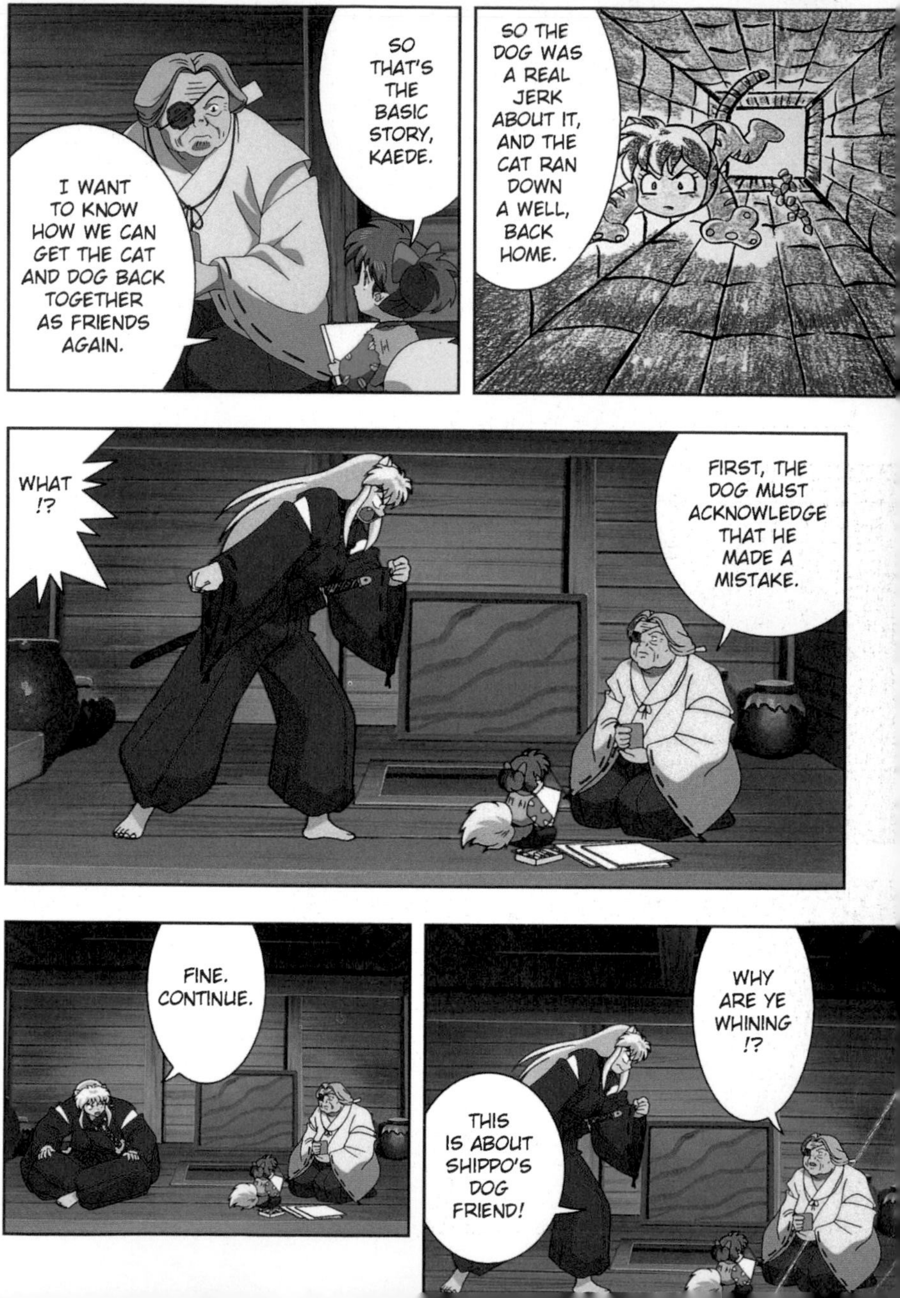
SO THE DOG WAS A REAL JERK ABOUT IT, AND THE CAT RAN DOWN A WELL, BACK HOME.
SO THAT'S THE BASIC STORY, KAEDE.
I WANT TO KNOW HOW WE CAN GET THE CAT AND DOG BACK TOGETHER AS FRIENDS AGAIN.
FIRST, THE DOG MUST ACKNOWLEDGE THAT HE MADE A MISTAKE.
WHAT!?
WHY ARE YE WHINING!?
THIS IS ABOUT SHIPPO'S DOG FRIEND!
FINE. CONTINUE.

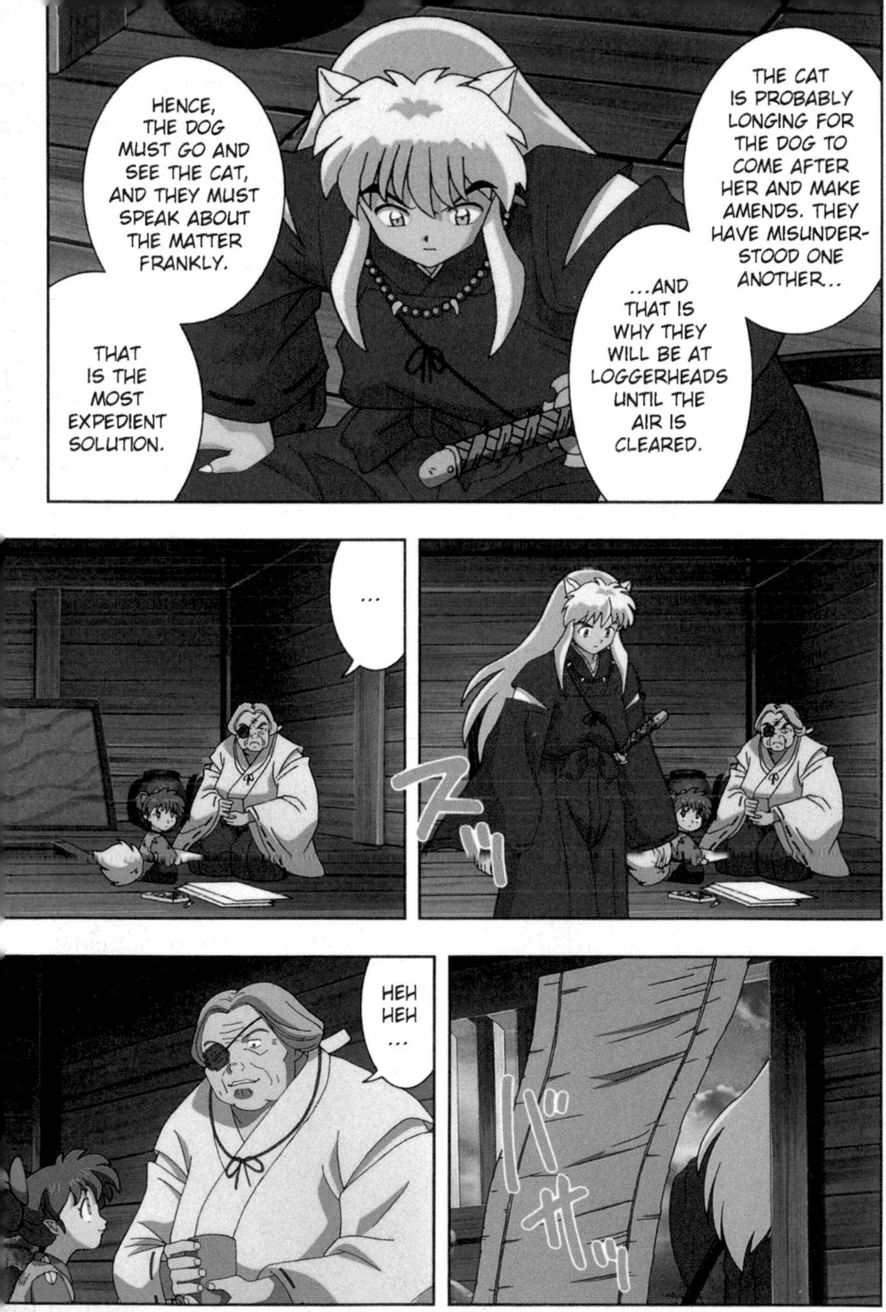
THE CAT IS PROBABLY LONGING FOR THE DOG TO COME AFTER HER AND MAKE AMENDS. THEY HAVE MISUNDER-STOOD ONE ANOTHER...
...AND THAT IS WHY THEY WILL BE AT LOGGERHEADS UNTIL THE AIR IS CLEARED.
HENCE, THE DOG MUST GO AND SEE THE CAT, AND THEY MUST SPEAK ABOUT THE MATTER FRANKLY.
THAT IS THE MOST EXPEDIENT SOLUTION.
ズッ
...
バサッ
HEH HEH ...

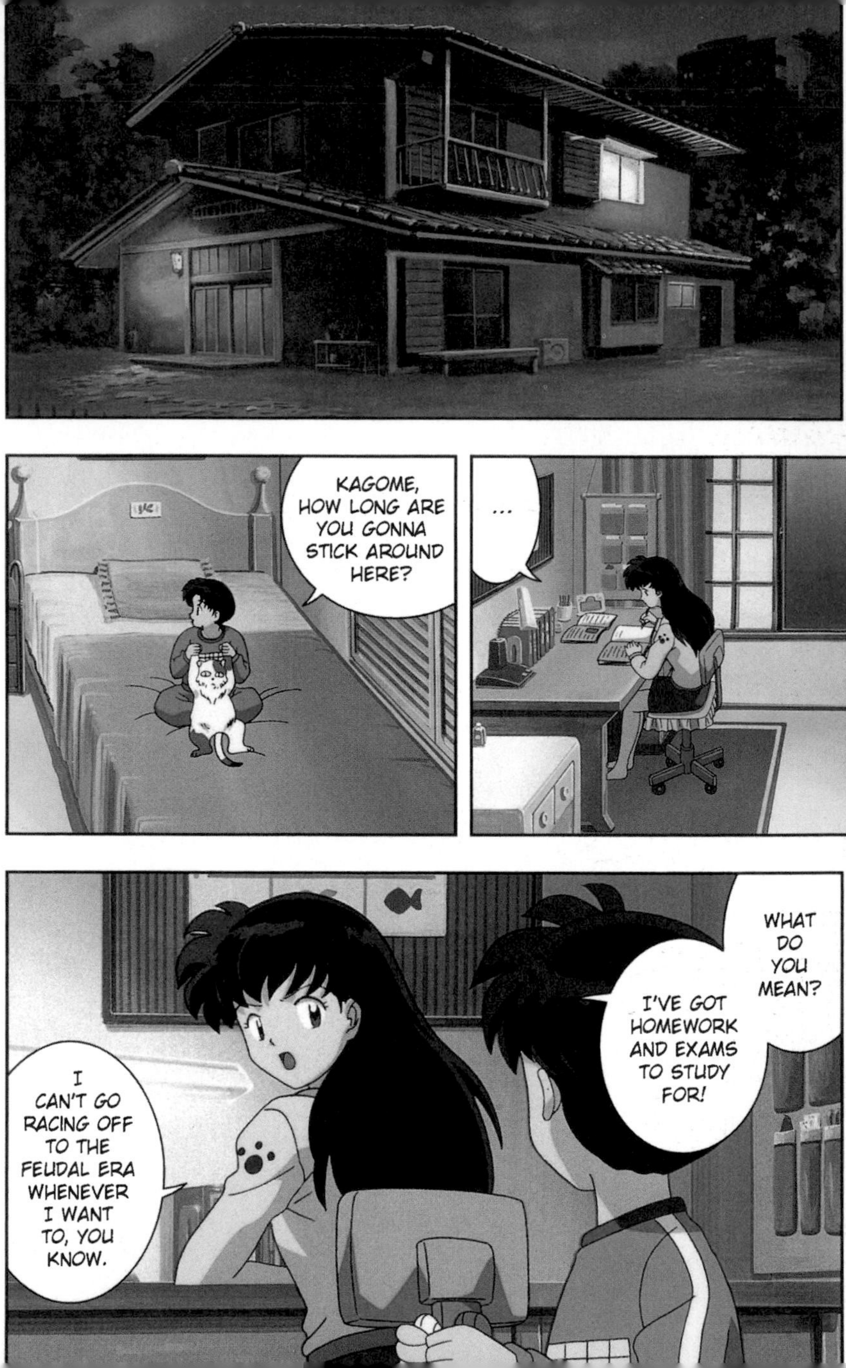
...
KAGOME, HOW LONG ARE YOU GONNA STICK AROUND HERE?
WHAT DO YOU MEAN?
I'VE GOT HOMEWORK AND EXAMS TO STUDY FOR!
I CAN'T GO RACING OFF TO THE FEUDAL ERA WHENEVER I WANT TO, YOU KNOW.

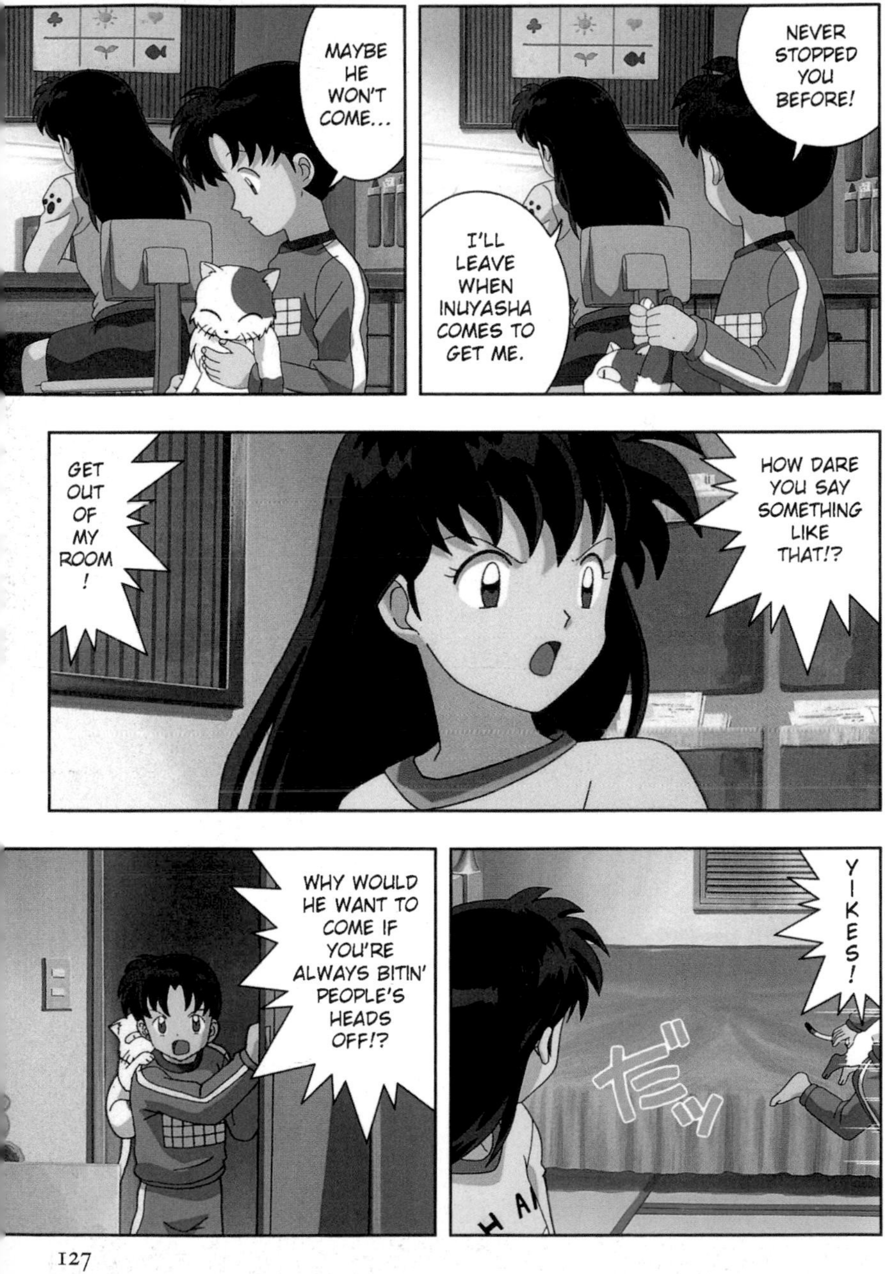
NEVER STOPPED YOU BEFORE!
I'LL LEAVE WHEN INUYASHA COMES TO GET ME.
MAYBE HE WON'T COME...
HOW DARE YOU SAY SOMETHING LIKE THAT!?
GET OUT OF MY ROOM!
YIKES!
ダッ
WHY WOULD HE WANT TO COME IF YOU'RE ALWAYS BITIN' PEOPLE'S HEADS OFF!?

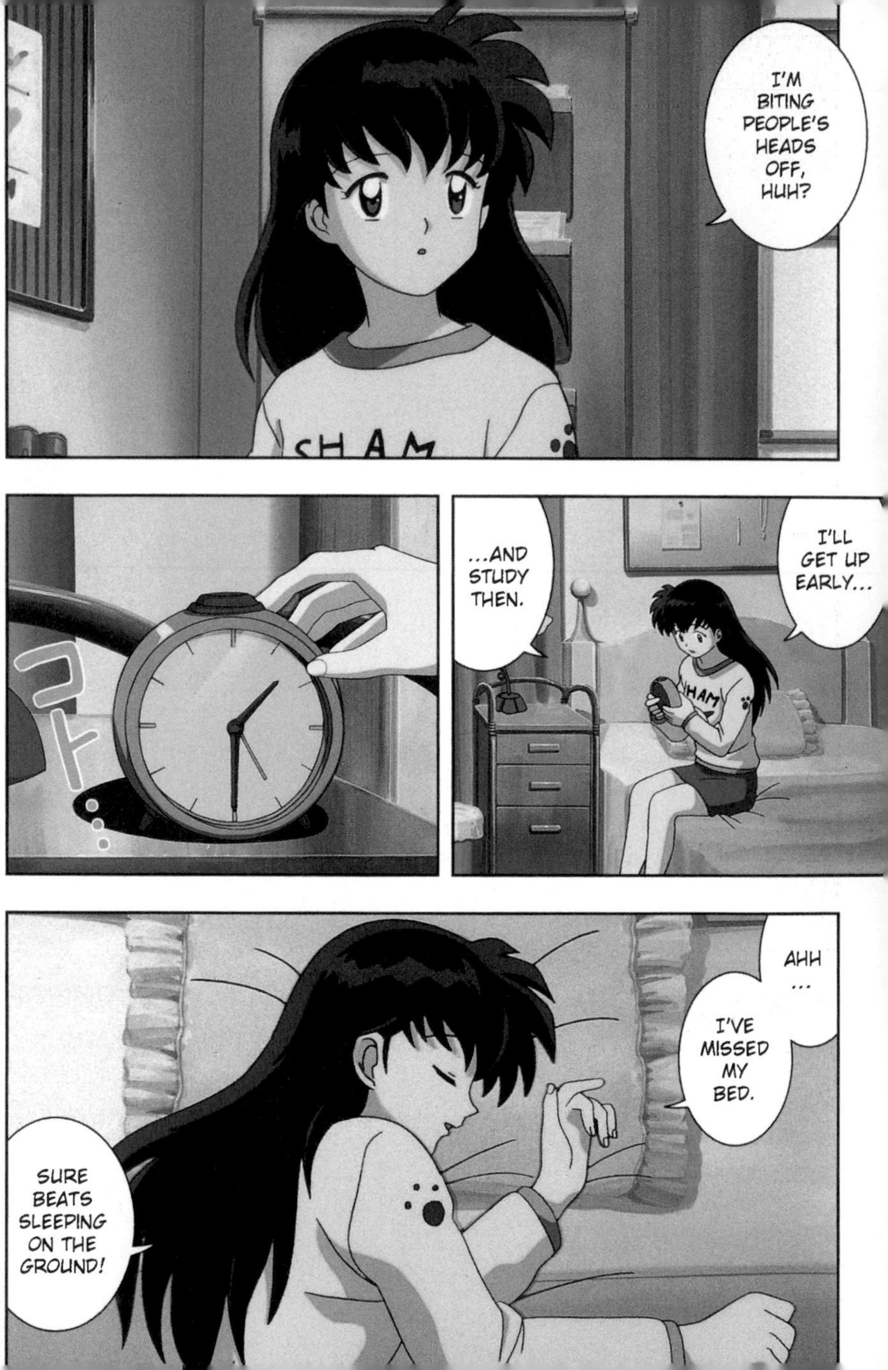
I'M BITING PEOPLE'S HEADS OFF, HUH?
I'LL GET UP EARLY...
...AND STUDY THEN.
コト
AHH ...
I'VE MISSED MY BED.
SURE BEATS SLEEPING ON THE GROUND!

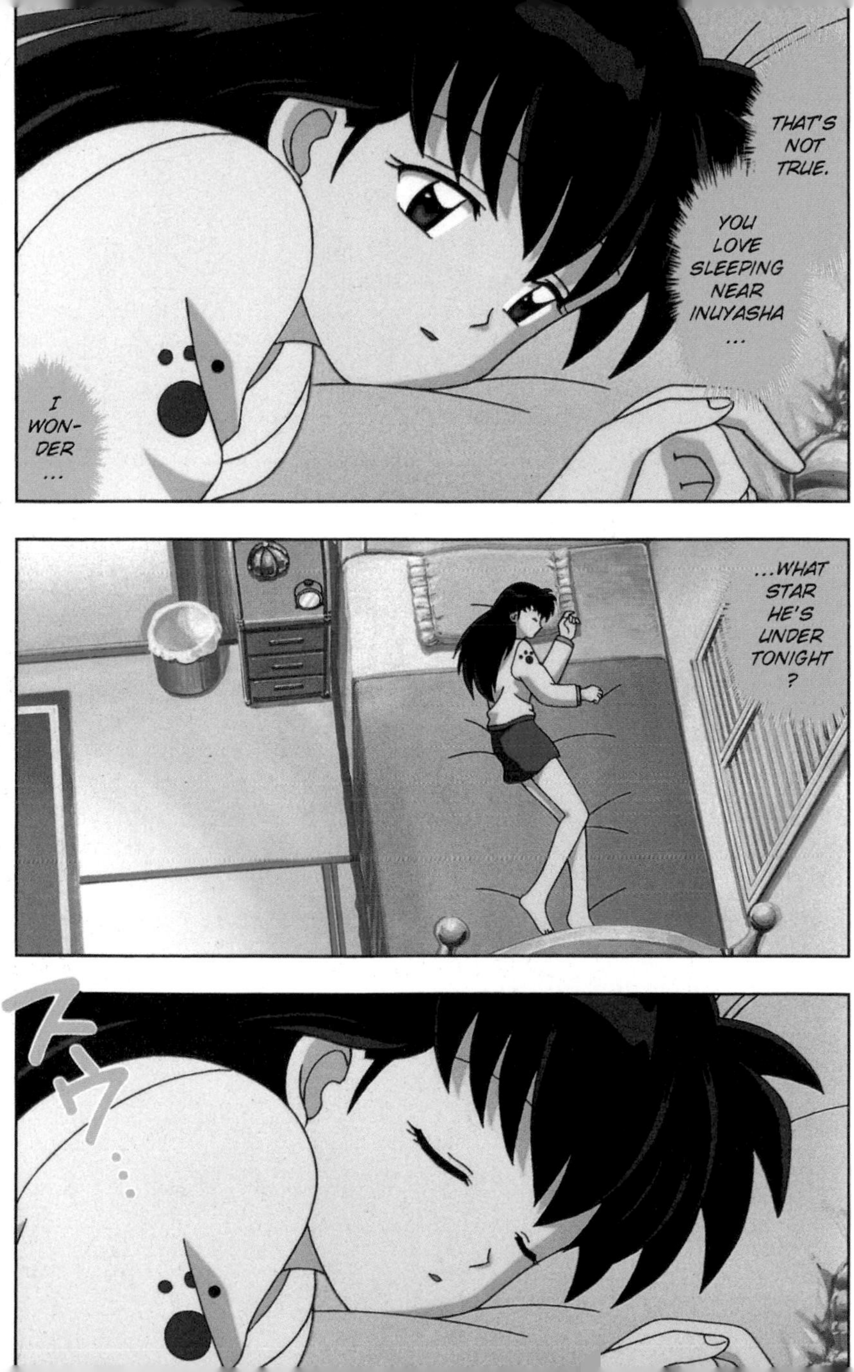
THAT'S NOT TRUE.
YOU LOVE SLEEPING NEAR INUYASHA ...
I WONDER ...
...WHAT STAR HE'S UNDER TONIGHT?
スゥ...

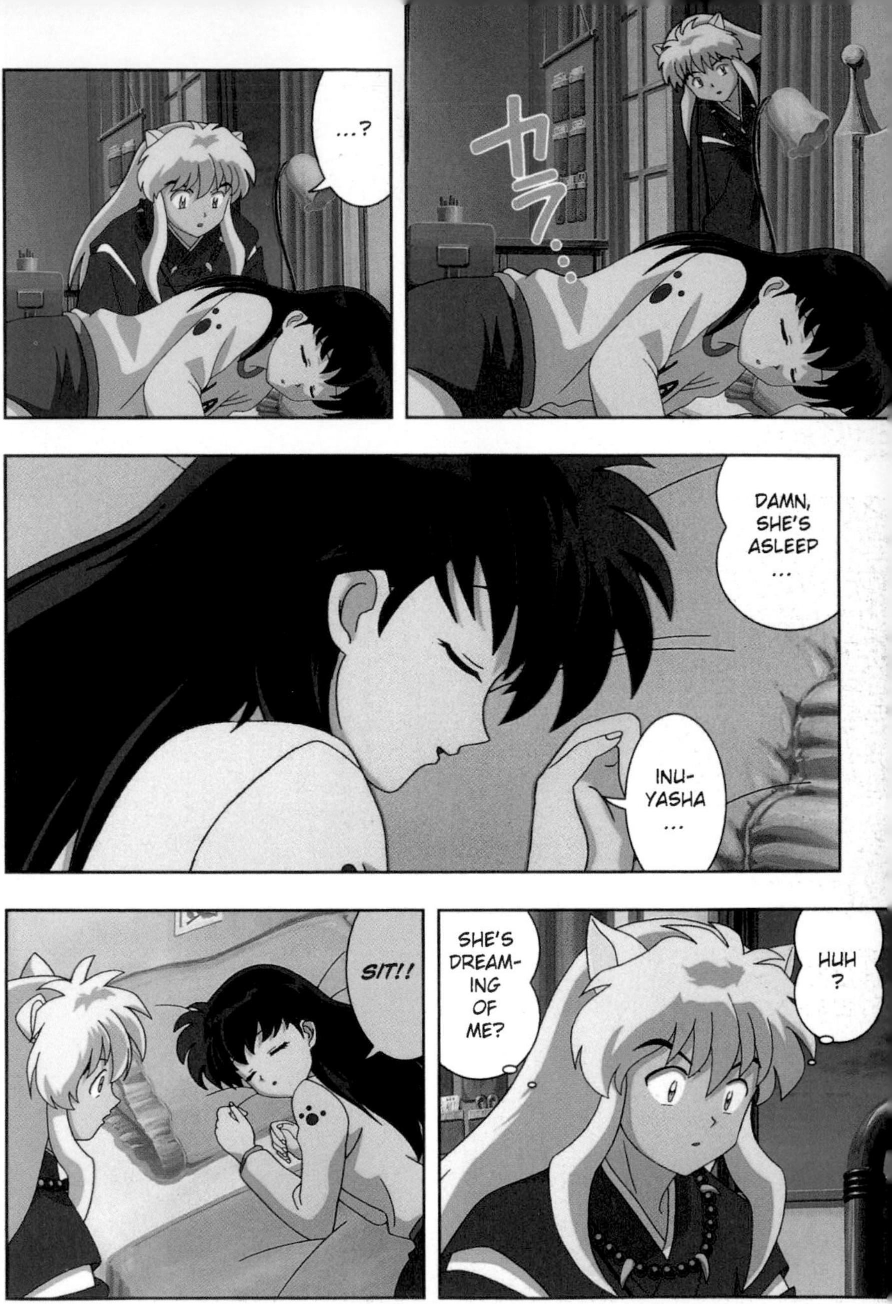
...?
DAMN, SHE'S ASLEEP ...
INU-YASHA ...
HUH ?
SHE'S DREAMING OF ME?
SIT!!

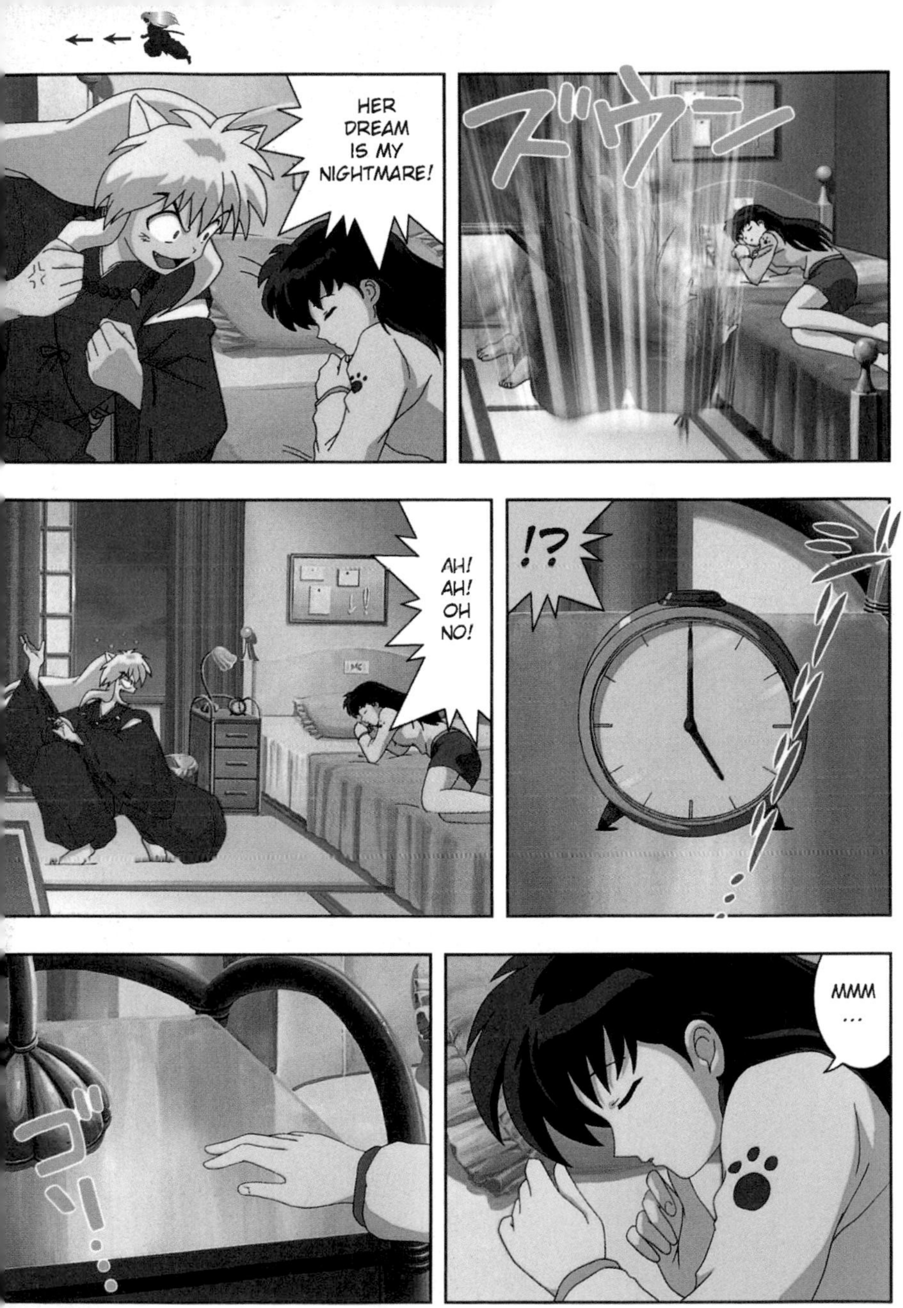
ズウーン
HER DREAM IS MY NIGHTMARE!
!?
AH! AH! OH NO!
MMM ...
ゴソ…

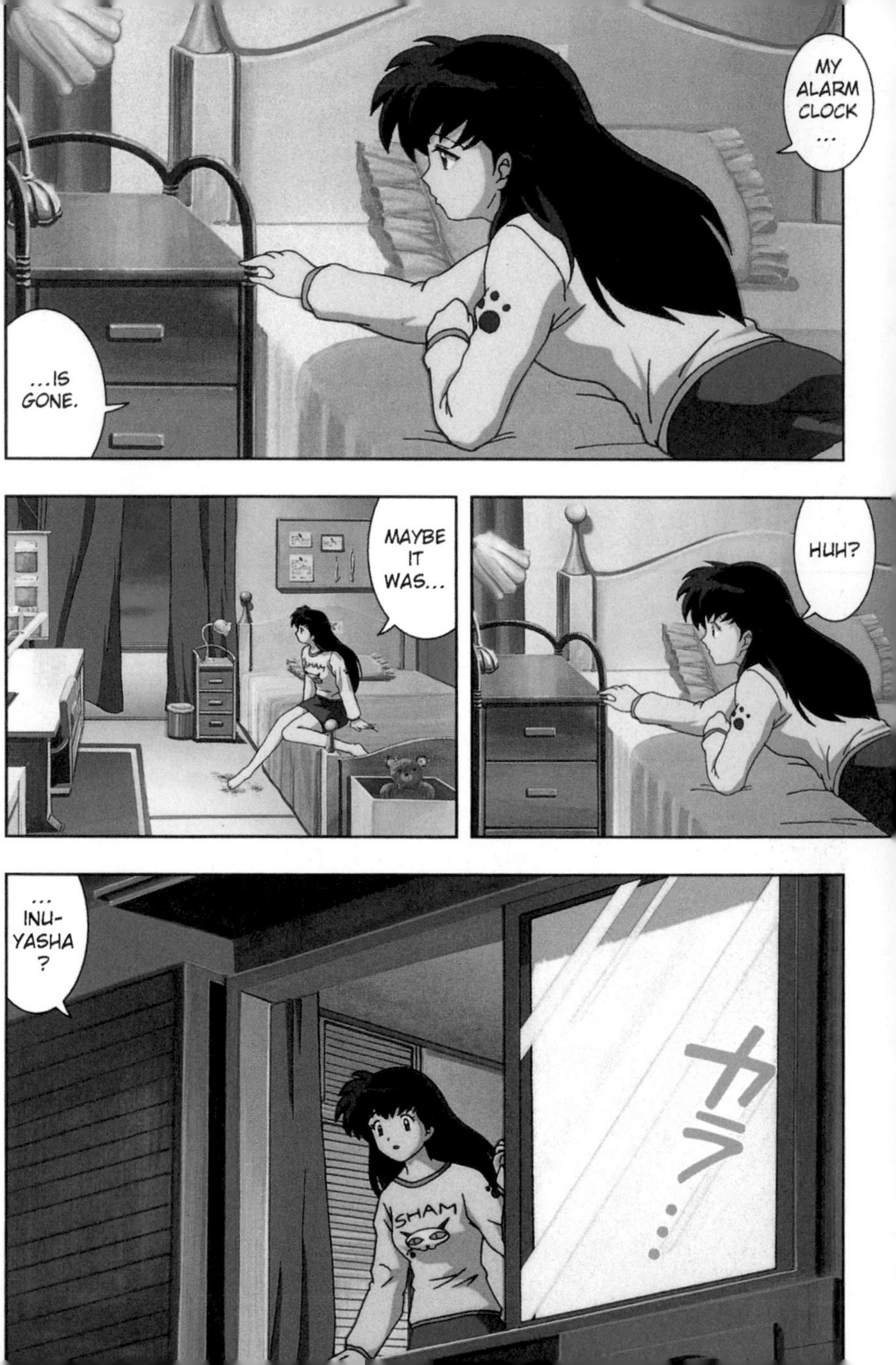
MY ALARM CLOCK ...
...IS GONE.
HUH?
MAYBE IT WAS...
... INU-YASHA ?
カラ...

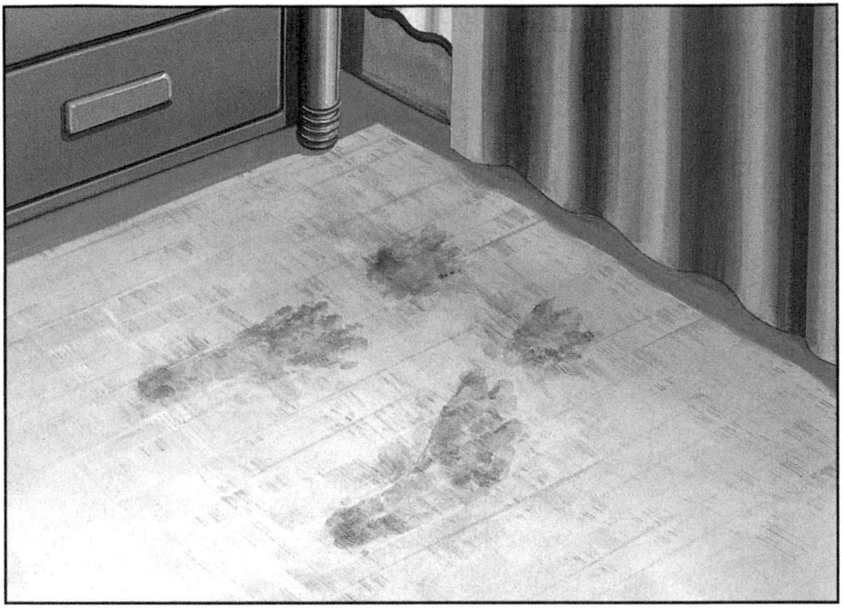

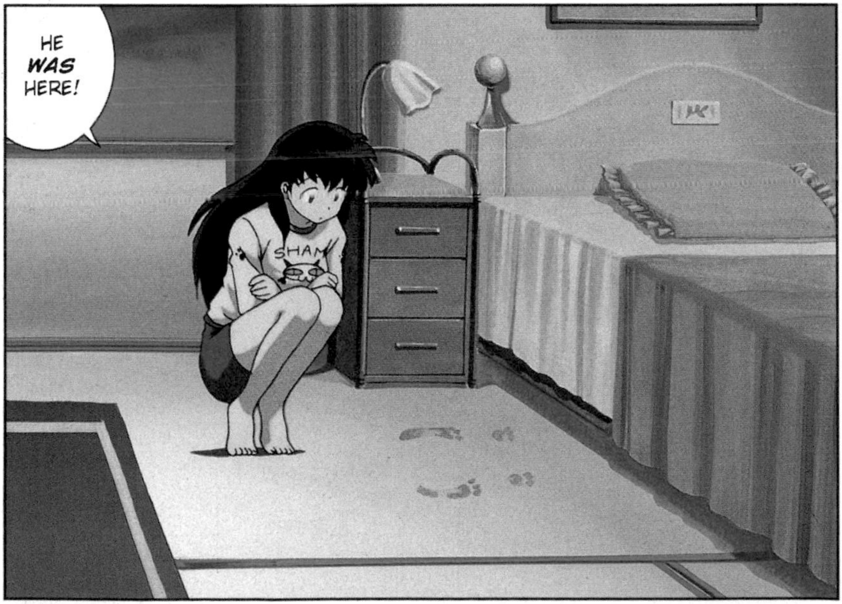
HE WAS HERE!

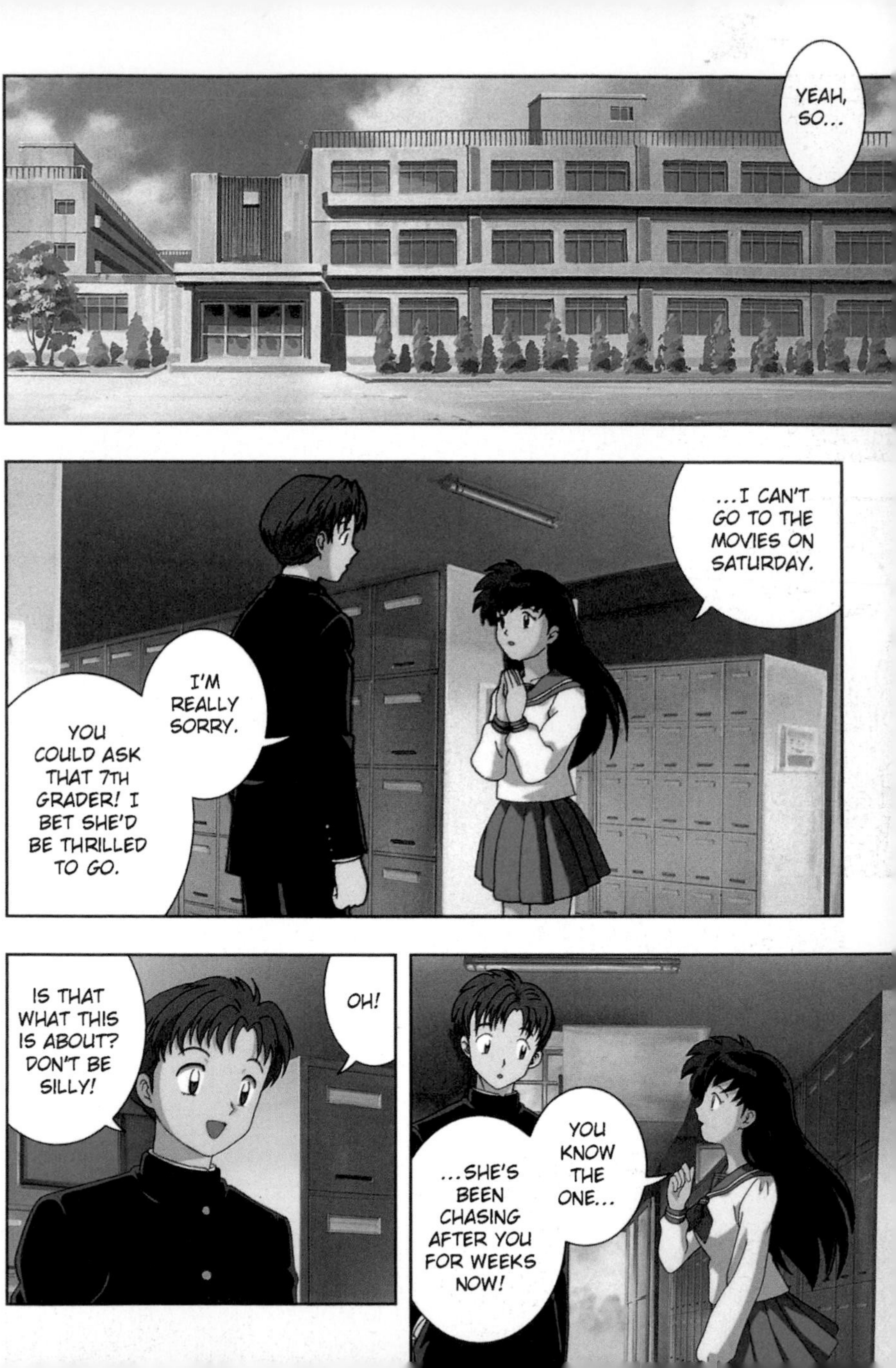
YEAH, SO...
...I CAN'T GO TO THE MOVIES ON SATURDAY.
I'M REALLY SORRY.
YOU COULD ASK THAT 7TH GRADER! I BET SHE'D BE THRILLED TO GO.
YOU KNOW THE ONE...
...SHE'S BEEN CHASING AFTER YOU FOR WEEKS NOW!
OH!
IS THAT WHAT THIS IS ABOUT? DON'T BE SILLY!

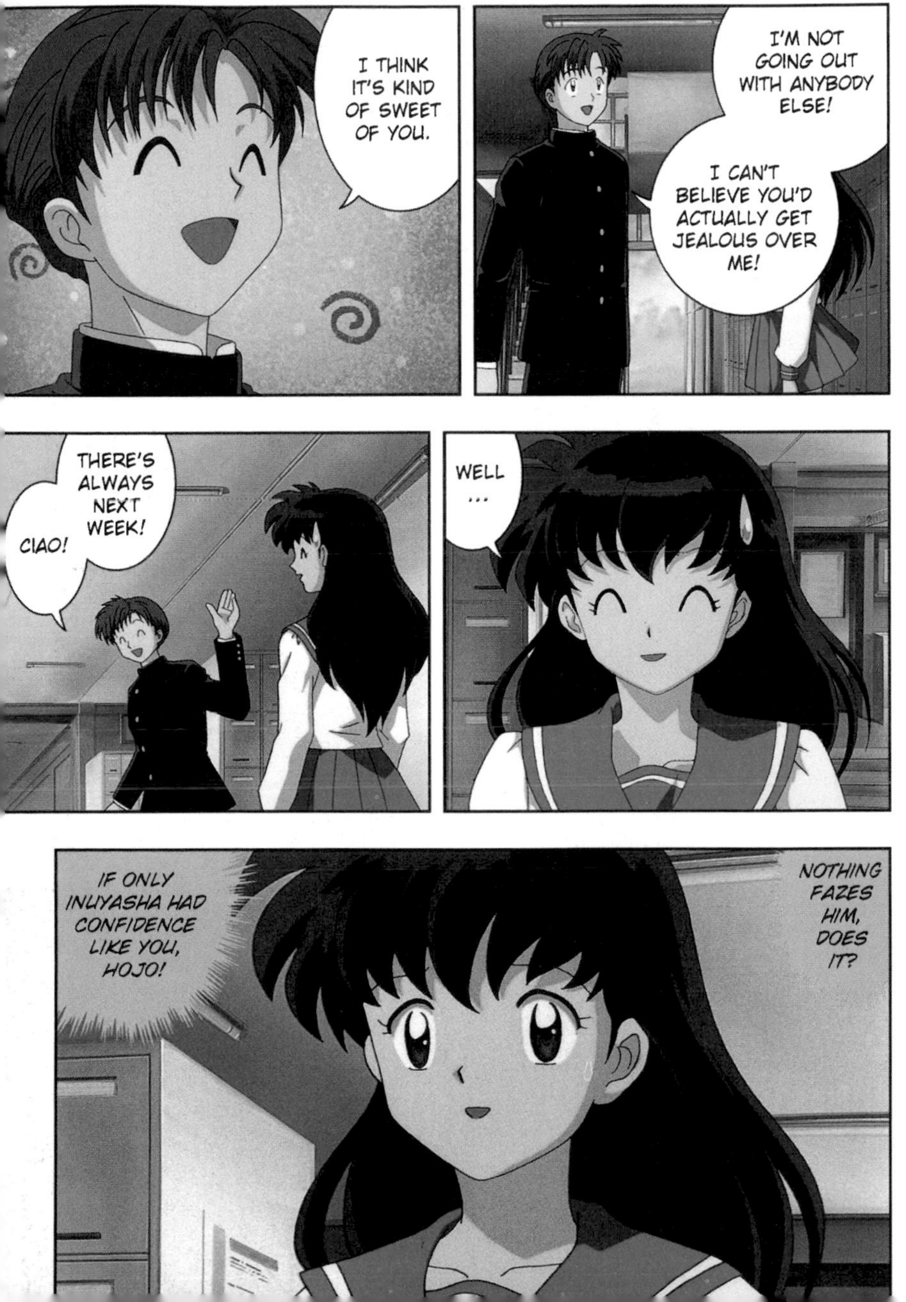
I'M NOT GOING OUT WITH ANYBODY ELSE!
I CAN'T BELIEVE YOU'D ACTUALLY GET JEALOUS OVER ME!
I THINK IT'S KIND OF SWEET OF YOU.
WELL ...
THERE'S ALWAYS NEXT WEEK!
CIAO!
NOTHING FAZES HIM, DOES IT?
IF ONLY INUYASHA HAD CONFIDENCE LIKE YOU, HOJO!

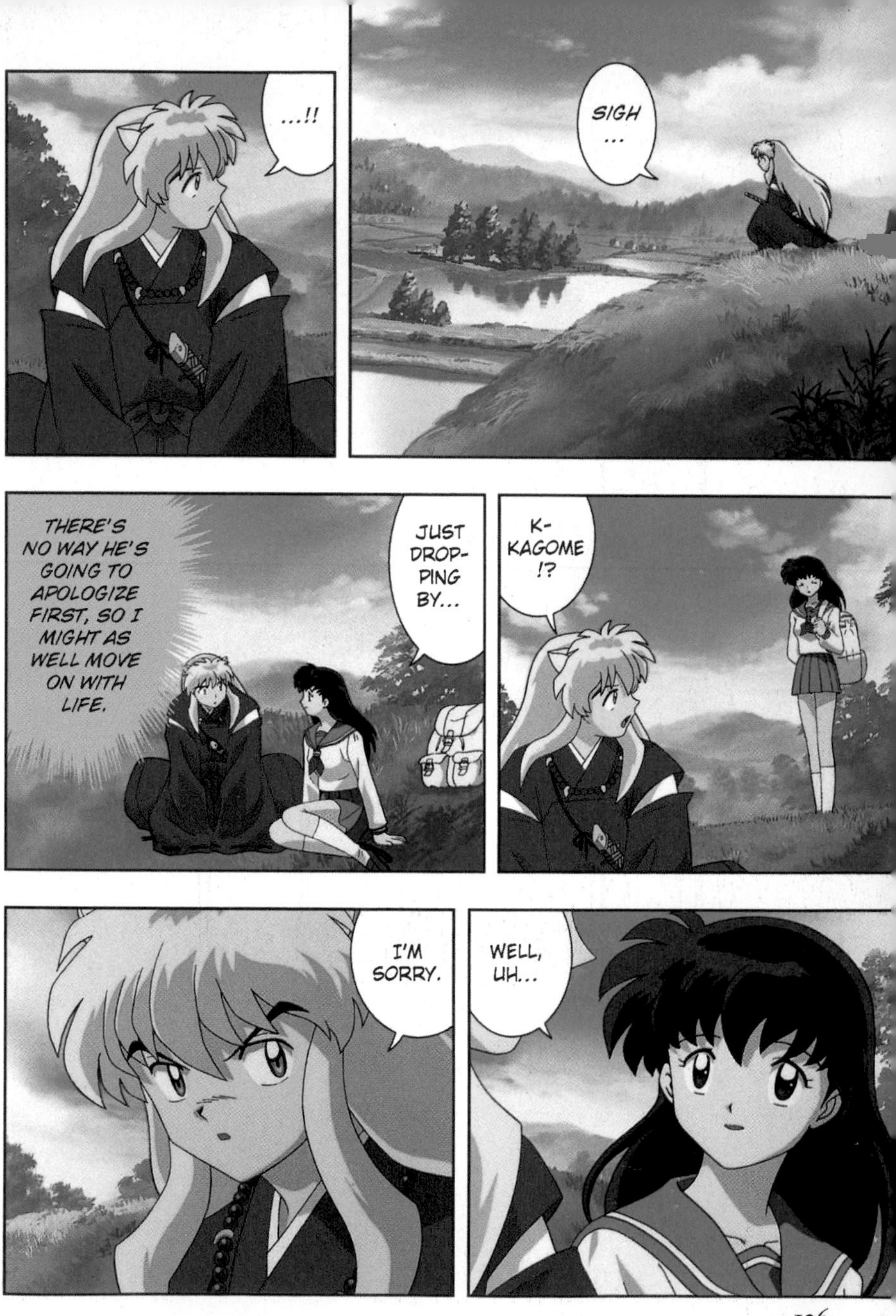
SIGH ...
...!!
K-KAGOME !?
JUST DROP-PING BY...
THERE'S NO WAY HE'S GOING TO APOLOGIZE FIRST, SO I MIGHT AS WELL MOVE ON WITH LIFE.
WELL, UH...
I'M SORRY.

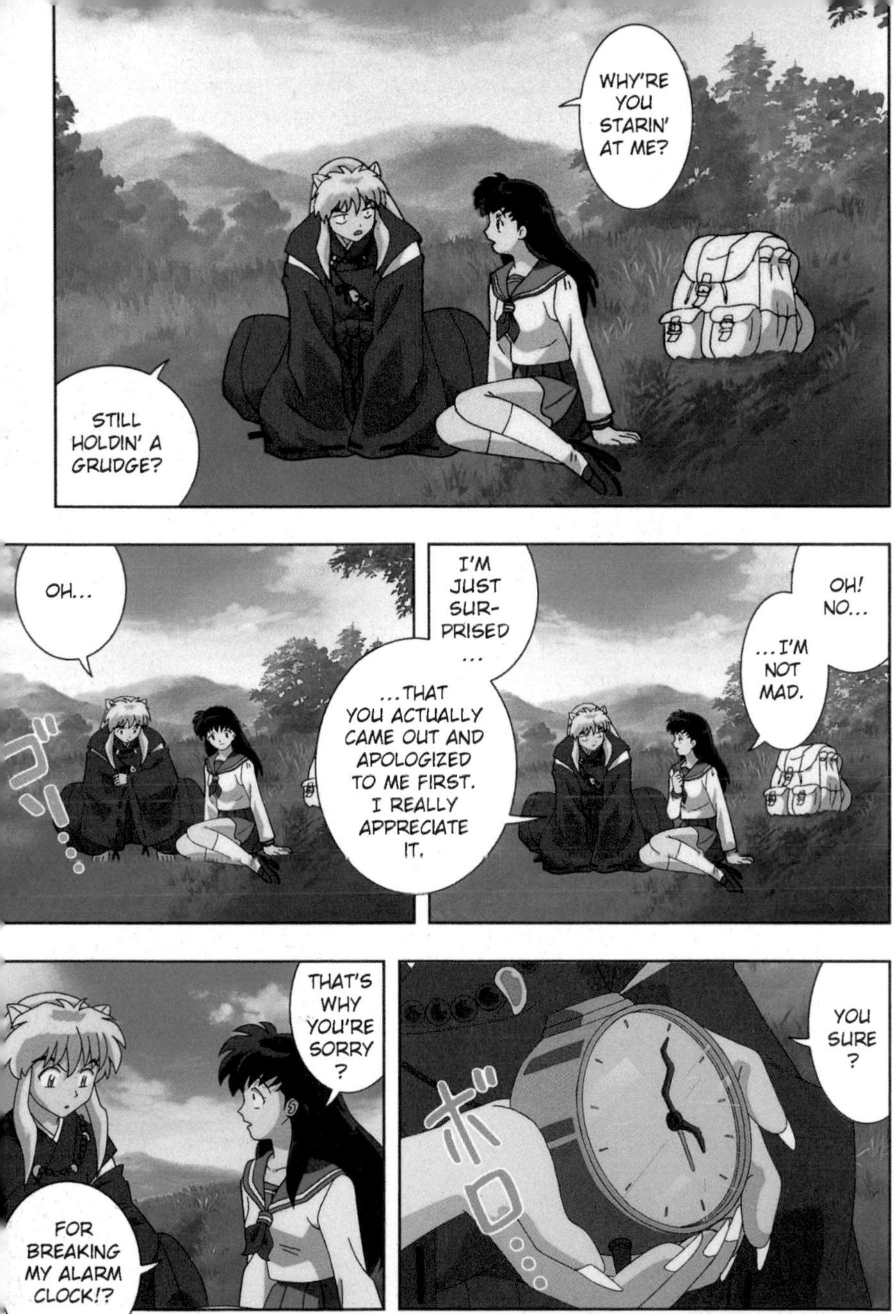
WHY'RE YOU STARIN' AT ME?
STILL HOLDIN' A GRUDGE?
OH! NO...
...I'M NOT MAD.
I'M JUST SUR-PRISED...
...THAT YOU ACTUALLY CAME OUT AND APOLOGIZED TO ME FIRST. I REALLY APPRECIATE IT.
OH...
YOU SURE?
ボロ...
THAT'S WHY YOU'RE SORRY?
FOR BREAKING MY ALARM CLOCK!?

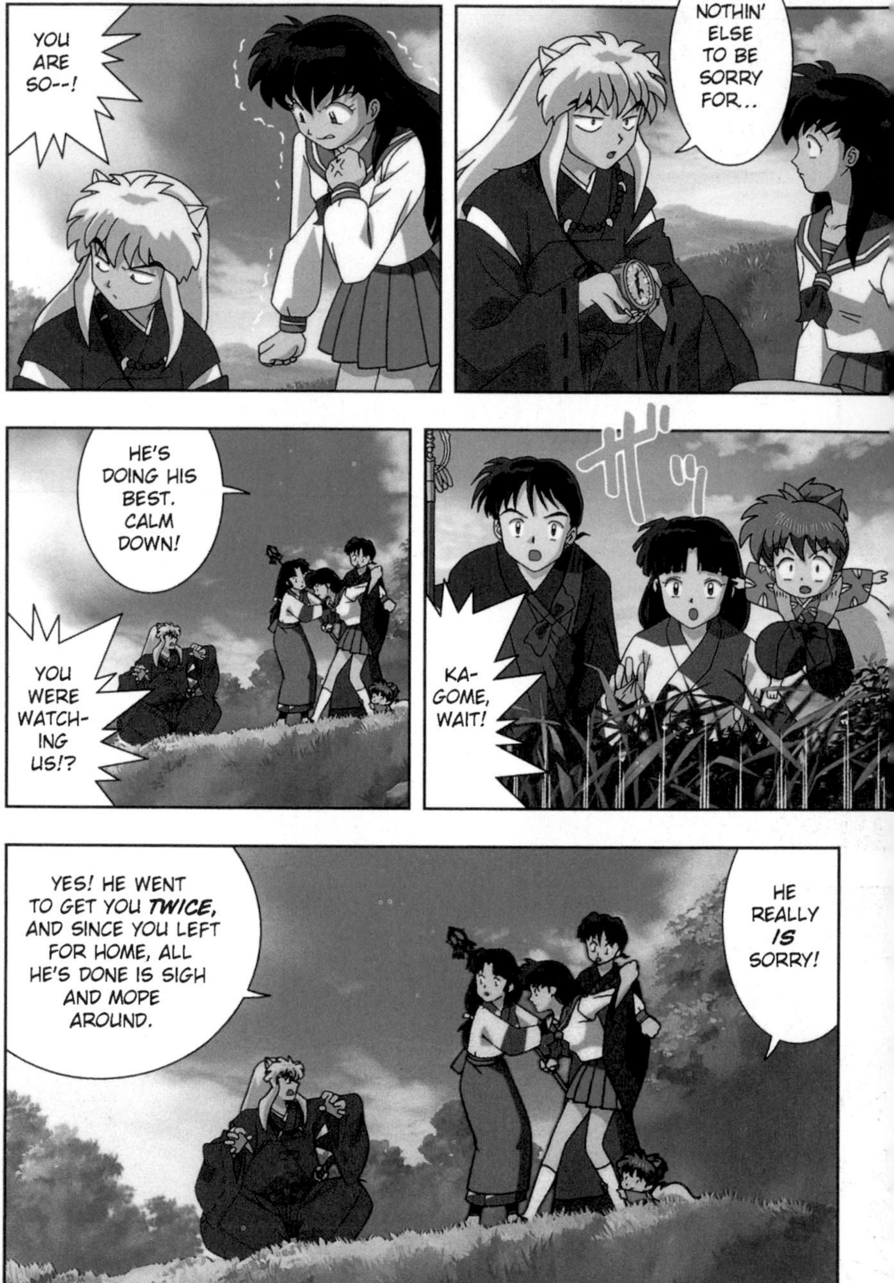
NOTHIN' ELSE TO BE SORRY FOR...
YOU ARE SO--!
ザッ
KA-GOME, WAIT!
HE'S DOING HIS BEST. CALM DOWN!
YOU WERE WATCHING US!?
HE REALLY *IS* SORRY!
YES! HE WENT TO GET YOU ***TWICE,*** AND SINCE YOU LEFT FOR HOME, ALL HE'S DONE IS SIGH AND MOPE AROUND.

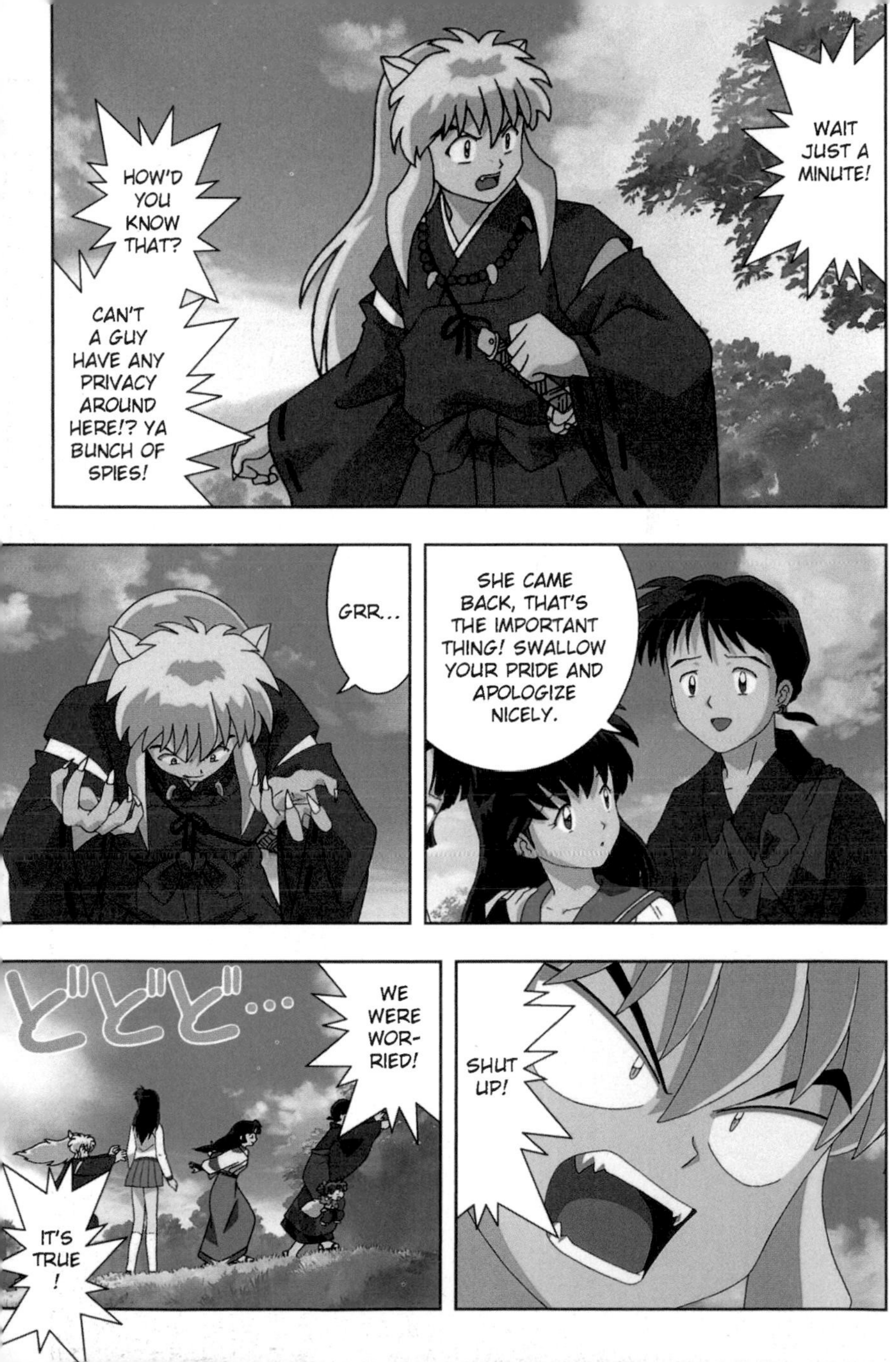
WAIT JUST A MINUTE!
HOW'D YOU KNOW THAT?
CAN'T A GUY HAVE ANY PRIVACY AROUND HERE!? YA BUNCH OF SPIES!
SHE CAME BACK, THAT'S THE IMPORTANT THING! SWALLOW YOUR PRIDE AND APOLOGIZE NICELY.
GRR...
SHUT UP!
WE WERE WOR-RIED!
どどど…
IT'S TRUE!

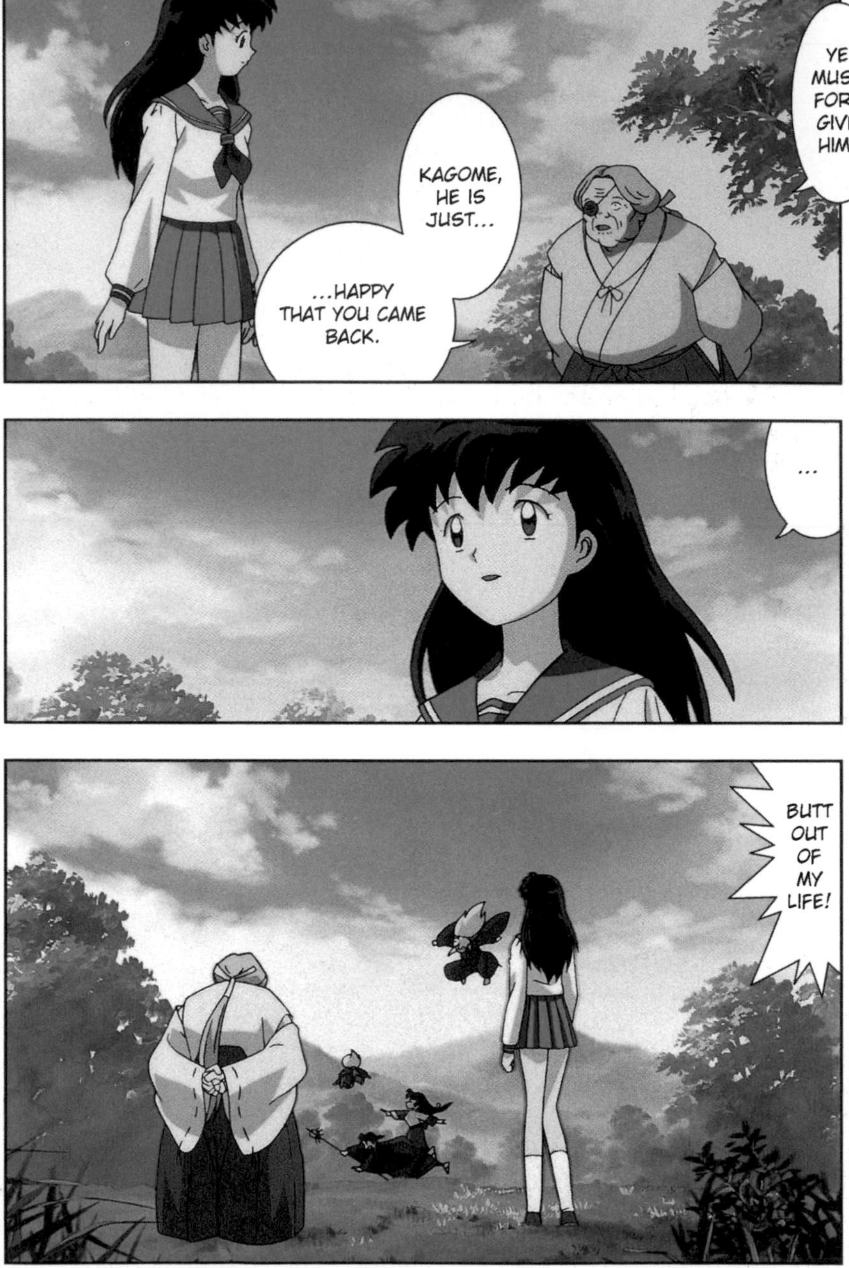
YE MUST FOR-GIVE HIM.
KAGOME, HE IS JUST...
...HAPPY THAT YOU CAME BACK.
...
BUTT OUT OF MY LIFE!

39
Trapped in a Duel to the Death!

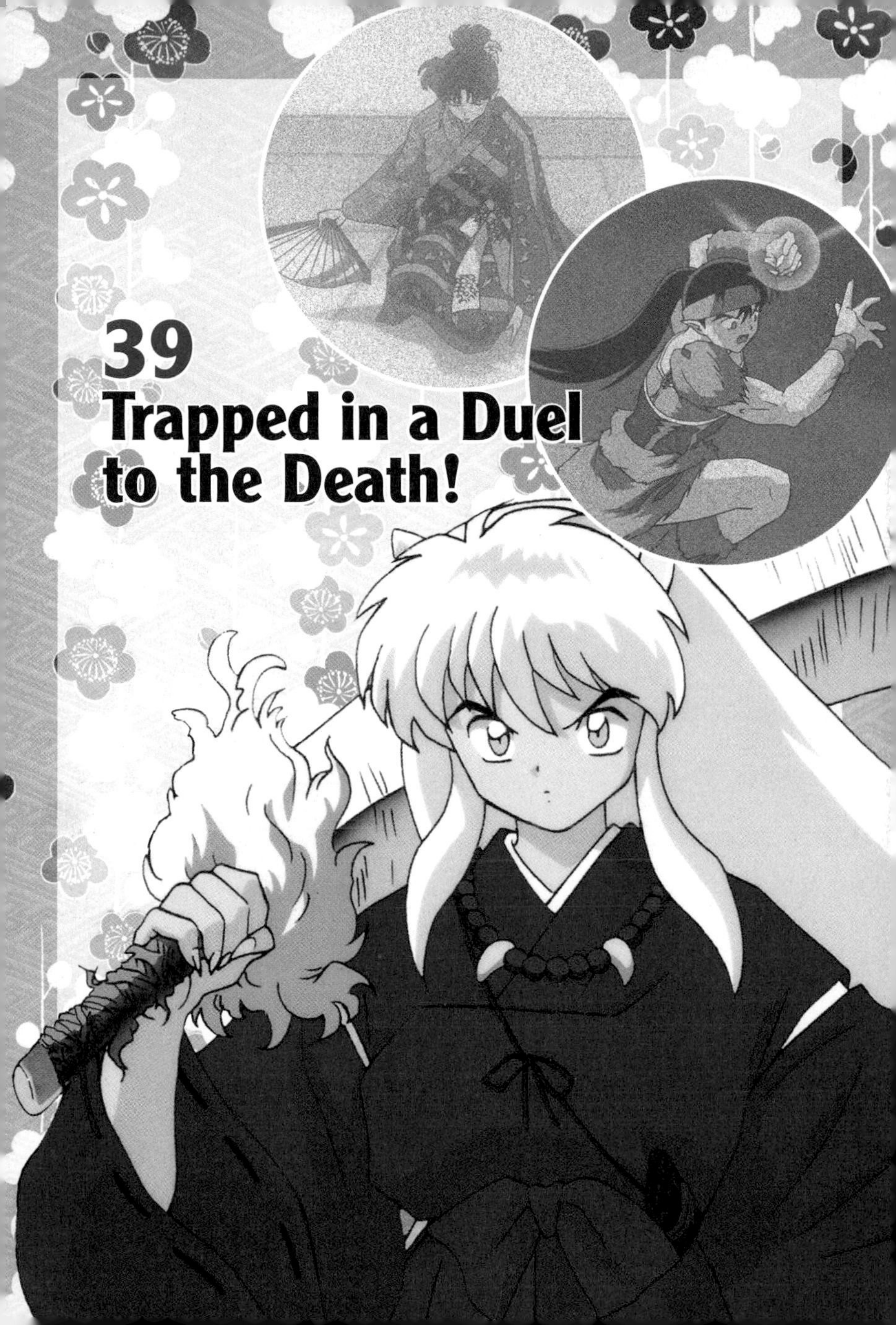

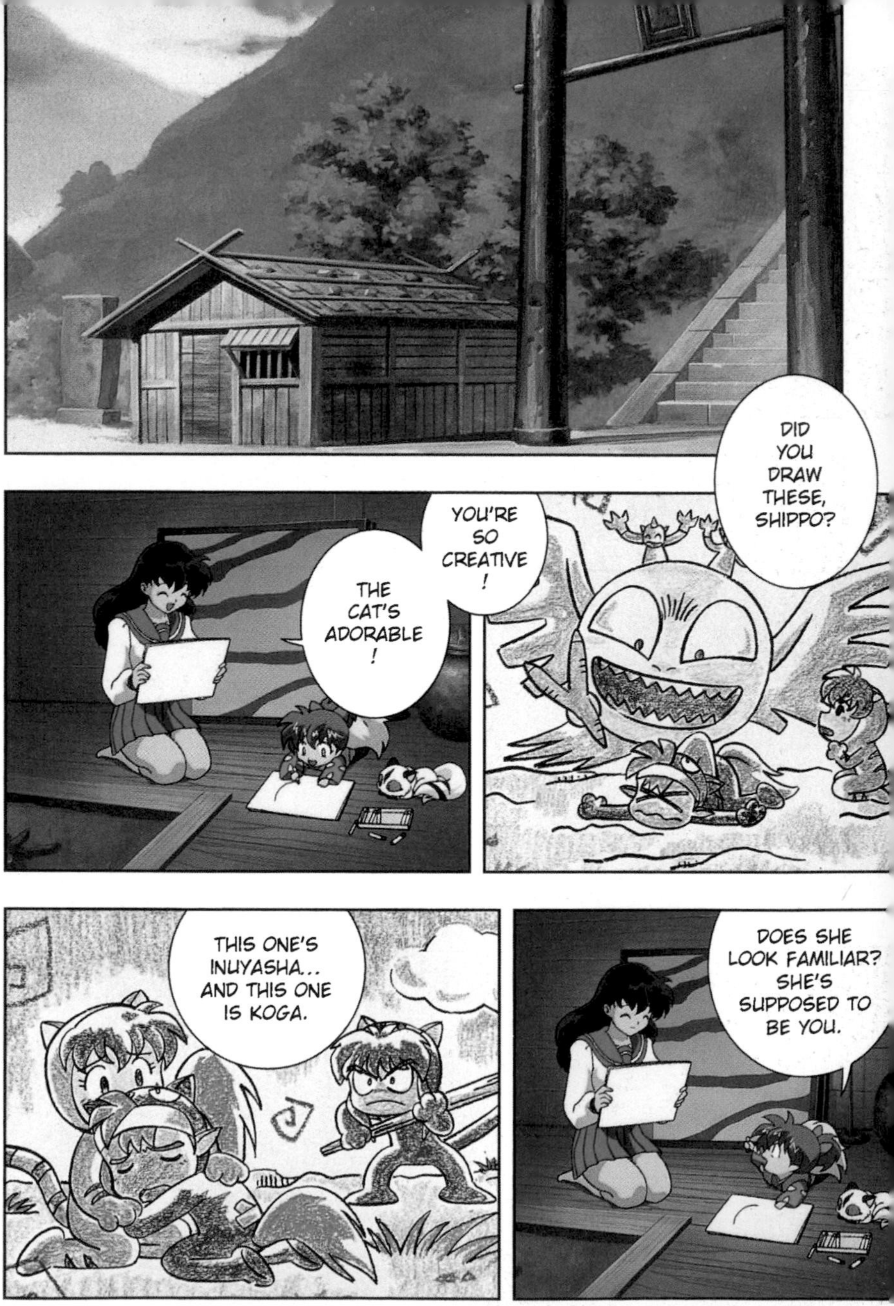
DID YOU DRAW THESE, SHIPPO?
YOU'RE SO CREATIVE!
THE CAT'S ADORABLE!
DOES SHE LOOK FAMILIAR? SHE'S SUPPOSED TO BE YOU.
THIS ONE'S INUYASHA... AND THIS ONE IS KOGA.

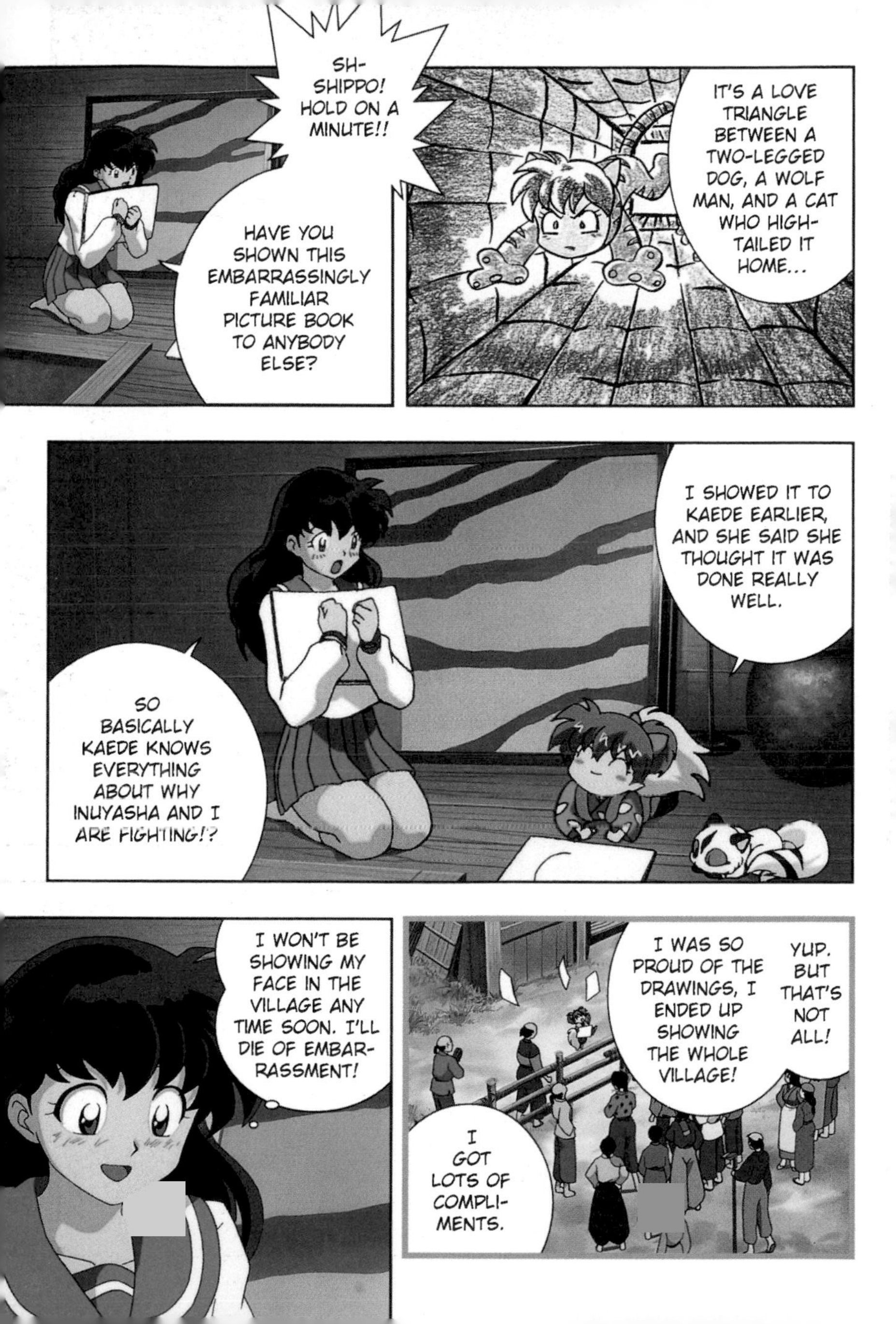

IT'S A LOVE TRIANGLE BETWEEN A TWO-LEGGED DOG, A WOLF MAN, AND A CAT WHO HIGH-TAILED IT HOME...
SH-SHIPPO! HOLD ON A MINUTE!!
HAVE YOU SHOWN THIS EMBARRASSINGLY FAMILIAR PICTURE BOOK TO ANYBODY ELSE?
I SHOWED IT TO KAEDE EARLIER, AND SHE SAID SHE THOUGHT IT WAS DONE REALLY WELL.
SO BASICALLY KAEDE KNOWS EVERYTHING ABOUT WHY INUYASHA AND I ARE FIGHTING!?
YUP. BUT THAT'S NOT ALL!
I WAS SO PROUD OF THE DRAWINGS, I ENDED UP SHOWING THE WHOLE VILLAGE!
I GOT LOTS OF COMPLI-MENTS.
I WON'T BE SHOWING MY FACE IN THE VILLAGE ANY TIME SOON. I'LL DIE OF EMBAR-RASSMENT!

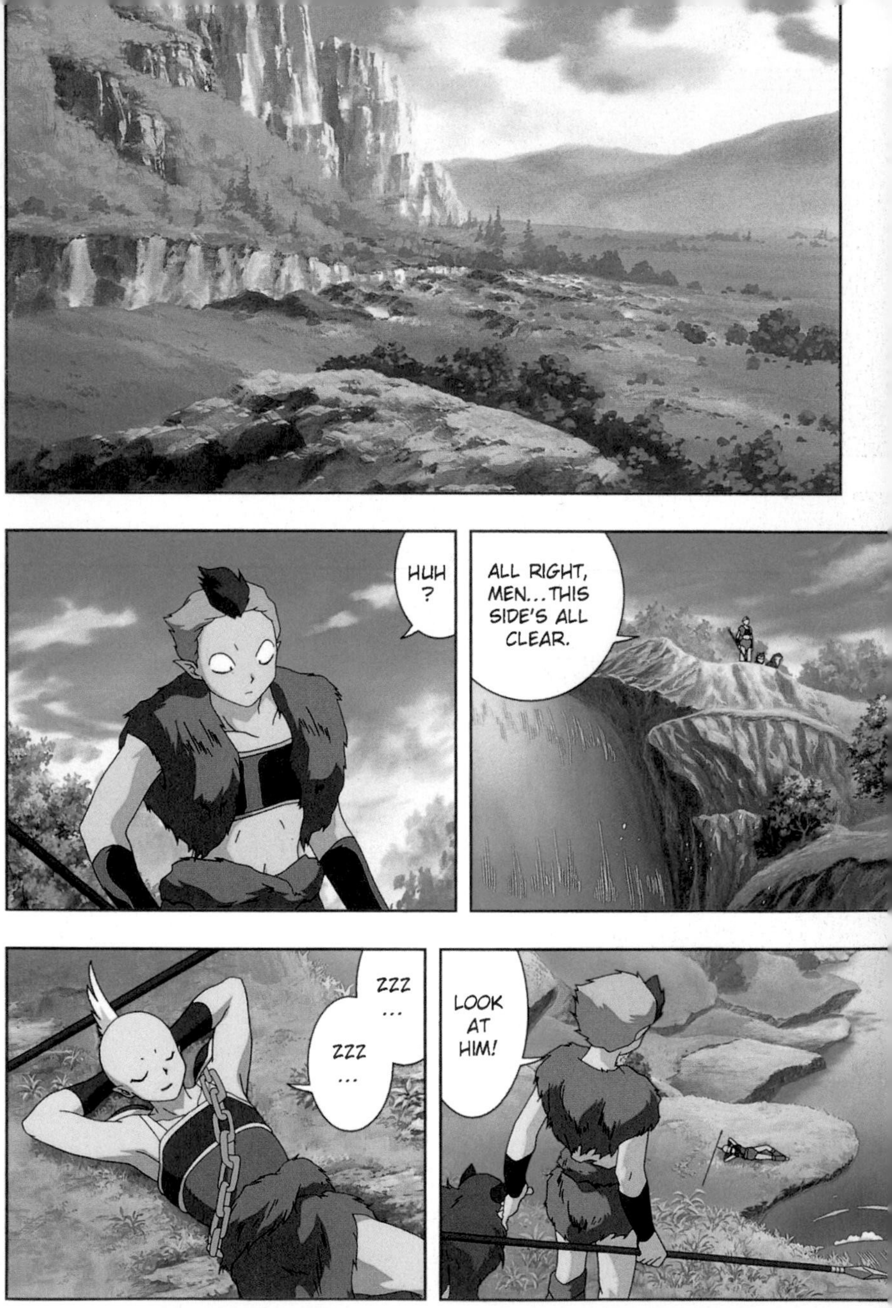
ALL RIGHT, MEN...THIS SIDE'S ALL CLEAR.
HUH?
LOOK AT HIM!
ZZZ...
ZZZ...

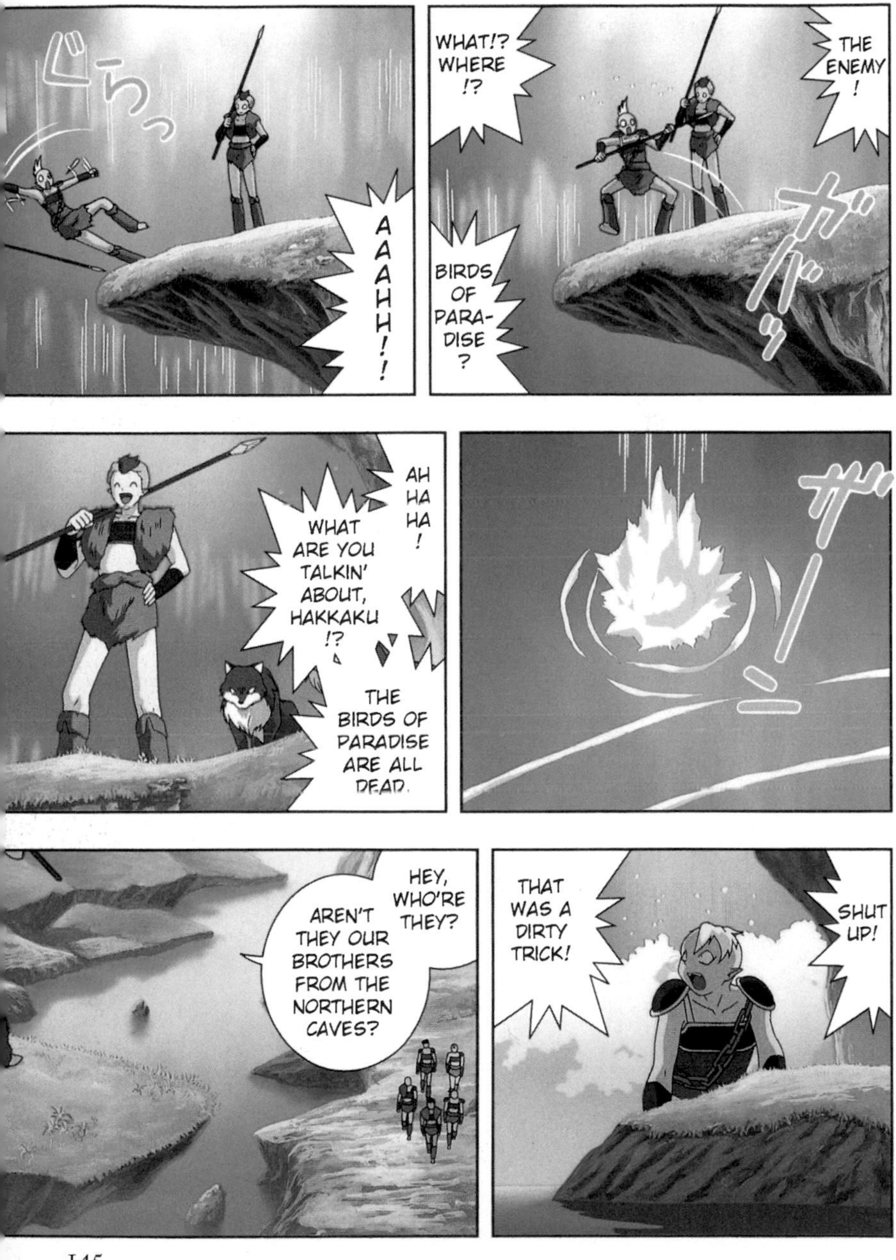
THE ENEMY!
WHAT!? WHERE!?
BIRDS OF PARADISE?
ガバッ
ぐらっ
AAAAHH!!
AH HA HA!
WHAT ARE YOU TALKIN' ABOUT, HAKKAKU!?
THE BIRDS OF PARADISE ARE ALL DEAD.
SHUT UP!
THAT WAS A DIRTY TRICK!
HEY, WHO'RE THEY?
AREN'T THEY OUR BROTHERS FROM THE NORTHERN CAVES?

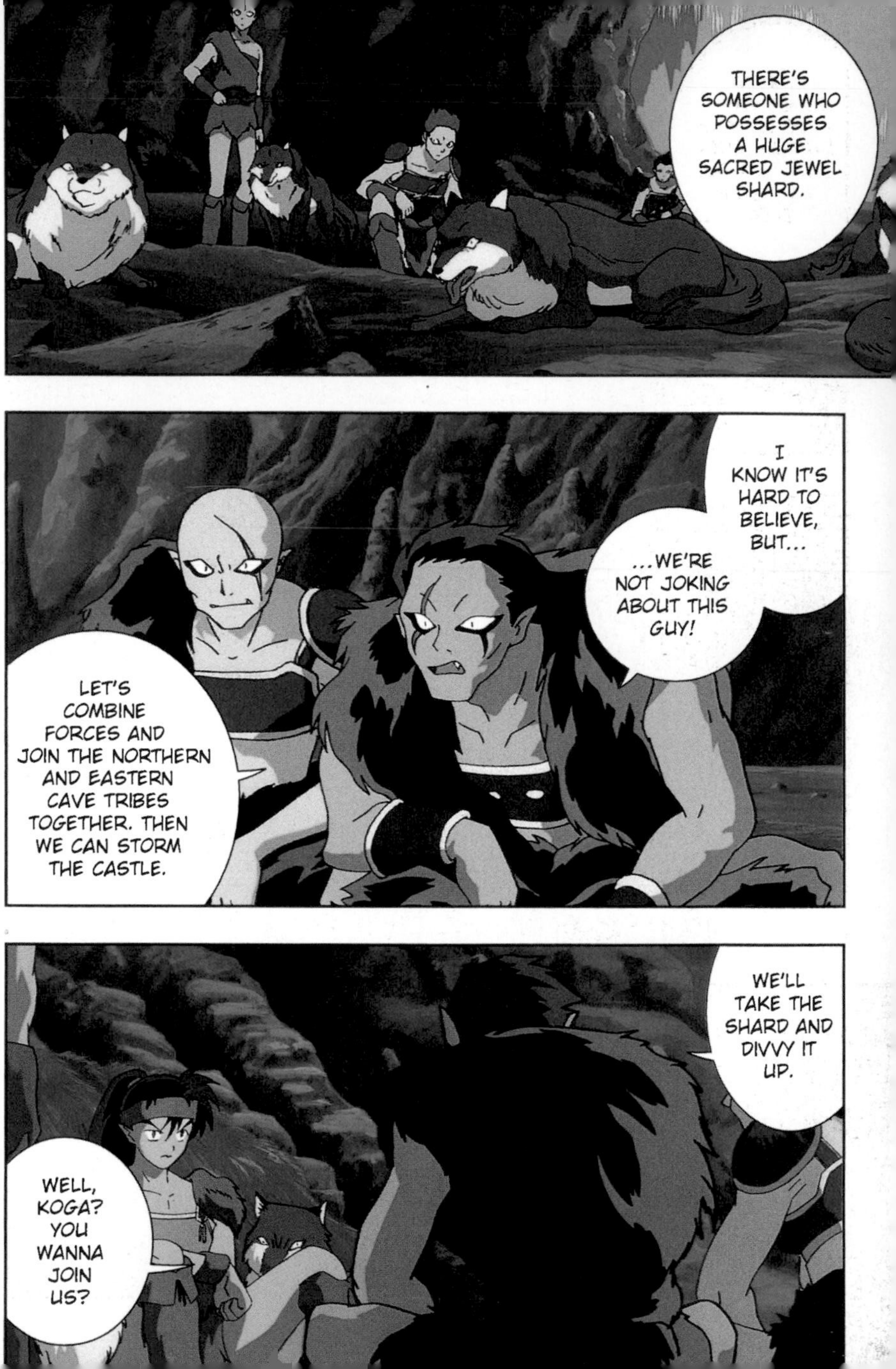
THERE'S SOMEONE WHO POSSESSES A HUGE SACRED JEWEL SHARD.
I KNOW IT'S HARD TO BELIEVE, BUT...
...WE'RE NOT JOKING ABOUT THIS GUY!
LET'S COMBINE FORCES AND JOIN THE NORTHERN AND EASTERN CAVE TRIBES TOGETHER. THEN WE CAN STORM THE CASTLE.
WE'LL TAKE THE SHARD AND DIVVY IT UP.
WELL, KOGA? YOU WANNA JOIN US?

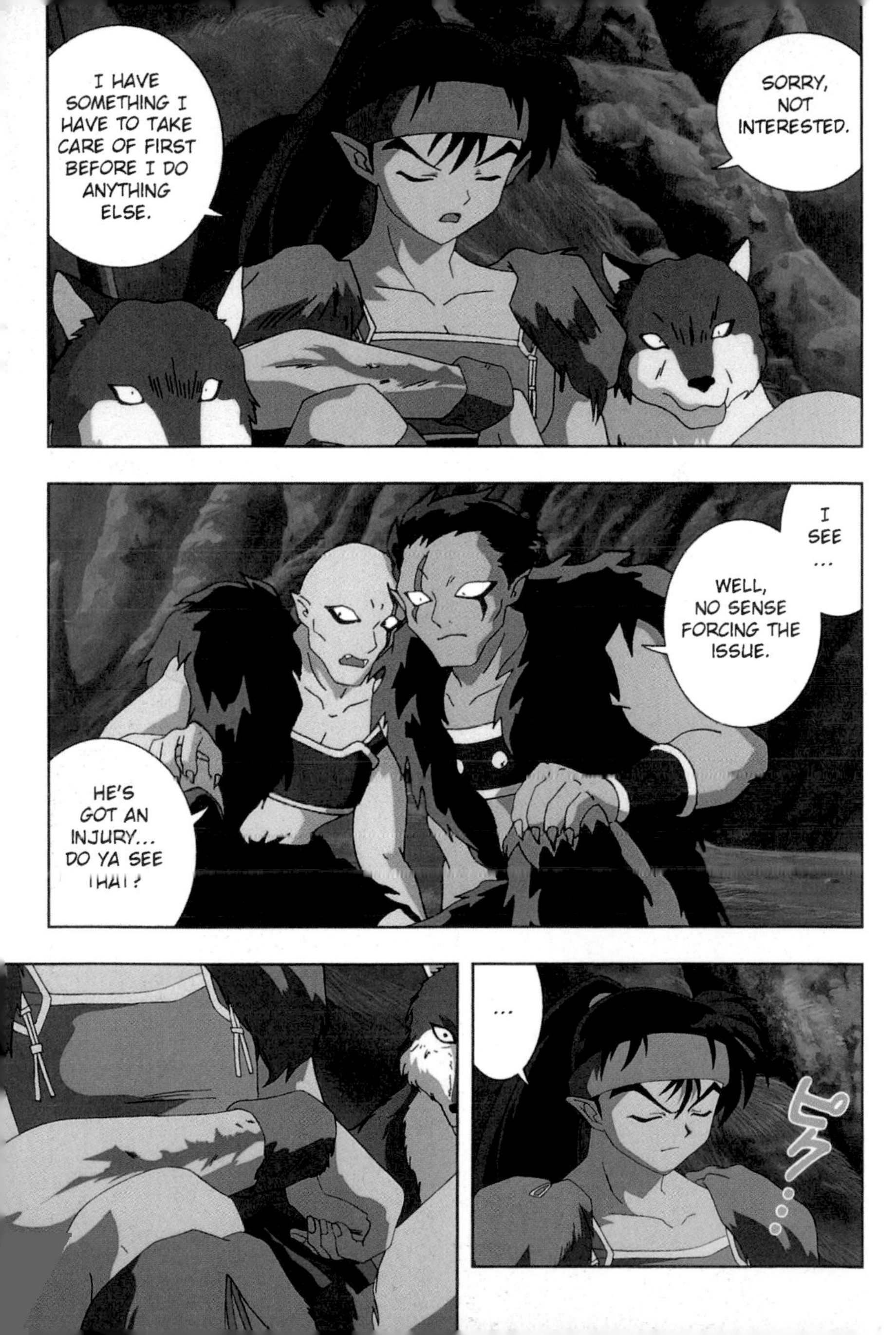
SORRY, NOT INTERESTED.
I HAVE SOMETHING I HAVE TO TAKE CARE OF FIRST BEFORE I DO ANYTHING ELSE.
I SEE... WELL, NO SENSE FORCING THE ISSUE.
HE'S GOT AN INJURY... DO YA SEE THAT?
...
ピク...

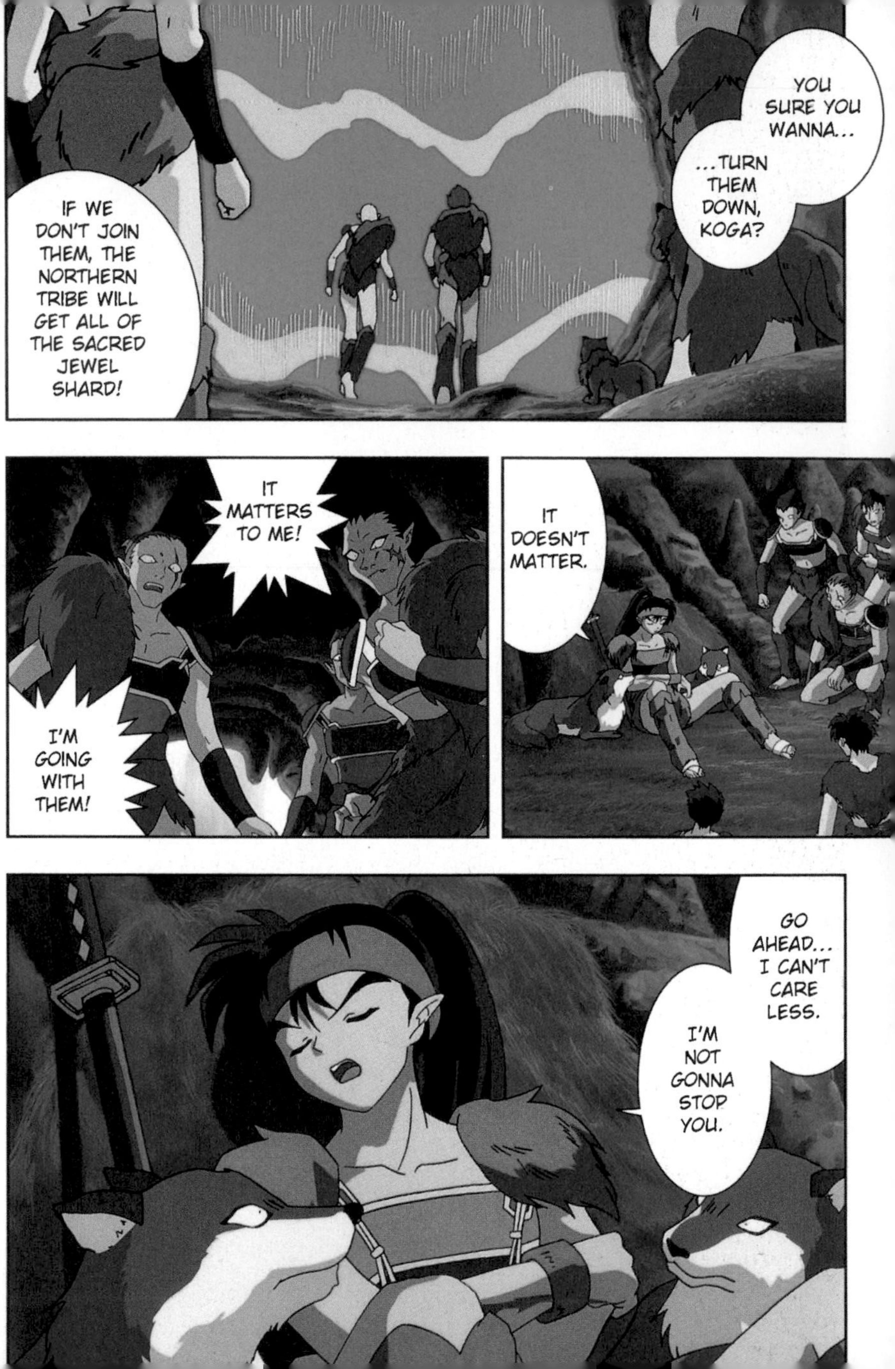
YOU SURE YOU WANNA...
...TURN THEM DOWN, KOGA?
IF WE DON'T JOIN THEM, THE NORTHERN TRIBE WILL GET ALL OF THE SACRED JEWEL SHARD!
IT DOESN'T MATTER.
IT MATTERS TO ME!
I'M GOING WITH THEM!
GO AHEAD... I CAN'T CARE LESS.
I'M NOT GONNA STOP YOU.

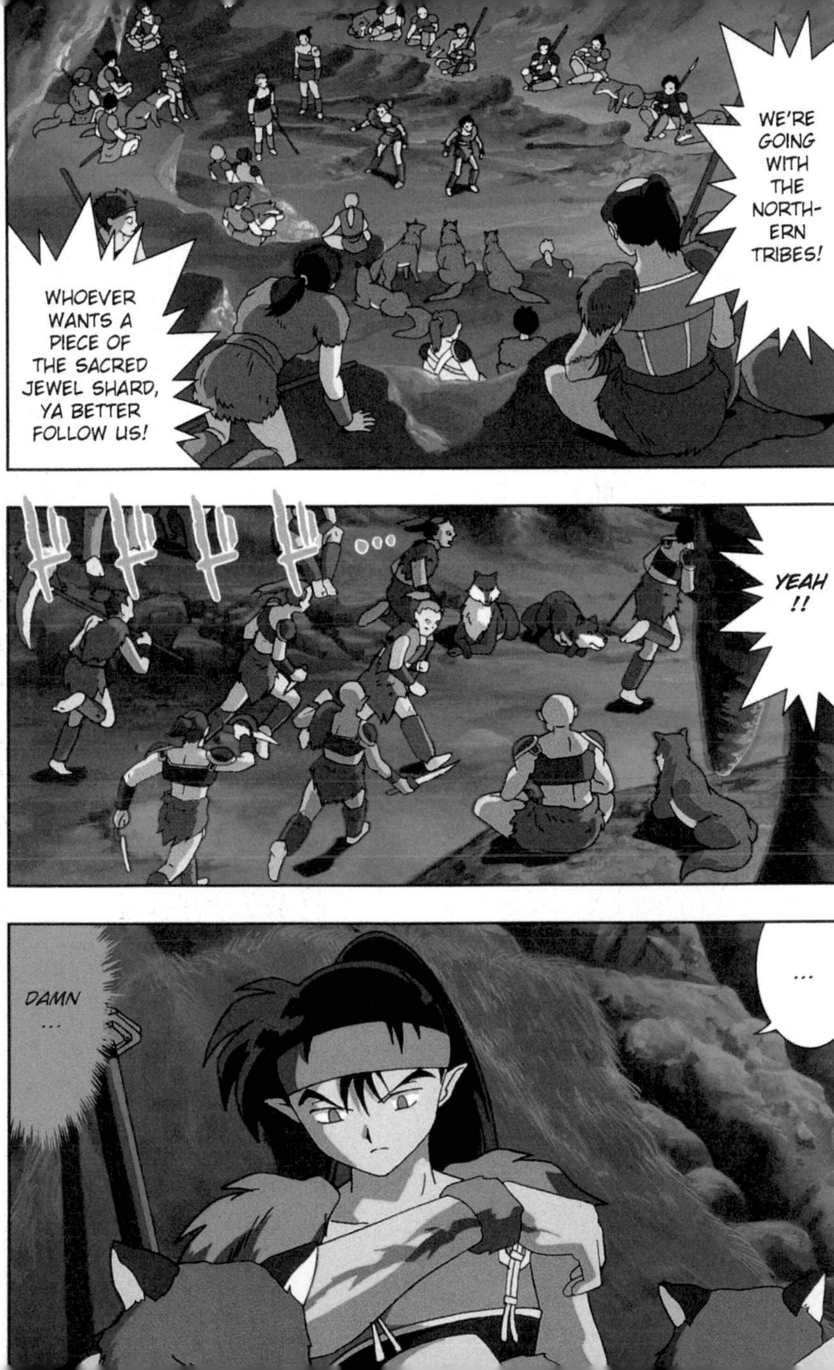
WE'RE GOING WITH THE NORTH-ERN TRIBES!
WHOEVER WANTS A PIECE OF THE SACRED JEWEL SHARD, YA BETTER FOLLOW US!
YEAH !!
...
...
DAMN ...

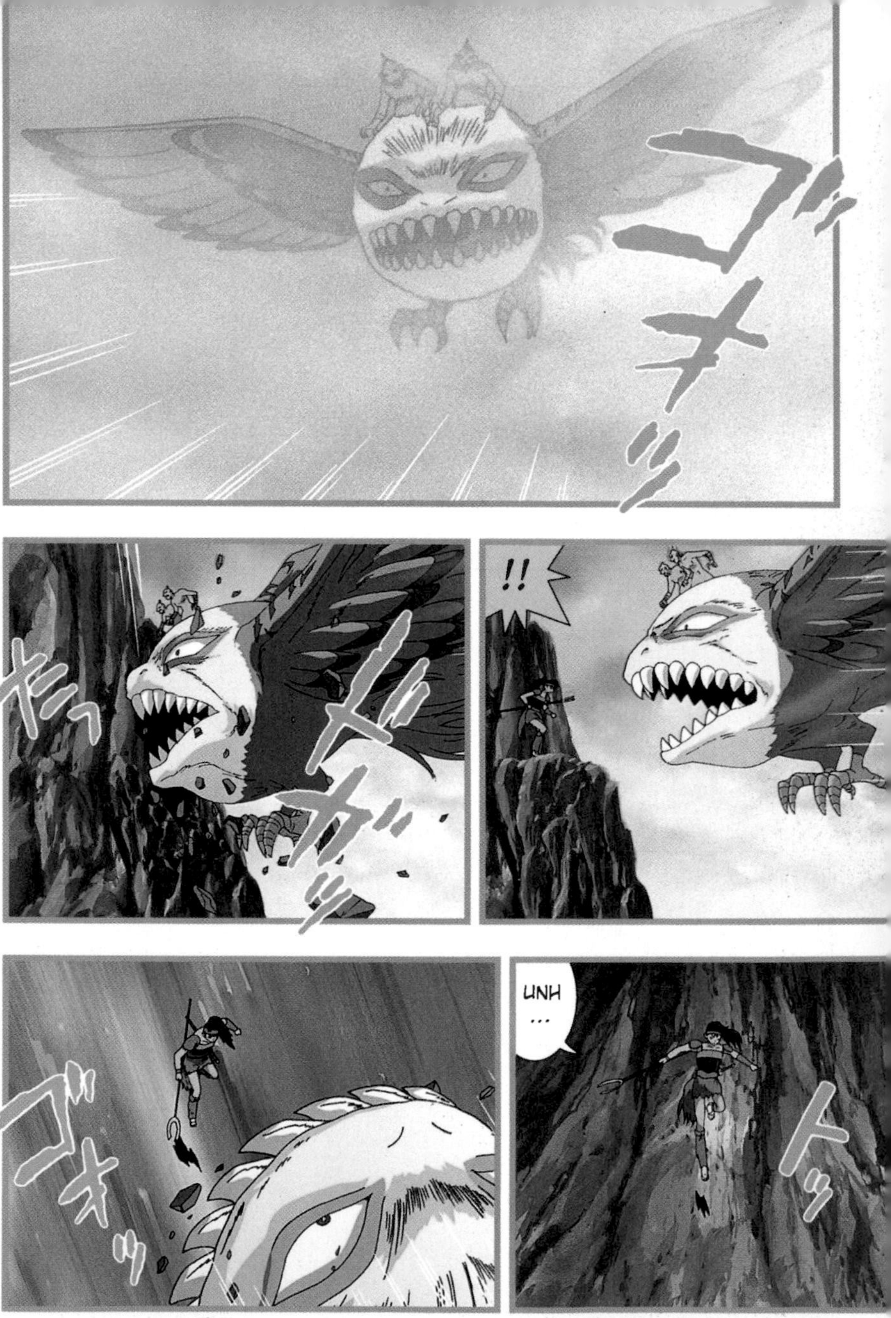
ゴオッ
!!
ドガッ
ダッ
UNH ...
トッ
ゴオッ

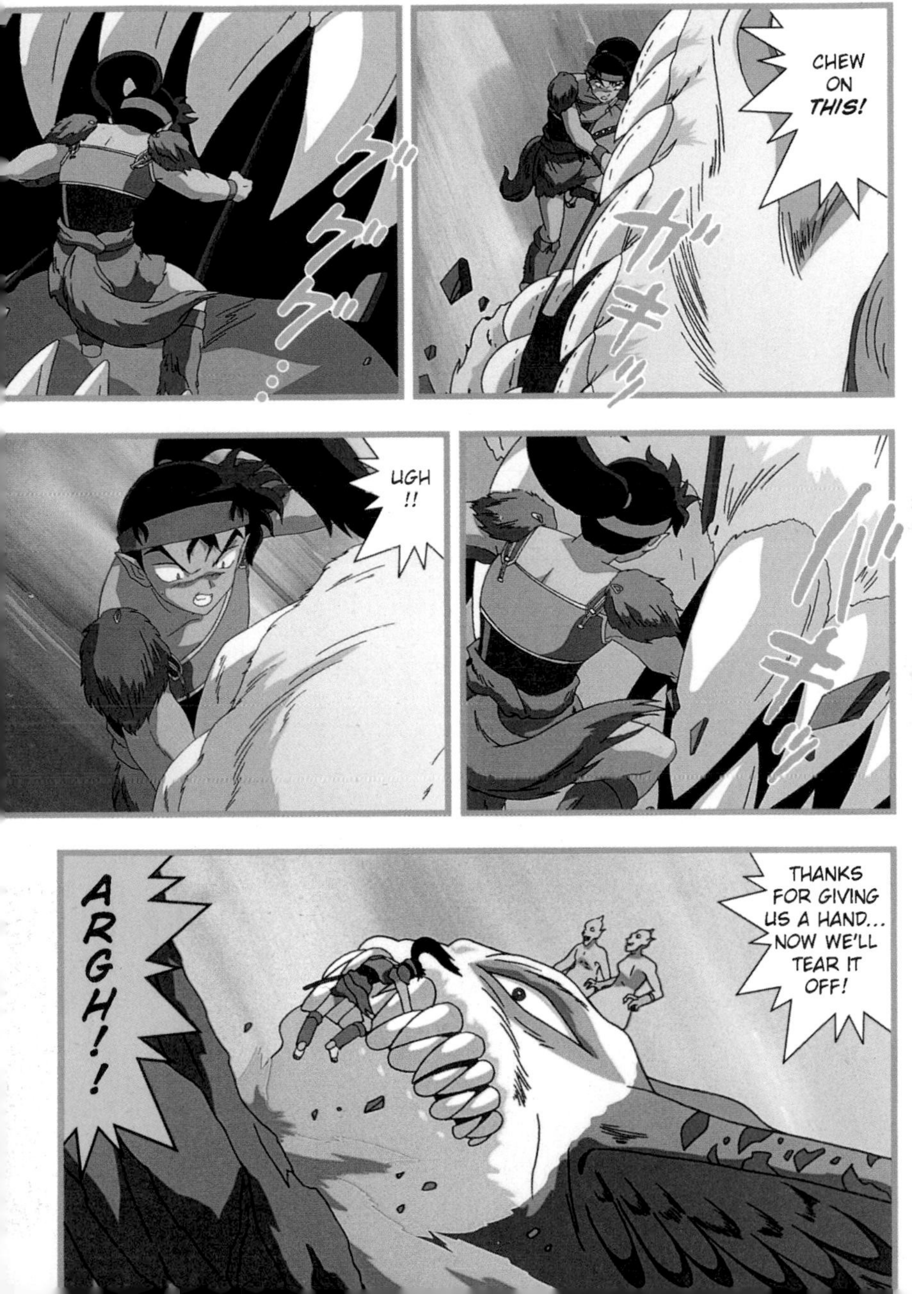
CHEW ON THIS!
UGH !!
THANKS FOR GIVING US A HAND... NOW WE'LL TEAR IT OFF!
ARGH!!

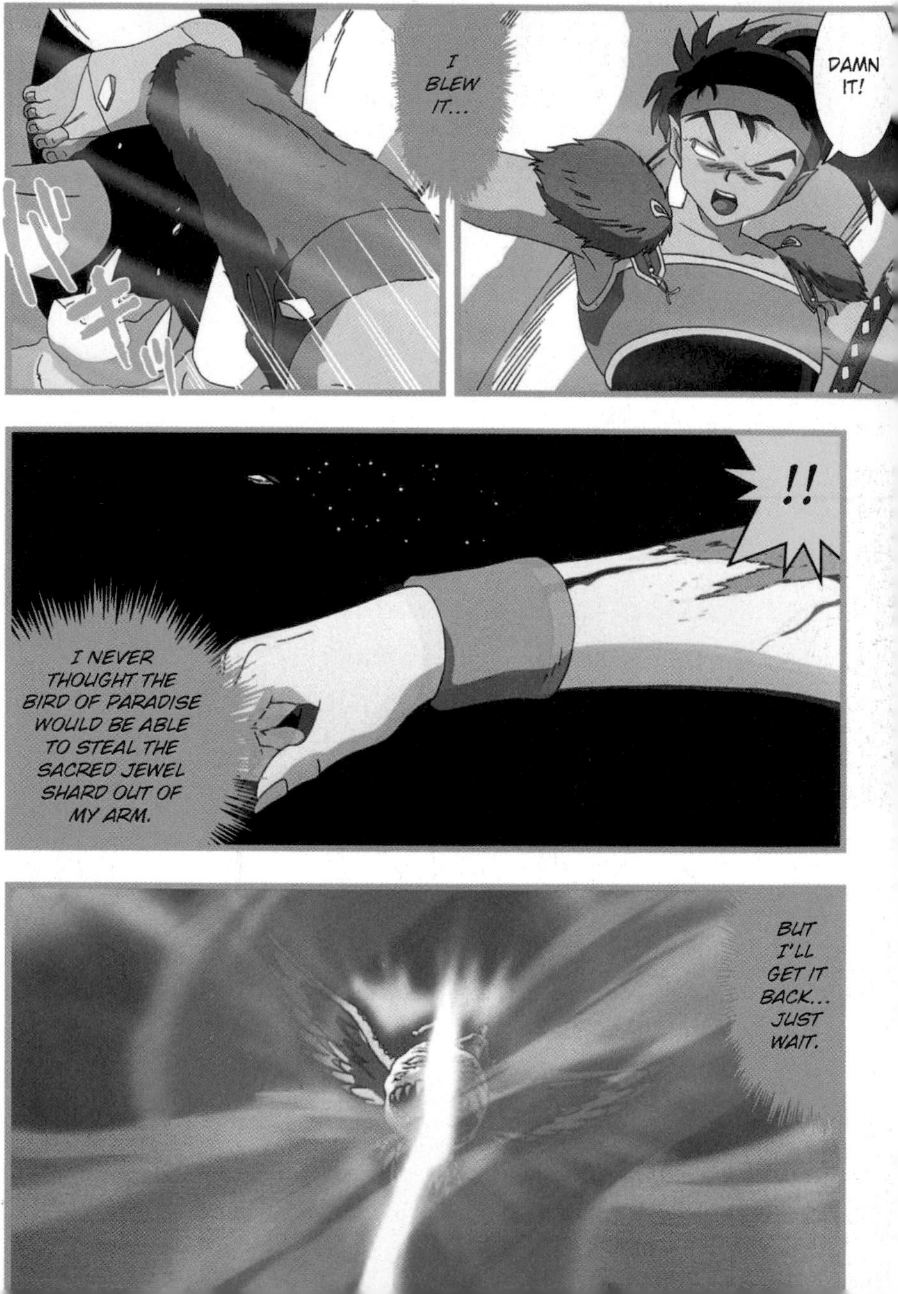
DAMN IT!
I BLEW IT...
!!
I NEVER THOUGHT THE BIRD OF PARADISE WOULD BE ABLE TO STEAL THE SACRED JEWEL SHARD OUT OF MY ARM.
BUT I'LL GET IT BACK... JUST WAIT.

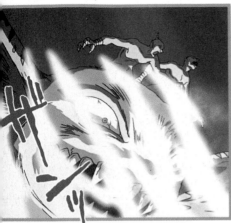

FIRST, I HAVE TO GET THAT DOG.

I CAN'T BELIEVE HE TOOK DOWN THAT BIRD WITH ONE SWEEP OF HIS SWORD.

THE JERK.

I WON'T BE SATISFIED UNTIL I WRING HIS NECK!

THIS WOUND...

...ISN'T HEALING AS QUICKLY AS I HOPED.

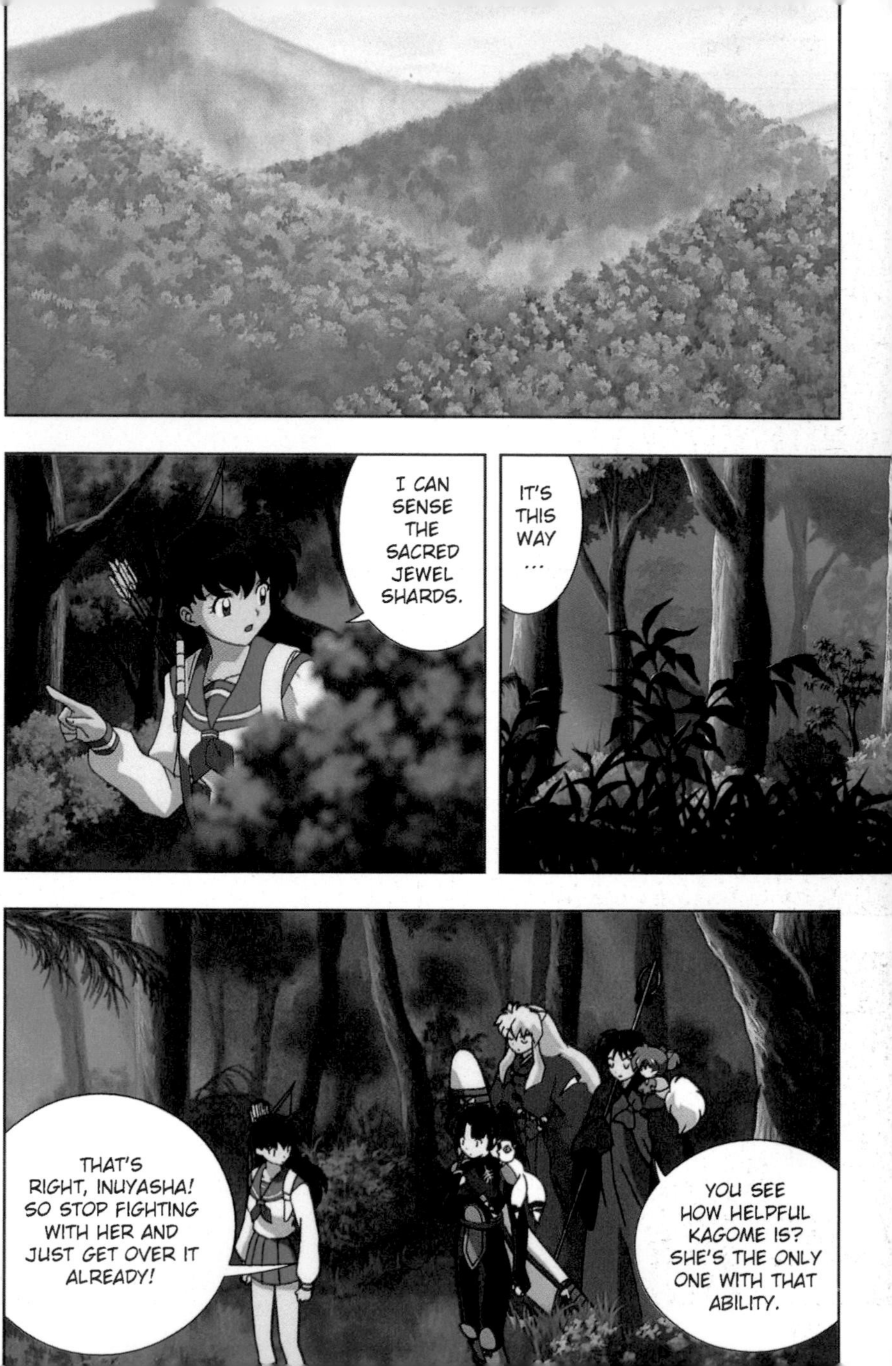
IT'S THIS WAY...
I CAN SENSE THE SACRED JEWEL SHARDS.
YOU SEE HOW HELPFUL KAGOME IS? SHE'S THE ONLY ONE WITH THAT ABILITY.
THAT'S RIGHT, INUYASHA! SO STOP FIGHTING WITH HER AND JUST GET OVER IT ALREADY!

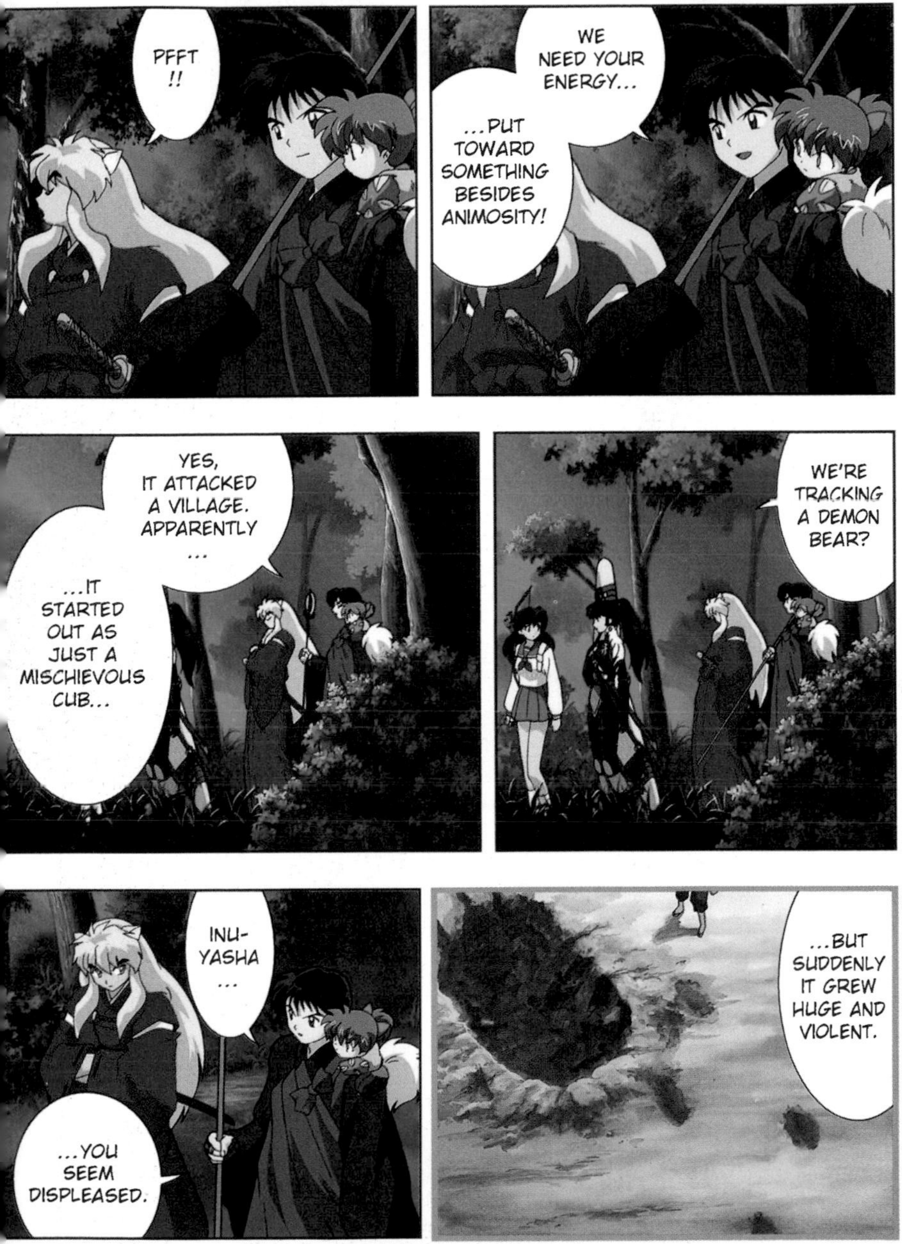
WE NEED YOUR ENERGY...
...PUT TOWARD SOMETHING BESIDES ANIMOSITY!
PFFT !!
WE'RE TRACKING A DEMON BEAR?
YES, IT ATTACKED A VILLAGE. APPARENTLY ...
...IT STARTED OUT AS JUST A MISCHIEVOUS CUB...
...BUT SUDDENLY IT GREW HUGE AND VIOLENT.
INU-YASHA ...
...YOU SEEM DISPLEASED.

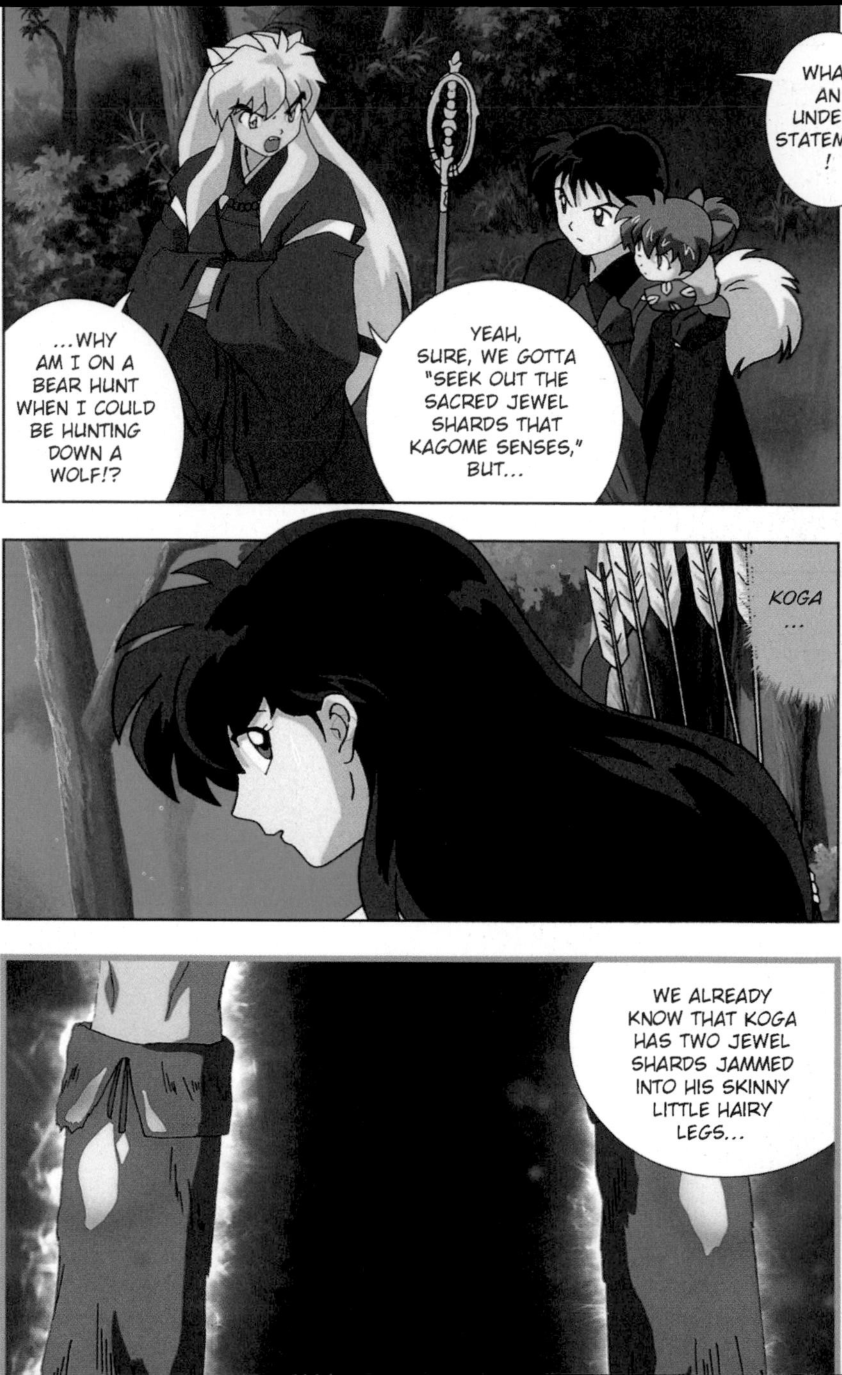
WHAT AN UNDER-STATEMENT!
YEAH, SURE, WE GOTTA "SEEK OUT THE SACRED JEWEL SHARDS THAT KAGOME SENSES," BUT...
...WHY AM I ON A BEAR HUNT WHEN I COULD BE HUNTING DOWN A WOLF!?
KOGA...
WE ALREADY KNOW THAT KOGA HAS TWO JEWEL SHARDS JAMMED INTO HIS SKINNY LITTLE HAIRY LEGS...

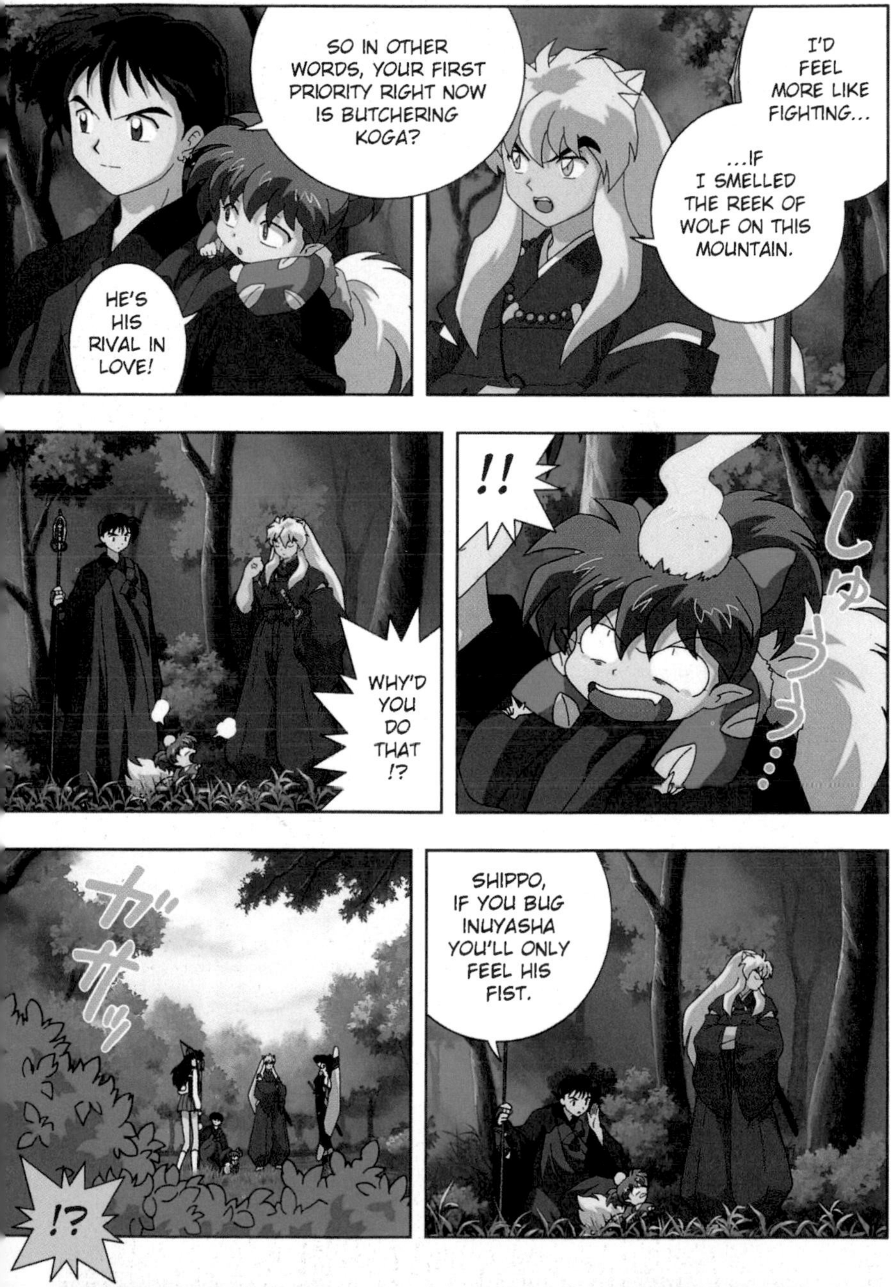

I'D FEEL MORE LIKE FIGHTING...
...IF I SMELLED THE REEK OF WOLF ON THIS MOUNTAIN.
SO IN OTHER WORDS, YOUR FIRST PRIORITY RIGHT NOW IS BUTCHERING KOGA?
HE'S HIS RIVAL IN LOVE!
!!
しゅうう
WHY'D YOU DO THAT !?
SHIPPO, IF YOU BUG INUYASHA YOU'LL ONLY FEEL HIS FIST.
ガサッ
!?

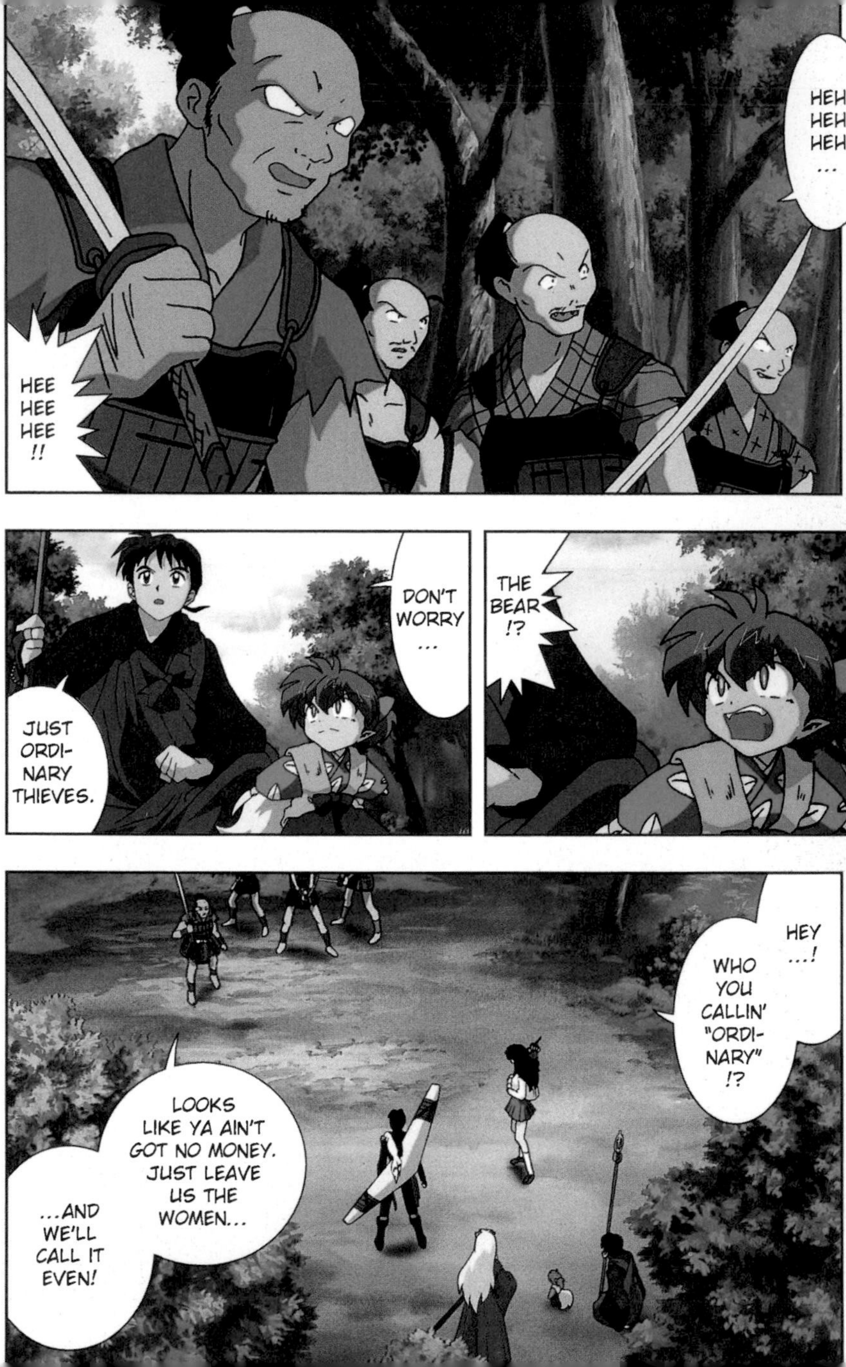
HEH HEH HEH ...
HEE HEE HEE !!
THE BEAR !?
DON'T WORRY ...
JUST ORDINARY THIEVES.
HEY ...!
WHO YOU CALLIN' "ORDINARY" !?
LOOKS LIKE YA AIN'T GOT NO MONEY. JUST LEAVE US THE WOMEN...
...AND WE'LL CALL IT EVEN!

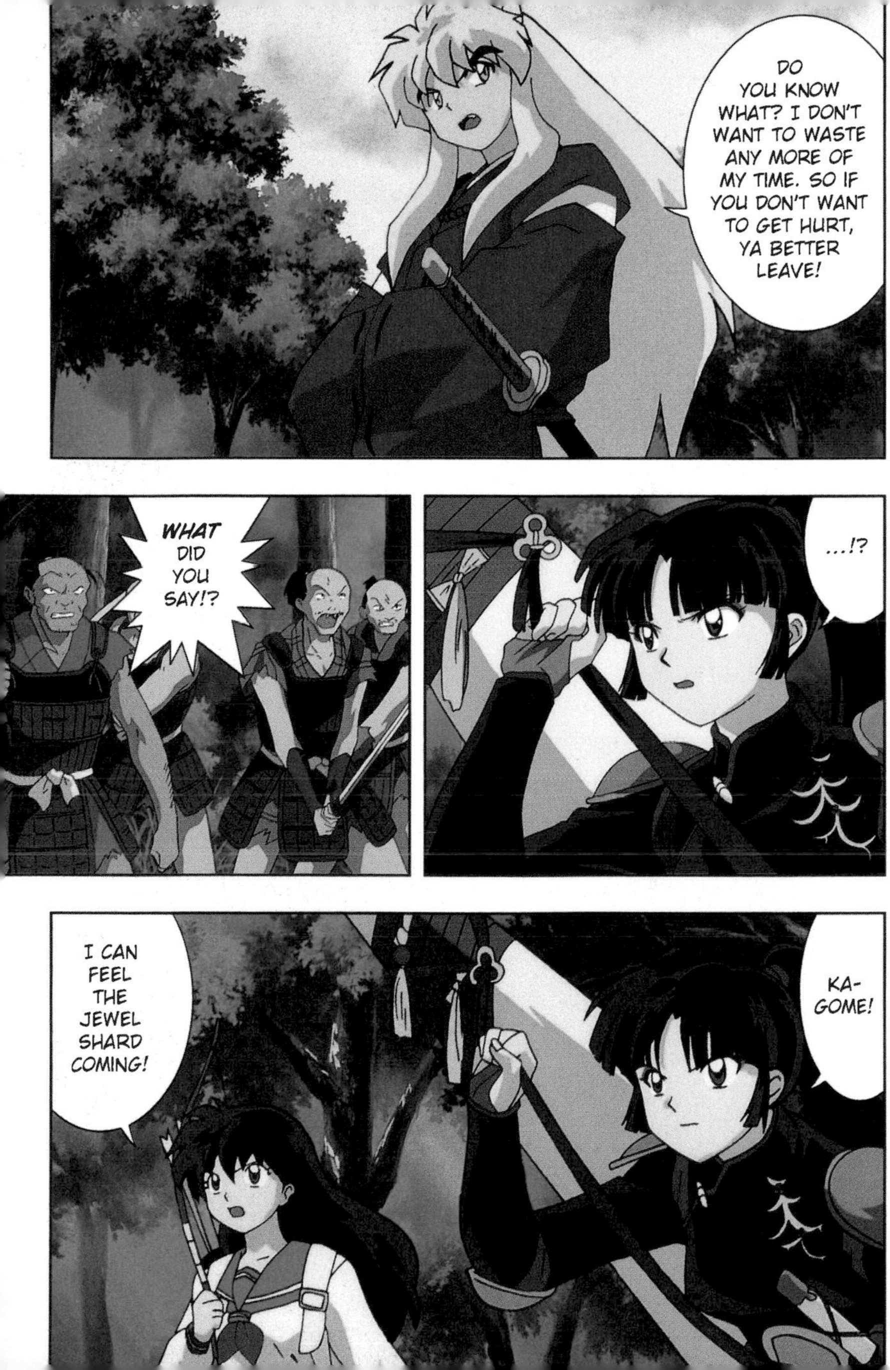
DO YOU KNOW WHAT? I DON'T WANT TO WASTE ANY MORE OF MY TIME. SO IF YOU DON'T WANT TO GET HURT, YA BETTER LEAVE!
...!?
WHAT DID YOU SAY!?
KA-GOME!
I CAN FEEL THE JEWEL SHARD COMING!

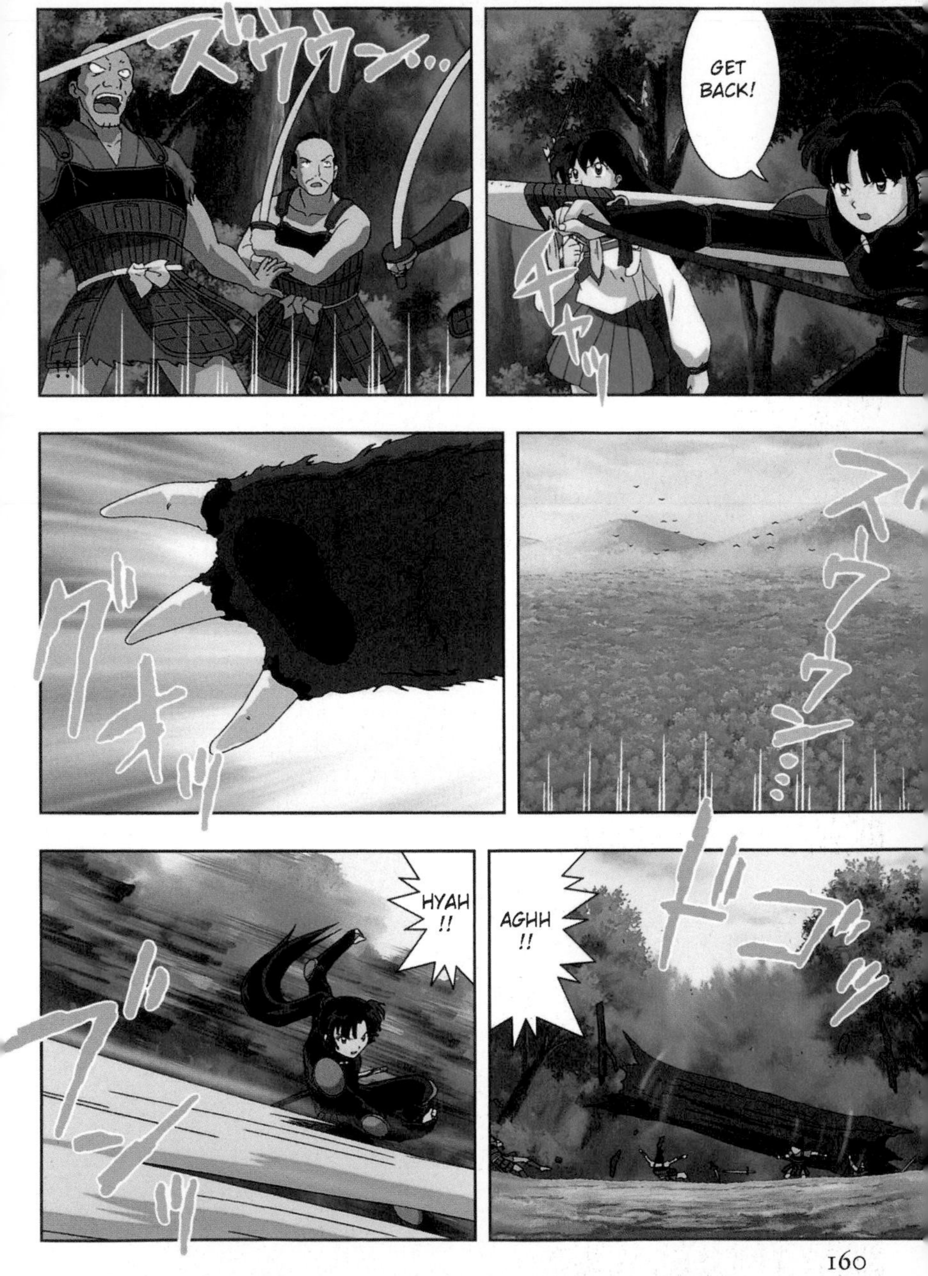
GET BACK!
AGHH !!
HYAH !!

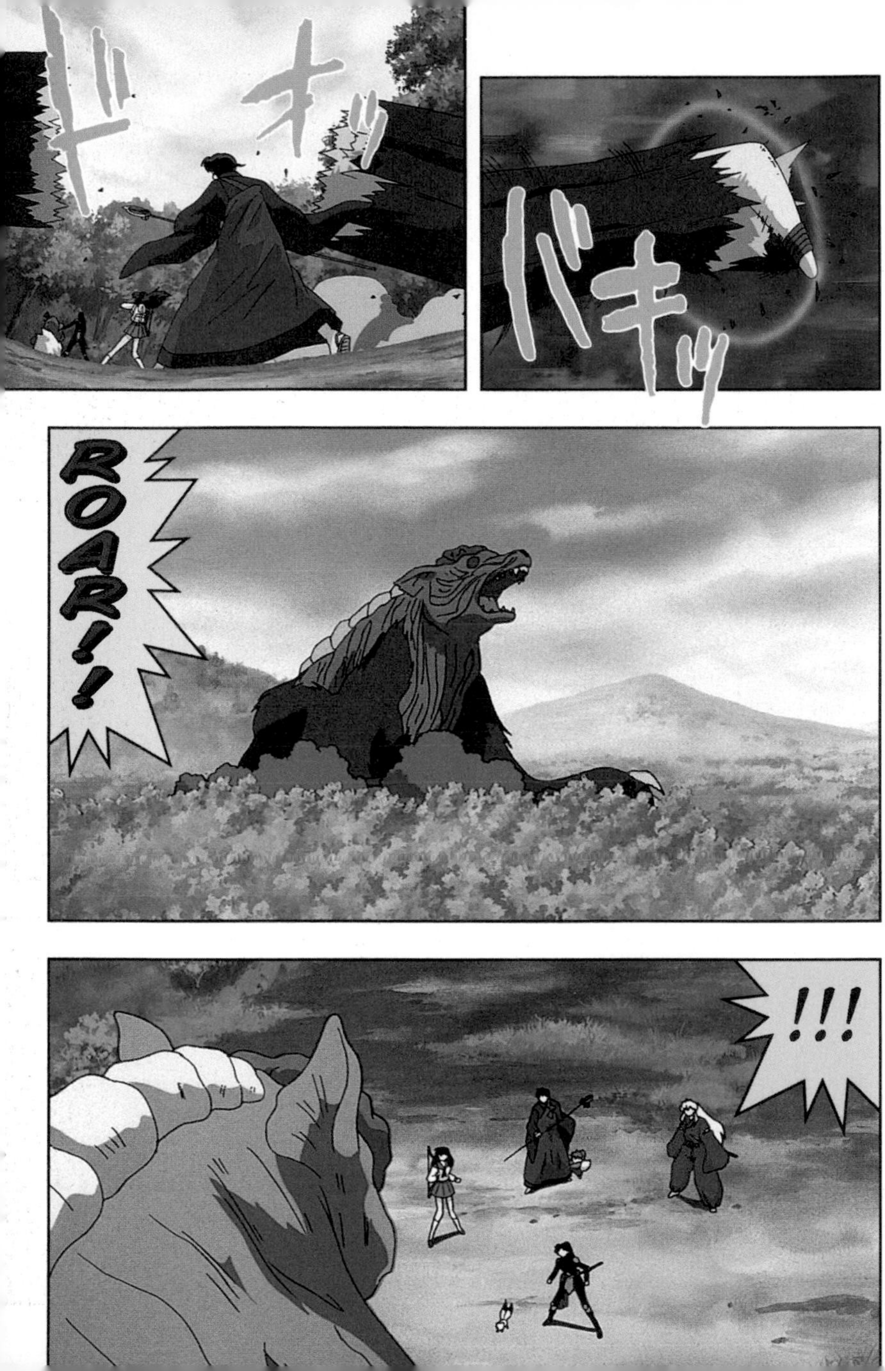
バキッ
ドオッ
ROAR!!
!!!

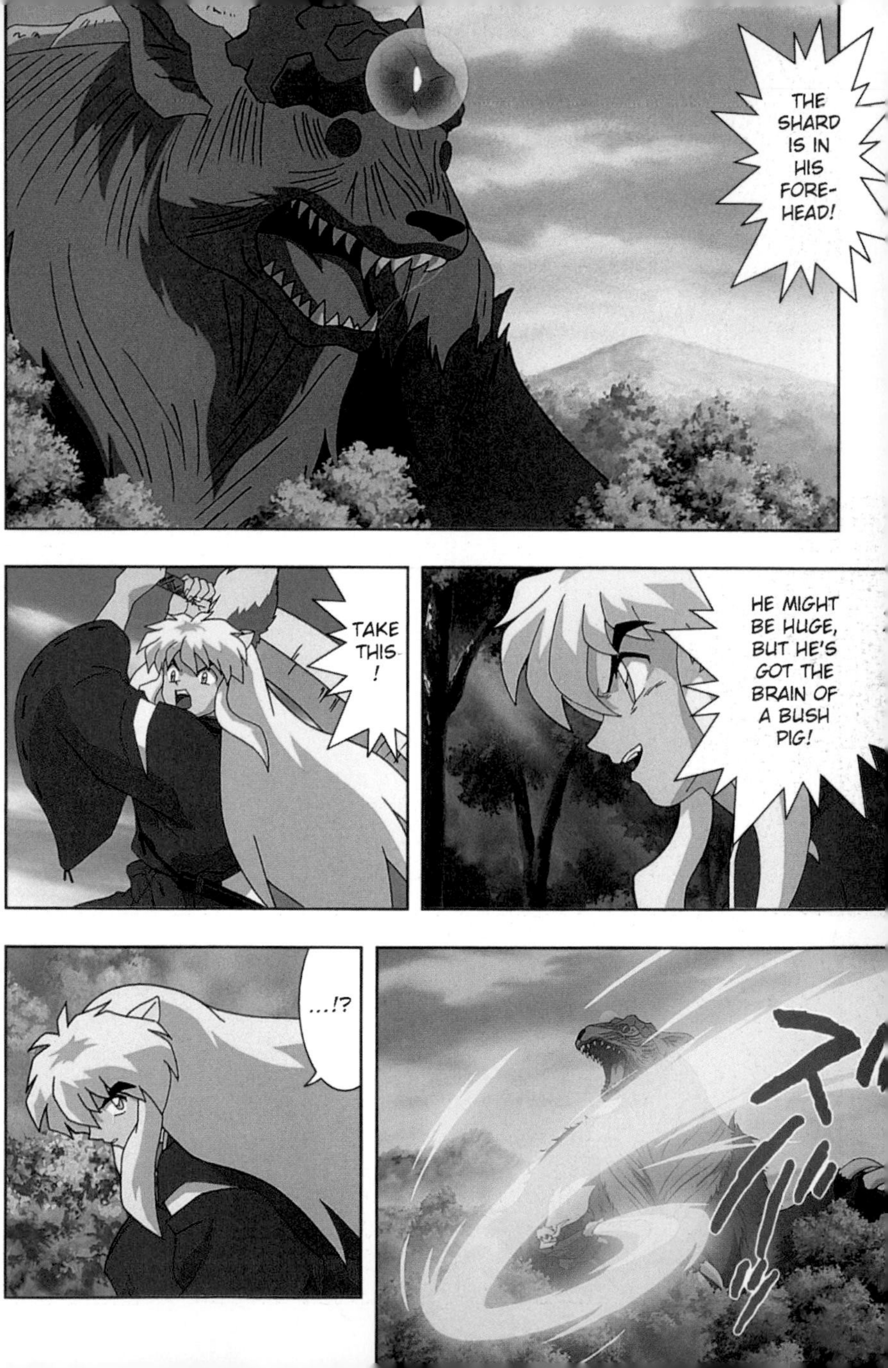
THE SHARD IS IN HIS FORE-HEAD!
HE MIGHT BE HUGE, BUT HE'S GOT THE BRAIN OF A BUSH PIG!
TAKE THIS-!
...!?

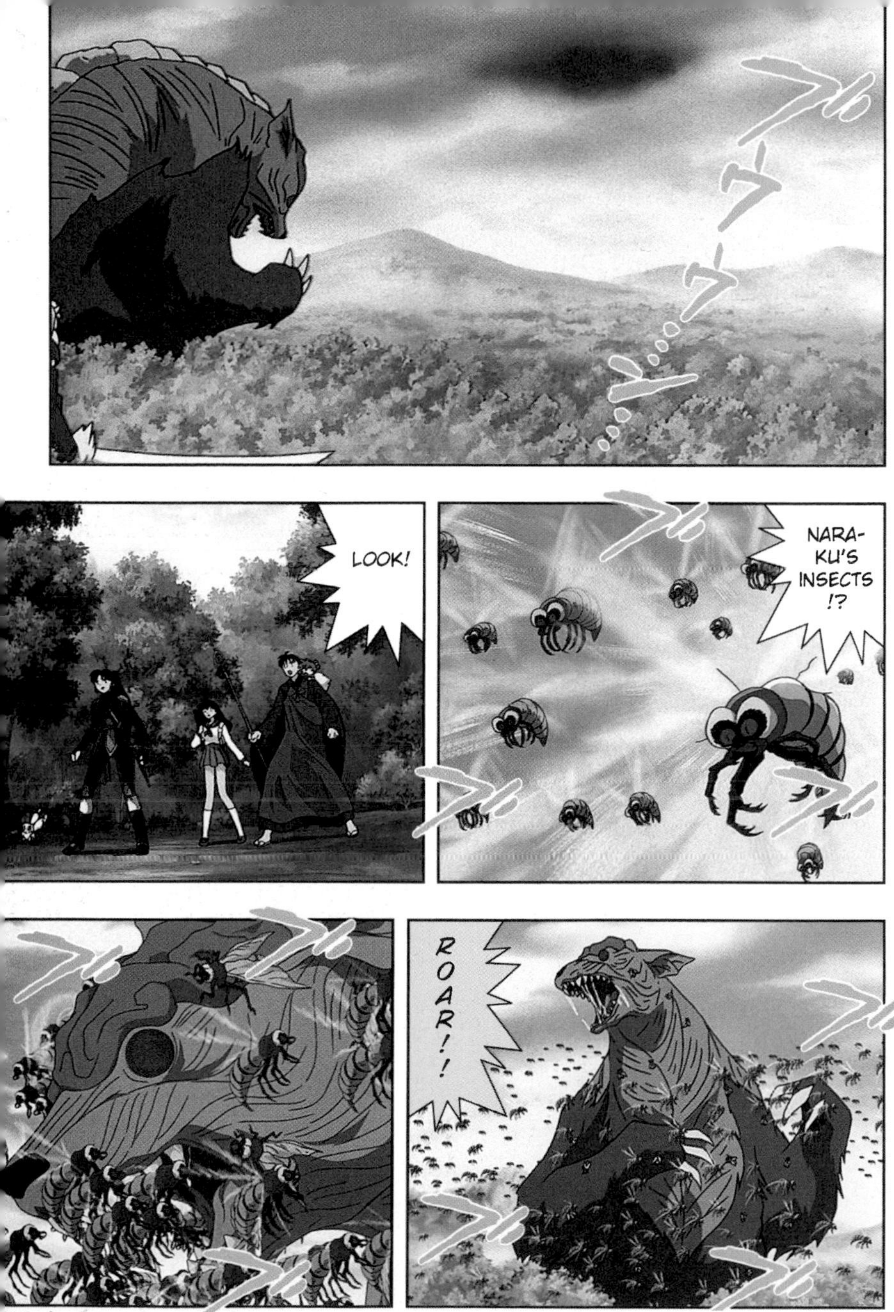
NARA-KU'S INSECTS !?
LOOK!
ROAR!!

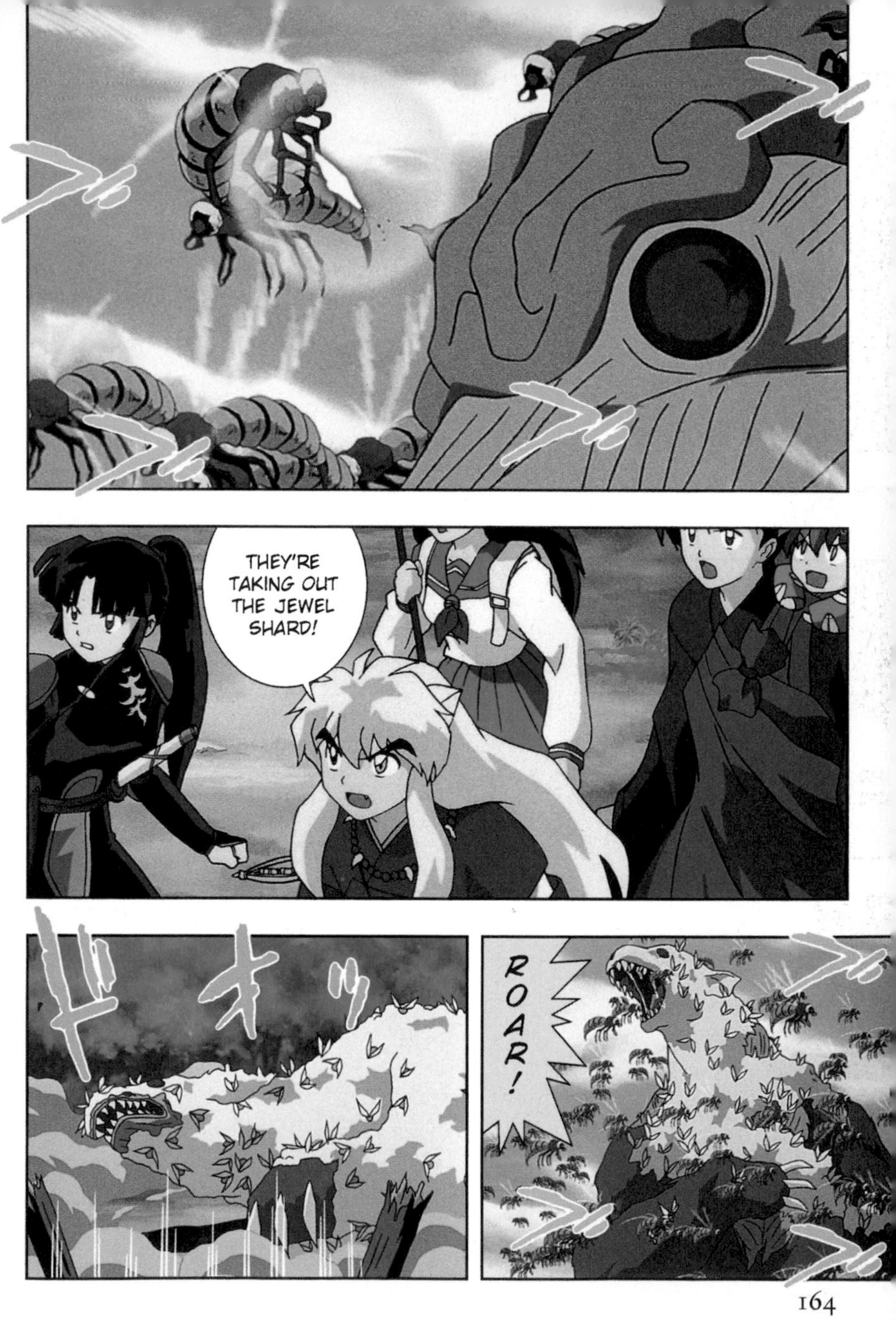
THEY'RE TAKING OUT THE JEWEL SHARD!
ROAR!

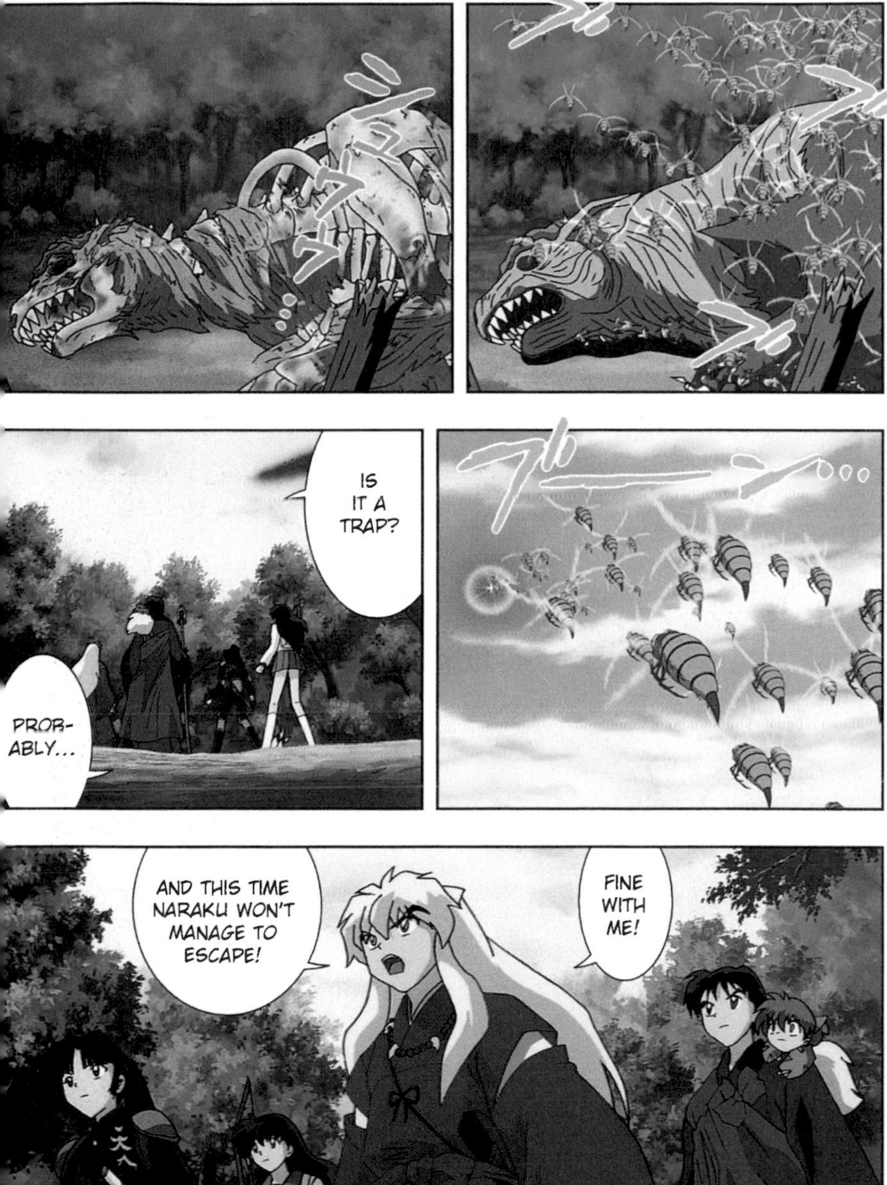
IS IT A TRAP?
PROB-ABLY...
FINE WITH ME!
AND THIS TIME NARAKU WON'T MANAGE TO ESCAPE!

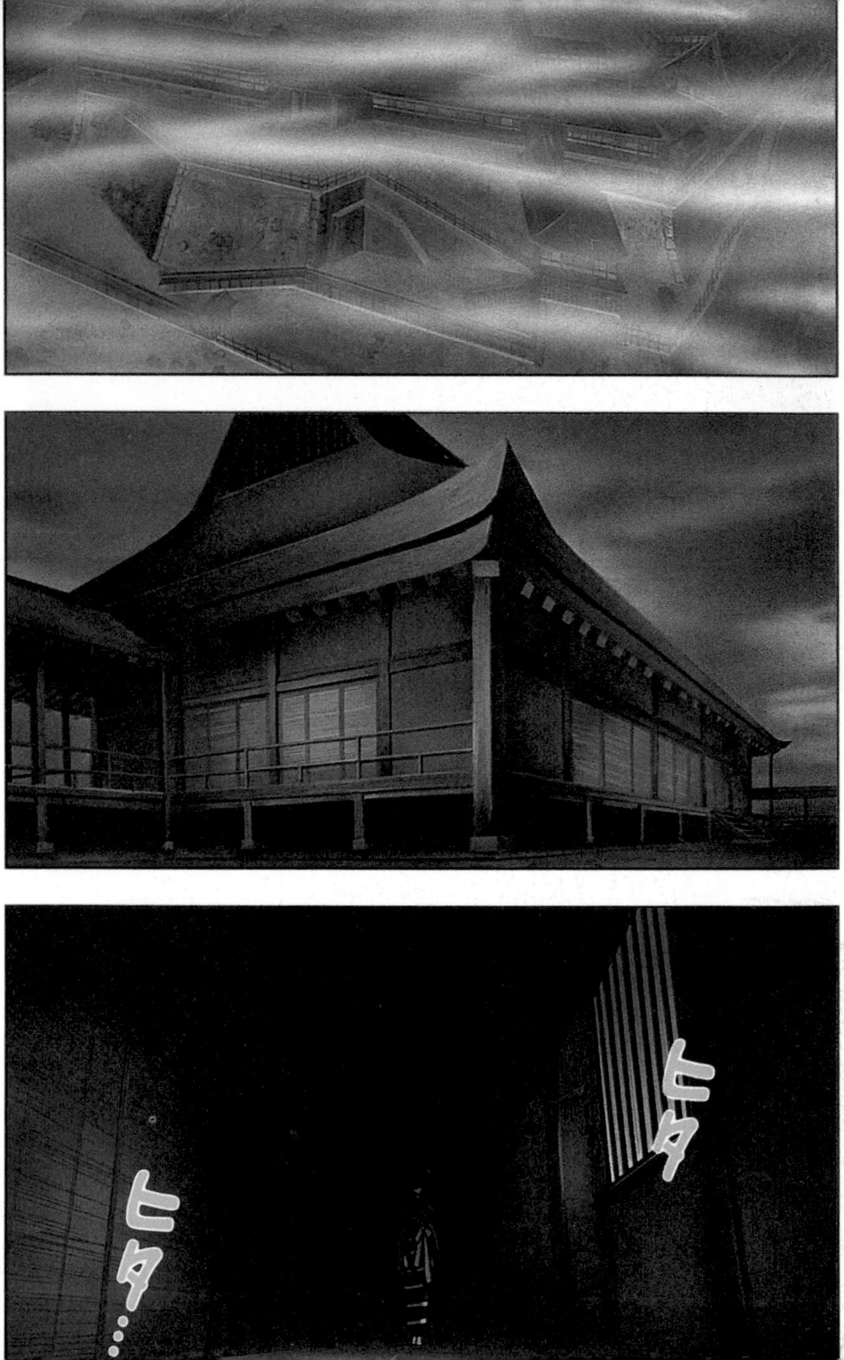
ヒタ
ヒタ…

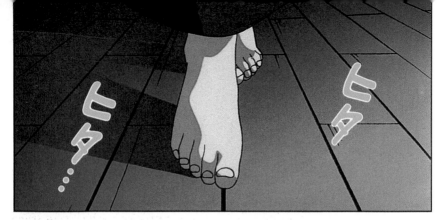

WELL, DEAR ...

YOU'VE DECIDED TO WATCH THIS FROM A DISTANCE, AND LET *ME* DO THE DIRTY WORK?

WELL, THAT MAKES THINGS EASIER IN THE LONG RUN.

THE SACRED JEWEL SHARDS...

...MAKE DEMONS EVEN STRONGER, DON'T THEY?

WHAT AN UTTERLY ENTICING OPIATE.

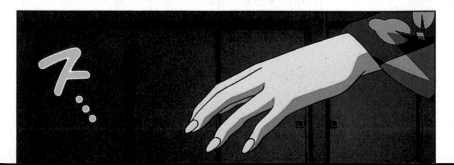

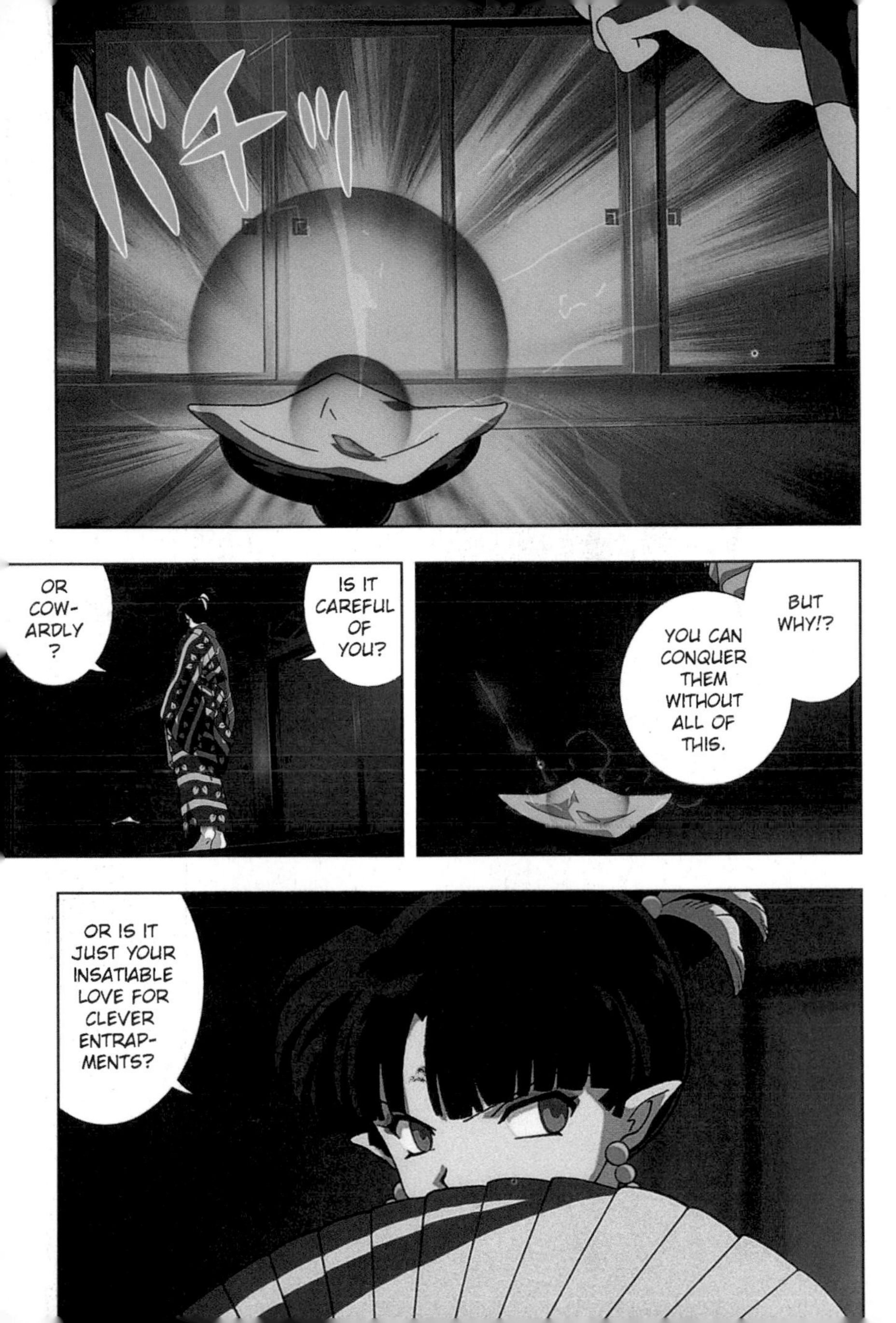
バチッ
BUT WHY!?
YOU CAN CONQUER THEM WITHOUT ALL OF THIS.
IS IT CAREFUL OF YOU?
OR COWARDLY?
OR IS IT JUST YOUR INSATIABLE LOVE FOR CLEVER ENTRAPMENTS?

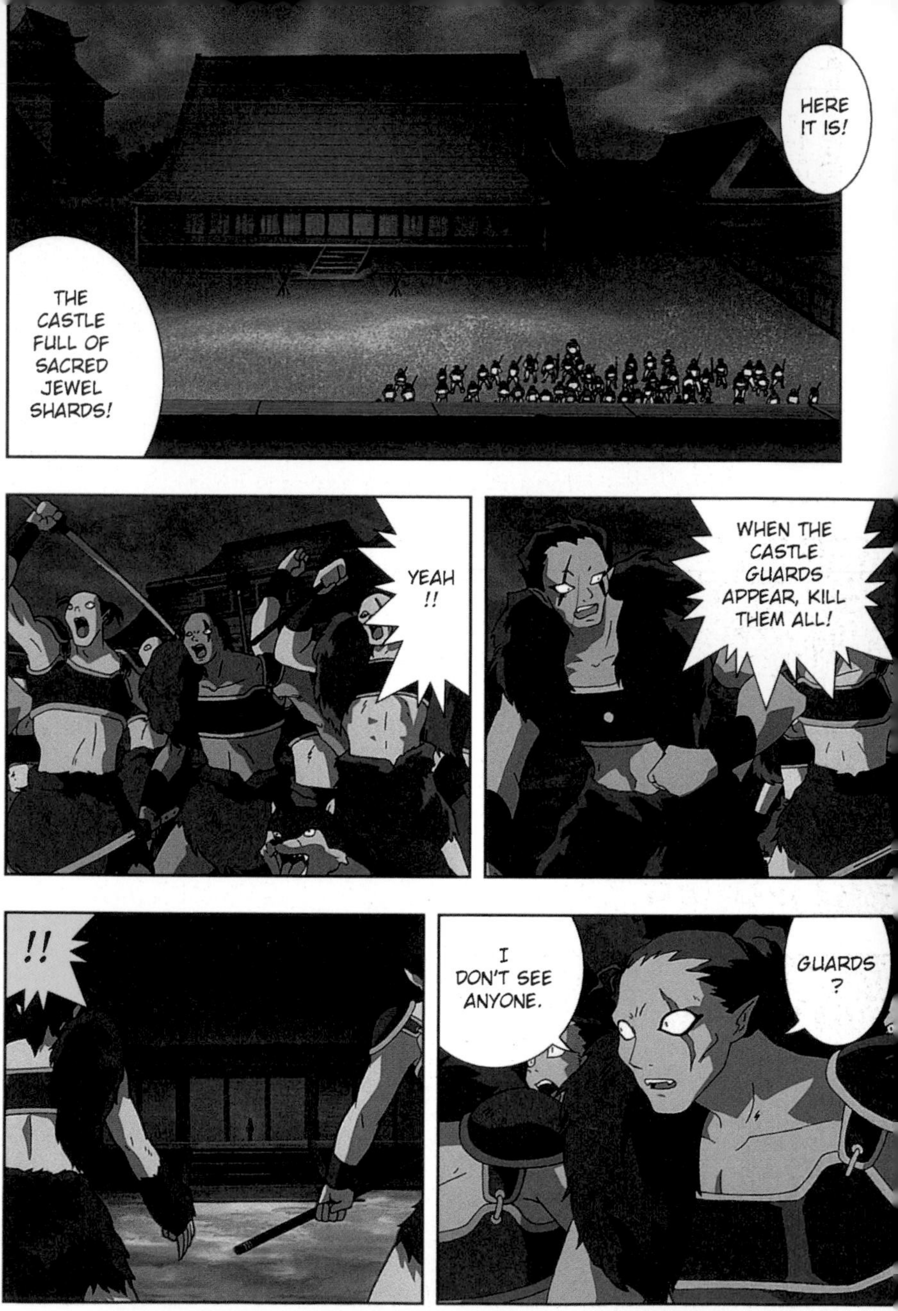
HERE IT IS!
THE CASTLE FULL OF SACRED JEWEL SHARDS!
WHEN THE CASTLE GUARDS APPEAR, KILL THEM ALL!
YEAH !!
GUARDS ?
I DON'T SEE ANYONE.
!!

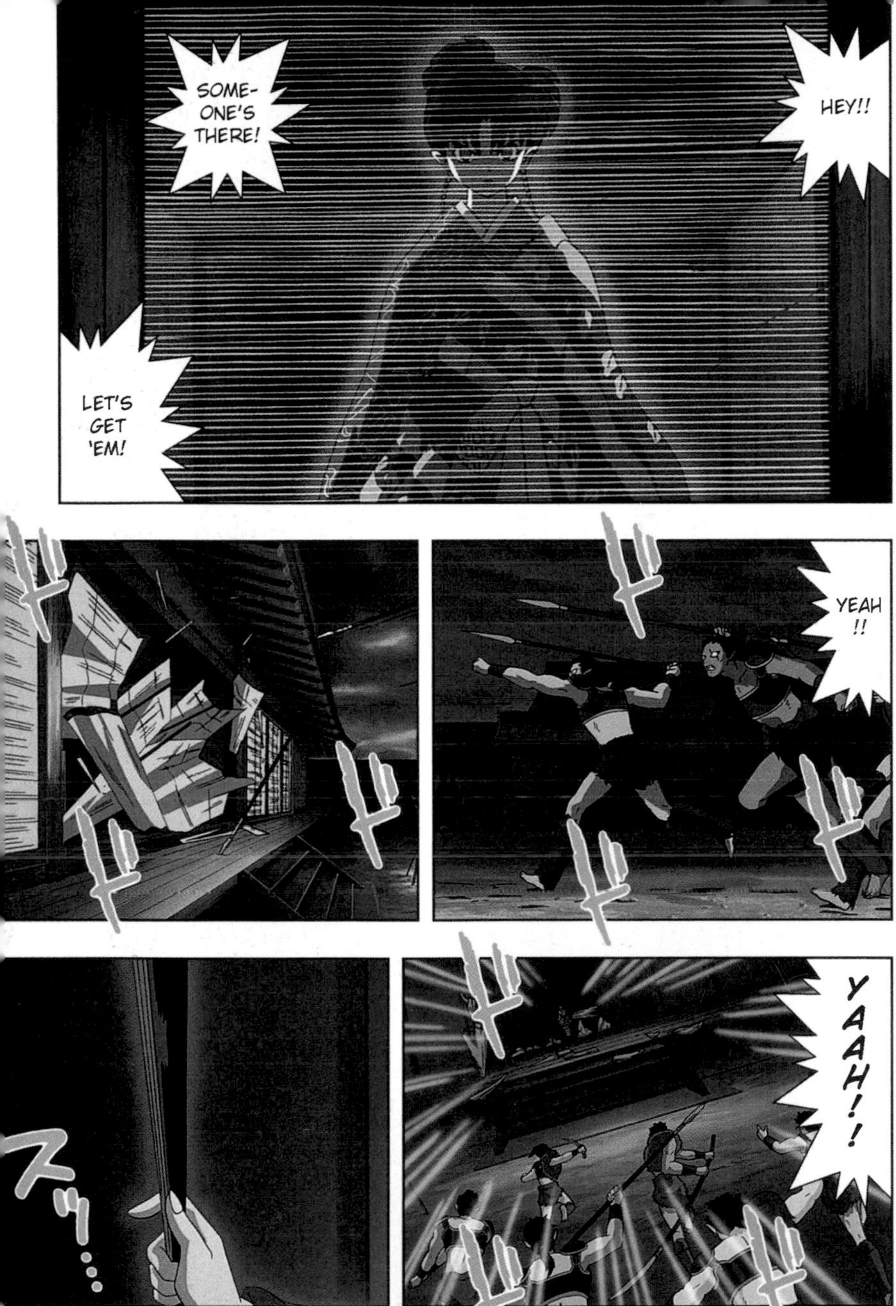
HEY!!
SOME-ONE'S THERE!
LET'S GET 'EM!
YEAH !!
YAAH!!
スッ…

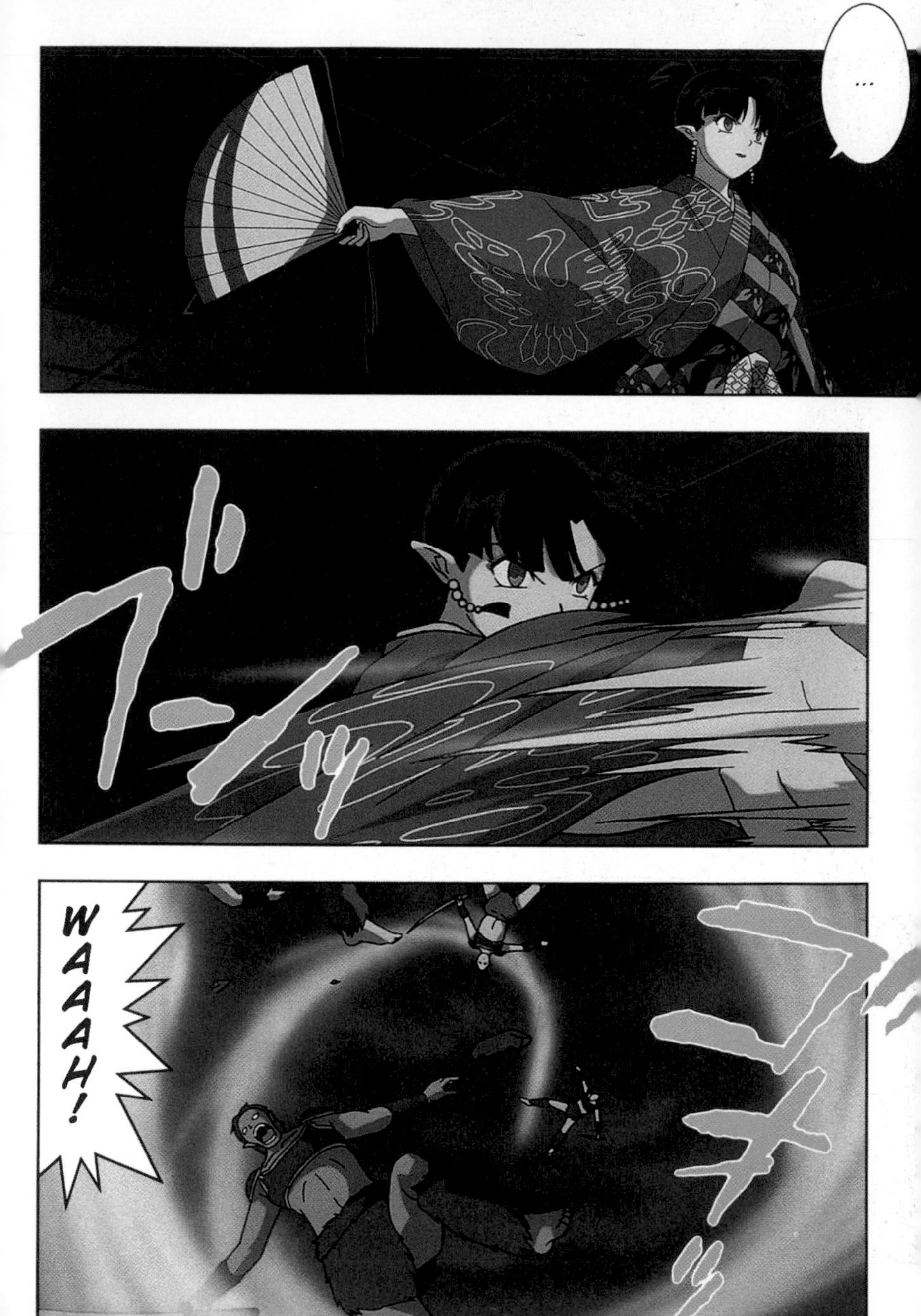
...
WAAAAH!

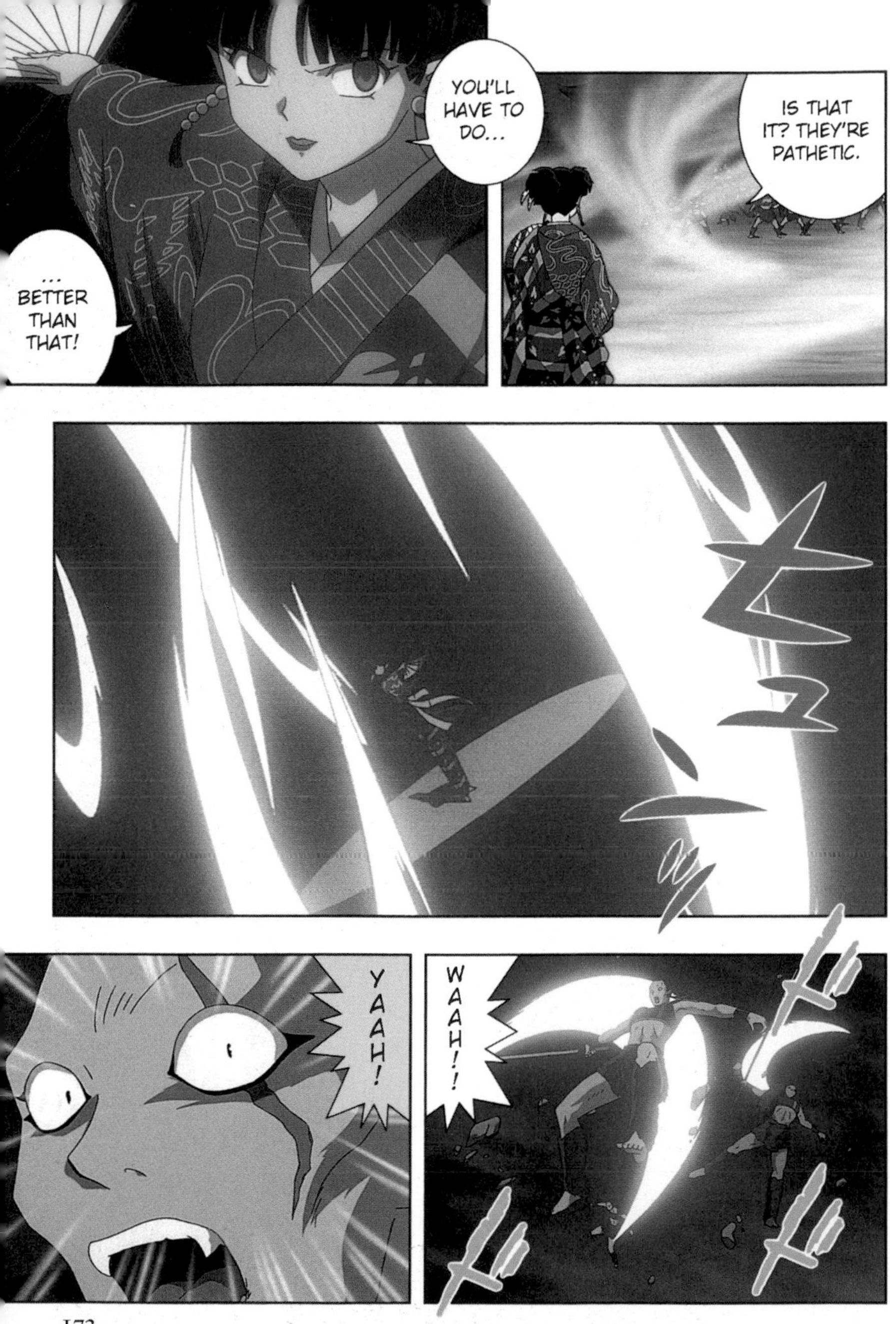
IS THAT IT? THEY'RE PATHETIC.
YOU'LL HAVE TO DO...
...BETTER THAN THAT!
WAAAH!!
YAAAH!

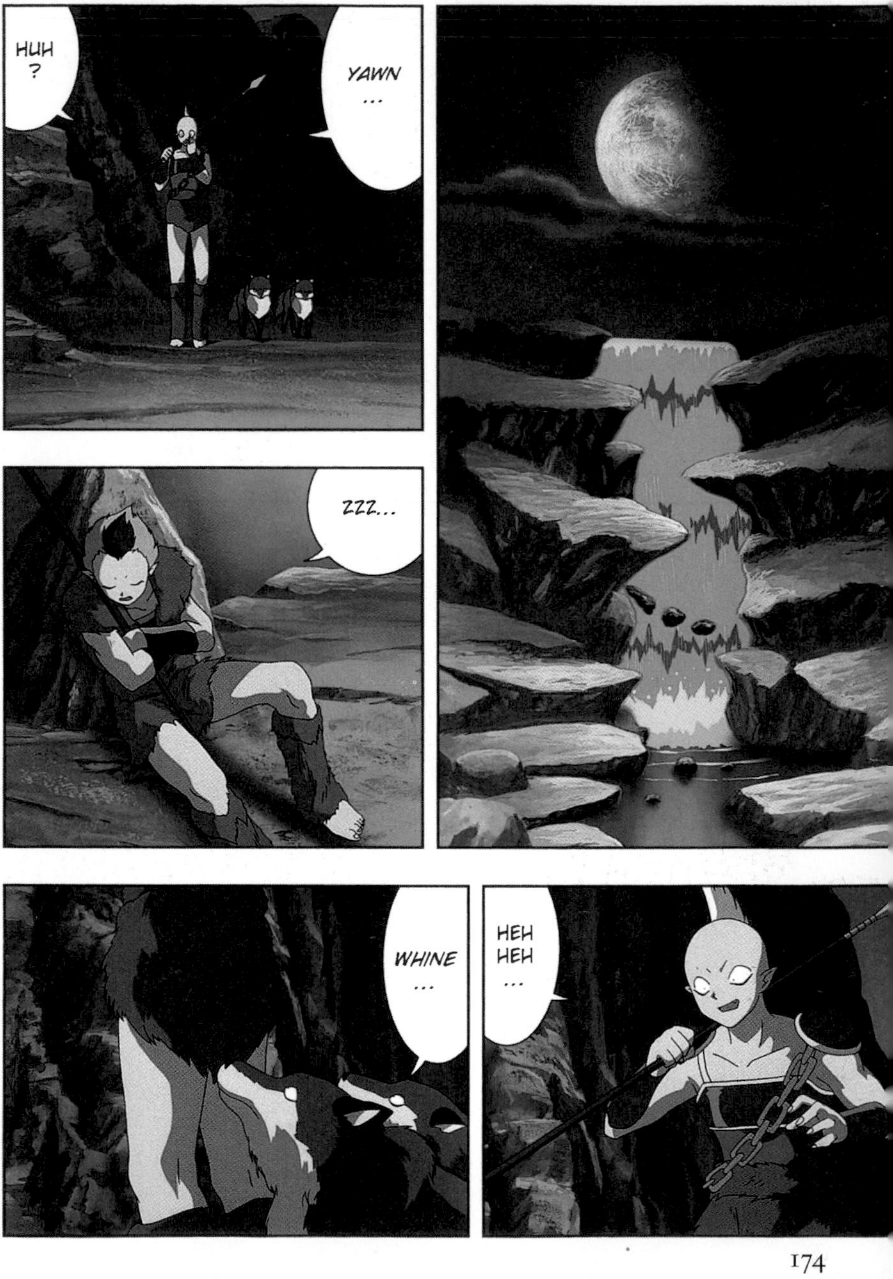
YAWN ...
HUH ?
ZZZ...
HEH HEH ...
WHINE ...

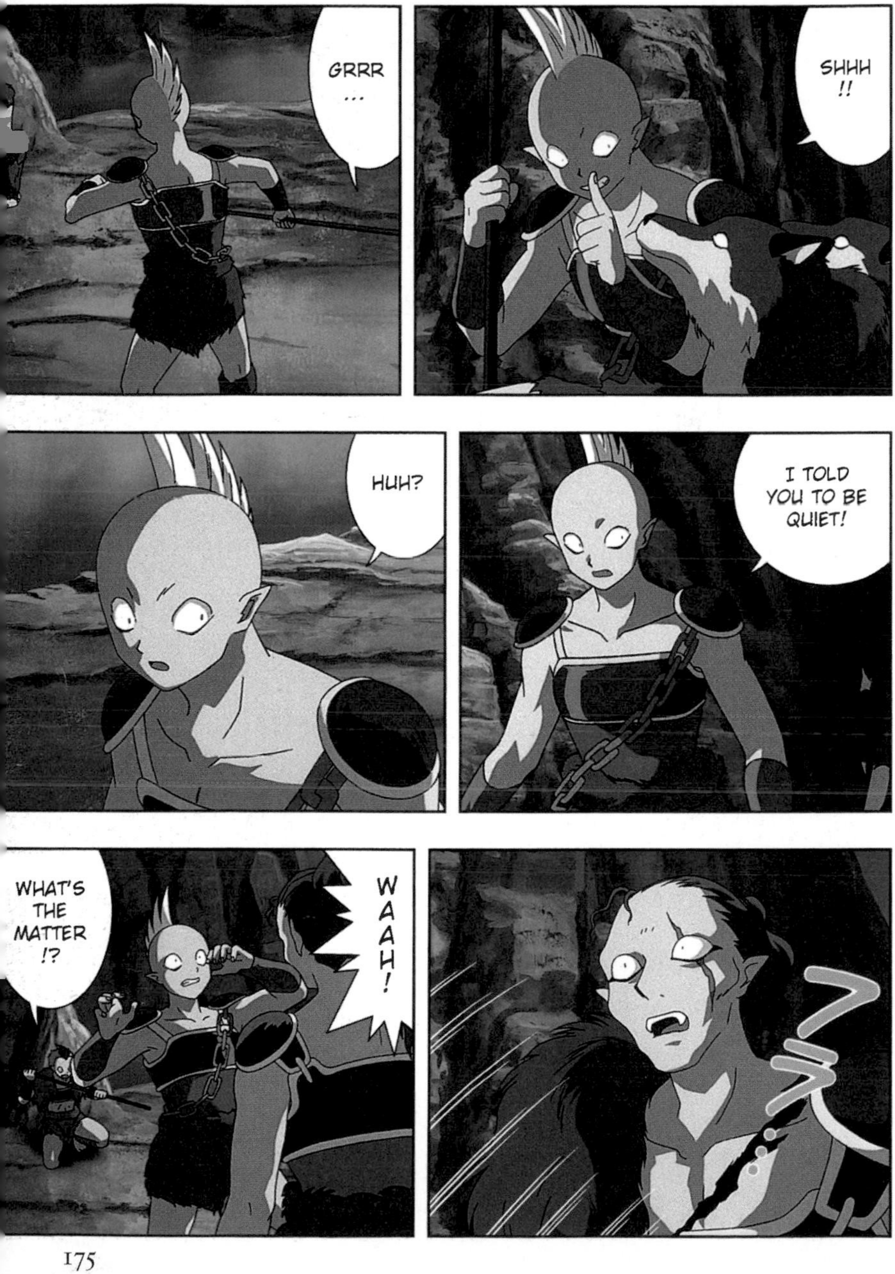
SHHH !!
GRRR ...
I TOLD YOU TO BE QUIET!
HUH?
WAAAH!
WHAT'S THE MATTER !?

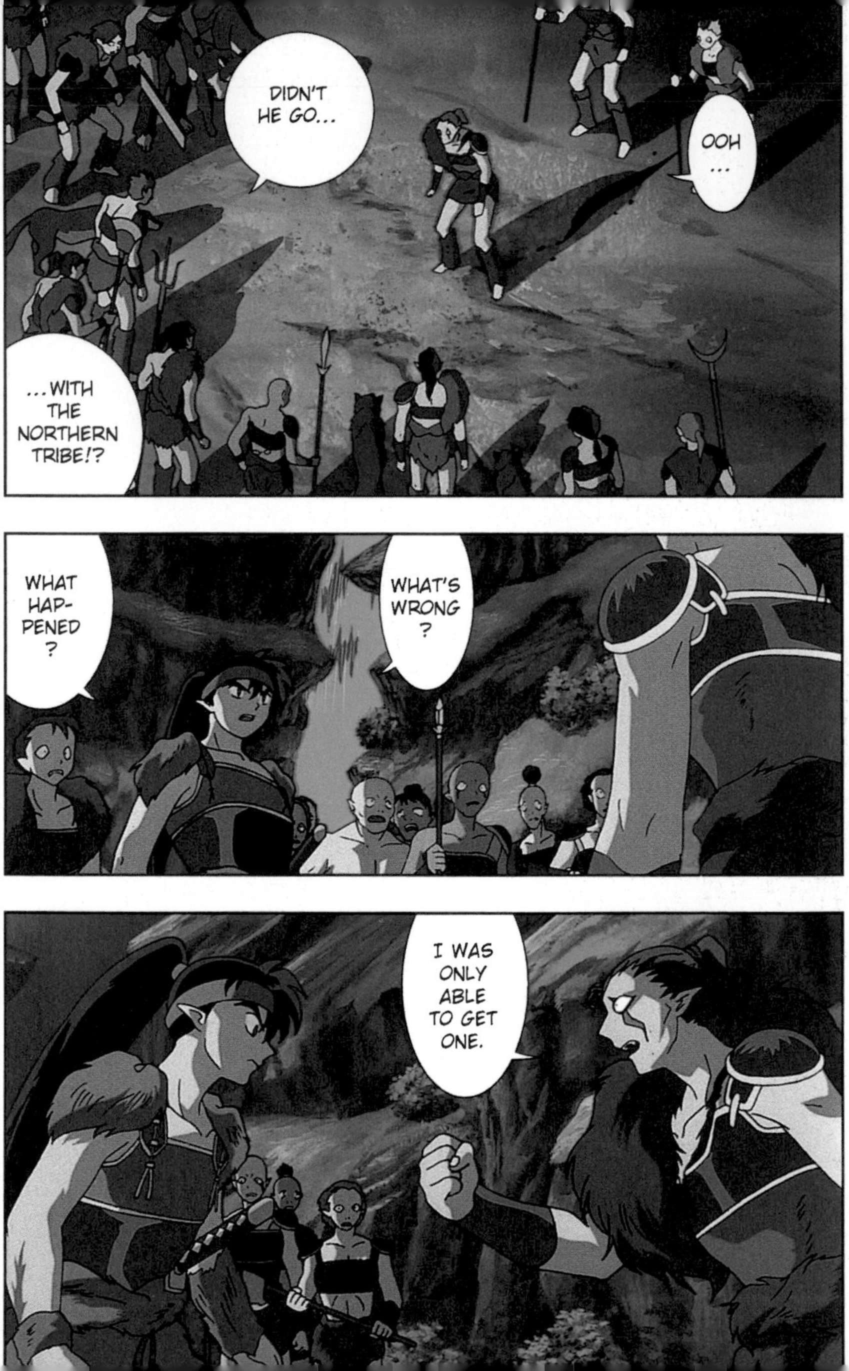
OOH...
DIDN'T HE GO...
...WITH THE NORTHERN TRIBE!?
WHAT'S WRONG?
WHAT HAPPENED?
I WAS ONLY ABLE TO GET ONE.

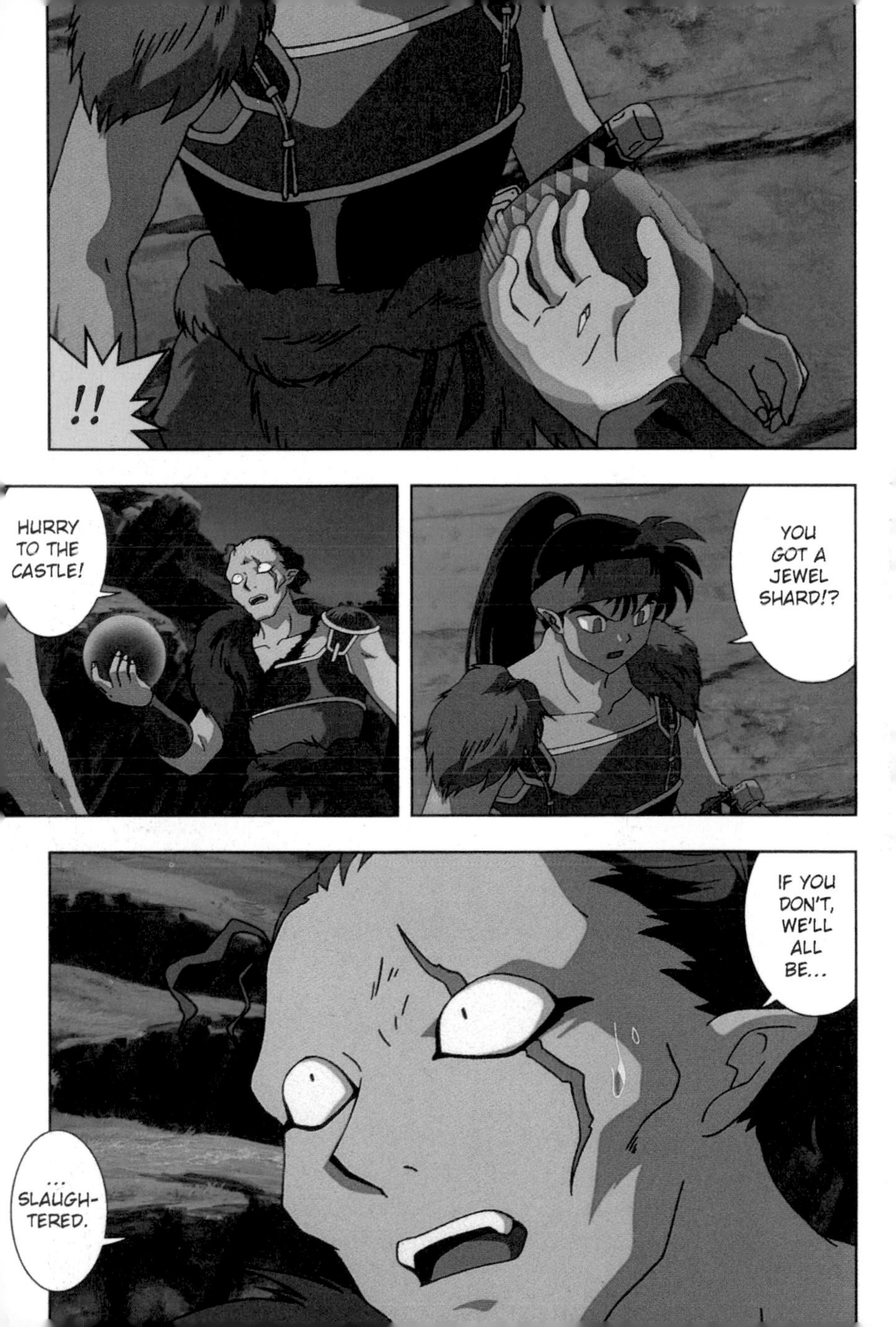
!!
YOU GOT A JEWEL SHARD!?
HURRY TO THE CASTLE!
IF YOU DON'T, WE'LL ALL BE...
...SLAUGHTERED.

たたたた…
たッ
たッ
ザッ
A JEWEL SHARD!

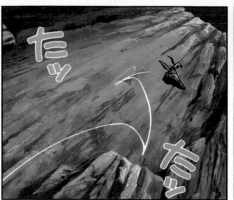

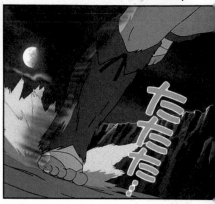

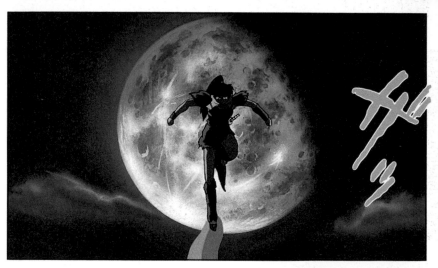

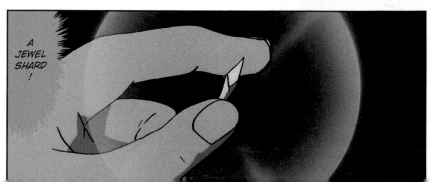

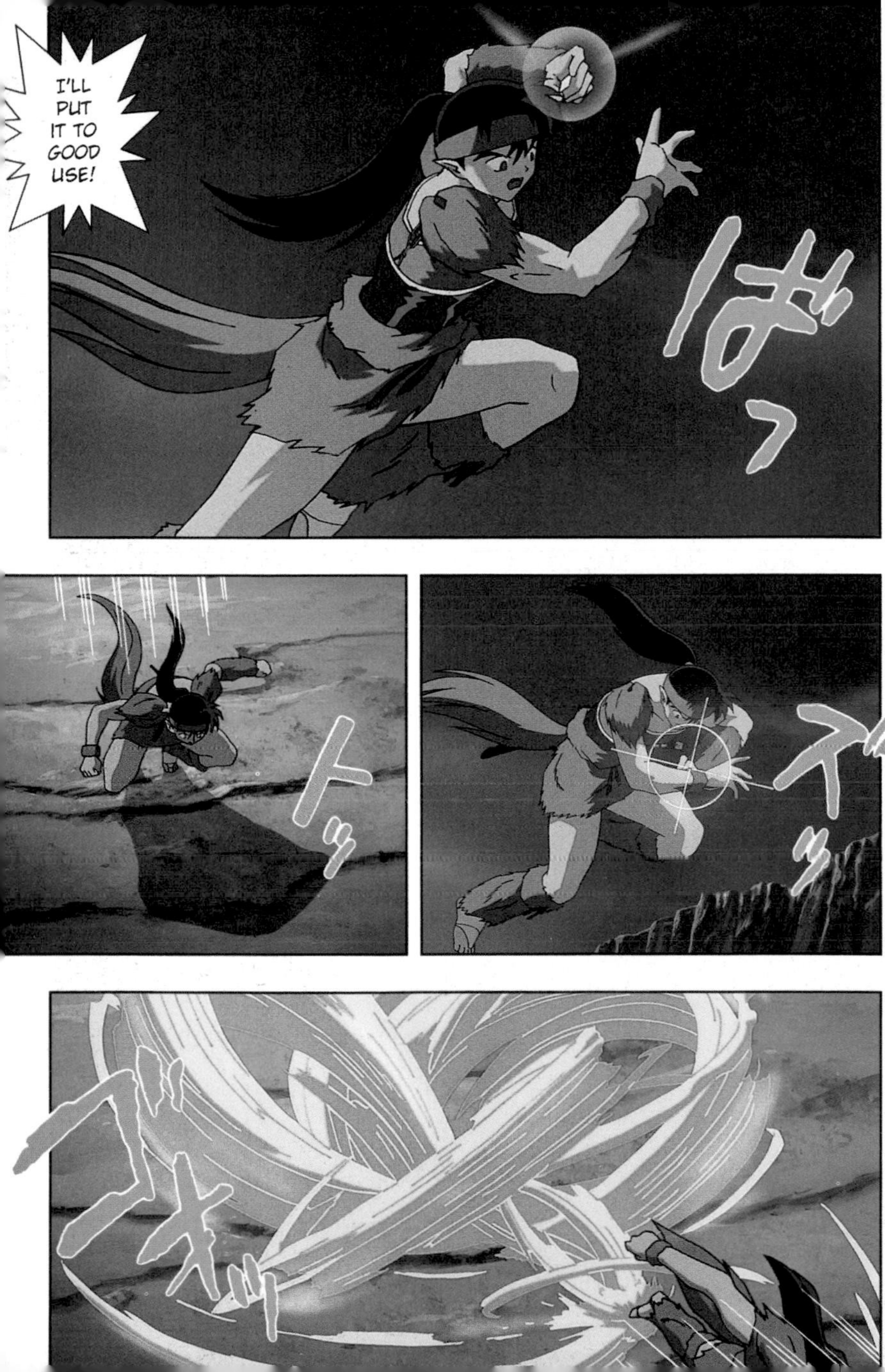
I'LL PUT IT TO GOOD USE!
トッ
ゴオッ

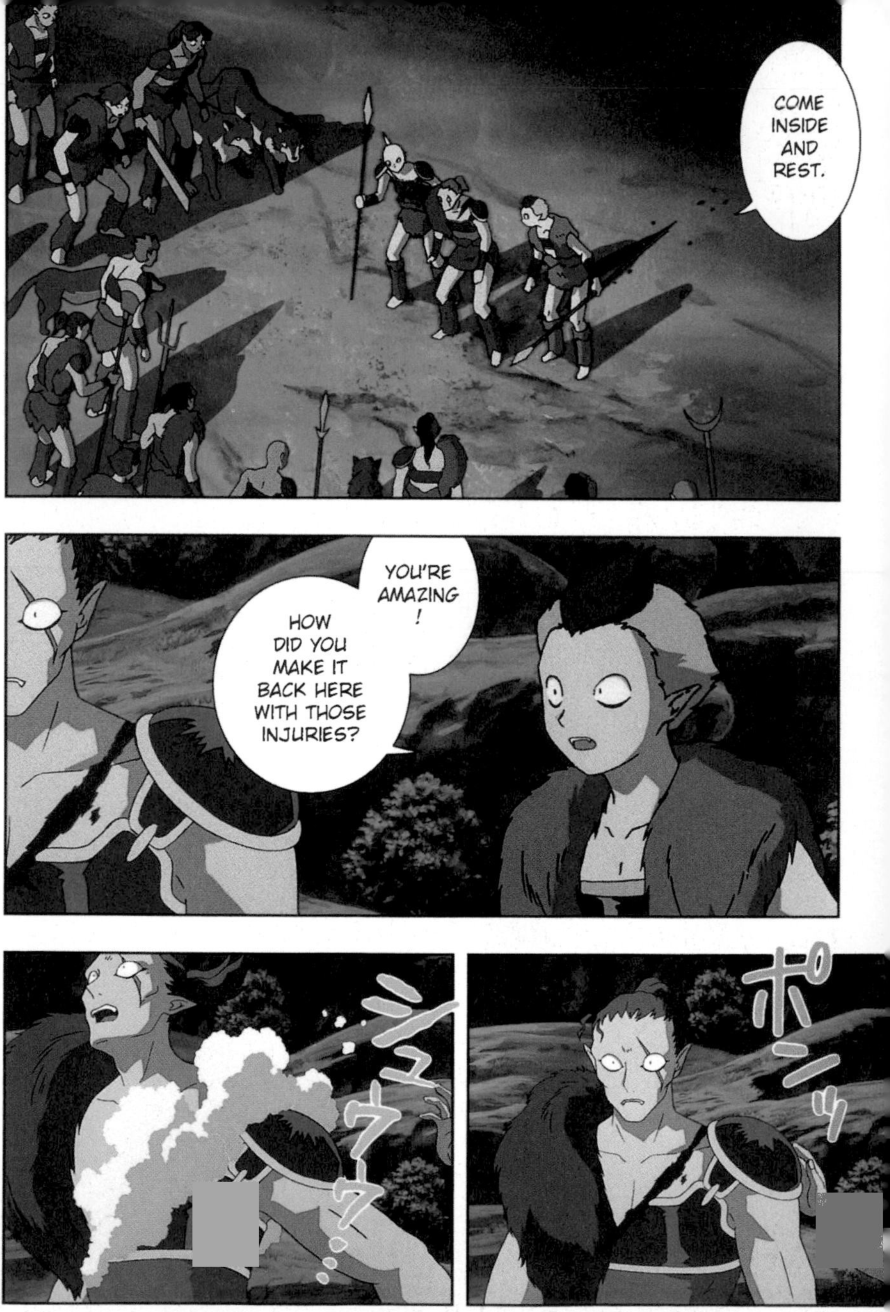
COME INSIDE AND REST.
YOU'RE AMAZING!
HOW DID YOU MAKE IT BACK HERE WITH THOSE INJURIES?
ポンッ
シュウウウ…

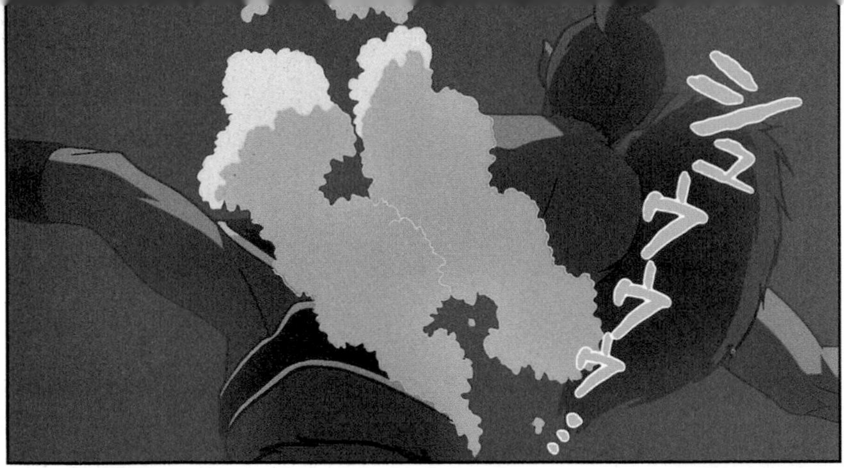

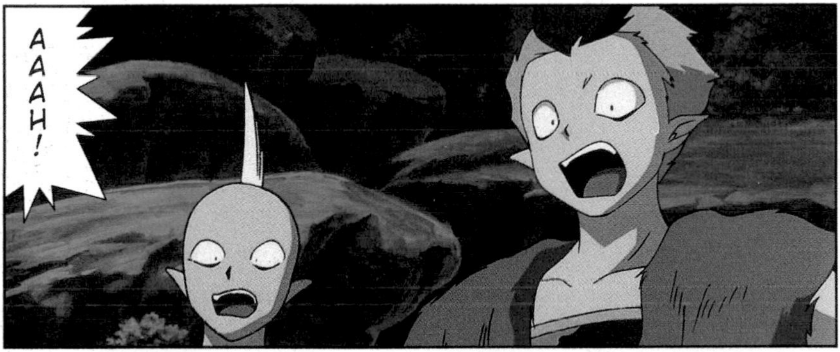
AAAAH!

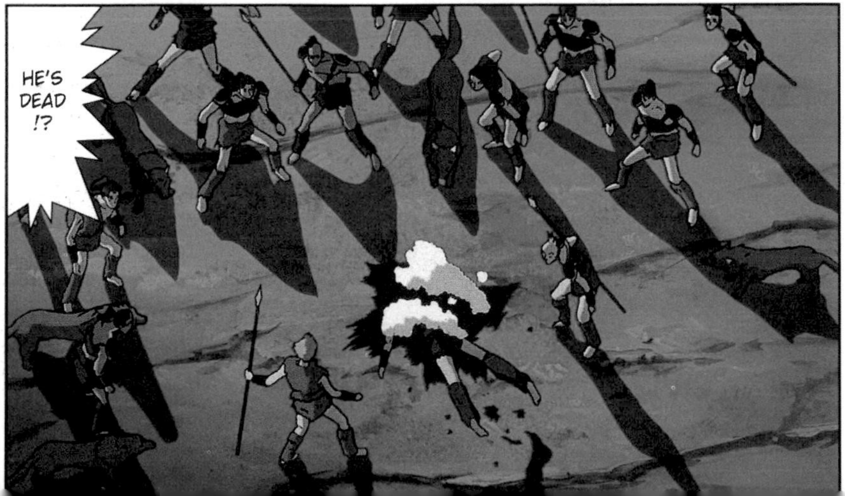
HE'S DEAD !?

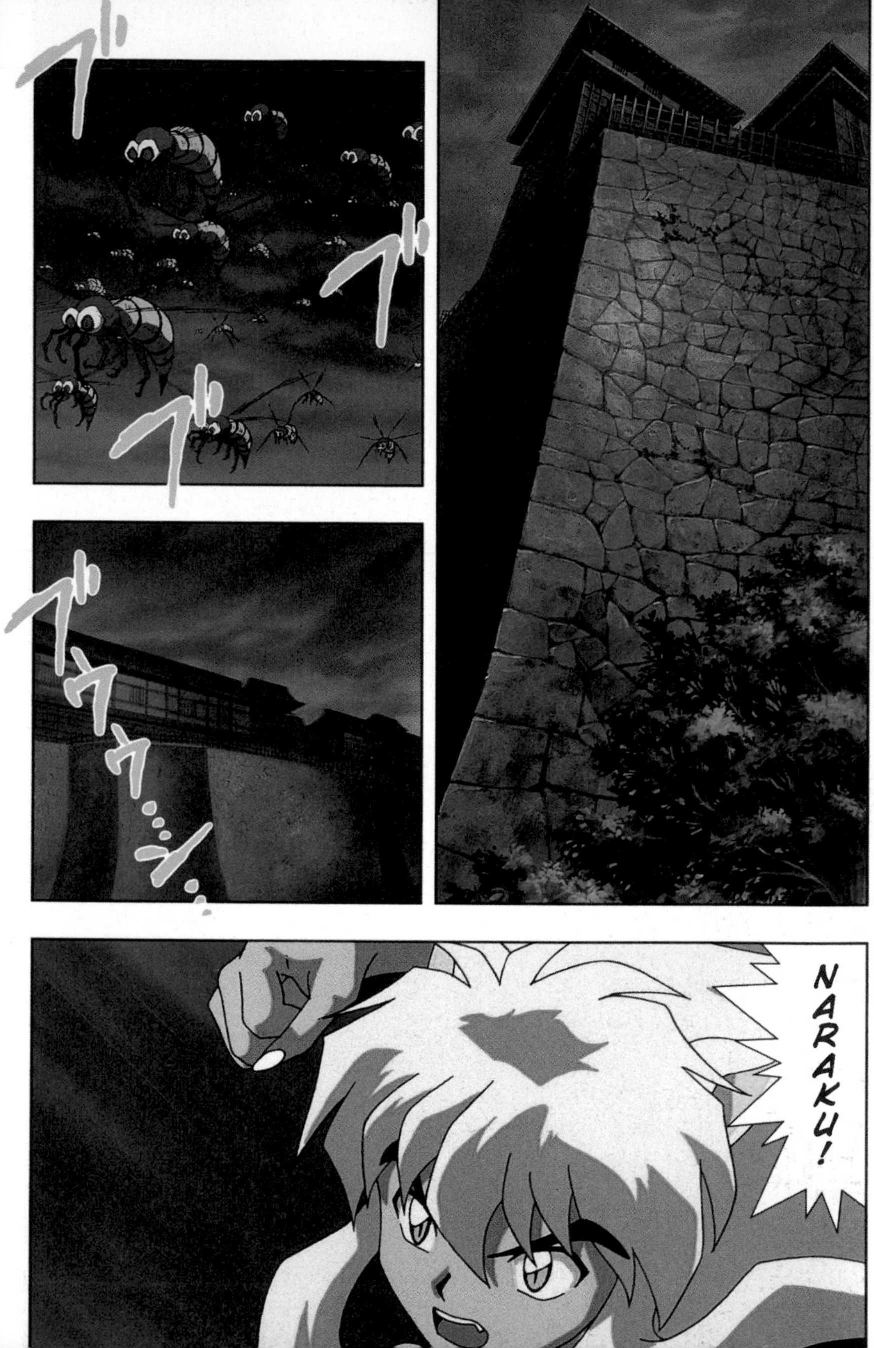
ブ
ブ
ブ
ブウウウ…ン…
NARAKU!

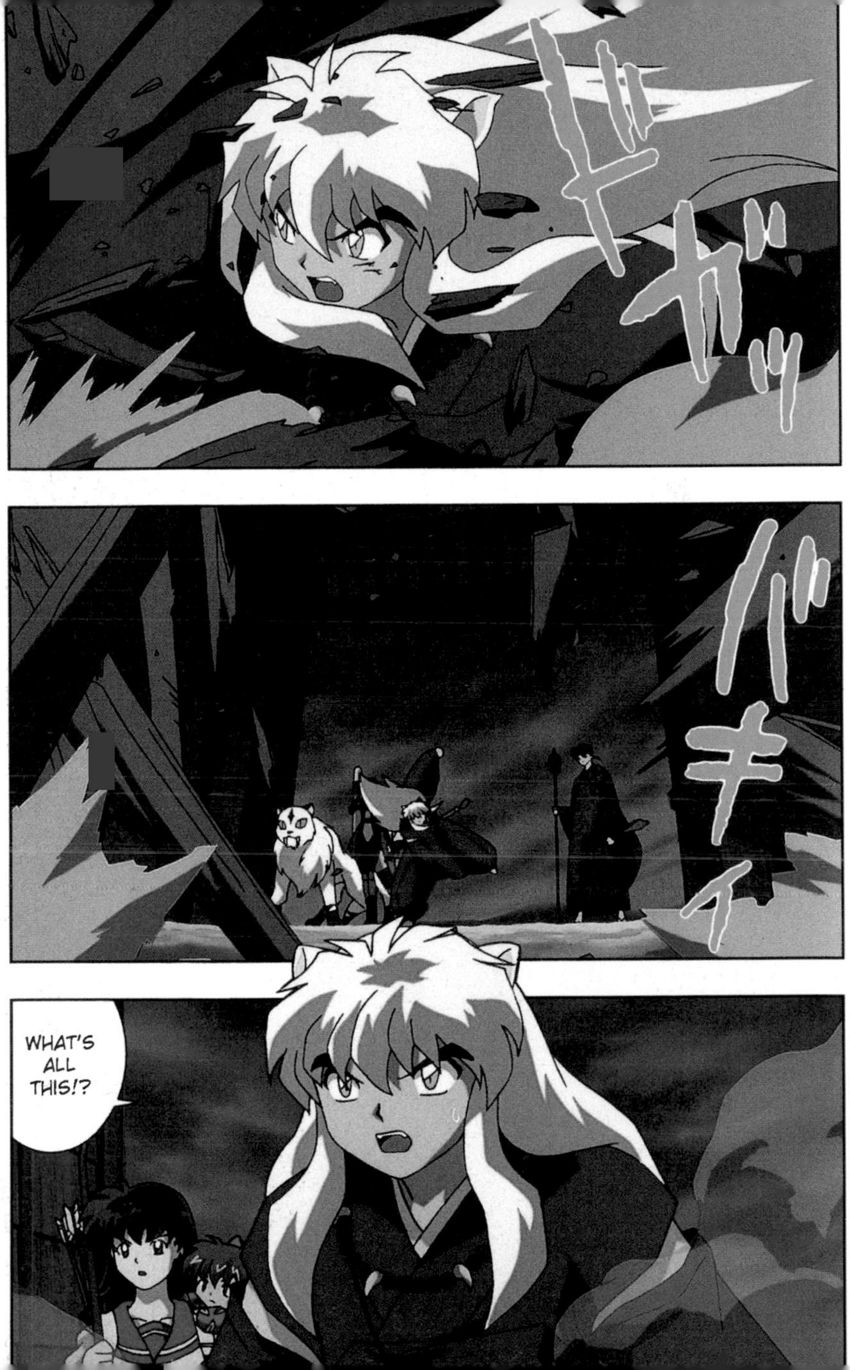
ドガッ
バキィ
WHAT'S ALL THIS!?

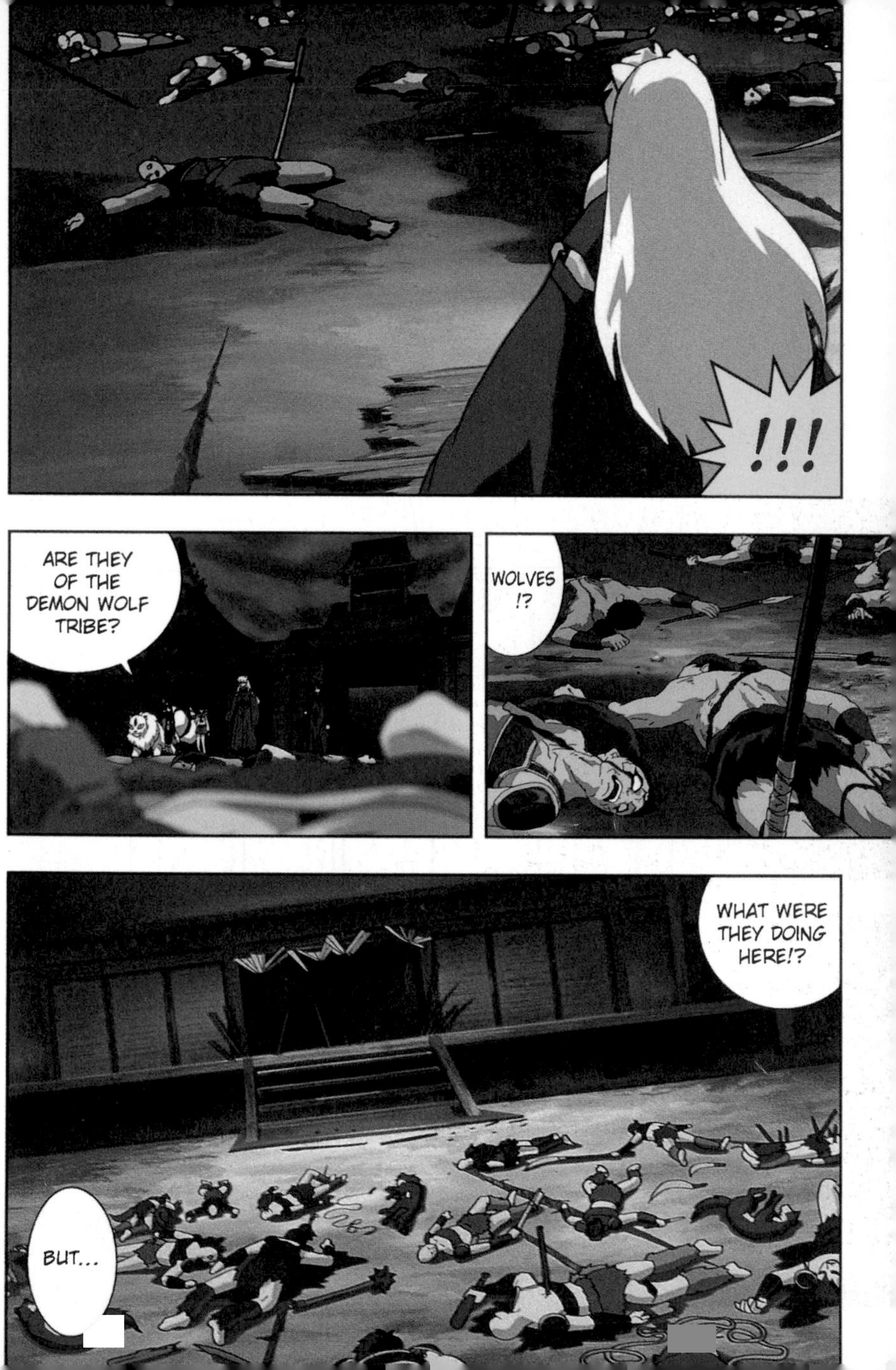
!!!
WOLVES !?
ARE THEY OF THE DEMON WOLF TRIBE?
WHAT WERE THEY DOING HERE!?
BUT...

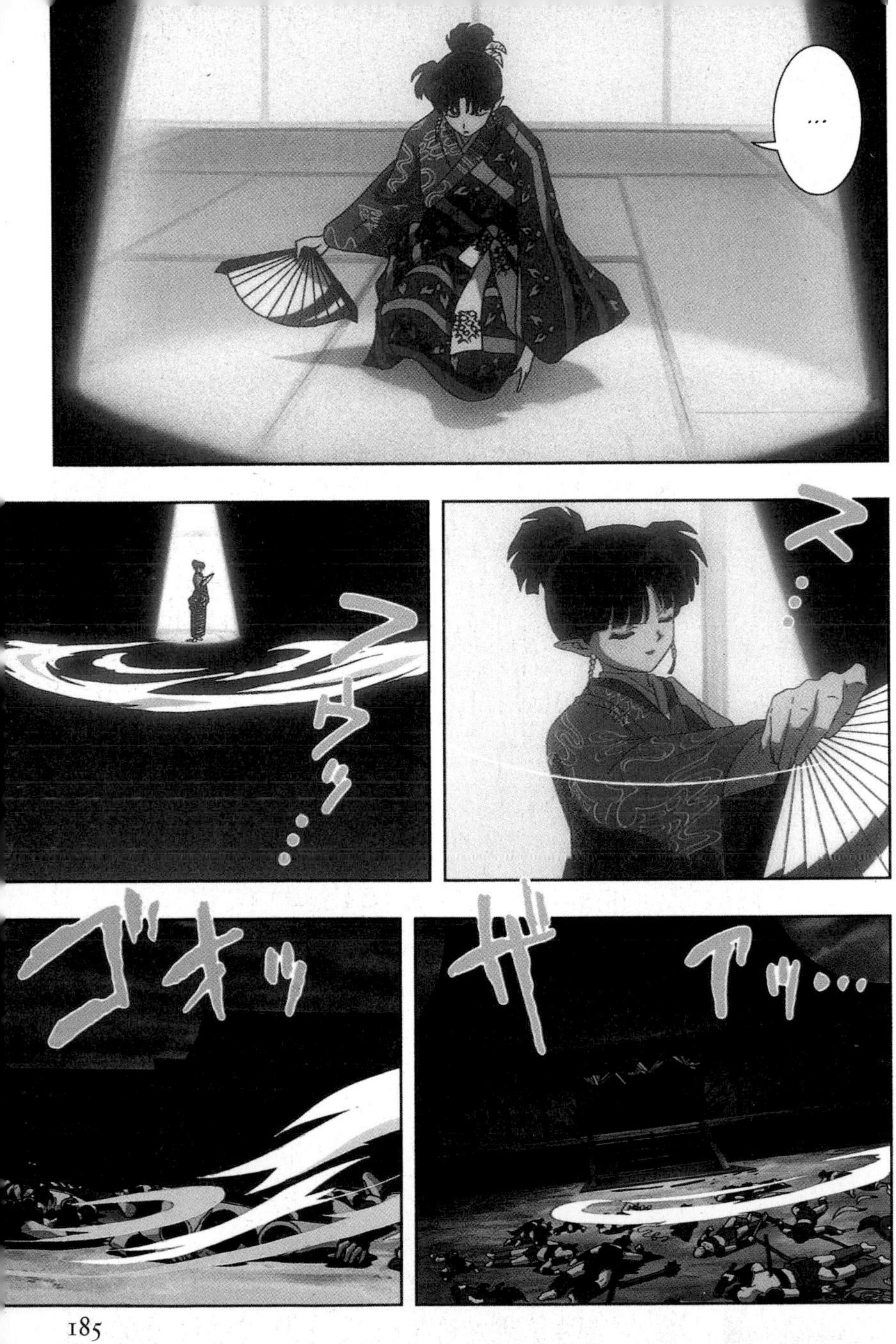
...
ス…
フワッ…
ザアッ…
ゴキッ

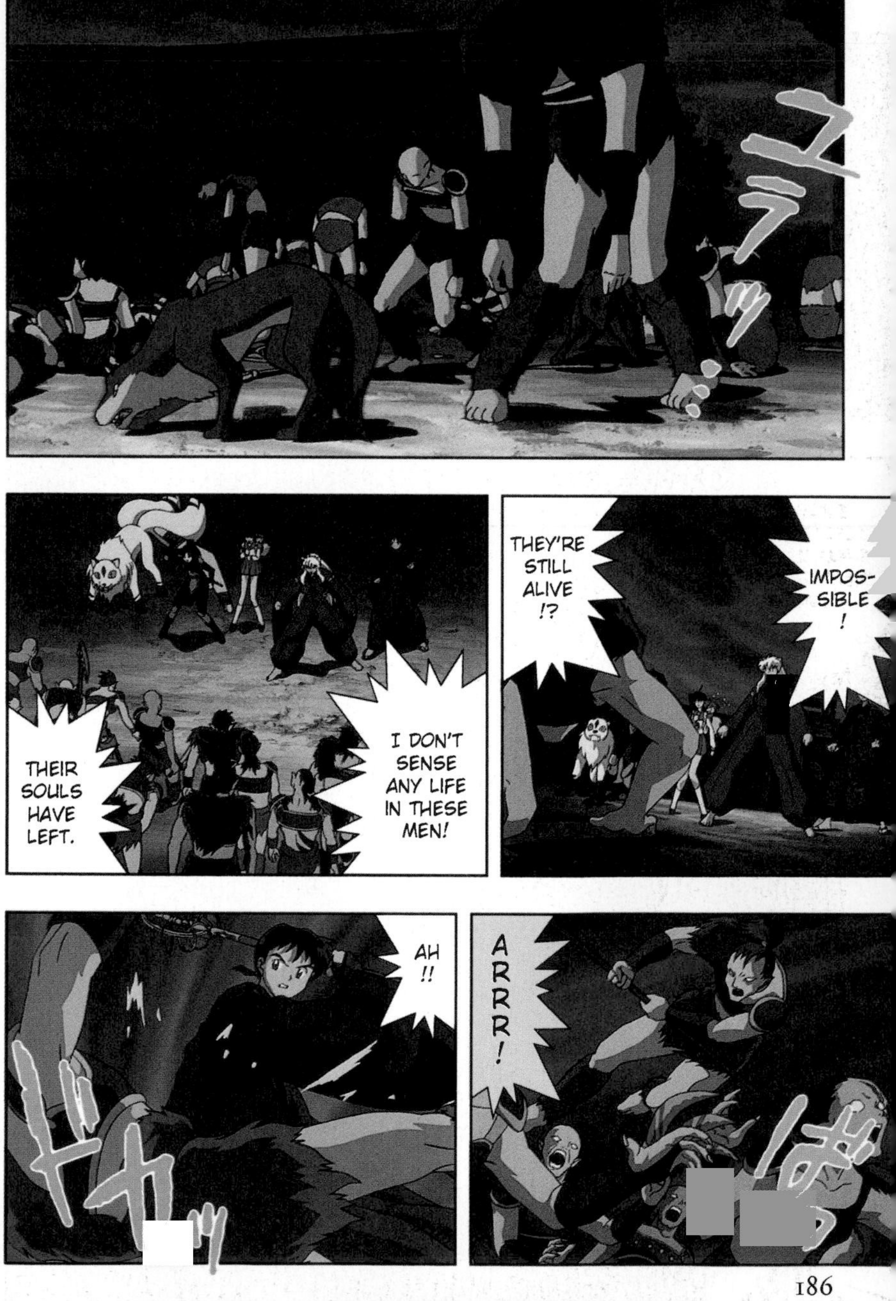
ユラッ
THEY'RE STILL ALIVE !?
IMPOS-SIBLE !
I DON'T SENSE ANY LIFE IN THESE MEN!
THEIR SOULS HAVE LEFT.
ARRR!
AH !!
ドカッ

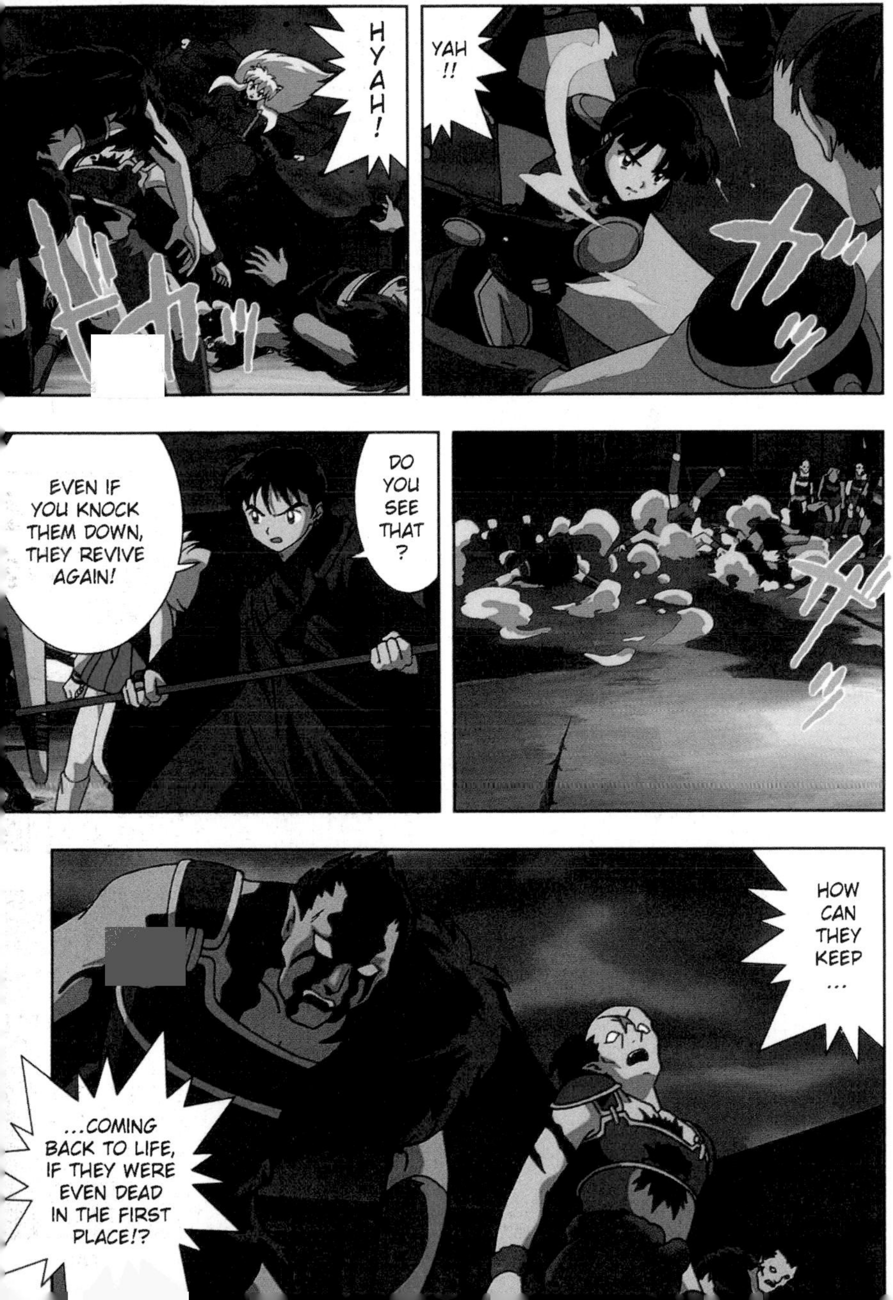
YAH!!
ガッ
HYAH!
ドカッ
DO YOU SEE THAT?
EVEN IF YOU KNOCK THEM DOWN, THEY REVIVE AGAIN!
HOW CAN THEY KEEP...
...COMING BACK TO LIFE, IF THEY WERE EVEN DEAD IN THE FIRST PLACE!?

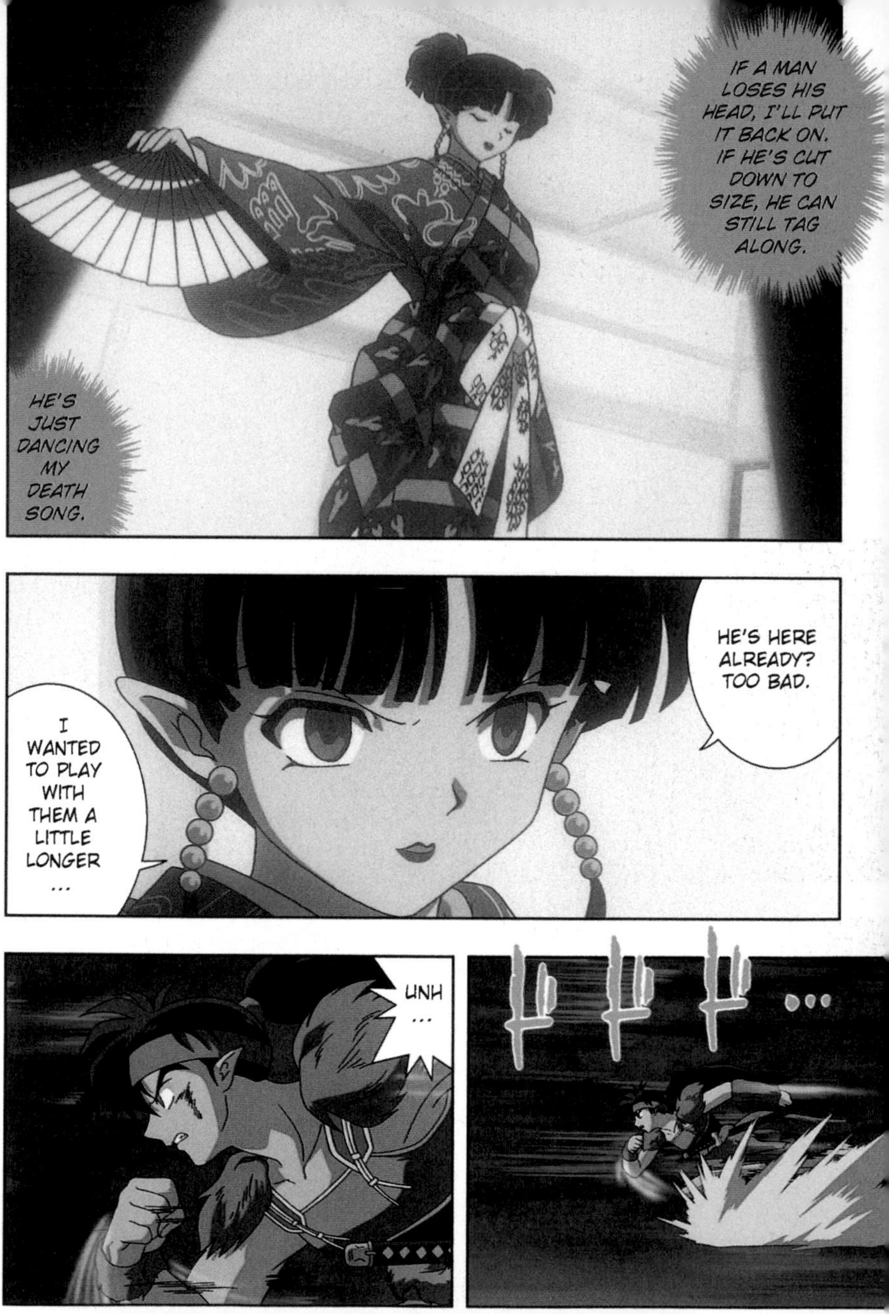
IF A MAN LOSES HIS HEAD, I'LL PUT IT BACK ON. IF HE'S CUT DOWN TO SIZE, HE CAN STILL TAG ALONG.
HE'S JUST DANCING MY DEATH SONG.
HE'S HERE ALREADY? TOO BAD.
I WANTED TO PLAY WITH THEM A LITTLE LONGER ...
ドドド...
UNH ...

WHAT
!?

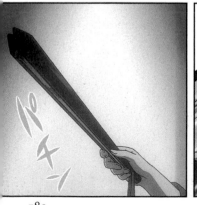

UGH
!!

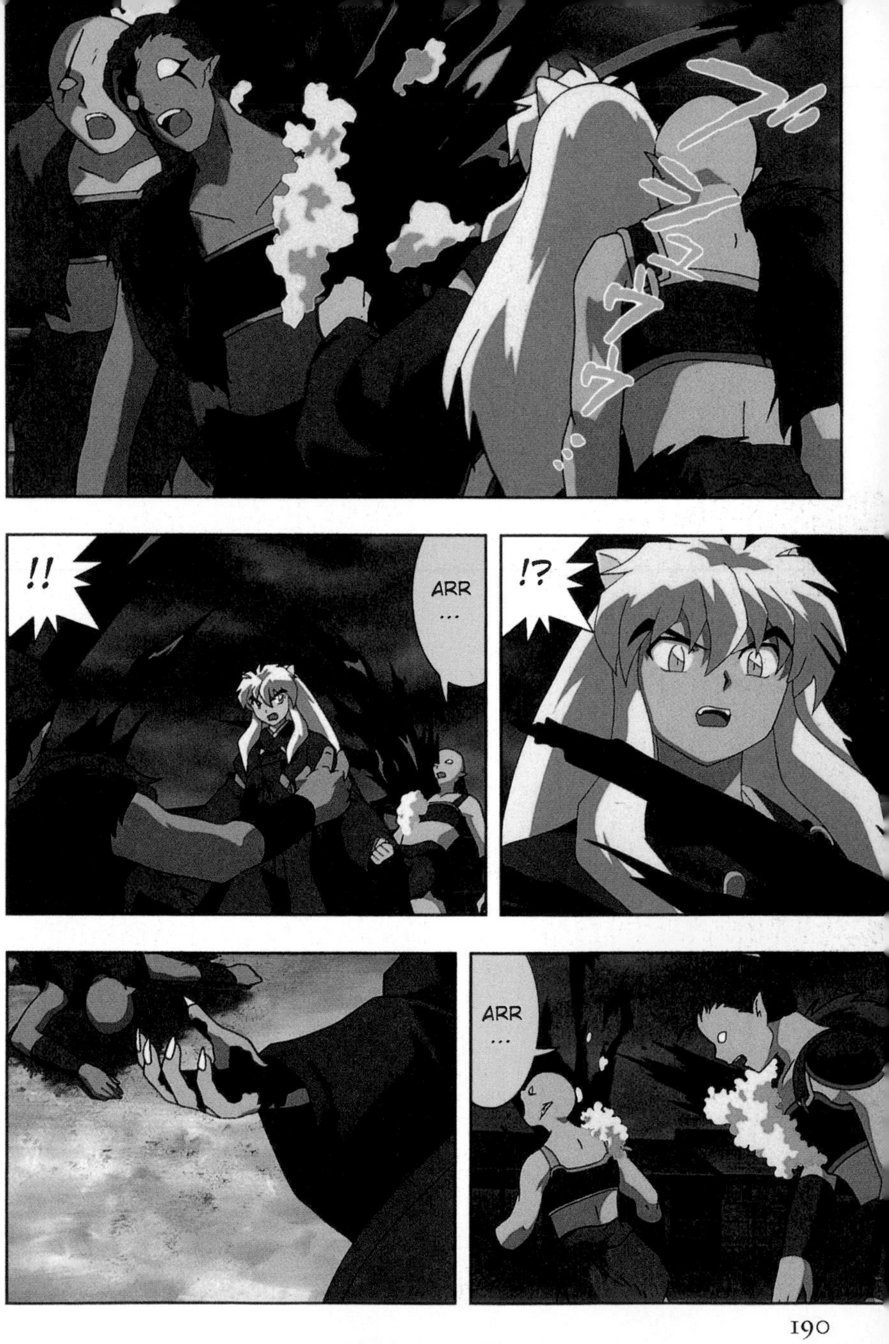
!?
ARR ...
!!
ARR ...

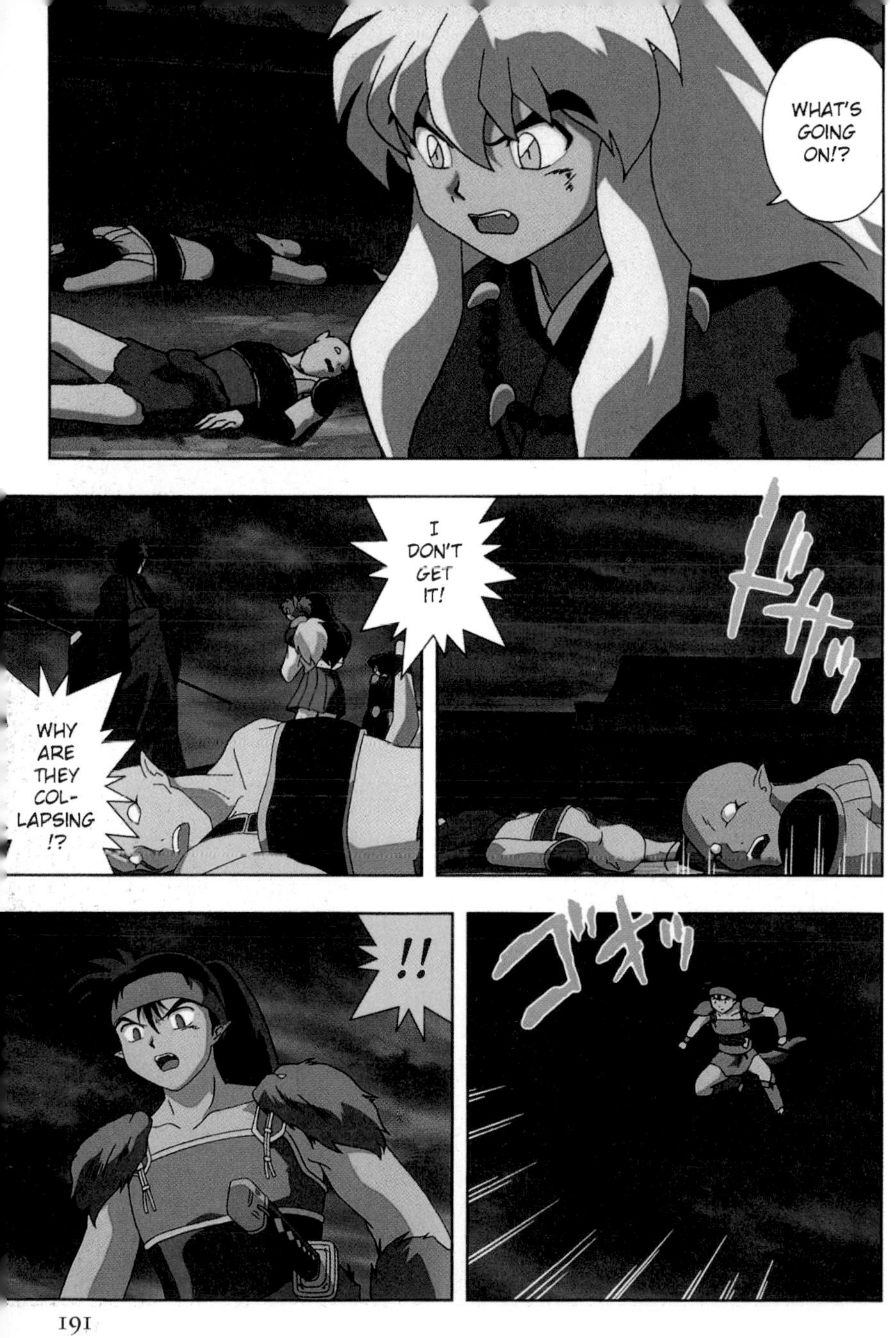
WHAT'S GOING ON!?
ドサッ
I DON'T GET IT!
WHY ARE THEY COL-LAPSING!?
ゴキッ
!!

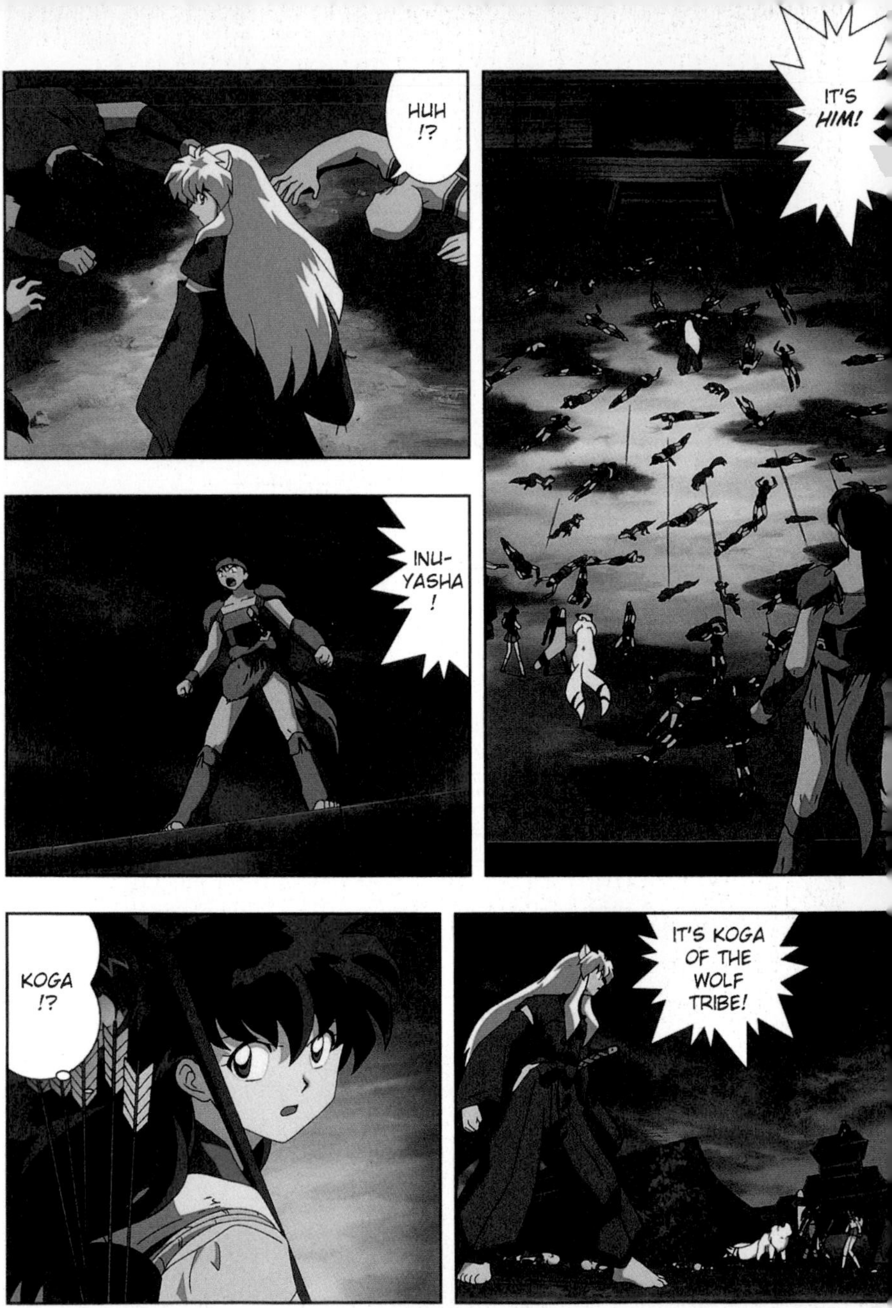
IT'S HIM!
HUH!?
INU-YASHA!
IT'S KOGA OF THE WOLF TRIBE!
KOGA!?

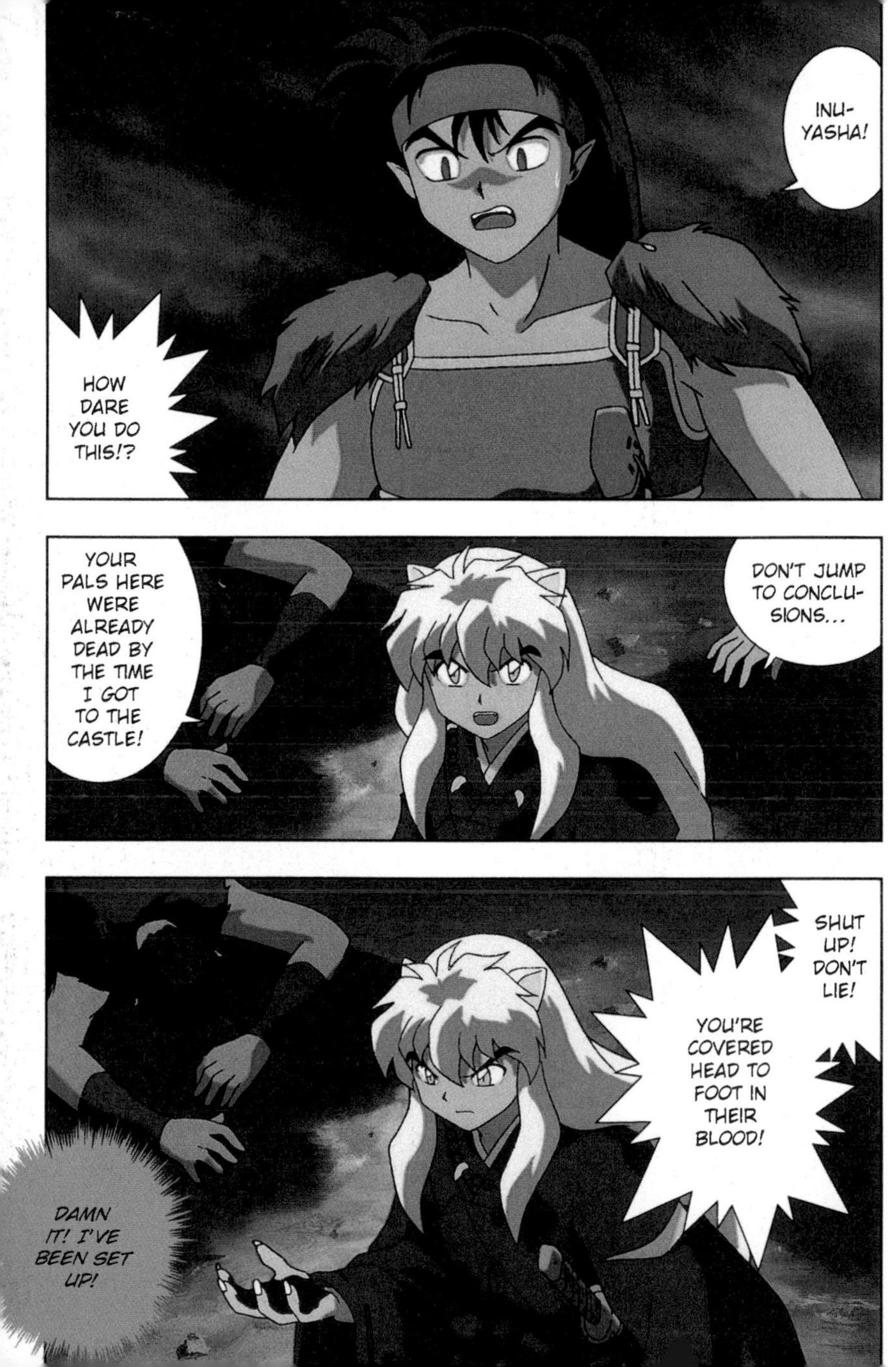
INU-YASHA!
HOW DARE YOU DO THIS!?
DON'T JUMP TO CONCLUSIONS...
YOUR PALS HERE WERE ALREADY DEAD BY THE TIME I GOT TO THE CASTLE!
SHUT UP! DON'T LIE!
YOU'RE COVERED HEAD TO FOOT IN THEIR BLOOD!
DAMN IT! I'VE BEEN SET UP!

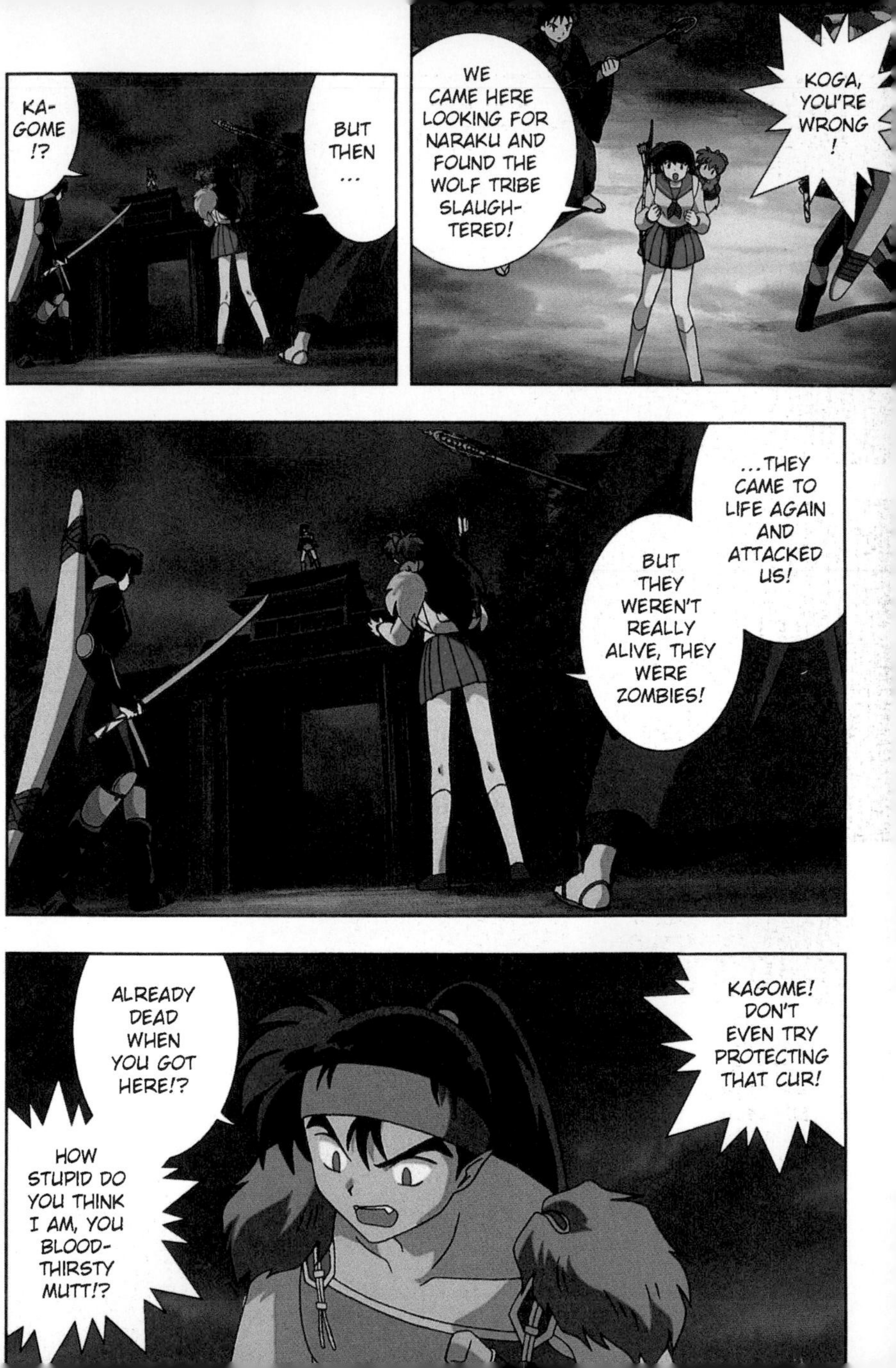
KOGA, YOU'RE WRONG!
WE CAME HERE LOOKING FOR NARAKU AND FOUND THE WOLF TRIBE SLAUGHTERED!
BUT THEN ...
KA-GOME!?
...THEY CAME TO LIFE AGAIN AND ATTACKED US!
BUT THEY WEREN'T REALLY ALIVE, THEY WERE ZOMBIES!
KAGOME! DON'T EVEN TRY PROTECTING THAT CUR!
ALREADY DEAD WHEN YOU GOT HERE!?
HOW STUPID DO YOU THINK I AM, YOU BLOOD-THIRSTY MUTT!?

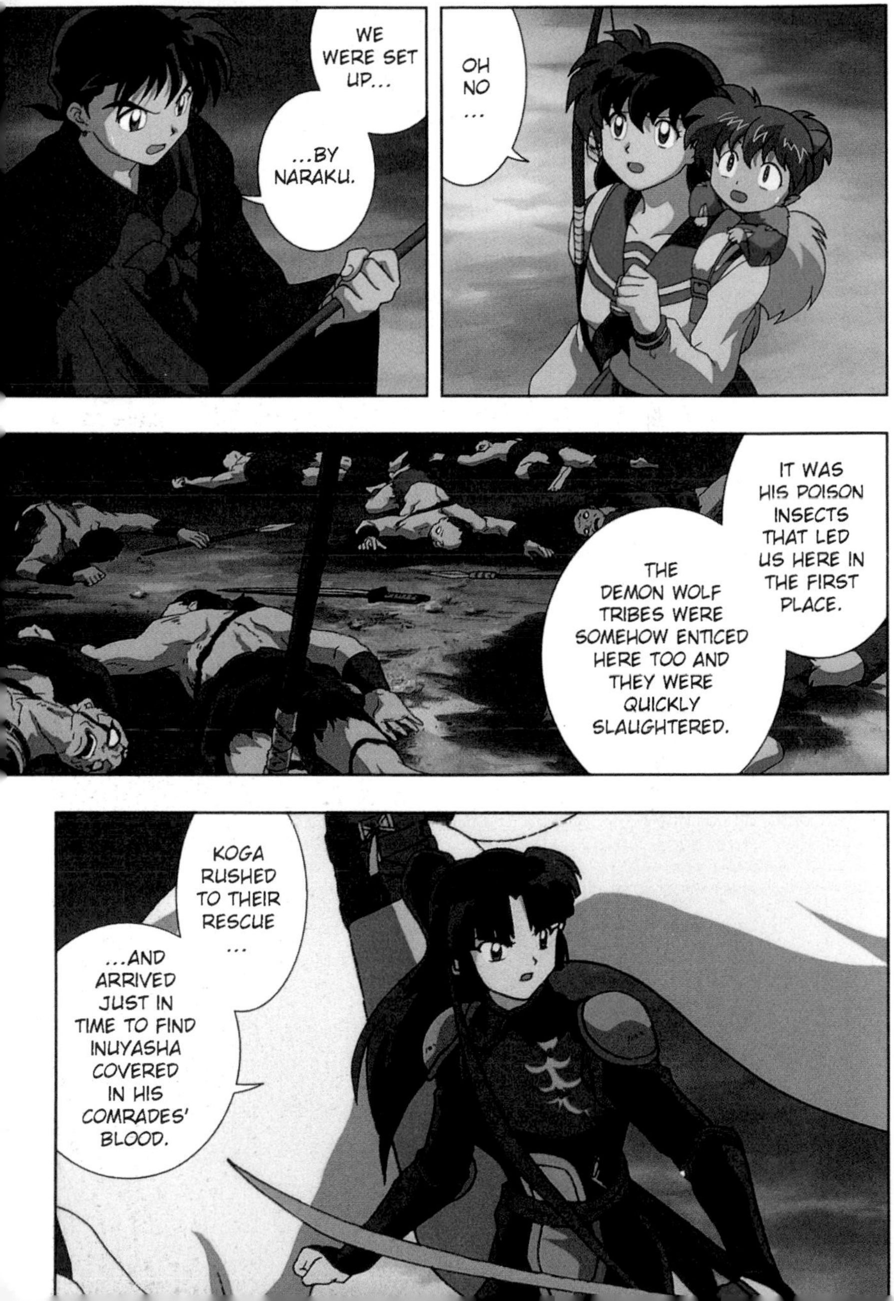
OH NO ...
WE WERE SET UP...
...BY NARAKU.
IT WAS HIS POISON INSECTS THAT LED US HERE IN THE FIRST PLACE.
THE DEMON WOLF TRIBES WERE SOMEHOW ENTICED HERE TOO AND THEY WERE QUICKLY SLAUGHTERED.
KOGA RUSHED TO THEIR RESCUE ...
...AND ARRIVED JUST IN TIME TO FIND INUYASHA COVERED IN HIS COMRADES' BLOOD.

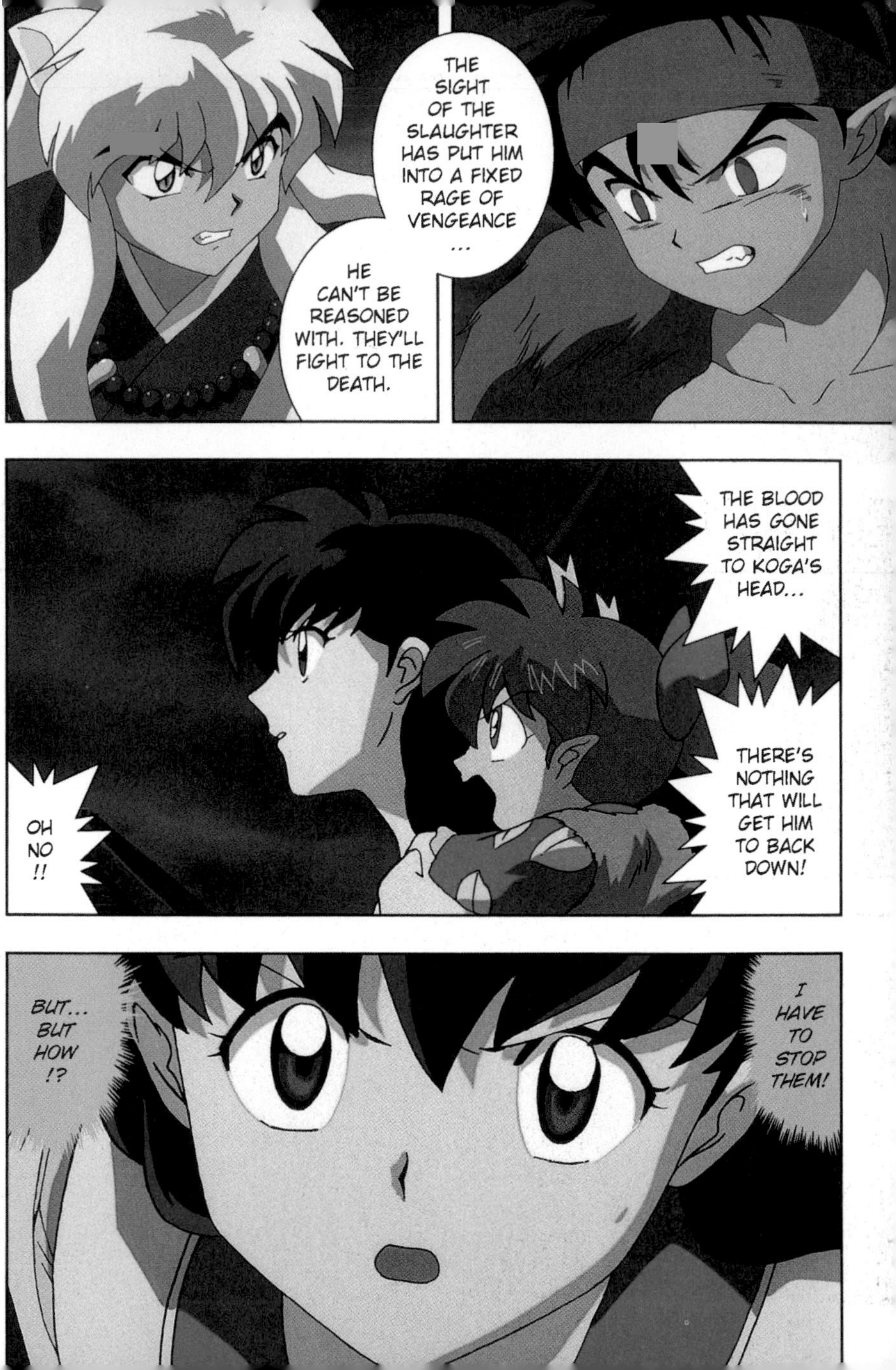
THE SIGHT OF THE SLAUGHTER HAS PUT HIM INTO A FIXED RAGE OF VENGEANCE ...
HE CAN'T BE REASONED WITH. THEY'LL FIGHT TO THE DEATH.
THE BLOOD HAS GONE STRAIGHT TO KOGA'S HEAD...
THERE'S NOTHING THAT WILL GET HIM TO BACK DOWN!
OH NO !!
I HAVE TO STOP THEM!
BUT... BUT HOW !?

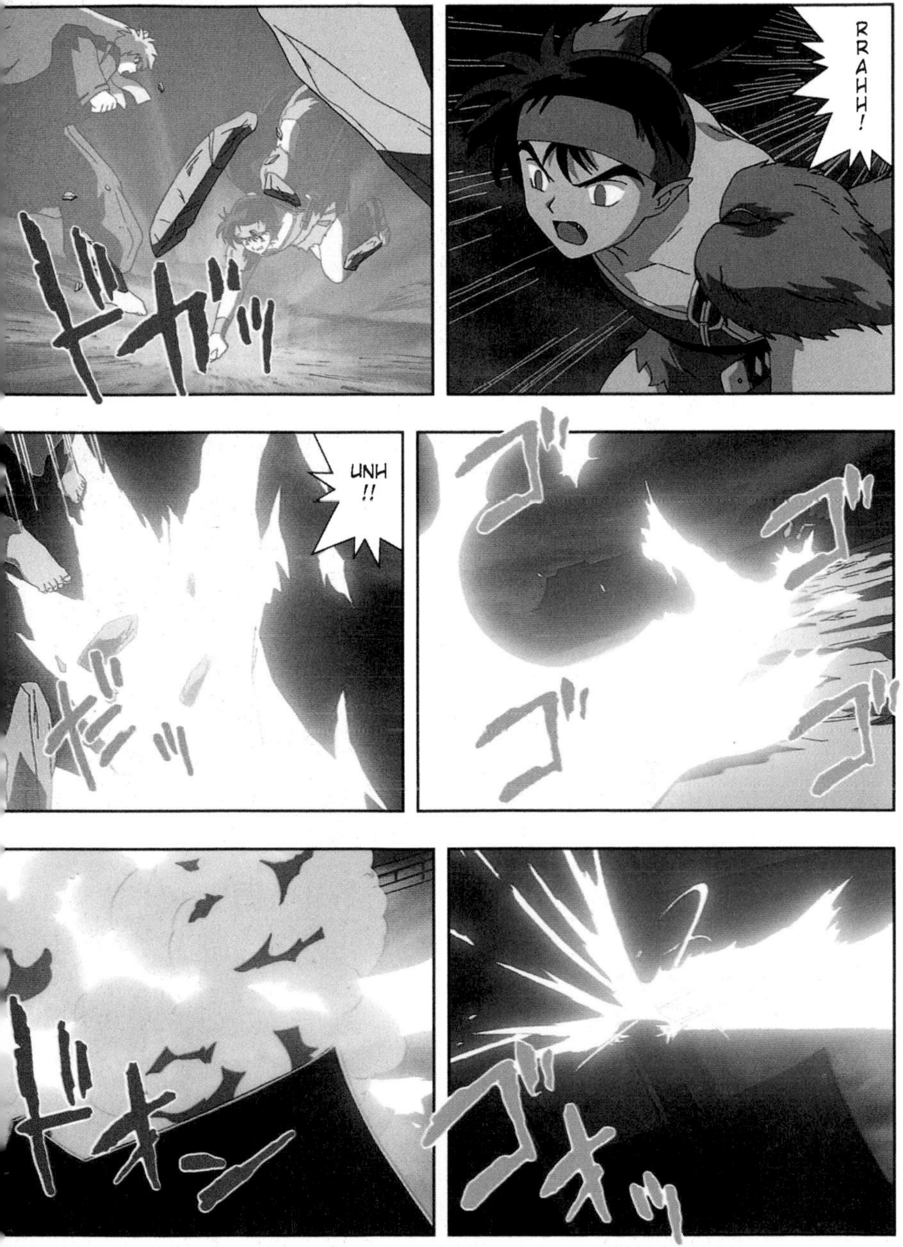
RRAHH!
UNH!!

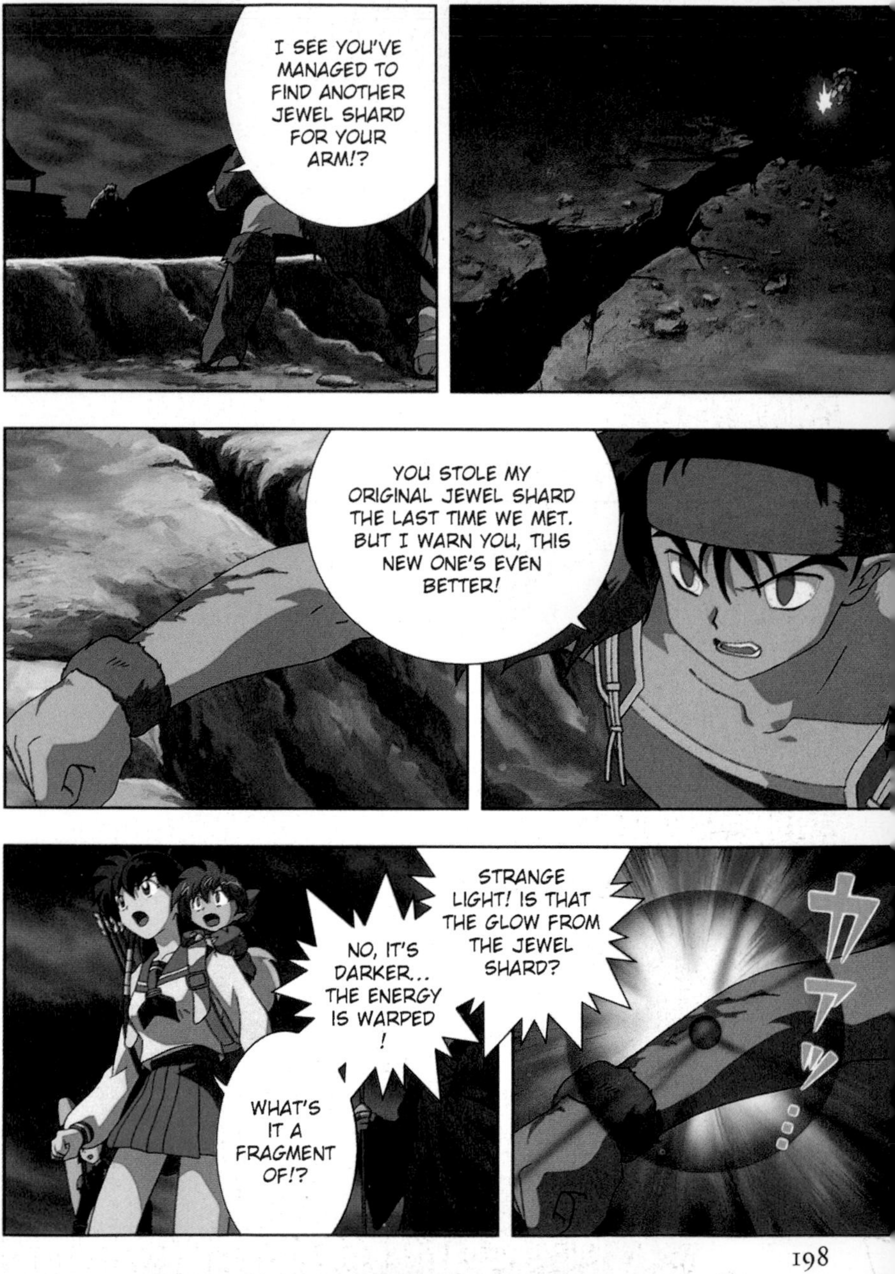
I SEE YOU'VE MANAGED TO FIND ANOTHER JEWEL SHARD FOR YOUR ARM!?
YOU STOLE MY ORIGINAL JEWEL SHARD THE LAST TIME WE MET. BUT I WARN YOU, THIS NEW ONE'S EVEN BETTER!
カァッ
STRANGE LIGHT! IS THAT THE GLOW FROM THE JEWEL SHARD?
NO, IT'S DARKER... THE ENERGY IS WARPED!
WHAT'S IT A FRAGMENT OF!?

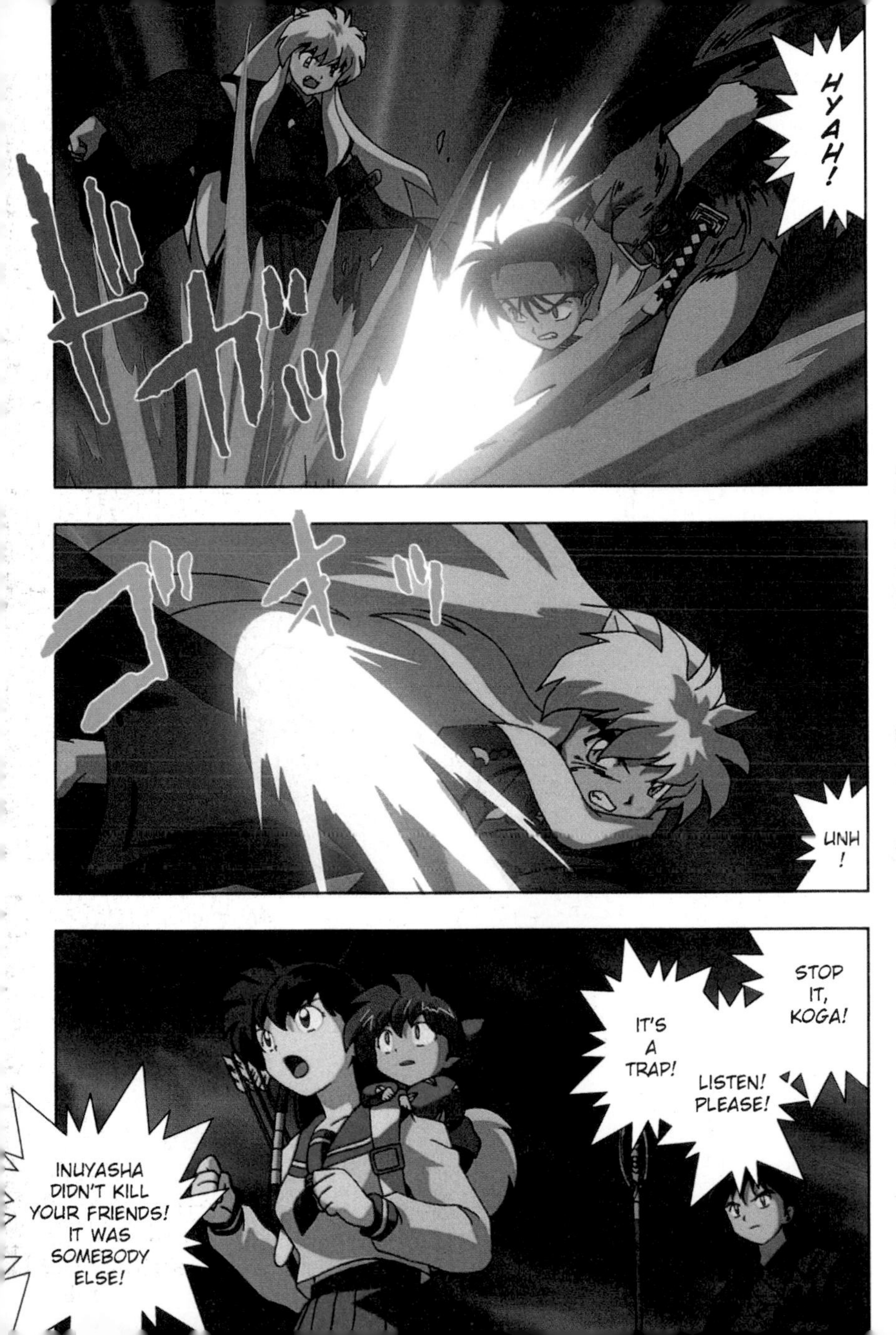
HYAH!
ドガッ
ゴオッ
UNH!
STOP IT, KOGA!
IT'S A TRAP!
LISTEN! PLEASE!
INUYASHA DIDN'T KILL YOUR FRIENDS! IT WAS SOMEBODY ELSE!

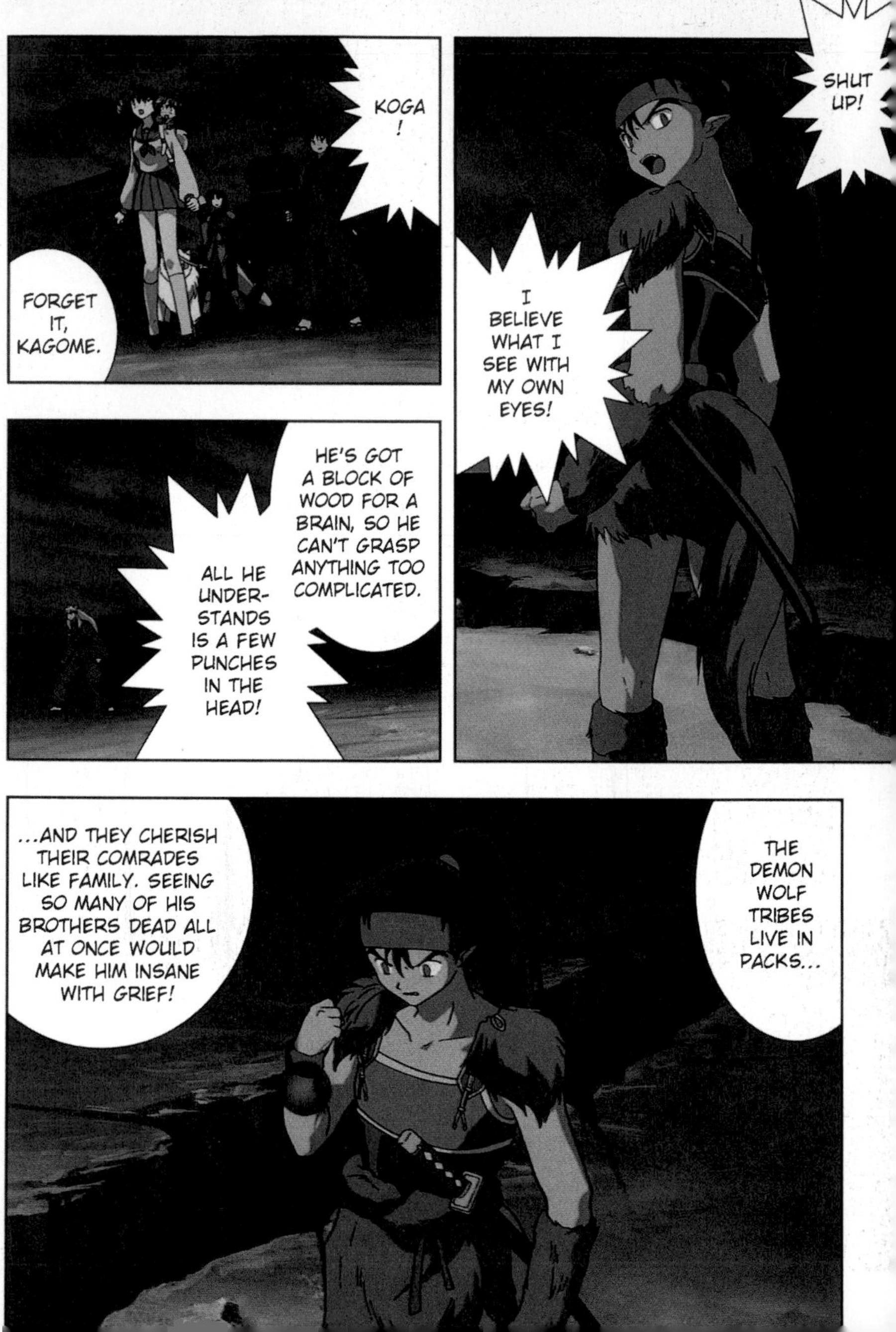
SHUT UP!
I BELIEVE WHAT I SEE WITH MY OWN EYES!
KOGA!
FORGET IT, KAGOME.
HE'S GOT A BLOCK OF WOOD FOR A BRAIN, SO HE CAN'T GRASP ANYTHING TOO COMPLICATED.
ALL HE UNDER-STANDS IS A FEW PUNCHES IN THE HEAD!
THE DEMON WOLF TRIBES LIVE IN PACKS...
...AND THEY CHERISH THEIR COMRADES LIKE FAMILY. SEEING SO MANY OF HIS BROTHERS DEAD ALL AT ONCE WOULD MAKE HIM INSANE WITH GRIEF!

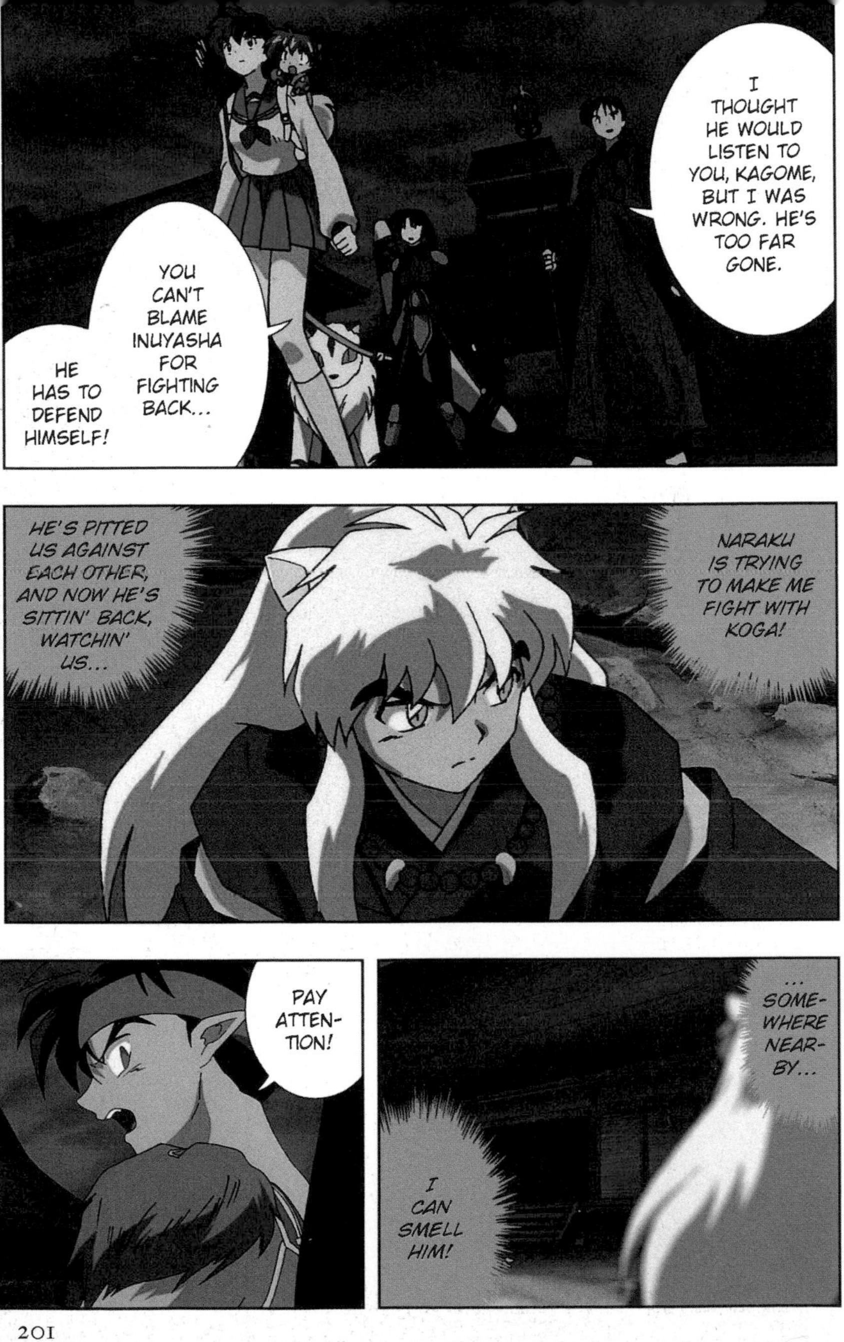
I THOUGHT HE WOULD LISTEN TO YOU, KAGOME, BUT I WAS WRONG. HE'S TOO FAR GONE.
YOU CAN'T BLAME INUYASHA FOR FIGHTING BACK...
HE HAS TO DEFEND HIMSELF!
NARAKU IS TRYING TO MAKE ME FIGHT WITH KOGA!
HE'S PITTED US AGAINST EACH OTHER, AND NOW HE'S SITTIN' BACK, WATCHIN' US...
...SOME-WHERE NEAR-BY...
I CAN SMELL HIM!
PAY ATTEN-TION!

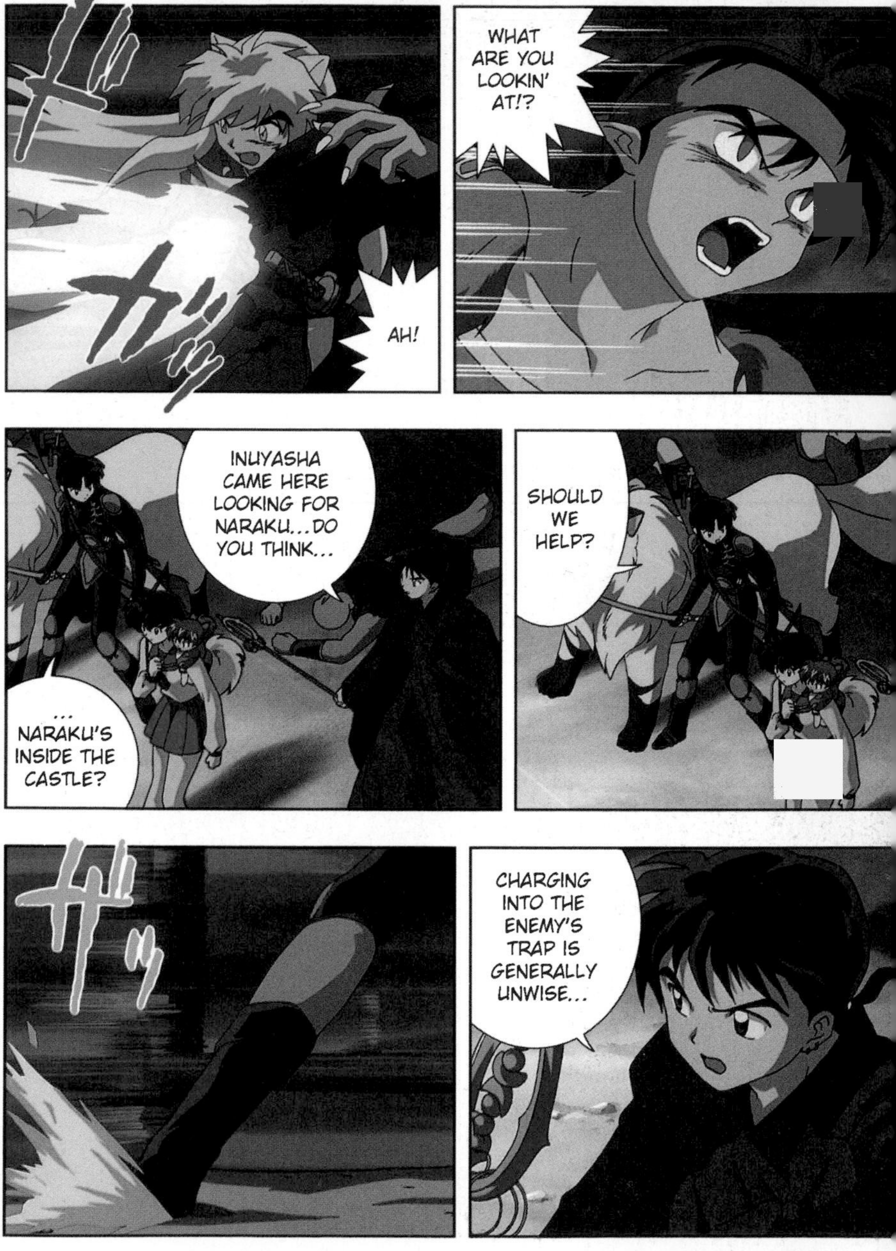
WHAT ARE YOU LOOKIN' AT!?
AH!
SHOULD WE HELP?
INUYASHA CAME HERE LOOKING FOR NARAKU...DO YOU THINK...
...NARAKU'S INSIDE THE CASTLE?
CHARGING INTO THE ENEMY'S TRAP IS GENERALLY UNWISE...

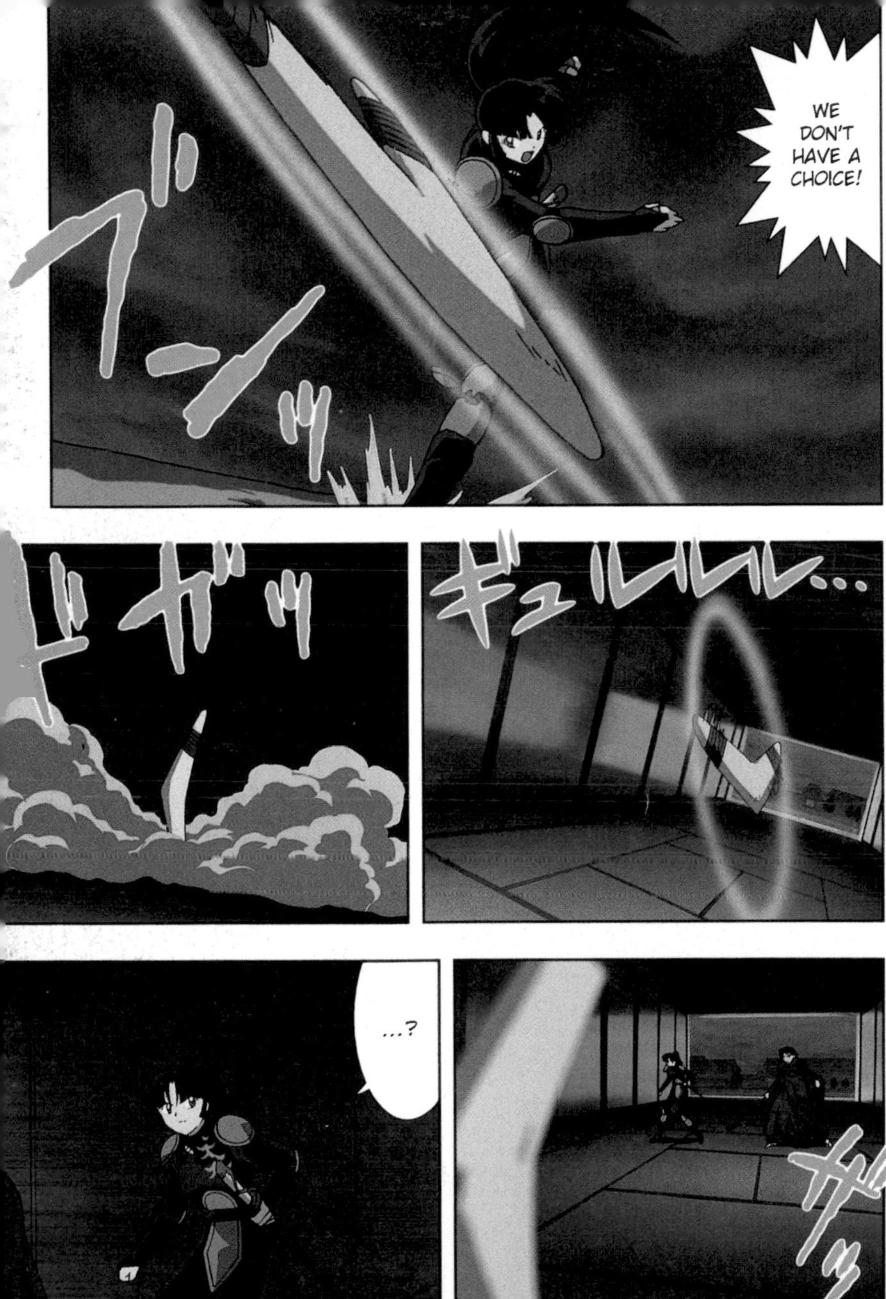
WE DON'T HAVE A CHOICE!
ブーンッ
ギュルルル...
ドガッ
ガッ
...?

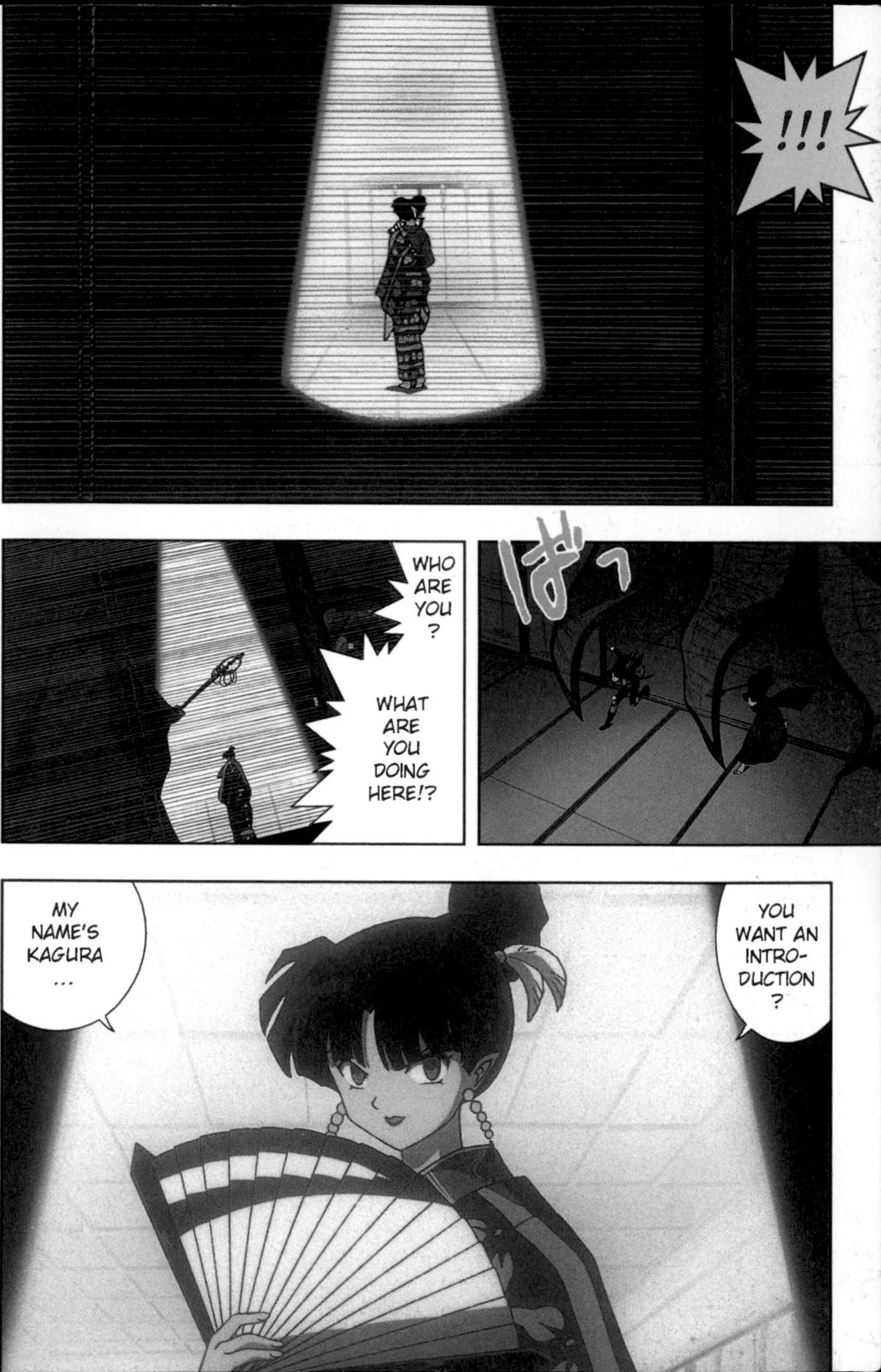
!!!
ぱっ
WHO ARE YOU?
WHAT ARE YOU DOING HERE!?
YOU WANT AN INTRO-DUCTION?
MY NAME'S KAGURA...

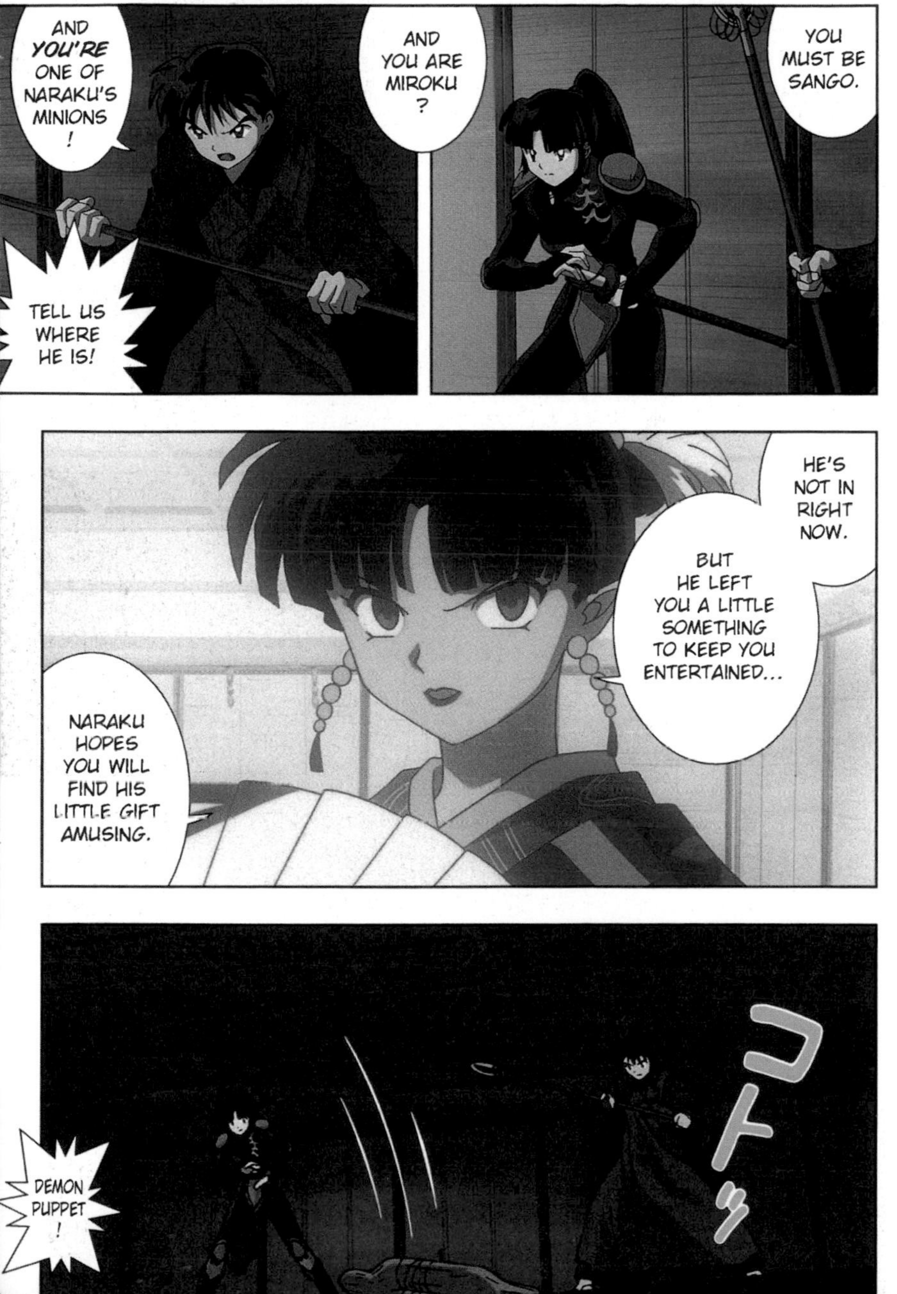
YOU MUST BE SANGO.
AND YOU ARE MIROKU?
AND *YOU'RE* ONE OF NARAKU'S MINIONS!
TELL US WHERE HE IS!
HE'S NOT IN RIGHT NOW.
BUT HE LEFT YOU A LITTLE SOMETHING TO KEEP YOU ENTERTAINED...
NARAKU HOPES YOU WILL FIND HIS LITTLE GIFT AMUSING.
コトッ
DEMON PUPPET!

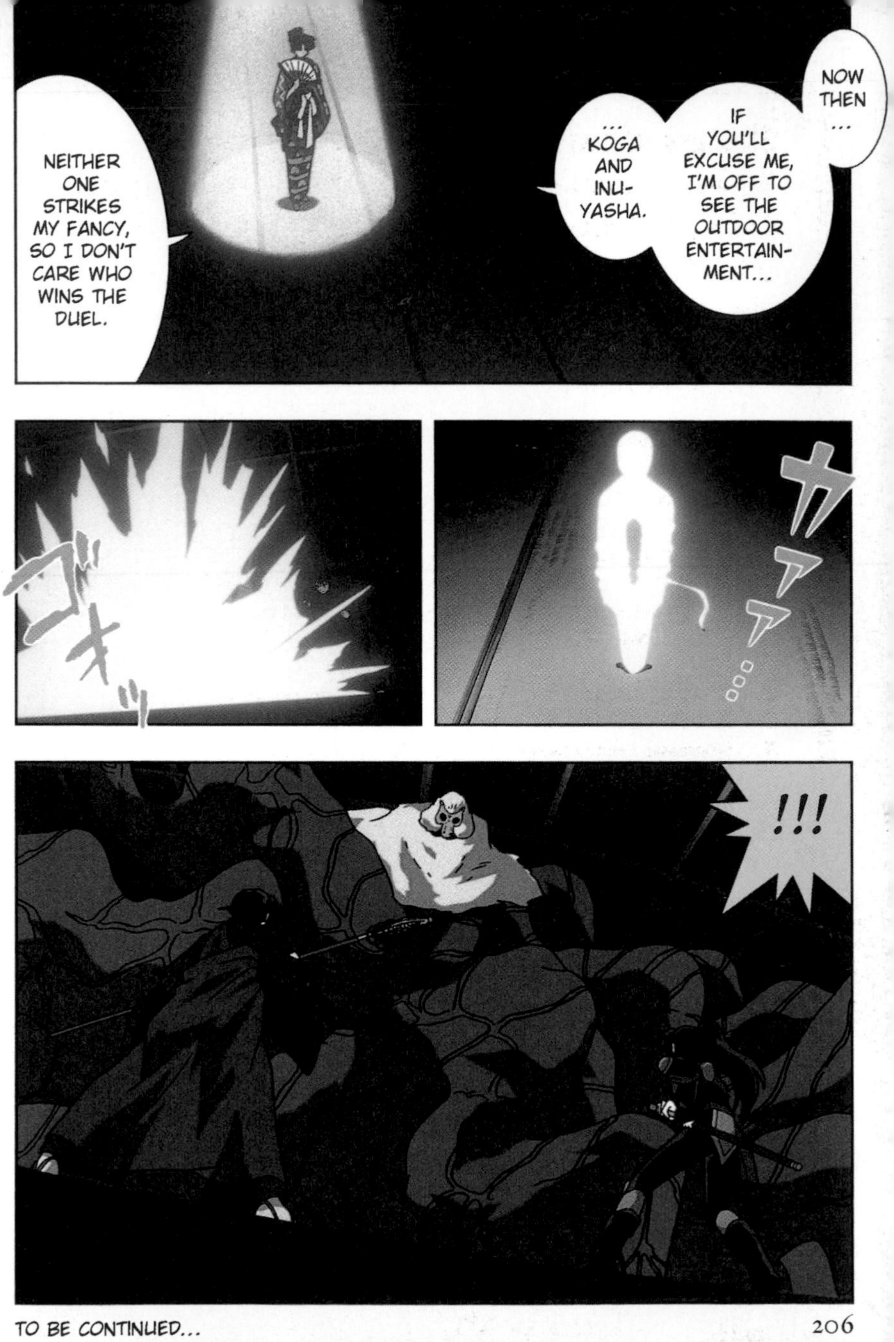
NOW THEN...
IF YOU'LL EXCUSE ME, I'M OFF TO SEE THE OUTDOOR ENTERTAIN-MENT...
...KOGA AND INU-YASHA.
NEITHER ONE STRIKES MY FANCY, SO I DON'T CARE WHO WINS THE DUEL.
ゴオッ
!!!

TO BE CONTINUED...

Glossary of Sound Effects

Each entry includes: the location, indicated by page number and panel number (so 3.1 means page 3, panel number 1); the phonetic romanization of the original Japanese; and our English "translation"—we offer as close an English equivalent as we can.

16.6 FX: Toh (touching down)

18.4 FX: Gui (grab)

19.4 FX: Pan (slap)

24.1 FX: Doga (smashing into cliff)
24.2 FX: Doh (hit)
24.3 FX: Bun (strike)
24.4 FX: Ta (Inuyasha lands)

27.1 FX: Ta ta ta… (running)
27.2 FX: Gohh (whoosh)
27.3 FX: Basa basa… (wings flapping)

29.1 FX: Ta ta ta… (running)
29.2 FX: Za za (skidding)
29.3 FX: Goh (whoosh)

31.2 FX: Doka (punch)
31.3 FX: Za (landing on bones)

33.5 FX: Ta (jump)

34.1 FX: Goh (whooshing)
34.2 FX: Zuba (slash)
34.3 FX: Doka (kick)

35.1 FX: Ta (leap)
35.3 FX: Dokun… (heartbeat)

Chapter 37:
The Man Who Fell in Love with Kagome!

6.1 FX: Doh doh doh… (waterfall crashing on rocks)

10.1 FX: Kun kun… (sniff sniff)
10.2 FX: Kun kun…(sniff sniff)
10.5 FX: Gabu (chomp)

11.2 FX: Pon (pop)
11.4 FX: Ga (spears clack together)
11.5 FX: Ta (running)
11.6 FX: Zan (splashing)

12.1 FX: Ta ta ta… (running)
12.2 FX: Doh doh doh doh (wolves galloping)

13.2 FX: Gui (yank)
13.3 FX: Bun (toss)
13.4 FX: Bun (throwing chain)
13.5 FX: Shururuму… (chain unfurls)

14.1 FX: Gin (chain hits spear)
14.2 FX: Pon (pop)

15.1 FX: Hyurururu… (flying through the air)
15.2 FX: Zun (pig falls)

16.5 FX: Ta (leap)

35.5 FX: Pishi (jewel shines)

36.1 FX: Ga (crashing through rock)
36.3 FX: Toh (jump)
36.4 FX: Basa (rocks collapse)
36.5 FX: Zu—n… (rocks collapse)

37.2 FX: Giro (beady eyes staring)

38.3 FX: Kaa… (jewel shard shines)

39.1 FX: Doga (bird attacks)
39.3 FX: Ta (running down cliff)
39.5 FX: Ta ta ta… (running)

40.5 FX: Doh doh doh… (running)

41.5 FX: Goh (whoosh)

42.1 FX: Goh (whoosh)

43.3 FX: Giri giri (pulling bowstring tight)
43.4 FX: Shun (arrow flies)
43.5 FX: Goh (arrow whooshes and glows)

44.1 FX: Zuba (slash)
44.2 FX: Dosa (bird falls to earth)
44.3 FX: Doh (guard falls)
44.4 FX: Ta (running)

45.4 FX: Gohh (whooshing)

46.2 FX: Zan (sword swing)
46.3 FX: Zuba (slash)
46.4 FX: Toh (Inuyasha lands)

48.2 FX: Ba (Miroku aims wind tunnel)
48.3 FX: Gohhh… (whooshing of wind tunnel)
48.4 FX: Gohhhh… (whooshing)
48.6 FX: Pashi (Miroku puts away Wind Tunnel)

52.5 FX: Da (leap)

53.2 FX: Ta (leap)
53.4 FX: Dokun… (heartbeat)

54.2 FX: Gohhh… (whoosh)
54.4 FX: Doga (crash)
54.4 FX: Ta (leap)

55.2 FX: Ga (impact)
55.3 FX: Giri… (spear bending)
55.4 FX: Ga (spear breaks)

56.4 FX: Baki (kick)

57.2 FX: Doh (smack)
57.3 FX: Gohhh… (whoosh)
57.5 FX: Za (walking)

59.1 FX: Kaa (shining)
59.4 FX: Gohh (whooshing of wind scar)

60.1 FX: Gohh (whoosh)
60.2 FX: Zan (slash)
60.3 FX: Gohhhh… (whoosh)

61.1 FX: Shuuuu… (bird disintegrates)

62.4 FX: Za (Kirara lands)

65.3 FX: Dohh (Inuyasha falls)

66.3 FX: Doh doh doh… (wolves run away)

72.2 FX: Gohh (whooshes)

Chapter 38:
Two Hearts, One Mind

75.2 FX: Mogu mogu (munch munch)

77.2 FX: Gata (chair pushed back)

82.3 FX: Ki—n ko—n (ding dong)
82.4 FX: Ta (rushing away)
82.5 FX: Da (friends dash after Kagome)

83.3 FX: Niko... (smile)

90.1 FX: Zawa zawa... (buzz of conversation)

94.2 FX: Ta ta ta... (running)
94.3 FX: Kyoro kyoro (furtive glances)

95.2 FX: Ba (leap)

100.2 FX: Za (rustling)
100.3 FX: Koso (sneaking around)
100.4 FX: Ta (leap)
100.4 FX: Gara (window opened)

101.1 FX: Ta (Inuyasha lands)
101.2 FX: Fuwa... (raising head)

103.4 FX: Ba (claps hand over mouth)

104.2 FX: Da (jump)
104.3 FX: Chya (opening door)
104.5 FX: Ta (running off)

105.2 FX: Za—(water splashes)
105.3 FX: Chapu (plops down in the tub)

107.1 FX: Ba ba (kicking dirt)

109.4 FX: Gashi (grab)

112.3 FX: Gara... (door sliding open)

115.2 FX: Za (toppling over)

117.4 FX: Bun bun (winding up arm to throw)
117.5 FX: Poi (toss)

119.4 FX: Da (running)

121.3 FX: Sa (holds up picture)

125.2 FX: Su (standing up)
125.4 FX: Basa (flutter)

127.4 FX: Da (running)

128.3 FX: Koto (putting alarm clock down)

129.3 FX: Suu... (sleeping)

130.1 FX: Gara... (window slides open)

131.1 FX: Zuun (bang)
131.3 FX: Jiririririri... (alarm rings)
131.6 FX: Goso... (reaching for alarm clock)

132.4 FX: Kara... (sliding window open)

137.3 FX: Gori (fumbling in sleeve)
137.4 FX: Boro... (holding out alarm clock)

138.3 FX: Sa (hopping up out of grass)

139.5 FX: Doh doh doh... (running)

Chapter 39:
Trapped in a Duel to the Death!

145.1 FX: Gaba (wobbling)
145.2 FX: Gura (falling)
145.3 FX: Za—n (splash)

147.3 FX: Piku (Koga shuts his eyes)

149.2 FX: Doh doh doh doh…
(wolfmen gallop off)

150.1 FX: Goh (whoosh)
150.3 FX: Doga (whack)
150.3 FX: Ta (leap)
150.4 FX: Toh (landing)
150.5 FX: Goh (whoosh)

151.1 FX: Gaki (breaking teeth)
151.2 FX: Gu gu gu…
(spear straining between jaws)
151.3 FX: Baki (spear snaps)

152.2 FX: Baki (kick)

153.2 FX: Zan (swipe)

157.3 FX: Shuuu… (swelling lump)
157.6 FX: Gasa (rustling in underbrush)

160.1 FX: Cha (readying weapon)
160.2 FX: Zuuun… (thunderous crashing in forest)
160.3 FX: Zuuun… (thunderous crashing)
160.4 FX: Guoh (swatting with paw)
160.5 FX: Dogo (tree falls)
160.6 FX: Bun (throwing weapon)

161.1 FX: Baki (tree breaks)

161.2 FX: Doh (tree falls)

162.4 FX: Zuba (slash)

163.1 FX: Buuu…n… (insects approaching)
163.2 FX: Bu bu (buzzing)
163.4 FX: Bu bu bu (buzz buzz buzz)
163.5 FX: Bu bu bu (buzz buzz buzz)

164.1 FX: Bu bu bu bu (buzz buzz buzz buzz)
164.3 FX: Bu bu bu (buzz buzz buzz)
164.4 FX: Doh (bear falls)

165.1 FX: Bu bu bu (buzz buzz buzz)
165.2 FX: Shuuu… (bees consume bear carcass)
165.3 FX: Bu—n… (buzz)

166.3 FX: Hita hita… (soft footfalls)

167.1 FX: Hita hita… (soft footfalls)
167.3 FX: Su… (moving screen aside)

168.3 FX: Su… (reaching for shard)

169.1 FX: Bachi (dark aura emanates)

171.2 FX: Doh doh doh (spears thrown)
171.3 FX: Doh doh doh (spears go into castle)
171.4 FX: Doh doh doh (wolfmen charge castle)
171.5 FX: Su… (holding up fan)

172.2 FX: Bun (launching wind attack)
172.3 FX: Goh (whoosh)

173.3 FX: Hyun (dancing of blades)
173.4 FX: Doh doh doh (slashing)

175.5 FX: Fura… (wobble)

178.1 FX: Ta ta ta… (running)
178.2 FX: Ta ta (leaping)
178.3 FX: Za (jumping)

179.1 FX: Ba (brandishing jewel fragment)
179.2 FX: Su (putting jewel in arm)
179.3 FX: Toh (Koga lands)
179.4 FX: Gohh (whooshing)

180.3 FX: Pon (patting)
180.4 FX: Shuuu… (body separating)

181.1 FX: Shuuuu… (body dissolving)

182.2 FX: Bu bu bu (buzzing)
182.3 FX: Buuuu…n… (buzzing)

183.1 FX: Doga (smack)
183.2 FX: Bakii (wood splintering)

185.2 FX: Su… (swish of fan)
185.3 FX: Fuu… (swishing fan)
185.4 FX: Zaa… (magic whooshes out)
185.5 FX: Gohh (whoosh)

186.1 FX: Yuru…
(wolf demons wobble as they stand)
186.4 FX: Ba (leap)
186.5 FX: Doka (whack)

187.1 FX: Ga (swinging weapon)
187.2 FX: Doka (kicking)
187.3 FX: Za (hitting the ground)

188.3 FX: Doh doh doh… (running with effort)

189.1 FX: Fuu… (zombies rise)
189.2 FX: Gohh (whooshing)

189.2 FX: Gohh (whooshing)
189.3 FX: Doh (striking)
189.5 FX: Pachi (gesturing with fan)

190.1 FX: Bushuuu… (dissolving)

191.2 FX: Dosa (collapsing)
191.4 FX: Gohh (whooshing)

197.2 FX: Doga (wham)
197.3 FX: Go go go go (big blasting strike)
197.4 FX: Da (leap)
197.5 FX: Goh (whoosh)
197.6 FX: Dohn (boom)

198.5 FX: Kaa… (jewel shining)

199.1 FX: Doga (strike)
199.2 FX: Goh (whoosh)

202.2 FX: Doga (wham)
202.6 FX: Za (skidding on gravel)

203.1 FX: Bun (throwing weapon)
203.2 FX: Gyururuु… (flying though the air)
203.3 FX: Doga (whack)
203.4 FX: Za (charging into castle)

204.2 FX: Ba (charging past screens)

205.4 FX: Koto (puppet drops on floor)

206.2 FX: Kaaa… (demon puppet glows)
206.3 FX: Goh (whoosh)